ANDY LAW

WORK
AND
DAYS

**DAILY WISDOM FROM THE
GREEKS AND ROMANS TO GET YOU
THROUGH YOUR WORKING DAY**

For Alessandra

υχὴν τοῦ ἐρῶντος ἐν ἀλλοτρίῳ σώματι ζῆν

Published by
LID Publishing Limited
The Record Hall, Studio 204,
16-16a Baldwins Gardens,
London EC1N 7RJ, UK

524 Broadway, 11th Floor, Suite 08-120,
New York, NY 10012, US

info@lidpublishing.com
www.lidpublishing.com

A member of:

www.businesspublishersroundtable.com

© Andy Law, 2019
© LID Publishing Limited, 2019

Printed in Latvia by Jelgavas Tipogrāfij
ISBN: 978-1-912555-10-9

Cover and page design: Caroline Li

ANDY LA

WO
ANI
DAY

τὴ

DAILY WISDOM F
GREEKS AND ROMAN
THROUGH YOUR WO

LONDON   NEW YORK
MADRID   BARCELONA
MEXICO CITY   MONTERREY

*"Latin and Greek are not dead languages;
they have merely ceased to be mortal."*

J. W. Mackail

CONTENTS

HALF A CENTURY OF HELP

I write this book for anyone in any business and at any level, hoping that it might prompt a certain thought or spur an action and (you never know) be useful too.

This is no more than a '*libellus*'. A small book. A fun thing. Something to dip in and out of on a daily basis, or whenever the mood takes your fancy.

Even so, I couldn't have done it without half a century's worth of serious help.

So, thank you to many people I haven't seen for many years, to many I should like to see more of, and to some I have never met.

My thanks to John Simpson (who was Head of Classics at The Portsmouth Grammar School) for 'strong-arming' me into taking the subject more seriously in the first place, way back in 1969.

Then gratitude goes to Niall Rudd for imprinting a permanent Horatian impression on me at Bristol University.

It has been an honour to know Dennis Riddiford (who was Head of Classics at Brentwood Grammar School) since my early twenties. His effortless, professional rigour naturally spills over and inspires.

Thank you to Messrs. Liddell & Scott, and Lewis and Short, for compiling their enormous Greek and Latin Dictionaries, respectively, over one hundred years ago. These were my first port of call as I started my search for relevant quotes.

And thanks also to the wonderful Classicists of today who constantly inspire me. There are so many, but recently I've been enjoying the work of Mary Beard (obviously), Edith Hall, Emily Gower, Nicholas Horsfall, Tom Holland and Stephen Harrison. I have never met any of them in person, only in books, and some of them through the internet, radio or TV.

I am grateful to those who have shaped and impacted my business life. Theodore Zeldin, Dave Stewart, Gerry Labourne, Anita and Gordon Roddick and Charles Handy were key allies in my more 'experimental' days.

Thanks, as always, to Martin Liu. He invited me to lunch in the spring of 2018. I am retired, so I went to meet him firm in my resolve not to write any more business books. It was his idea to combine my business career with my love of classics – and write something.

I left lunch raring to go.

Finally, the biggest thank you is to my wife Alessandra, *'animae dimidium meae'*.

INTRODUCTION

MOTHERS OF INVENTION

The Classics for me has always been more than a hobby, but less than a career.

When I left university in 1978, I went straight into business. After a brief and undistinguished stint in grain commodity trading, (a business the Greeks and Romans would have approved of and raised to elevated status), I entered the world of advertising. This industry is about persuasion. 'Advertising' is by origin a Latin word, 'advertere', meaning 'turn towards'. Good advertising is persuasive enough if it motivates the customer to turn towards the product or service in question. Oratory is important in advertising. You have to win over your client, often in a contest. And once you've won your client, you will have to sell a creative idea that you ardently believe will do the trick. Every week someone would be using their oratorical skills to pitch some concept or another to someone else. I often fancied that the judicious use of Ciceronian rising tricolons could better serve my sales pitches. Today, as I look back, I am not so sure.[1]

My career developed into international business consulting and I spent many hours flying between completely different types of businesses, a number of which were multinationals. Like the Mediterranean traders of 3,000 years ago, I would dip in and out of (air) ports, dropping off my business advice and picking up new lessons to take away with me and then recycle back into my trade. One day I would be China with a washing machine manufacturer. The next, an automobile factory in California.

But one thing remained a constant. I could never leave the world of Classical Greece and Rome too far behind. English is the global language of business and peppered amongst the conversations or documents, the cultures and even the buildings, I would always find the Greeks and the Romans.

In the boardrooms and washrooms of companies the world over, I would come across the kind of banter that Menander, the Greek comedy playwright, and Juvenal, the Roman satirist, would have heard many times over. Both these writers would have marshalled and polished the banter to their own ends. They created persuasive, lively pieces about people, work, politics and society that resonate loudly and clearly. Many read as if they were written only yesterday.

But it is the tutorials discussing the extraordinary Roman poet Horace with the inestimable Niall Rudd[2] that lie at the heart of my passion for the Classics, a passion which has remained undimmed by both time and the demands of business life. "Horace is not a young man's poet", Professor Rudd would sigh, as we struggled to unweave the subtle language constructions that Horace would craft, and then agonize over the right word or phrase in English to match the nuance of his Latin. The older I get, the clearer Professor Rudd's observations become, and the further I travel into Horace's labyrinthine world.

Alongside my 'day job' I have written business books, absorbed business theory and collected business thoughts, so that sitting on shelves not too far from Plato, Plautus, Propertius and Pliny, you can find Marshall McLuhan, Charles Handy, Tom Peters and Peter Drucker.

The business world and the classical world might not seem at first glance to be happy bedfellows. Themes in business change regularly and radically and very few business books remain contemporary for very long. This stands in stark contrast to the literature of Greece and Rome. Greek and Latin texts, for obvious reasons, don't change very much, if at all, over time. Even some books of classical literary criticism or history have stood the test of time, still standing upright and proud like their stone counterparts, the Parthenon in Athens (completed 2,500 years ago, in 432 BCE), or the Colosseum in Rome (completed almost 2,000 years ago, in 80 CE).[3] The words of the Greek playwright Euripides and Roman poet Ovid, for example, still burn furiously, lighting up the imagination, delighting audiences and raising still more questions.

Few business books can rival Eduard Fraenkel's *Agamemnon*, or Ronald Syme's *The Roman Revolution* for depth of scholarship and lasting relevance. Most business books jump on current day bandwagons and are discounted fast, both financially and intellectually.

Not all, though. There are some which, for me, have clearly stood the test of time; Marshal McLuhan's *Understanding Media*, Theodore Levitt's

HBR paper *Marketing Myopia*, Peter Drucker's *The End of Economic Man* and *The Cluetrain Manifesto*, for example.

In a business career spanning over 40 years, I've been in every management position, from temp and trainee to CEO and Chairman. I've also been an Ernst & Young Entrepreneur of the Year, was profiled by the Harvard Business Review, joined UK government think tanks in Downing Street and steered meetings at The World Economic Forum, Davos. I'm not showing off; there's a big 'But' coming right now.

But . . .

Very few business books have taught me how to react in the present moment, or act for a future opportunity. So many of these books are post rationalizations, seeking clues from already established success stories.

I've scratched my head many times trying to adopt or adapt a specific company's winning ways into my own businesses, usually with little success.

So, for clues to business success and a reminder of my many and varied 'ups and downs' during my career, I've returned to where I started – The Classics.

Greece and Rome could well be called the 'Mothers of Invention' when it comes to business strategy.

You see, the Ancient Greeks and Romans were as industrious in business as they were in architecture, art, dance, drama, education, innovation, leisure, literature, oratory, philosophy, science, technology and warfare.

They had sophisticated legal systems and well recognized commercial practices. Many of these were based on long-established trade systems, supply chains, product inventories and distribution ports that had been forged for them earlier by superlative businessmen – the Phoenicians. This was an ancient race, traceable back to 3400 BCE, but who were certainly operating in an extremely businesslike way in and around the Mediterranean from at least 1200 BCE.

Although we know very little about the Phoenicians, we can deduce this much: they were extremely enterprising. They were traders and marketeers. They were wheeler-dealers and middlemen. You name it, they traded it. Wood, silver, linens, their famed crimson/purple cloth, even monkeys. They had business empires rather than militaristic empires. They operated separate business units from separate towns, such as Tyre, Sidon and Byblos (in modern day Lebanon); Carthage (in Tunisia); and Cadiz (in southern Spain). The units had a boss (a King) but they also had a 'Board of Directors', (a kind of Advisory Council) to monitor the actions and decisions of the boss. The Phoenicians developed the alphabetic script, possibly as a 'lingua franca' since they traded widely amongst many different Mediterranean languages and cultures. This alphabet, you might conjecture, would have allowed them to at least write stock inventories, commercial contracts and ownership credentials. But in fact, there is very little Phoenician literature of substance and there is evidence that they chose at times to be deliberately secretive. Ultimately the Phoenician alphabet was adopted by the Greeks and eventually it came down to the keyboard with which I write this book.

But it's important to remember that there were no 'businesses' in the sense of the protected legal entities we would recognize today. Indeed, businesses, as we understand them, are relatively new concepts.

Both work and employment in Greece and Rome bear very little resemblance to the way we work now, but what structures there were give clues and definition to the sophisticated economies that were in play in those times. They send echoes from the past, strong reminders, of how and why business terms have come to us. They send cautionary notes to us, such as how we might deal with employees and the purpose of profit. And these ancient business structures also throw into relief characters and characteristics that we would instantly recognize in the workplace today.

Well over 60% of English words have Greek or Latin roots, as do almost all our scientific and technical terms. The word 'profit', for example, comes from the Latin '*profectus*', which means 'progress' or 'success', reminding us that the purpose of profit is to advance the business. Profit is not merely a term to denote good financial housekeeping, nor is it something you just pile up and look at. Profit, in its purest sense, must be put to work to advance the company.

The word 'strategy' comes to us from the Greek 'στρᾰτηγός', meaning 'a leader' or 'a general'. This usefully reminds us, as all good business books do, that the best company strategy comes from the top and leads from the front. Good strategy, like a good general, will marshal its forces behind a clear objective and will know when the job is done.

Putting these quotes together has demonstrated to me one thing very clearly. In trade, medicine, manufacture, science and technology, we have made obvious advances over the Greek and Roman cultures of 2,000 years ago.

But intellectually, I am not sure that we have moved any further forward.

The Greeks and the Romans were as intelligent then as we are today, and their advice remains stunningly relevant.

'GREECE AND ROME' IS BIGGER
THAN GREECE AND ROME

When I refer in the book to 'Greece and Rome', I am really talking about a period that loosely starts around 750 BCE and roughly ends around 450 CE.

Geographically, 'Greece and Rome' covers what today we call Greece and Italy; but of course both these civilizations travelled and traded widely, and conquered and plundered liberally. 'Greece and Rome' is an area much bigger than the countries of Greece and Italy.

When I use the term 'Greece', I mean the first half of our period of time, from 750 BCE to 146 BCE. This huge expanse of time sweeps up Homer, Plato, Aristotle and Herodotus amongst many others. Greece was highly sophisticated, politically astute, creatively advanced and philosophically perceptive a long, long time before the Rome of Julius Caesar and Cicero.

In 146 BCE, Rome delivered a mighty two-punch power blow that took out both Corinth, in Greece, and Carthage, a city on the North African shore of modern-day Tunisia. The two cities were completely razed to the ground. Both Greece and an important, strategic part of the North African coast were brought under Roman control. It was an astonishing show of power.

The year 146 BCE saw a display of military muscle that would eventually create an empire which, by 211 CE, was made up of 46 provinces stretching from northern Britain to the Mediterranean coast of Africa, and from Spain in the west to the Iran/Iraq border in the east. It was an empire of many peoples, races, languages, religions, cultures and histories.

This empire is estimated to have embraced 35% of the world's population.[4] If it were transplanted into our world today, the Roman Empire "would constitute the seventh-largest country in the world, at some 6.5 million square kilometres approaching the area of Australia or Brazil."[5] It would be almost twice the size of India.

It was Greece, of all the provinces, that helped to sculpt the culture of the Roman Empire. You can't have Rome without Greece. The art, philosophy and scientific achievements that came from Greece were assimilated wholesale by the Romans. In fact, Rome plundered Greek art on an industrial scale.

The Romans appropriated Greek academia. The Roman equivalent of 'Harvard' or 'Oxbridge' was Athens. Both Cicero and his son were taught by a certain Cratippus in Athens at what was known as the 'Peripatetic School'. An Athenian education was what every aspiring young

Roman needed on his *'Curriculum Vitae'* (the Latin expression we like to abbreviate to 'CV').

Simply put, the Romans could not do much of what the Greeks were able to do, and so over time they went on to incorporate and take ownership of the entire Greek 'cultural achievement'.

Yes, the glory of Greece had been captured by the Romans, but the Romans were in turn captivated. They were entranced by what Greece had to offer. Horace famously wrote:

> "Once Greece was captured, it then took its savage conqueror captive
> and inserted some Culture into those Latin bumpkins."[6]

Both cultures used each other, and the colonization of Greece regularly came back to bite the 'Latin bumpkins' in a way we would certainly recognize today. Over time the Greeks had absorbed and incorporated themselves fully into the Roman labour force, taking maximum advantage of the opportunities their 'captors' had given them. There was all manner of employment to be had, particularly for the intellectually skilled: in teaching, in the sciences, in middle-management and in medicine, for example.

LAND OF THE GIANTS

From the legacy of Homer right down to the primacy of Vergil, the Greeks and the Romans had it all. Power, influence, money, creativity, innovation, immigration, intellectuals, politics, sex, drugs and, (well, it was at times), 'rock and roll'.

Just think about this for a moment. If you were born in Athens in 500 BCE, you would have lived through the era-defining and still famous Persian War. You could have been at the opening night of Aeschylus' masterly *Oresteia* performed at the Literary Festival and you would have seen him win first prize. For a 69th birthday present your kids would have sorted tickets for you for the premiere of Euripides' *Medea* and the following year you would have sat in stunned silence as you listened to Pericles' funeral oration. Sophocles was your peer and you see him in 468 BCE beat Aeschylus at the Dionysia Award Show. (He goes on to win a further 23 times.)

Socrates was born when you were 31 and the world's first historian, Herodotus, when you were 40; and Thucydides too. You might have heard Thucydides' rationale in 431 BCE for writing the History of the Peloponnesian War, a conflict you would have thankfully seen little of, although your children would no doubt be caught up in it. These children would have thoroughly enjoyed watching Aristophanes attend his own plays. He was born when you were 52. They would have been around to read Xenophon's exciting tales of derring-do and could have sent their kids to sit at the feet of Plato, who was born just 73 years after you were. The mighty Xerxes, the great Persian King of Thermopylae fame, died during your lifetime, in 465 BCE.

Extraordinary times indeed. But it goes on.

If you were born in Rome, 400 years later, you might well have bumped into the following: Julius Caesar; Brutus, who famously assassinated Caesar; the orator Cicero; the hugely successful general, Pompey the Great; Catullus, the love poet; Spartacus, who led the famous slave rebellion; the great poet Vergil; the infamous Cleopatra; Horace; the billionaire Crassus; Mark Antony and the powerhouse Roman matron Livia. Oh, and the Emperor Augustus.

Between these times lived Alexander the Great; Hannibal; Euclid, the 'father of geometry'; and Archimedes, the 'grandfather of innovation'.

We are talking about massive cultures, with massive histories. We are dealing with big, world-famous thinkers and even bigger ambitions.

In the daily quotes that follow, we are going to meet these world class strategists, proven leaders, inspirational innovators and successful power brokers as well as orators, poets, historians, teachers and philosophers.

In short, we will hear from men and women who, thousands of years ago, wrestled with exactly the same daily dilemmas that we wrestle with today and who, one way or another, found the right words to offer motivating advice.

HOW TO USE
THIS BOOK

There is a quote for each day. All the translations are my own. My objective is to make the Greek and Latin instantly intelligible to the modern reader. I make no attempt to match ancient poetic meters, or to slavishly translate each and every word if that means demolishing flow and comprehension. I know that I occasionally take small liberties because of this.

The translated quote is followed by the original Greek or Latin text and the author, book and chapter, or line.

The quote gives us the Theme of the day. There are 20 Themes. Not surprisingly, given the philosophical, rhetorical and military strengths of the Greeks and Romans, Personal Development, Presentations and Leadership are Themes which regularly appear.

The Theme is followed by some more thoughts on the quote under two headings:

CHECKPOINT: elaborates on the quote. You might be asked to consider whether the point has any direct meaning or relevance to you personally. What are you doing, or about to do, that the quote might reference? At the very least it might give you some food for thought.

WANT TO KNOW MORE? gives you a little more context. Who was the author? What was happening at the time the quote was written? Did something of note happen on that particular day?

You might like to pluck a quote out every now and then and spice up that internal memo.

The Themes build as they repeat throughout the days, weeks and months. At the end of the book you can find the quotes organized into the 20 business Themes that this book embraces. This means that if, for example, Time Management is something you are thinking about, you can quickly find the days on which this is discussed and build a fuller picture of how the Greeks and Romans tackled such an issue.

THEMES:

Communicating	Competitors
Consumer Insights	Entertaining
Finance	Human Resources
Innovation	Internet
Leadership	Legal
Personal Development	Presentations/Meetings/Documents
Project Management	Reorganization
Risk	Sales
Social and Environmental	Strategy
The Watercooler	Time Management

WORK AND DAYS

> **The most important part of every endeavour is the beginning.**
>
> *(οἶσθ᾽ ὅτι ἀρχὴ παντὸς ἔργου μέγιστον)*
>
> Plato. Republic 377a

THEME: PROJECT MANAGEMENT

CHECKPOINT: It's New Year's Day. New Year, New Plans. New Resolutions to keep. So, start!

What have you told yourself you need to achieve? Maybe you are just starting a first career, or a new career? Where do you want to be in three years' time? Sit down and map out the steps to get there. It could be forming a team; having difficult conversations with seniors and/or juniors; it could be that you have made certain plans but haven't talked them through with those close to you yet.

Write pros and cons if you need to. There are 'decision-making trees' that can help too – check them out, they are more helpful than you might think.

WANT TO KNOW MORE? Just about everyone's heard of Plato (approximately 429 BCE – 347 BCE). He is the colossus and foundation stone of Western philosophical thinking, who was taught by none other than Socrates. It was Plato who then went on to teach Aristotle. And Aristotle taught Alexander the Great. Great success was clearly forged from great education!

Plato's influence is immense. He was innovative, transformative and few have reached his depth of thinking across such a breadth of subject matters. Today's quote comes from one his most famous and influential works, *The Republic*.

Plato is talking about education. The most important first step, he says, is training the mind. We must tell toddlers stories to establish early patterns of thinking, and decision-making, about what is right and what is wrong.

> ## The biggest benefit of language is clarity.
>
> *(μεγίστην λέξεως ἀρετὴν σαφήνειαν εἶναι)*
>
> Galen. On The Natural Faculties 1.2

THEME: COMMUNICATING

CHECKPOINT: Are you expressing yourself clearly? Communication is essential in business yet so often it fails to deliver the key message successfully. Think about a simple piece of verbal communication. You assemble the thought in your head. The thought is transmitted to your mouth. You speak. The words travel (albeit briefly) through the air. The recipients' ears receive the message. The ears send the transmission to the brain, where it is finally decoded. Think there's any chance the message might get misunderstood at any stage?!

Language, as Galen, a celebrated physician and philosopher, points out, can clarify where confusion reigns. Think carefully about how, when and, indeed, whether you communicate. Is it by email, verbally, or via tweeting? Is it late at night or first thing in the morning? These things really do matter. Aim to be as clear as possible through your communication, then your intentions will be clearly understood. As a rule, send less (and clearer) messages rather than more.

WANT TO KNOW MORE? Galen (who was born in 129 CE and died about 210 CE) was at first medical supervisor to the gladiators of Pergamum. It wasn't much of a career, so to improve himself he did the obvious and moved to Rome. Galen's success was to summarize all past and current thinking on medicine and position himself as an expert source of medical knowledge. He did well, soon winning wide acclaim and becoming personal physician to the Imperial court and emperors such as Marcus Aurelius, Commodus and Septimius Severus.

> **There are as many opinions as there are people in the room.**
>
> *(quot homines, tot sententiae)*
>
> Cicero. De Finibus Bonorum et Malorum 1.15

THEME: PRESENTATIONS/MEETINGS/DOCUMENTS

CHECKPOINT: It's usually around this time that many people will be heading back into work after the Christmas break. There will be 'kick-start' meetings, documents to catch up on and presentations to make. Try not to have too many people in meetings or presentations and copy only the relevant people on any documents. People don't like to be left out of things – they see it as a political move. So be sensitive about the way you do it. Clearly communicate who's involved and who needs to know, and why.

What Cicero is reminding us is that 'too many cooks can spoil the broth'.

WANT TO KNOW MORE? January 3 is notable for two things.

Today, in 106 BCE, the magnificent Roman orator Marcus Tullius Cicero was born in Arpinum, about 100 kilometres south-east of Rome. Cicero is valuable to us because *he was there*! He wrote about real events and real people in real time. He witnessed for real what other historians can only speculate about. This is the first of 21 entries for Cicero, whose comments and observations about people and politics ring very true today.

Also, between January 3 and 5, the Romans celebrated the festival of the '*Compitalia*', held once a year in honour of the '*Lares Compitales*', household deities of the crossroads, to whom sacrifices were offered at the places where two or more pathways meet.

Businesses find themselves 'at the crossroads' many times, often agonizing over which strategic route to take. Today's advice helps to cut down the number of routes.

Set end dates to your ambitions.

(sit finis quaerendi)

Horace. Satires 1.1.92

THEME: PERSONAL DEVELOPMENT

CHECKPOINT: The purpose of end dates in your personal development is not just for you to work out what you need to achieve (financially, professionally and personally), and by when, but to understand what external influences you might need to help you move forward.

These influences could be straightforward training courses, extra-curricular talks, socializing amongst the right people and constant engagement with headhunters. To develop, you must be networked and you must stay contemporary. Have you got something interesting to say? If so, who will you say it to?

We use all sorts of project management tools when running a project. If the project is 'you', do the same. Manage yourself, set targets, set ambitions. Know when you should have reached them.

WANT TO KNOW MORE? Almost every single book written about the Roman poet Horace will start with, or include, these lines: "Horace was born in Venusia, Apulia, on December 8, 65 BCE." But in some respects this is the least interesting and helpful fact about Horace.

What makes Horace interesting is his phenomenal poetry.

Horace carefully chose his words so that every single one mattered. You have to start here, with Horace. With the exact words he wrote.

His sentence construction is often tortuous, making sensitively accurate translation difficult (certainly within meter) but at the same time it reveals a poet whose words are like tiles in an ever-revealing mosaic. With astonishing skill and sensitivity Horace marshalled the Latin language into the vocabulary of romance, rancour and reflection. In each of his works his words connect in surprising ways, producing an end piece of extraordinary emotional resonance.

> **I urge you. Take the route the traffic avoids. Don't travel down tracks trodden by others. Avoid the wide-open road and take the narrow one. The one the others don't go down.**
>
> *(καὶ τόδ' ἄνωγα, τὰ μὴ πατέουσιν ἅμαξαι τὰ στείβειν,*
> *ἑτέρων ἴχνια μὴ καθ' ὁμά δίφρον ἐλᾶν μηδ' οἷμον ἀνὰ πλατύν,*
> *ἀλλὰ κελεύθους ἀτρίπτους, εἰ καὶ στεινοτέρην ἐλάσεις)*
>
> Callimachus. Aetia 1.25

THEME: INNOVATION

CHECKPOINT: It's so easy to become creatures of habit. We get into cosy routines at work. The commute, the coffee, the desk, the meeting, lunch, and so on, all become normalized very quickly. New routines become difficult. Innovation becomes tiresome.

Yet innovative thinking is essential in today's business world. Competitors can copy you fast and consumers can be fickle, jumping from one idea to the next as they are digitally notified about what's new, improved or substantially better.

When it comes to thinking innovatively, creatively or 'out of the box', you have to break those habit-forming routines. It will help unlock and unblock your mind. That's the first important step. Be somewhere different. Be with different people. It doesn't have to be uncomfortable. It just has to be something that forces a change of behaviour.

WANT TO KNOW MORE? Callimachus was born in Cyrene in Libya (around 310 BCE) and studied philosophy in Athens. He returned to North Africa to become a teacher of poetry and grammar and, while still young, was persuaded to become the librarian at the new Library of Alexandria, a famous and important library of the ancient world.

That was his day job, but his real passion was for poetry, of which we have, alas, precious little. We just have tantalizing fragments of what appear to be a large output of work.

What we do know is that he was a hugely significant influence on important Roman poets like Horace, Catullus and Propertius.

Today was also the birthday of an ancient Roman goddess – Vicae Potae – who can be likened to the idea of Victory.

Perhaps a good day for brainstorming?

> ### While I'm talking, time is flying by.
>
> **(dum loquor, hora fugit)**
>
> Ovid. Amores 1.11

THEME: TIME MANAGEMENT

CHECKPOINT: We all have deadlines. The closer we get to the deadline, the more stressful the process. The Greeks and Romans pondered time as much as we do today. But they weren't as persecuted by it; after all they had only rudimentary time-keeping methods (the most widely used of which was watching the sun come up in the morning and go down at night!).

We have saddled ourselves with time-keeping impediments.

Carving out quiet time to get things done is important, though often difficult in modern open plan offices. Sending out 'Do Not Disturb' signals helps. Like putting on headphones or even putting up physical signs communicating that you need to focus on work – both sensible ideas when the last thing you want is an unwelcome chatty visitor.

WANT TO KNOW MORE? One minute Ovid (born March 20, 43 BCE) was the talk of the town, Rome's leading poet. The next he was banished by the Emperor Augustus for, as Ovid himself says, "*carmen et error*"; a poem (we assume the *Ars Amatoria*) and a mistake. (The 'mistake' remains a mystery, although Augustus' granddaughter, Julia, was also banished that year – 8 CE – and that's enough to get tongues wagging).

Ovid was an outstanding literary force. If you have to read just one piece of Latin in translation read his *Heroides*. The concept of the book alone is enough to make you want to pick it up. It takes the form of a series of letters written by famous (mythological) women to their lovers. These women are aggrieved, and the letters express all manner of feelings from hope to loss. Latin from the female perspective. You don't come across that very often.

> **On the whole, a properly deliberated action plan leads to a job well done.**
>
> *(τῷ δὲ εὖ βουλευθέντι πρήγματι τελευτὴ ὡς τὸ ἐπίπαν χρηστὴ ἐθέλει ἐπιγίνεσθαι)*
>
> Herodotus. Histories 7.157

THEME: PROJECT MANAGEMENT

CHECKPOINT: There's a thrill to new projects which often means that 'hitting the floor running' can be an exciting prospect. Don't do that.

Press the pause button.

The upfront planning of a project is as important as the processing of the project itself. Properly thought-through plans will include time and cost estimates, client expectations as well as the perfect composition and management of the team who are to perform the task.

WANT TO KNOW MORE? We don't know a great deal about the man Cicero called *"pater historiae"*, the Father of History,[7] but Herodotus' legacy is undisputed. If you've ever heard of The Battle of Marathon, or seen the movie *300*, you're living his legacy. Born around 480 BCE in Halicarnassus (Bodrum, Turkey) – then a city under Persian rule – it looks like he was drummed out of town for dissident behaviour. He eventually wound up in Athens, where he seems to have earned some serious money for creating a positive image of Athens' role in The Persian Wars. Herodotus, having lost his citizenship of birth, successfully gained citizenship of a new Greek town based in southern Italy, Thurii, and lived there, we think, until his death around 425 BCE.

Herodotus was an innovator, bringing a lively personal tone and a dramatic storytelling technique to his invaluable history of a pivotal time in the journey of the Greek people.

> **Don't try and find difficulties that aren't there.**
>
> *(in scirpo nodum quaeris[8])*
>
> Plautus. The Brothers Menaechmus 247

THEME: PROJECT MANAGEMENT

CHECKPOINT: Projects need 'an arrow of direction'. They need to move as swiftly and as effortlessly as possible. Don't overcomplicate the process by trying, as the expression goes, 'to boil the ocean'. Not every single stone needs to be turned over and not every eventuality needs to be anticipated.

There will be problems, of course, but there is nothing worse than chasing rabbits down rabbit holes. Decide if the problem is a genuine problem. Does it represent 'clear and present danger' to the progress of the project? Make your mind up decisively, and then make your move.

In a team, there will always be someone whose 'glass is always half empty'. It's tempting to listen to these people because you don't want to appear cavalier about the way you run things. Just be careful the person isn't being negative for negativity's sake (as is sometimes the case).

WANT TO KNOW MORE? Plautus (born around 254 BCE, died about 184 BCE) was a right rollicking playwright whose plays influenced Shakespeare and many others, right up to the present day. Importantly, his plays are the earliest works in Latin to survive in complete form. They are funny, rude, slapstick and dramatic. The plays are adapted from Greek plays and developed to suit Roman audiences.

Plautus had the theatre running through his veins. He started the hard way, as a stagehand and then as an actor, often playing, we think, a character called Maccus – a kind of 'Coco the Clown'. He was a massive success and if budding theatre companies or playwrights could somehow attach his name to their productions, they would.

He was a prolific writer of around 60 plays, two-thirds of which are sadly lost.

> **There is risk in every business.**
>
> *(πᾶσι δέ τοι κίνδυνος ἐπ' ἔργμασιν)*
>
> Solon. Fragment 13.65

THEME: RISK

CHECKPOINT: The metaphors, similes and aphorisms used to describe business life tell us everything. 'Choppy waters ahead'; 'plain sailing'; 'there's no such thing as a free lunch'; 'no pain no gain'; 'you have to speculate to accumulate'.

You get the idea.

Businesses operate in a constant state of fragility. But to make matters worse, you can't move the business forward without taking some risk. A bold strategy might pay off. Some entrepreneurs win where others fail.

Good managers have always tried to manage risk by ensuring that there is always a budget for research, development and innovation. Successful companies don't sideline this activity, they make it a core part of the organizational structure so that quality market intelligence flows through risk assessment as much as it does the other departments which are managing more day-to-day activities.

WANT TO KNOW MORE? Solon (approximately 640 BCE – 550 BCE), was one of the 'Seven Wise Men' of Greece and is often cited as the man who kick-started Greek democracy. What is less often mentioned is that before he got into politics, he was a businessman. Solon entered commerce to put some distance between himself and his father, who was, it seems, charitably de-wealthing at an alarming rate. (Well, it was alarming to Solon).

Solon's business career was brief, and he soon moved into significant military and legal roles, eventually becoming the chief lawmaker in Athens.

His achievement was to completely overhaul the legislative system of Athens, thereby ending the exclusive grip on the system by the ruling aristocrats. He was offered a kingship but turned it down and eventually stood down from his role, demanding that his revised system stay in place for at least ten years. Sadly, his reforms were overturned just four years later.

> **People so easily believe what they want to believe.**
>
> *(quod fere libenter homines id quod volunt credunt)*
>
> Caesar. The Gallic War 3.18

THEME: CONSUMER INSIGHTS

CHECKPOINT: Social Psychology matters to businesses. How customers think and make decisions, how they select or deselect brands, are important enough questions that an entire industry has been built to answer them.

Self-confirmation bias is the diagnosis of events, facts and messaging according to your own pre-existing beliefs.

You will not persuade customers to buy your product if their mindset is not aligned with that of your business.

Businesses that spend time on their values find that they communicate and resonate more easily with customers who have similar mindsets. And remember, it takes time to establish a relationship with customers. It is a fair objective to want to change a consumer mindset and attract them to your product or service, but simply bombarding them with blunt messages is a scattergun approach which will most likely come up against well-entrenched views, and fail.

WANT TO KNOW MORE? What a day. Today in 49 BCE, Julius Caesar crossed the Rubicon. To say it was decisive is an understatement.

Caesar was caught in a political trap. His unprecedented military success in Gaul (France) made him praised and feared in equal measure. If he continued extending the Roman Republic with his trademark cold-blooded, efficient brutality, he would remain untouchable. After all, he had a hugely successful army at his disposal. If he returned to Rome to seek high political office, he would have to relinquish his command. This would have weakened him. His enemies claimed they had enough on him to get him arrested and put on trial. Whether they did or not, Caesar decided not to risk it.

Crossing the Rubicon was a throw of the dice for Caesar. And it worked.

> **Even springs and wells have a habit of drying up,**
> **if you draw from them excessively, and non-stop.**
>
> *(καὶ γὰρ τὰς κρήνας καὶ τὰ φρέατ᾽ ἐπιλείπειν πέφυκεν,*
> *ἐάν τις ἀπ᾽ αὐτῶν ἀθρόα πολλὰ λαμβάνῃ)*
>
> Demosthenes. On The Navy Boards 31

THEME: INNOVATION

CHECKPOINT: Constantly relying on the same consumer base is dangerous. Consumers are fickle and promiscuous. They can jump from one better, cheaper or more useful product to the next at the drop of a hat.

Communicating to consumers by constantly utilizing the same media, also gets tiring and, as they say, familiarity breeds contempt.

It's the same principle as crop rotation. You need to keep moving things around so that you plant your ideas in fresh fields. You should refresh your propositions, your products, your media choices. Look for new customers, in new places – even internationally – and understand how your existing customers have changed. The likelihood is your customers are transforming faster than you can transform your business.

WANT TO KNOW MORE? If the Romans had Cicero, the Greeks had Demosthenes (384 BCE – 322 BCE). A lawyer of some distinction, Demosthenes was the genuine article. Sincere, resolute and crystal clear in his thinking, his speeches treat us to vivid snapshots of public and private life in ancient Athens.

Most of his big speeches were directed squarely at Philip II of Macedon, who threatened Athens from the north. Demosthenes' speeches were understandably called 'Philippics'. Cicero was to follow in his footsteps over 300 years later, with his own 'Philippics', this time against Mark Antony.

> **Man is by nature a political animal.**
>
> *(ὁ ἄνθρωπος φύσει πολιτικὸν ζῷον)*
>
> Aristotle. Politics 1.1

THEME: HUMAN RESOURCES

CHECKPOINT: Could any phrase be truer? Particularly in the workplace? Office politics surely account for a significant amount of your time at work. Often the politicking can be mild and manageable but often it is conducted on an industrial scale and for reasons of power-grabbing, envy, fear, money and fame.

The victims of office politics will spend an even greater percentage of time processing the hassle they receive. Office stress and even breakdowns can be credited to this pernicious behaviour.

Check online for strategies to deal with the backstabbers, parasites and saboteurs – there is plenty of good advice to be found. Most urge you to document everything that happens in as much detail as possible and not to openly respond or retaliate. The bigger the issue, the higher up the ladder you ultimately need to take your claim. If you have a Human Resources (HR) official, inform them.

Alternatively, as a last resort, seek professional help. Remember, politics in the office should not be a reason to have to leave a business.

WANT TO KNOW MORE? Aristotle (384 BCE – 322 BCE), pupil of Plato and tutor to Alexander the Great, is one of the giants of Greek philosophical thinking, despite the fact that almost everything he planned to publish is lost. Instead, though, we have his notes, lecture materials and various other aide-memoirs attesting to his substantial thinking.

He was a polymath, lecturing and writing on astronomy, biology, botany, ethics, mathematics, metaphysics, meteorology, philosophy, science and theology.

Aristotle wasn't just a 'head-in-the-clouds' academic. He liked to think about things from a practical point of view. This makes much of his thinking extremely valuable. His Nicomachean Ethics, for example, is often cited when issues of business ethics crop up.

> **When you're everywhere, you're nowhere.**
>
> *(nusquam est, qui ubique est)*
>
> Seneca. Epistles 2.2

THEME: INTERNET

CHECKPOINT: The internet has become a numbers game. Whether it's global reach, 'netizenship' of Facebook, advertising monies poured into the web, or the sheer capacity of the net to handle data, we're talking more noughts than we have ever been used to.

The temptation to flood sites with your presence is enormous. But step back for a moment.

How do you use the internet yourself? What are your expectations of what information to receive and what to reject? How often do you buy something, only to see it advertised back to you the very next moment? ('Too often' is the answer).

Being everywhere on the internet is not a strategy. Careful targeting is. It's the line-by-line manicuring of relationships that count; the paradox is that putting together your strategy is a tiny steps affair and a slower-than-you-think process. You have to incubate your messaging with your customers over time and be where they expect, and want, you to be.

WANT TO KNOW MORE? Could Seneca be any more prescient?

We'll hear a lot from Seneca (the Younger). His dad (The Elder) makes an entry too in mid-October.

Seneca was born around 1 BCE and his life came to an abrupt end when he was ordered by the Emperor Nero to kill himself in 65 CE.

Seneca's writing leant itself to the ready quote, and so on the button was he when it came to 'the human condition' that we marvel at how perfectly suited to our times he is. He understood anxiety and stress and provided bon mots to help his contemporaries navigate the perilous climate created by the bonkers Emperor Nero.

Seneca wrote philosophy, plays (all tragedies) and letters in an accessible and, for its time, modern way. After his death, his style of writing became de rigeur amongst the younger generation.

....

> **Speed is essential.**
>
> *(celeritate autem opus est)*
>
> Cicero. Philippic 5.53

THEME: STRATEGY

CHECKPOINT: Business books can be frustrating. You find yourself reading that you have to plan, plan and plan. Strategy is too important to rush. Then you turn over the page and the next chapter tells you all about speed of the competition, speed of change, 'first mover advantage' and all that.

The only way I reconcile these two equally valid points is with the old carpenter's adage 'measure twice, cut once'. By all means strategize, it's essential. Test your ideas, even do a dummy run. But when you press the 'Go Button' it has to be 'Action Stations'.

Speed to market provides competitive advantage. And speed of change – adaptability – provides consumer advantage.

WANT TO KNOW MORE? If you were in Rome on this day in 83 BCE, and you were friends or neighbours of Marcus Antonius Creticus and his wife Julia Antonia, you'd be hearing the unmistakable cries of baby Marcus Antonius. That's Mark Antony, the Mark Antony of Shakespeare's "Friends, Romans, countrymen, lend me your ears" fame.

Mark Antony was one of Julius Caesar's generals and a close ally. But after Caesar's assassination his life went awry. Always a womanizer, boozer and gambler, he was a lad's lad, who commanded tremendous loyalty from his troops. As Shakespeare and Hollywood have reminded us, he hooked up with Cleopatra and gave the world a mega love story.

As he starts to spin out of control, Cicero denounces him in a series of 'Philippics', (see January 11). Today's quote is in fact from one such Philippic.

....

> **The truth is, people are influenced by different objectives and different interests.**
>
> *(verum esto aliis alios rebus studiisque teneri)*
>
> Horace. Epistles 1.1.80

THEME: HUMAN RESOURCES

CHECKPOINT: It's incredible how different people are. A truism, you might think. But when you've managed a number of people over a number of years you recognize that each individual has their own unique threshold of pride, ability, ambition, greed, tolerance and moral judgement.

What's a good deal for one is not so good for the other. What's a joke to one person is inflammatory to another.

Some people love to strategize, others like to sell.

Some like to lead, others like to follow.

In HR terms, of course, these differences can become an asset. Personality profiling can help you to create teams of different individuals with different interests and objectives. Combining differences can create strong teams.

WANT TO KNOW MORE? The general Marcus Salvius Otho was driven by ambition and the need for cash, it seems, to depose his mate Galba as emperor of Rome on this day, January 15, 69 CE. Galba had been emperor for only seven months. Otho himself only lasted three months, in what became a year of turmoil called by historians the 'Year of the Four Emperors'.

Horace wrote these words almost 100 years earlier (around 23 BCE). He himself had seen differing objectives and interests battle it out for power, until the Emperor Augustus defeated Mark Antony in 31 BCE and became undisputed master of the Roman world.

Horace was a complex man. His relationships with people were never straightforward. He was inconsistent and often contrary. He was intense at times, passionate at others. He could weave melancholy into joy and cruelty into flattery at the stroke of a stilus. There is no evidence that Horace married.

> **Know thyself.**
>
> *(γνῶθι σαυτόν)*
>
> Inscription on the Temple of Apollo (attr. Thales)

THEME: **PERSONAL DEVELOPMENT**

CHECKPOINT: 'Know yourself' is the cornerstone of personal development. One of the biggest mistakes you can make in your career is to pretend to be someone you're not, or hide aspects of your personality. People with a clear understanding of their own strengths, weaknesses and character attributes are much easier to work with.

'Know yourself' is in essence an injunction to understand that we are driven by both conscious and unconscious wishes, feelings, intentions and desires which, for whatever reason, have been suppressed. (See Freud for more info!)

The more we know about ourselves, the more we avoid getting stuck in adverse patterns of behaviour.

WANT TO KNOW MORE? This is such a fabulous quote, claimed by many, and some attribute it to other fine wordsmiths (including Heraclitus, Socrates and Pythagoras). The Roman poet Juvenal says the saying simply dropped down from heaven (*'ex caelo'*). And why not?

One person who understood himself very well was Octavian, the adopted heir of Julius Caesar. On this day in 27 BCE he rebranded himself 'Augustus' – a name dripping in religious connotation and gravitas.

The journey from teen Octavian to esteemed Emperor Augustus was one of continued growth and development. Where he ended up cannot have been planned when he tentatively landed in Italy to claim his due inheritance from the estate of the assassinated Julius Caesar. But he was confident enough in himself at each stage to make the moves he did, with the team he had. His strategy was a huge success.

> **Leaders are wise because they keep the company of wise men.**
>
> *(σοφοὶ τύραννοι τῶν σοφῶν ξυνουσίᾳ)*
>
> Sophocles. Ajax The Locrian Frag. 14

THEME: LEADERSHIP

CHECKPOINT: Three days of quotes about Leadership now follow. One expression that constantly irritates me in the world of business is 'it's lonely at the top'.

No, it's not. Well, I guess it is if you decide to make it like that.

Clever leaders network like mad. They share experiences. There are all sorts of formal and informal get-togethers that offer training and support. Even if you're the head of a tiny company, you can join an association and meet and hear other business experts.

Networking needs to be diarized. If you make it a spontaneous affair you won't reap the important benefits of rubbing shoulders with an increasingly broad spectrum of expertise.

Finally, there's an essential element to keeping the right company. It's one that we so often avoid but which in my experience brings the greatest gain.

Make sure you occasionally put yourself in the company of people you wouldn't normally meet. You learn as much, if not more, from people who have experiences of completely different types of problems.

WANT TO KNOW MORE? Ever heard of Oedipus? Or the Oedipus Complex? Sophocles, the master playwright, brought us Oedipus in all his glory.

Sophocles was a great innovator, whose intelligent, powerful scripts, and ability to create real suspense, made him the foremost playwright of his era. The big award ceremonies of his day were the Dionysia and the Lenaea, where you staged your play to win. Sophocles entered 30 competitions, winning 24. His plays are absolutely stunning and his themes timeless. His characters are beautifully drawn out and his plots are exciting. They twist and turn with great surprise. No wonder they are still performed today. Sophocles produced at least 123 plays, but only seven have survived.

> **Give me a night with sleep and a day without disputes.**
>
> *(sit nox cum somno, sit sine lite dies)*
>
> Martial. Epigrams 2.90

THEME: **DISPUTES**

CHECKPOINT: Nothing much changes over the years, does it? Here is the satirist Martial echoing what so many CEOs of today must surely be thinking.

Modern business is a 24-hour machine with constantly moving parts. It is inevitable that some of these parts will come loose, either by themselves or by outside influence.

Disputes will arise.

Resorting to litigation at the drop of a hat is becoming more commonplace, whether it's over disgruntled employees, angry customers or aggressive competitors.

Every business needs to be protected and that means either building-in a legal resource (if you're big enough) or bolting one on.

The earlier your contracts get the OK from the lawyers, the better. And if you want to avoid heart palpitations and sweats, refer potentially worrisome matters to them for a view.

And tell them you'll hear their view the next day. After a good night's sleep.

WANT TO KNOW MORE? If you want to hear the sounds of ancient Rome, smell the city and witness the detail of daily life, then pick up a copy of Martial's epigrams. Like the great comedians of today, he casts a critical, witty, rude eye over the day-to-day characters living in the biggest city in the world and brings them all down to size.

They're all here, the posh, the pompous and the perverted. Most modern translations only reproduce selected Epigrams. Try and get your hands on the complete set. The naughty ones that are often left out are a lot of fun.

Martial was born around 40 CE in northeast Spain and left in his early twenties for the big city, Rome, where he was to live for 34 years.

> **It's not a good idea to have too many leaders.**
>
> *(οὐκ ἀγαθὸν πολυκοιρανίη)*
>
> Homer. Iliad 2.204

THEME: LEADERSHIP

CHECKPOINT: Leadership is about setting an overall direction, and then inspiring the workforce to get behind it. Too many 'leaders' delay that process, create confusion over who's in charge of what, and prompt political games as employees play one 'leader' off another.

The delivery of the plan is the bread-and-butter activity of the business and requires plenty of day-to-day decision-making.

Decision-making in business is the motor that moves a business forward. Having too many decision-makers will slow a business down. But too many steps up to the decision-maker will also create delay. Businesses like to be careful, for reasons we have already seen, but some businesses overcomplicate the route to getting a Yea or Nay decision.

Make sure that the right budget approvals lie with the right people. There can only be one leader in a business, but the clever ones put the right managers in the right place, with the ability to read the situation on the ground and deliver. Just check that your leadership is creating the flow that's needed.

WANT TO KNOW MORE? All Western literature begins with *The Iliad*. Homer exploded a literary bomb with his extraordinary war epic and the aftershock is felt as powerfully today as it was felt in ancient times. They say all roads lead to Rome, but in terms of classical literature, all roads lead to Homer and The Trojan War. This conflict spawned tragedy, epic, love and travelogue genres like no other event. The stories before, during and after the war are as gripping as any tale ever told since. This is not surprising. This was the tale that gave birth to a thousand different storylines. Homer's characters constantly appear and reappear in ancient and modern literature. Maybe you want to take your interest in the Classics further? Then, if you haven't already done so, read the *Iliad*.

> ## We can't all do everything.
>
> *(non omnia possumus omnes)*
>
> Vergil. Eclogues 8.63

THEME: PROJECT MANAGEMENT

CHECKPOINT: Vergil's quote, a kind of proverb that goes all the way back to Homer, has enormous ramifications for modern business. Times change fast, certainly faster than you can adapt your employee base. Not everyone in the organization can do everything that needs to be done.

Teams of experts can more easily respond accurately than one 'generalist' employee. The higher up the pyramid structure the manager goes, the less likely he will have all the skills needed. Assessing recommendations then becomes the real role of senior management. Businesses will always find themselves with specific skills shortages and, let's be honest, training courses can only take you so far.

The obvious solution is to hire in expertise as and when you need it. Management consultants and PR firms are good examples of this. And sometimes you need to have the skills in-house.

But remember, recruiting new skill sets will change the company and redefine the business you are in. Every now and then, take a look at how the market has changed your recruitment policy, and ask yourself, 'What Business Am I Now In?'. The answer could be illuminating.

WANT TO KNOW MORE? Vergil's book of *Eclogues* (meaning 'selections') was the first collection of poetry he wrote. He composed them between 42 BCE and 38 BCE when he was in his early thirties.

Rome at this time was in turmoil. Julius Caesar had been assassinated and the 'pro-Caesar' forces were in bloody battle against the 'anti-Caesar' brigade.

It looks like one of the motivations for writing the *Eclogues* was the trauma of the forced confiscation of Vergil's home in order to house 'pro-Caesar' troops.

Despite the turmoil, Vergil turned out an exquisite set of ten poems set in an idyllic countryside, immaculately connected in terms of theme, and interwoven with beautiful and subtle messaging.

> **As often as you can, think about what you're about to say, think about what you're saying about someone and think about who you're saying it to.**
>
> *(quid de quoque viro et cui dicas, saepe videto)*
>
> Horace. Epistles 1.18.68

THEME: COMMUNICATING

CHECKPOINT: 'Comments' and 'chats' are small things, aren't they? Not in the business world, I'm afraid. It could be 'how's it going?', or the 'can we have a quick chat?' type of comment, or it could be stronger than that. "I've got a few comments to make." Private room. Door closed. You know the drill. So often we do not think through these chats, and the danger here is that when you get a response you didn't expect, you can be thrown off balance.

Age, sexual orientation, gender and ethnicity, for example, might all play a big part in the misinterpretation of what you have to say.

As a general rule, never discuss people who are not present unless there is a specific reason.

Just think before you speak.

Tailor what you say to the person or people you are speaking to.

WANT TO KNOW MORE? Horace was a poet, not a historian or a letter writer. He was influenced by many things, experimented with them all and drew on the most useful in his forceful direction of opinion.

Indeed, Horace is often sketchy about factual detail and contemporary readers can be quick to accuse him of being nebulous, contradictory and frustrating.

His poems are none of these. Horace clearly heeded his own advice. He thought very carefully before he spoke to us. His words have a clarity and an intellectual depth that stuns. Horace can smuggle nuance into ambivalence and drop conflict into platitudes, such that each generation, reading the poetry against the background of different times, moods and fashions, peels back in wonder yet another layer of deep and meaningful insight.

> **We need not prolong this meeting any further.**
> **There's proper work to be done.**
>
> *(μηκέτι νῦν δήθ᾽ αὖθι λεγώμεθα μηδ᾽ ἔτι δηρὸνἀμβαλλώμεθα ἔργον)*
>
> Homer. Iliad 2.435

THEME: TIME MANAGEMENT

CHECKPOINT: Could Homer have come up with one of the most valuable and relevant quotes for modern business?

Yes.

Those chairs who are able to bring meetings to a close exactly when they are slated to end are to be applauded.

Meetings should have strict agendas. Presentations should have strict timing. Individual comments should be strictly monitored. Am I sounding strict? I guess so, but for a reason.

Meetings that overrun are a sign of lack of preparation, lazy management and a complete absence of common courtesy. They create stress and signal problems. They permit too much discussion. Importantly, meetings that run over time represent a significant breach of trust, given the expectation of a time frame that is not being respected.

Real business is done outside of meetings – sales calls, brainstorms, customer interaction, etc.

Long meetings have become the scourge of modern-day business.

WANT TO KNOW MORE? If you want to know more about Homer, I'm about to disappoint you. For someone who has made such an extraordinary impact on global literature, almost nothing is known about him; or her; or them. Homer could be more than one person. This could be a team at work. The *Iliad* and *Odyssey* are the two works that make Homer forever famous, but they would have been sung, semi-chanted or rapped. Maybe a little bit of all three.

You'll find that Homer repeats many phrases – they are called Homeric formulas. These repetitions served a number of purposes. They prompted the singer to remember what was coming next. A prompt for a handover maybe? A chance to grab a cup of wine? Or even a quick toilet break? The *Iliad* and *Odyssey* are long pieces to get through.

> **I am afraid I've expressed it badly;
> let me try to make my calculations clearer.**
>
> *(vereor ne parum expresserim: apertius calculo ostendam)*
>
> Pliny The Younger. Letters 8.2.5

THEME: COMMUNICATING

CHECKPOINT: Communicating sales or financial information is extremely difficult. Often it will be generated on a spreadsheet. Usually the only person who will understand the spreadsheet is the person putting it together. The problem with spreadsheets is that they're so seductive. They're indispensable. The functionality of automated calculations has made them the go-to tool for all businesses. But the end result can be complicated.

When you are discussing the data with colleagues, try to be more creative with your approach. There's nothing worse than a roomful of people staring blankly at rows and columns of numbers, each too embarrassed to put their hand up and say they can't understand it.

Work backwards. What does your audience most need to know? How can that be best presented? It could be that you don't use the spreadsheet at all. Don't forget that the common spreadsheet formats today, such as Excel, have a whole range of tools, including graphs and charts. These might help to clarify the points you are making.

Analyzed information carries a message. What is that message?

Now, make the message crystal clear.

WANT TO KNOW MORE? Pliny (approximately 61 CE – 112 CE) is a wonderful source of information on the day-to-day goings on in ancient Rome and its provinces. But his most obvious claim to fame is his quite amazing eye-witness account of Vesuvius erupting in 79 CE. He describes the event in some detail, including the death of his uncle in the chaos of Pompeii.

Pliny was an orator and a poet. But it's mainly his letters that have come down to us. He's often writing to friends who lived outside Rome in order to keep them up to date on the hustle and bustle of life in the Big City.

....

> **And, as you see, we don't need to search far afield**
> **for enemies: they surround our walls on every side.**
>
> *(nec longe scilicet hostes quaerendi nobis; circumstant undique muros)*
>
> Vergil. Aeneid 11.387

THEME: COMPETITORS

CHECKPOINT: Wherever you look, competitors lurk. Fast-moving copy-cat companies operating from less-regulated places overseas can swamp your market. Disgruntled ex-employees, an audacious start-up, new products, fighting in the boardroom. All these produce enemies at the gate, waiting to watch you slip, to get a slice of your business pie or, worse, to bring you down.

The point to be made here is: don't be complacent. There are things you can do about ferocious competition.

Legal protection certainly helps – we've looked at how important that is – but legitimate threats arise all the time.

Take a look at how unique and competitive your product or service really is. What is the status of your reputation and customer relationships? It's a crazy thought, but companies with strong reputations can ride out threats just because of their history of quality commitment to customer service.

WANT TO KNOW MORE? Vergil was born near Mantua in Northern Italy in 70 BCE and died in Brindisi, in 19 BCE. The death of Vergil is a story in its own right. He was on his way back to Rome (from a trip to Athens) intending to finalize his '*magnum opus*', the *Aeneid*. When he realized he couldn't make it back to Rome, he asked two companions to destroy the one and only existing version of the *Aeneid*, saying he hadn't perfected it and so wasn't happy with it. Luckily Augustus stepped in quickly and told them not to be so daft.

He wasn't happy with it? Ye Gods! It's an extraordinary piece of work, with layers and layers and layers of detail. Yes, there are a couple of nips and tucks he obviously could have made – but it was, and remains, a work of utter genius. Talk about being a perfectionist!

....

> **'To talk' is derived from the word 'place', so they say.**
>
> *(loqui ab loco dictum)*
>
> Varro. On The Latin Language 6.56

THEME: COMMUNICATING

CHECKPOINT: There's a time and a place for speaking to people about important matters such as a review, a promotion, a pay rise, or an awkward issue.

The meeting should be diarized to be mutually agreeable and to allow enough time for any preparation.

The location needs thinking about. It sends a message.

The 'come to my office' request is fine, but unless it is going to be a negative meeting, it's best to elucidate, for example: 'nothing to worry about, it's about tomorrow's meeting'.

It could be a restaurant – that transmits a positive message. A bar perhaps?

The place of the meeting says more than we think about what words will be spoken there.

So, give a moment's thought to the choice of meeting place.

WANT TO KNOW MORE? Marcus Terentius Varro (116 BCE – 27 BCE) was an academic, a polymath really, in both the arts and sciences. He was an agriculturalist, antiquarian, encyclopaedist, epidemiologist, historian, librarian, microbiologist, philologist, poet, politician and soldier.

He was a prolific writer with over 70 literary projects to his name. Only two of his works survive.

Varro was nearly put to death by Mark Antony, despite being a (late) supporter of Julius Caesar, but he was saved by Augustus and slid quietly and further into a life of academia.

....

> ## Our current system is a joke.
>
> *(ἐπεὶ νῦν γε γέλως ἔσθ᾽ ὡς χρώμεθα τοῖς πράγμασιν)*
>
> Demosthenes. First Philippic 25

THEME: REORGANIZATION

CHECKPOINT: We all know the old adage of the frog and boiling water, don't we? Maybe not. The adage goes like this: drop a frog into boiling hot water and he'll hop out to safety immediately. Drop a frog into cold water and then slowly heat it up, and the frog will start swimming happily until it is eventually boiled alive. Nice.

The point is that we can work in a set routine day in and day out, moaning about this system or that *'modus operandi'* (way of working), but never realize it's not working until it's too late.

It's important to review your organizational arrangements regularly. Are they contemporary (i.e. fit for purpose in today's environment), and are they satisfying (i.e. do people find them easy and, ideally, do they put people in a good frame of mind)?

So often systems are exposed as they are falling apart. That's when you'll hear Demosthenes' quote spoken out loud.

Stay ahead of the game. Form teams to take a quick look at how things could be improved.

WANT TO KNOW MORE? Demosthenes was born in 384 BCE and died on October 12, 322 BCE. Despite achieving enormous status, he was a weak and somewhat frail man.

But what makes his rise to the top of oratory even more remarkable is that he had a stammer. He conquered this speech impediment by filling his mouth with pebbles and speaking on the beach against the sound of the waves. He would also go for a run and then start speaking when out of breath. He found it helped his frustrating ailment. He laboured at this for a while, hiding in an underground bunker until he felt able to address the world.

His hard work and dedication paid off and he spoke his way to the top!

....

Courage grows by daring, fear grows by delay.

(audendo virtus crescit, tardando timor)

Publilius Syrus. Sententiae 43

THEME: LEADERSHIP

CHECKPOINT: Nervous shrew-like leaders who hide behind their desk and play things 'by the book' are unlikely to be a success. They may have the qualifications and the CV to do the job but in today's 'open world', leading from the front, being 'out there' and crafting big bold strategies is what cuts the mustard.

CEOs who have been in place for a long time tend to want to keep things as they are, claiming downturns will always lead to an upturn.

The problem is that businesses have 'stakeholders'. These comprise shareholders, employees, customers, suppliers – anyone affected by the company.

Being bold is an art and the more you do it, the easier it gets. Doing nothing, but just 'pottering along' and putting off the difficult but obvious conversations, actually increases the fear factor within a company, as stakeholders start to imagine potential unpleasant future scenarios.

WANT TO KNOW MORE? What would we do without dear old Publilius Syrus? He was a Syrian slave who through his ready wit and repartee made it out of slavery, freed by a master who clearly rated him and who then went on to educate him. What a break.

Publilius wrote 'mimes' which were improvised and knockabout scenarios, and so very few written examples remain. The educated Publilius, however, went on to write over 700 '*sententiae*', or clever one-liners. This has fuelled books of Latin quotations since such books (like this one) first appeared.

Ten of his quotes that pertain to business have found their way into this book.

> **You cannot step into the same river twice.**
>
> *(δὶς ἐς τὸν αὐτὸν ποταμὸν οὐκ ἂν ἐμβαίης)*
>
> Plato. Cratylus 402a (attr. Heraclitus)

THEME: PERSONAL DEVELOPMENT

CHECKPOINT: Over the years I've heard the quote "You cannot step into the same river twice" many times. But what does it really mean?

It means the flow of activity every day is different. You can't go back to yesterday's events and recreate them (although some people go to enormous lengths to try!). Change is a defining feature of our lives.

Managing change is a business theme that eats up considerable shelf space in the business section of bookshops.

But the 'change' aspect of the quote is only half the story. The real message inherent in Heraclitus' quote is that you have to manage the 'unknowable'. There are considerably fewer books in the shops on this subject.

Keep your ears and eyes open. Learn to accept that things change, and relish jumping into new challenges. If you're managing a department or an entire business, keep innovative thinking central and the framework of teams as flexible as possible.

WANT TO KNOW MORE? Let's talk about Heraclitus, who speaks to us here via Plato.

Good News: We have lots of fragments of his thoughts because he is so often quoted by others.

Bad News: Not all of them make a lot of sense.

We don't know when he was born or when he died, but he seemed to be alive and well around 500 BCE, according to ancient writers.

Heraclitus was one of the 'Pre-Socratics'. That means he was issuing astute food for thought before Socrates, who appeared on the scene some 50 or so years after Heraclitus.

It's a clever man who can condense down many words
into a brief space. And do it well.

(σοφοῦ πρὸς ἀνδρός, ὅστις ἐν βραχεῖ
πολλοὺς καλῶς οἷός τε συντέμνειν λόγους)

Euripides. Aeolus 28

THEME: COMMUNICATING

CHECKPOINT: Most people go weak at the knees at the thought of sitting down (or even standing up) in front of a few people and summarizing a large subject. Condensing a large research document down to a one-pager for the boss is a difficult task.

Presenting it is even harder. What to leave in? What to cut out?

Break the information down into its component parts.

What am I going to say? How will images or charts amplify my message? These are two completely different modes of communication, by the way. Hearing is absolutely not the same as Seeing.

A shortcut to how this is done well is to watch a professional network TV news bulletin, like the BBC or CNN. Notice how the anchor talks and the visuals amplify the points being made.

Use the charts as summary lines to embellish what you say; speak to embellish the charts.

And cut down the information to be looked at to the barest minimum, or your audience will read the charts and not hear what you are saying.

One sentence per slide/page only.

WANT TO KNOW MORE? Euripides is one of the 'big three' Greek playwrights. We met Sophocles, who was just a generation ahead of Euripides, earlier this month and we'll meet the third, Aeschylus, in early February.

Euripides was an extraordinary playwright. If you can, watch the 1972 movie, *The Trojan Women*, with Katharine Hepburn and Vanessa Redgrave, and you can see for yourself. His understanding of women suggests he conversed deeply with them, which might have raised a few eyebrows in his day.

He also (well, almost certainly) rubbed shoulders with Sophocles, Socrates and Aristophanes. An evening in the bar with those four would have been quite something.

> ## This dispute needs an arbitrator.
>
> *(ἐπιτρεπτέον τινί ἐστι περὶ τούτων)*
>
> Menander. Men At Arbitration 219

THEME: **DISPUTES**

CHECKPOINT: Disputes are a big subject because they range from small one-on-one arguments to full-blown legal.

In many cases, disputes need third-party involvement. A trusted senior manager can help to avoid escalation, but trained professionals are better. In ancient Greece, private arbitrators were regularly used to settle disputes.

Try not to get too personal when explaining your perspective on the disagreement. That only inflames matters and does you no credit. Facts speak for themselves. If you have quality witnesses to events who are prepared to get involved, certainly involve them.

If you are proved to be right in your contention, follow the rules of international diplomacy and let the other side leave the arbitration with their dignity intact. It will pay off in the long term.

WANT TO KNOW MORE? We have to thank the ever-developing science of modern archaeology for the few plays of Menander that we now have. In fact, if it wasn't for 20th century discoveries, there would be almost nothing of his work, despite the fact that he wrote over 100 comedies.

Menander was known as the Prince of New Comedy, a refreshingly new form of comedy and a complete break from the harsh satirical comedy of Aristophanes.

Menander wrote about real people, ordinary people, domestic situations, love affairs, children and so on.

Menander is a big figure in the history of Greek theatre, whose brilliance is sadly dimmed by the loss of his work. He is said to have drowned in about 293 BCE at the age of 52 while swimming off the beach near the Athenian port of Piraeus.

> **You're young! Get up off your behind and head abroad! There's a lot more to come from you.**
>
> *(linque tuas sedes alienaque litora quaere, o iuvenis: maior rerum tibi nascitur ordo)*
>
> Petronius. Poems 6

THEME: PERSONAL DEVELOPMENT

CHECKPOINT: Travel broadens the mind. A cliché that happens to be true.

All of us are connected into a thriving global marketplace, with goods and services traded daily from every corner of the globe.

In terms of career development, a stint abroad adds so much to your experience, perspective, skill sets and ultimately your CV. You learn about different ways of doing things, you understand the motivations behind certain decision-making, you pick up lessons and language you would never learn, by definition, if you just stayed in the country of your birth.

People have hidden depths and one of the barriers to revealing them and bringing up different, wide-ranging skills is that they are never truly challenged.

Travel is a challenge easily met and handsomely rewarded.

WANT TO KNOW MORE? It is highly possible you've heard of Petronius' *Satyricon*. The book achieved fame in the same way as *Lady Chatterley's Lover* did – it was deemed 'naughty' and certainly not suitable for schoolchildren. But like D. H. Lawrence's work, Petronius' book is much more than the naughty bits.

Petronius wrote with confidence and some '*brio*', embracing parody and satire alongside neat and elegant Latin. The Satyricon is a rare example of the 'Latin Novel'.

Petronius also wrote (well, almost certainly wrote) poetry. Some poems are just as bawdy as the *Satyricon*, you'll be pleased to know. Many are about his love of the country and the seaside.

Petronius was a member of the highest ranks of the senatorial class and was close to the Emperor Nero, for whom he appeared to be a kind of contemporary cultural fashion advisor. He was also at one point in his career Governor of Bythinia (northern Turkey).

> **Money does not turn into wealth unless you know how to use it.**
>
> *(οὐδὲ τὸ ἀργύριόν ἐστι χρήματα, εἰ μή τις ἐπίσταιτο χρῆσθαι αὐτῷ)*
>
> Xenophon. Economics 1.12

THEME: FINANCE

CHECKPOINT: Putting your profits to good use is essential in a business if you are to maximize your growth potential. But you need to seek expert advice. Having someone with you who understands money management is key to business success and is the first thing you need if you're setting up a business.

When choosing who should manage your money, take plenty of advice. Finance directors come in many shapes and sizes. Some are in the background, others are highly influential. Many will rise to become CEOs. Sometimes, businesses will split the finance function between a Commercial Director and a Finance Director. If you run a small business, you will need an outsourced function, or you will end up as finance, commercial, sales and marketing all rolled into one. Not a good idea.

Everyone is in business to make money, but the most important question to ask is: what do you want to do with the money you make?

Spend time thinking carefully about this; it's a harder question than you might imagine.

WANT TO KNOW MORE? The word 'economy' is – surprise, surprise – a Greek word. But *'οἰκονομία'* (economy) is more akin to 'household management' or 'housekeeping'. Not that this difference would have worried Margaret Thatcher, who famously said in 1979, the year she became prime minister: "Any woman who understands the problems of running a home will be nearer to understanding the problems of running a country."

But did the Greeks and Romans write books about the economy as we understand it today? Not really.

However, Xenophon's book, *Economics*, although about the domestic economy, does include such things as 'the role of profit' and 'the importance of record keeping'.

> **From one wrong-doing, learn everything.**
>
> *(et crimine ab uno disce omnis)*
>
> Vergil. Aeneid 2.65

THEME: PERSONAL DEVELOPMENT

CHECKPOINT: The faulty 'O' ring (a rubber seal) on the Space Shuttle *Challenger* caused the flight to explode in the air, killing all seven crew members. The 'O' ring disaster (the seals were not suitable for purpose) was thoroughly investigated by NASA, of course, and what was discovered became a case history on poor internal communication and 'groupthink', a psychological phenomenon whereby the desire for a team to harmonize overwhelms correct decision-making.

From the 'O' ring screw-up, an enormous amount was learned.

When you make an honest mistake, or your team does not win an all-important sales pitch, it's important to look back to see what happened.

This should not be about recrimination but about learning and continual improvement.

WANT TO KNOW MORE? If Homer's *Iliad* was a literary bomb and foundation stone of Western literature, then Vergil, 700 or so years later, was the master craftsman who turned the gift of literature into a consummate art form and influenced generations who came after him.

Vergil wrote only three major pieces, but his legacy was to invent the art of modern writing. He revolutionized the way symbolism and wordplay would add many-layered textures to events and characters, so that you can spend a lifetime reading Vergil's masterpiece The *Aeneid* and find that new things emerge every time you do so. It is not an understatement to call Vergil a genius.

The structure of the *Aeneid* is clever and complex. He uses themes and memes from both Homer's *Iliad* and *Odyssey*, but despite the intricate craftsmanship involved, he also creates a tale that is fresh, fast and fun to read.

> **Work divided up is done faster.**
>
> *(divisum sic breve fiet opus)*
>
> Martial. Epigrams 4.82.8

THEME: PROJECT MANAGEMENT

CHECKPOINT: When asking someone to do something, consider how much work might be involved. Maybe you'll need to discuss it with the person in some detail to get an idea yourself.

Throwaway requests for 'information on this' or 'an analysis of that' can come back to haunt you when you realize the task was too big for just one person and that it wasn't achievable in the time allotted.

The time aspect, though, is only part of the problem. If you overburden an individual with too much work, you fall prey to the law of diminishing returns. They might start out enthusiastically but as the size of the task becomes apparent, their work rate will dwindle and, worse, they could start to experience mental and physical fatigue.

Look at the scope of the work in a three-dimensional way. How many people will it take to do how much work in how much time?

WANT TO KNOW MORE? Martial (approximately 40 CE – 103 CE) lived for most of his life in Rome, the city he loved to lampoon. He retired in his old age back to Spain, where he was born. Rome at that time was host to people from all over the vast empire, and beyond. During his time in Rome, Martial would have witnessed some crazy and hair-raising events, such as in the year 69 CE when four generals in succession pitched for the top job of emperor.

Martial would have witnessed the construction of the Colosseum, the largest amphitheatre ever built – so huge in fact that special roads had to be built between Tivoli and Rome to carry the travertine stone used to construct the monumental edifice.

Today the Colosseum still attracts tourists and the centre of Rome retains the multicultural cosmopolitan feeling it would have had when Martial was there.

> **There were no sales of anything to anyone when everyone had everything they needed.**
>
> *(διάθεσις γὰρ ἦν οὐδενὸς πρὸς οὐδένα πάντων εὐπορούντων)*
>
> Plutarch. Lucullus 14.1

THEME: STRATEGY

CHECKPOINT: The first question for all new product development ideas is: are you launching your product into a saturated market?

The question defines the next step. If you are launching into a saturated market, what is your point of difference? Is your product actually needed?

Did the world need another taxi service? Uber offered something unique in the way it linked drivers to customers. It offered new access, not new taxis.

Did the world need another iPod? Seems not. In 2006 the Zune (from Microsoft) died an almost instant death.

Products that launch into a market that is already saturated with the same idea are called 'me-too' products. To succeed you have to be cheaper, or prettier, or more useful, or ideally all three.

Double-check what you're planning to launch into the marketplace. Is it really filling a need?

WANT TO KNOW MORE? Plutarch (approximately 46 CE – 120 CE) had a number of jobs, which he held simultaneously. He was a priest at Delphi and a philosopher, biographer and essayist. He became quite a celebrity in Rome and, although a home-loving Greek, received Roman citizenship at some point in his career. The Emperor Hadrian gave him the management task of governing Achaea (mainland Greece).

By all accounts, he was a much-loved man who wrote over 200 books.

Plutarch's *Lives* are accounts of famous Greeks and Romans, such as Pericles and Julius Caesar. They are wonderful portraits that flesh out the characters, making them feel very real.

We also have a wonderful and extremely personal letter from Plutarch to his wife, consoling her following the unexpected death of their daughter, aged just two.

> **Make sure you have goods that retail at a fifty percent markup.**
>
> *(pares quod vendere possis pluris dimidio)*
>
> Juvenal. Satires 14.200

THEME: FINANCE

CHECKPOINT: Let's be clear what Juvenal is advocating here. A 50% markup means the cost of producing your product is doubled when it comes to being sold.

Pricing is one of the four important 'Ps' of marketing (Price, Product, Place, Promotion).

If you price too high, you can get passed over. Too cheap and your margin is so low you can't efficiently and effectively run your business.

There's an old adage in the sales promotion world that 'the best consumer promotion is free money'. It's true a lot of the time, but not all of the time. When you discount your product, there's an effect on image. The words 'cheap', 'budget' and 'discount' all add slightly different connotations, don't they?

On the other hand, if you want to create a 'premium image', a higher price can help. There's a lot to think about.

But Juvenal's rule of thumb is the best place to start when planning your pricing strategy.

WANT TO KNOW MORE? Juvenal gives us pictures of ancient Rome which are often caustic at times. Be that as it may, they are a blast and allow us to dive head first into the nooks and crooks, and luxuries and latrines of a city contending with all the issues we contend with today. Racism, commercial wheeler-dealers and crooked lawyers. All modern life is there in Juvenal.

Which makes not knowing a great deal about his personal life particularly frustrating.

We do know that Juvenal was a contemporary of Martial and the two knew each other. If they were writing their satirical sketches today, they would surely have had their own late-night TV show!

> **A great deal is lost through slowness and stupidity.**
>
> *(multa amittuntur tarditie et socordia)*
>
> Accius. Diomedes Frag. 270

THEME: TIME MANAGEMENT

CHECKPOINT: There's a kind of Goldilocks 'sweet spot' in processing your business-day's work. Not too fast, and not too slow.

Efficiency is measurable now and often appears on analyses of employee timesheets. Time is money and employees who are taking a long time to get things done may provide the first clue in understanding why revenues are moving slowly.

Make sure you are giving as much support as you can to the workforce and avoid leaving people alone for long periods to 'get on with it'.

Be careful that plain stupid mistakes aren't being made – such as entering data incorrectly or making daft assumptions. It happens more often than you'd think.

WANT TO KNOW MORE? Lucius Accius was born around 170 BCE and is thought to have died around 86 BCE. He was a writer of tragedies, historical plays and, apparently, erotic poetry. Today we only have some fragments of his work.

He was regularly referred to by writers of his age, suggesting he was well respected.

Many of his plays take inspiration from the Trojan War. This quote comes from a fragment of one of his tragedies, *Diomedes*. Diomedes was one of the more prominent Greeks, and one who hid in the famous Trojan Horse.

> **Fake news and events are created by rumour-mongering.**
>
> *(ἡ δὲ λογοποιία ἐστὶ σύνθεσις ψευδῶν λόγων καὶ πράξεων)*
>
> Theophrastus. Characters 8.1

THEME: THE WATERCOOLER

CHECKPOINT: Think 'fake news' was a term first coined by Donald Trump?

Think again. Theophrastus shows us that there's nothing new in politics or journalism.

Rumour and gossip were as big an issue for the Greeks and Romans as they are for us.

Rumours are not individual opinions. They are pieces of information presented as news that have a grain of believability in the context of known events.

They are a form of entertainment, which is why people perpetuate them.

They are a currency of communication exchanged over lunch, or during a coffee break.

They can be personally very damaging and debilitating when targeted at an individual.

A rumour is the verbal equivalent of Japanese knotweed. Once it takes root, it spreads fast and is very hard to eradicate.

If you feel fake news and rumours are gripping your organization, move extremely quickly to stamp them out.

WANT TO KNOW MORE? Theophrastus (approximately 371 BCE – 287 BCE) was probably a student of Plato and was certainly a friend of Aristotle. He lived in the time of Philip of Macedon and his famous son, Alexander the Great.

Theophrastus was a renowned botanist, but he also wrote the amusing character sketches from which today's quote is taken.

The characters are pure entertainment, but they give us a very good understanding of the motivations of people living in Greece during one of the most extraordinary periods in all its history. The characters Theophrastus introduces to us include flatterers, chatterers, fake-newsmakers and slanderers.

Each one a very contemporary personality trait, particularly in the workplace!

> ## You're never too old to learn.
>
> *(αἰεὶ γὰρ ἡβᾷ τοῖς γέρουσιν εὐμαθεῖν)*
>
> Aeschylus. Agamemnon 584

THEME: PERSONAL DEVELOPMENT

CHECKPOINT: The rate of change and new developments means we have to keep ourselves constantly up to date. Opting out is not an option.

Many businesses have embraced this with personal development programmes, both formal (such as presentation courses) and informal (such as self-learning groups).

But don't rely on the workplace to provide this. Upgrade yourself!

It's never been easier to learn a language or study a course. And we should! We are all living longer. The capacity for learning is not one of the faculties which is lost with age (as Aeschylus reminds us). Keeping mentally agile is as important as keeping physically fit.

I guess with so many options at our disposal these days, you can teach an old dog new tricks.

WANT TO KNOW MORE? Aeschylus witnessed the greatest revolution in the history of Athens, fought in one of the greatest battles in the history of Europe, and wrote some of the greatest plays ever written and performed in the world today.

You can say, with some confidence, that he was 'one of the greats'.

When Aeschylus was a teenager he witnessed the overthrow of tyrants and the establishment of the world's first democracy in Athens. The rest is history, as they say.

When he was in his thirties he fought with his fellow citizens against the invasion of the Persians in 490 BCE. Ten thousand Athenians marched to Marathon to meet an invading force of over 125,000 Persians. The Athenians won. Greece was saved. And the rise of Classical Greece (Socrates, Plato and all that) followed. Again, the rest is history.

Aeschylus was the 'Father of Tragedy'. It all starts with him. In the 21st century, his play, *The Persians*, was voted The Greatest Play Ever Written. And he was up against Shakespeare.

> ## Wow. What unbelievable speed.
>
> *(o celeritatem incredibilem!)*
>
> Cicero. Letters To Atticus 7.22.1

THEME: PROJECT MANAGEMENT

CHECKPOINT: Speed is a measure of the distance covered and the time within which it is achieved.

Speed, today, shocks and surprises us all the time. We 'travel' so far on the internet within the normal timespan of a day that it feels like we are moving faster than ever. Competitors' speed has demolished businesses before they even knew a threat was coming. Speed of delivery is now a new and hugely important competitive advantage. Urgency in business is the result of aggressive competitors and promiscuous consumers breathing down our necks.

As a manager of the process, take a big top-down view of the whole effect of speed on quality, efficiency, morale and general well-being, and make sure all of these are attended to. Make sure the team gets on with each other and is appropriately rewarded. Make sure the end product is as good as it possibly can be by providing the right resources. And make sure the end of the process is duly recognized.

WANT TO KNOW MORE? Cicero was, and still is, a hugely important figure. He witnessed first-hand the assassination of Julius Caesar and he wrote vividly about the chaotic period before and after Caesar's death.

From the get-go he was the undisputed master of written Latin, whether it be vicious attacks on Rome's political opponents, in-depth philosophy or more personal letters to his wife, Terentia.

Cicero's output was huge. He spent his entire life writing. So much so that ever since his dramatic death in 43 BCE, he has been constantly quoted by people wishing to add weight to their views on education, ethics, politics and literature. In fact, this very book could have been put together using only quotes from the great man himself.

> **If you are sensible you will recover in full what's duly yours.**
>
> *(ἐὰν οὖν σωφρονῆτε, τὰ ὑμέτερ᾽ αὐτῶν κομιεῖσθε)*
>
> Lysias. Against Philocrates 14

THEME: LEGAL

CHECKPOINT: You have to protect your business. In some respects, from a legal point of view, limited companies are treated very much as if they are human beings.

They have rights. They cannot be mistreated. They have responsibilities. They have to pay taxes and they have to act with respect toward the people closely engaged with them.

When your business is unfairly treated, you must act. Whether it's a financial hit or a reputation loss, you need to repair the problem as soon as you possibly can.

Businesses can very quickly gain 'a reputation'. You don't want to be thought of as 'badly run', or 'bad payers' or 'easy to dupe'.

Businesses have 'assets', like people have 'belongings'. Money, people, goods and services.

Look after them.

WANT TO KNOW MORE? Lysias came to Athens from Sicily with his father, a wealthy arms manufacturer and an acquaintance of Plato.

Lysias was therefore not an Athenian citizen, but he was granted resident alien status, which was almost upgraded to full citizenship, but for a technical mistake in the process.

So Lysias, a superb, crystal-clear writer with an extremely clever legal brain, was not able to participate in Athenian court proceedings himself.

This didn't hold him back; he became a much sought-after writer of speeches for other eminent legal professionals.

His speeches are adapted to the character of each of his clients, but all display wit, intelligence, diplomacy and a laser-sharp understanding of the speech writer's skill to turn the heads of the jury.

Lysias opens up Athenian life for us, giving us insight into both the everyday disputes of ordinary people and the big power plays of the day.

> ## The pleasure is in the work itself.
>
> *(labor est etiam ipse voluptas)*
>
> Manlius. Astronomica 4.155

THEME: PROJECT MANAGEMENT

CHECKPOINT: Here's a useful piece advice.

Enjoy what you're doing!

I'm not suggesting you come to work high-fiving everyone every day, but it's important to understand that there can be delight in the work you do and how you do it.

Some people love what they do. And, have you noticed, they tell you that? A lot.

Others find work a bit of a grind. Monotonous maybe.

If you find your work a tad dull, look around.

There's likely to be enjoyment where you least expect it.

It could be colleagues, or simply the journey to work itself.

When embarking on a project, it's always worth being optimistic about the process ahead.

Before you start, sit down with your co-workers on the project and work out how to build genuine fun into the process.

WANT TO KNOW MORE? You have to feel a little bit sorry for Marcus Manlius. He is completely ignored by all Latin writers and yet he wrote his *Astronomica* to be a celebrity scientist.

Oh dear.

Manlius wrote his epic poem on Astronomy sometime around the period of the death of Augustus and the appointment of Tiberius as emperor (14 CE).

Forgotten by his contemporaries and overlooked by posterity, he was eventually uncovered and dusted off by an Italian scholar in about 1415 CE.

That could have been Manlius' big chance to get into the limelight, but sadly he was overshadowed when the same scholar also unearthed another scientific work called *On the Nature of Things*, written by Lucretius a hundred years before Manlius put stylus to wax.

On the Nature of Things, as we shall see, was significantly more important.

And so, Manlius remains in a corner of the classical world, still hoping his big day will come.

> **Give to the one who delivers. Do not give to the one who does not.**
>
> *(καὶ δόμεν ὅς κεν δῷ, καὶ μὴ δόμεν ὅς κεν μὴ δῷ·)*
>
> Hesiod. Works And Days 354

THEME: HUMAN RESOURCES

CHECKPOINT: Incentives play an invaluable part in business life.

Annual bonuses, pay rises, benefits and on-the-spot rewards are all part of keeping employees motivated.

But HR has an important role here. (If you don't have an HR department, get outside advice).

Factors to keep in mind are 'how much' and 'to whom'. Is it an ongoing bonus scheme or a one-off? Is it anticipated, or even expected?

Remember that if the reward is part of an incentive programme it is essential, as Hesiod advises, to make sure that the people who deserve it get the reward and those who don't, don't.

That means you have to have an objective system that calibrates who deserves what (and why).

Without a system, you can be accused of favouritism.

Incentives build businesses. Favouritism can destroy them.

WANT TO KNOW MORE? If Homer came first, then Hesiod came a very close second.

Hesiod was the son of an immigrant who came to settle in Greece around 700 BCE and started life as a shepherd.

Unlike Homer, we know Hesiod was the name of a person. Not that Homer wasn't a person, it's just that he could have been more than one. Where Homer might have been 'people', Hesoid was definitely a 'person', a guy with a name and address.

Justifiably, this gives him some claim to fame.

And fame he has.

One day, Hesiod just drops the shepherding and becomes a poet, inspired by the power of words. He does well in his new profession, winning at least one poetry competition that we know of.

As you have spotted, Hesiod obviously copied the title of this book for his major and influential work on the 'ins' and 'out' of work life in (very) ancient Greece. I'm flattered.

> ### Let the tree live a long time!
> ### It is a remarkable declaration of our serious commitment.
> *(vive diu nostri pignus memorabile voti)*
>
> Statius. Silvae 2.3

THEME: SOCIAL AND ENVIRONMENTAL

CHECKPOINT: If the Greeks and Romans did not look after the earth, they would be biting, as one might say, the land that fed them.

Our relationship with Planet Earth comes into daily life more and more. Rachel Carson fired the starting gun in 1962, with her book *Silent Spring*, which made the public aware of what mankind was doing to the natural world.

We have moved from a world of almost zero corporate concern to almost every business on the planet playing a role. Social and environmental actions are now one huge issue and, often, a major political concern.

How businesses play their part can range from having a paper recycling bin in the corner of the office to making it a full-blown business strategy. It can even be put at the very heart of the business, like The Body Shop did in its heyday.

If you are developing a social or environmental, or even ethical, strategy you must make sure it connects to the core product or service you produce.

If you don't it will become, at first, a 'nice' thing to do, and then a sideshow, then an expensive luxury.

WANT TO KNOW MORE? Statius is the boy from Naples, who, when he was about 40 years old, tried his luck in Rome.

But nine years later, Statius went back to Naples, having failed to crack the poetry awards. He died there two years later in 96 CE.

Statius composed the *Silvae* (a collection of 35 poems) sometime between 89 CE and 96 CE while in Naples.

The *Silvae* are light and charming and reveal a painter's eye view at times. The Emperor Domitian is present in spirit throughout the poems, which are in essence commentaries and reflexions on the life and times under the authoritarian regime of the imperial family and various powerful patrons.

> **If you want to be loved, be lovable.**
>
> *(ut ameris, amabilis esto)*
>
> Ovid. The Art Of Love 2.107

THEME: PERSONAL DEVELOPMENT

CHECKPOINT: Oh, is it Valentine's Day? I hadn't noticed.

Once the roses and cards have finished circulating around the office, it's worth thinking about love and the office. And I don't mean affairs.

Whilst you'll still hear people say things like "I don't care what people say about me," being liked by employees and/or colleagues leaves a very strong, positive and warm feeling.

Actually, it does more than that.

It improves communication, it relaxes tensions and it makes the work day function like a well-oiled machine.

To be loved in the workplace, if that is a personal target (and why not), you have to be approachable; you have to have an 'open-door' policy and you have to be trustworthy. You have to positively demonstrate that you are someone who listens and who takes action when necessary.

WANT TO KNOW MORE? Ovid has been fated to fall in and out of fashion both in his own life and throughout the centuries that followed.

He's very much in fashion now. And I'm pretty certain he's here to stay.

Ovid was born in March 43 BCE, almost a year to the day after Julius Caesar was assassinated. He was born into a wealthy family from Sulmona, a town to the east of Rome. As was the way in those days, he was sent to Rome to study; in Ovid's case, his subject was law.

However, he gave up studying law when he was still quite young and opted to become a poet instead. Much to his father's disapproval.

Ovid remained a bit of a rebel with early erotic poetry that created quite a storm when it was first recited.

Ovid's themes of sexual transformation, love, the body and effects of time and distance on relationships make him more pertinent today than ever before.

> ## You really shouldn't forget those things!
>
> *(ὧν οὐκ εἰκὸς ἀμνημονεῖν)*
>
> Thucydides. The Peloponnesian War 3.54.5

THEME: PROJECT MANAGEMENT

CHECKPOINT: We live very busy, very hectic lives. We are 'always on'. With all the virtual assistance available today, the assumption must be that we don't need to remember things. But these alerts can shunt out reminders of things that need to be done in a more orderly fashion.

Control the chaos of your day by planning your workload in the morning. You can do it over breakfast or on your commute. What are the events of the day that define your workload and give it its importance? Keep your 'note-to-self' at hand.

If you're worried a colleague might forget something important, a gentle prompt can help. Mark the prompt with a memorable action – something as simple as offering a coffee will do.

That way, you'll be happy they'll remember, and they'll be happy not to have forgotten.

WANT TO KNOW MORE? Thucydides was born 20 years after Herodotus, in Athens.

Herodotus wrote a history, *The Persian Wars*, Thucydides wrote the follow-up, *The Peloponnesian Wars*.

There is no evidence that the two ever met.

In fact, Thucydides never once formally mentions his incredibly famous predecessor. If he does make a passing vague reference, it's a rather sniffy comment about a couple of disputed facts. So, he'd obviously read Herodotus, but never met him. Strange. A rival perhaps?

Thucydides was undoubtedly a genius. The work, whilst it may not be 'history' as we might understand it (with events, facts, corroboration), is a masterpiece.

For evidence of this skip to Part Two of the book and read the oration which Pericles gives at a memorial ceremony for the war dead.

It's a morale booster for the war-weary Athenians and is the template for many such great public addresses throughout history, including *The Gettysburg Address*.

> **Stop doing those jobs that get you running around in circles.**
>
> *(relinque ista iamdudum, ad quae discurritur)*
>
> Seneca. Epistles 84.11

THEME: TIME MANAGEMENT

CHECKPOINT: Sometimes you can end a day's work and wonder what you've been doing.

How many times have you looked for a document on your computer only to find it was wrongly labelled or filed? So, you fix the problem, and while you're at it you double-check that everything else is filed correctly. That leads you to end up deleting a load of redundant stuff and then you think you'd better run the anti-virus software. Just in case. Suddenly it's lunchtime and you haven't done a stroke of work.

How often do you start a project only to find that you're stuck on one particular point? You go around in circles and you keep staring at the same difficult point.

Suddenly you've lost an hour.

Stop. Focus.

You can't be super-efficient 100% of the time and actually a little displacement activity can help keep you sane. When you're stuck, walk around, have a coffee or a large glass of water.

But if you've jobs to do, then do them. If necessary, devote a day to the 'running-around-like-a-mad-thing' jobs and get them out of the way.

WANT TO KNOW MORE? Seneca was an asthmatic. Curiously, it was ill health that kept him alive. Seneca was a rising star in the Senate who, despite his asthma attacks, was a very fine orator. Rising stars unfortunately are noticeable, and the Emperor Caligula noted his fame and became jealous enough to want have Seneca put to death.

Fortunately for Seneca, there were people in the Imperial household who had his back and one young lady advised Caligula that Seneca was in fact suffering from tuberculosis and would be dead in a very short time. Caligula took notice and left Seneca to die by himself.

Wisely Seneca 'retired' from politics for a while, and when Caligula was assassinated in 41 CE, Seneca's 'tuberculosis' miraculously disappeared, and he was able to get back to work.

> **People are really keen on just two things: lunches and fun.**
>
> *(duas tantum res anxius optat, panem et circenses)*
>
> Juvenal. Satires 10.80

THEME: ENTERTAINING

CHECKPOINT: In most businesses there will, at some point, be some kind of get-together or party. The office day out, team lunch, summer party, Christmas party, new-business win celebration. You name it. They are important and, managed correctly, can be a real morale booster.

But the opposite is also true. Badly organized entertainment can send out all the wrong messages.

Ideally, as many of these events as possible should be put in the diary at the beginning of the year, so that they are seen to be planned, are clearly part of work life and have a rationale.

More spontaneous get togethers, however valid, are better conducted out-of-hours.

Office celebrations should be built into the natural rhythm of the business and not bolted on hastily as an afterthought (unless something very special has happened, of course).

WANT TO KNOW MORE? In many respects Juvenal is a bit of a mystery man.

His own writings tell us almost nothing about him. He seems to be on the side of the underdog, bemoaning the low standard of living of schoolteachers and writers (and, amazing but true, lawyers) and some of his earlier satires suggest he was pretty poverty-stricken himself.

If true, this was unusual. Most of the literature we have from ancient Rome was written by well-off individuals who had rich parents, patrons or substantial enterprises (usually farms) from which to enjoy a good living.

To write, publish and perform you needed an infrastructure and a workforce. You had to bribe people to get things done, or to appear in front of key celebrities. You might think that slaves would be a good source of support for the struggling artist, but even slave-labour required financial upkeep.

Juvenal certainly supported the underdog, but he was not one himself.

> **Time takes everything away, even our minds.**
>
> *(omnia fert aetas, animum quoque)*
>
> Vergil. Eclogues 9.51

THEME: **PERSONAL DEVELOPMENT**

CHECKPOINT: Very few businesses ever review the successes and failures of past times. It's as if the only valid timeframe in which to analyse decisions is one year at the most.

New managers come and go, at every level. Short-term, incentive-based contracts designed to pep up the business and pump up the value are part and parcel of business life today.

Memory of the past in businesses is usually reserved for 'they were the good old days' type comment.

Today the internet holds so much data. A digital memory bank built over many years is now at our disposal. Do we use it for library information? Very rarely.

It's human nature to erase or bury or forget bad times and to remember the good ones, so that history is rewritten just before it repeats itself.

The message? The better you train your mind to remember, the less likely you are to repeat mistakes.

WANT TO KNOW MORE? Vergil loved the countryside. Apart from the obvious peace and quiet and 'honest labour' of shepherds, ploughman and goatherds, he felt it evoked a simplicity that his modern times of war and strife had forgotten. We'll see later how long it took Vergil to write (spoiler alert: a very long time) but his hard work paid off. The story goes that his *Eclogues* ('Selections') were an immediate, massive hit on the stage. Vergil became an overnight sensation.

On the stage? Yes, these poems were performed, and in a melodic fashion. In the *Eclogues* a singing competition is taking place between shepherds. Just like Shakespeare, reading them to yourself doesn't do them justice; they need to be brought to life with stage direction and even a talented director.

> ## A message sent, flies off. Irrevocably.
>
> *(et simul emissum volat irrevocabile verbum)*
>
> Horace. Epistles I.18.71

THEME: INTERNET

CHECKPOINT: Oh, the woes of instant messaging, emails, tweets and so on.

Hardly a day goes by without a news story of some celebrity, businessman or politician regretting pressing 'send' on an ill thought-out message.

Remember, once you've sent your message, you can never recall it. The sender gets your message the instant it is sent.

Not only can you not recall the message, you can't completely erase it. It lives forever and can be copied and shared endlessly. Cancelling an embarrassing tweet is fine, but what about the person who took a screen shot and shared that?

Once you've sent your message, assume the world will see it.

The wisest thing to do is to engage your brain and think 'pause' before you press 'send'.

WANT TO KNOW MORE? Horace's father was wealthy enough to buy a proper education for his son. That meant being sent to Rome, which was over 200 miles away from the family home in Venosa. By foot or cart that was a long journey to make. When he was about 18 he went on to study at Athens (our equivalent of Cambridge, Harvard or Oxford) to complete his education. While at Athens, Horace met Brutus (Julius Caesar's assassin) and was recruited into the Republican army to fight against Mark Antony and a young man called Octavian, who would later change his name to Augustus.

The Republican Army was beaten, and Horace left the battlefield a loser.

Horace was smart enough and wealthy enough to obtain a pardon from Octavian and buy a job in the treasury at Rome. (Yes, you could buy yourself into work in those days).

Once settled in Rome with a nice job, Horace, who had always been writing odd bits and pieces of poetry since his early twenties, starts to write. And in so doing, he writes himself into history.

> **Rumour. Of all the things sent to plague us,
> nothing moves faster. Its speed gives it momentum
> and the more it moves on, the stronger it gets.**
>
> *(fama, malum qua non aliud velocius ullum.
> mobilitate viget viresque adquirit eundo)*
>
> Vergil. Aeneid 4.174

THEME: THE WATERCOOLER

CHECKPOINT: Once rumours are out in the open, everyone hears about them, makes assumptions and draws conclusions. Rumour spreads far, and fast.

It is impossible to live without rumours. They act as a kind of early warning system. We need them and, in some cases, thrive on them, particularly when there is obvious change in the air.

It's important to understand the nature of rumours, as the Greeks and Romans certainly did.

If you hear a rumour, assume everyone has heard it. Don't try and manage it, unless you know the absolute truth about the detail of the story being passed around. In that situation, calmly address the content and then provide the truth, with as much evidence as you can.

It's worth remembering the old adage 'truth is stranger than fiction', or as we like to say nowadays 'you couldn't make it up!'.

It's because real-life events can be so extraordinary, even unbelievable at times, that rumour is such a strong currency.

WANT TO KNOW MORE? After his first works were performed, Vergil became a sensation. But he was a painstakingly slow writer. It took him 3 years to write his first book, the *Eclogues*, 7 years to write his next book, the *Georgics*, and 12 years to write the *Aeneid*. In fact, he wrote just a few words a day. The *Aeneid* is woven together like a three-dimensional tapestry. Almost every word he wrote counted, and was connected and interconnected. He thought long and hard about the names he gave to people and places, and he made sure they divulged a hidden element to the story. He constructed his giant epic so that each chapter reconnects with another in an extraordinary display of symmetry.

> **Keep an eye on whatever it is possible to lose.**
>
> *(adspicere oportet quicquid possis perdere)*
>
> Publilius Syrus. Sententiae 9

THEME: PERSONAL DEVELOPMENT

CHECKPOINT: Despite how much care we think we are taking, there is so much we can, and do, lose.

We can lose house keys. Annoying.

We can lose data. Frustrating.

We can lose our jobs. Devastating.

We can lose relationships. Awful.

We can even lose our minds.

Speed has the effect of making it less easy to organize both our work and private lives.

Get into the habit of recognizing the things that are important.

From saving a document in the right folder to seeing a friend for a drink, everything we do needs more attention than ever.

Otherwise we just keep forgetting and losing.

WANT TO KNOW MORE? Publilius Syrus, a slave from Syria, is a good example of how, if you were smart enough, you could rise through Roman society.

He came to Rome on the same boat as Manlius (see February 11) and was later freed, no doubt because of his intelligence and wit.

Publius could read people and society very well and we have over 700 of his simple yet apposite one-liners. He also wrote plays, none of which have been unearthed yet.

Slaves were freed through a process of 'manumission', which was a very straightforward and brief ceremony in front of a magistrate with the owner basically saying: "I want this man to be free."

Freed slaves were called Freedmen. They could hold junior civil servant roles only, but were free to work and amass as much wealth as they could.

> **Every organization is, as we can see, a sort of partnership.**
>
> (Ἐπειδὴ πᾶσαν πόλιν ὁρῶμεν κοινωνίαν τινὰ οὖσαν)
>
> Aristotle. Politics 1.1

THEME: LEGAL

CHECKPOINT: It doesn't matter what kind of company yours is, it will always be a partnership of some kind. Of course, some businesses are actually legally formed 'partnerships'. But beyond the legal definition, limited companies, sole traders and PLCs are 'in partnership' with suppliers, customers and employees; even with the local community in many cases.

Understanding 'the company you keep' is now an essential part of running a business. It defines your reputation.

Businesses are interlinked (now even more so thanks to the internet,) with a greater number of stakeholders than ever before. Everybody who interacts with a business (and often many who never have and never will) has a view on the business.

Understanding that you are in partnership with a wide community of people can help you to build your business. A good and trusted employer embraces as much of the community as possible.

WANT TO KNOW MORE? Aristotle left a will when he died in 322 BCE, aged 62. Reading it today, it feels remarkably like a contemporary Last Will and Testament. After his first wife died, Aristotle took up with her slave, Herpyllis. He had children from both women.

In the will, he appoints an executor and makes provision for his children, including naming legal guardians for them until his eldest reaches legal maturity.

He also makes sure that Herpyllis is properly looked after.

Aristotle left instructions for various statues of his family to be completed and he also requests that his first wife be reburied with him.

This is one of those documents that reminds us how very little emotional distance actually separates us from those people living 2,500 years ago.

> **For these people I'm setting no boundaries or time constraints; I've empowered them – no limitations!**
>
> *(his ego nec metas rerum nec tempora pono; imperium sine fine dedi)*
>
> Vergil. Aeneid 1.278

THEME: INNOVATION

CHECKPOINT: Today, innovation is more important than ever, as new technologies create new competitors and superior products.

Make sure innovation doesn't come too late for your business and that it is managed from the centre of the company. Put your best people on the team, give them the tools and the time to do the job. Empower them to think as widely as possible and , importantly, don't give them boundaries.

'Evolution, not Revolution' is often the mantra of cautious management, but neither of these words are correct.

'Execution' is the right mantra. Innovate properly; then execute the results properly.

WANT TO KNOW MORE? Vergil knew trauma. His father went blind, and both his brothers died before him. His family were country folk from northern Italy, working with bees and cattle. They had enough money to send Vergil to schools in Cremona and Milan and then to university in Rome, to learn rhetoric. But Vergil was a sensitive lad and he found the competitive nature of his subject too much. He left Rome and went to Naples, where he studied philosophy.

While at Naples, the other students nicknamed him 'Parthenias', meaning 'girly'. The misspelling of his name as 'Virgil' may have come at this time as an attempt to label him a 'virgo', or young female virgin. Teasing at college is no new thing.

Vergil never married and was very close to confirmed bachelor and fellow poet Horace.

Horace called Vergil 'my other half'.

Vergil was tall, dark, shy and softly spoken. He cared little for how he looked and regularly suffered from ill health.

Nothing created dies.

(θνῄσκει δ᾽ οὐδὲν τῶν γιγνομένων)

Euripides. Chrysippus Frag. 839

THEME: INTERNET

CHECKPOINT: Tomorrow's memories are all the stored actions of today. The traces on the tracks of our online journeys never disappear.

The interactions of our relationships are compiled over time to eventually create a composite picture of exactly how we feel about something or someone (customer, boss, family member, friend).

We are each defined by two memories.

An online one. And an embodied one.

Our online memory just gets bigger and bigger. We have created a universe of information bigger than our own world. And it keeps growing. Stored memory allows people to play tricks. They can discover your past actions and can persecute you or delight you as they wish.

Our embodied memory can play tricks too. We can forget what we said.

But the person we said it to may remember.

The lesson here? Be careful what you store up. Everything you do creates a picture of you.

WANT TO KNOW MORE? Euripides (approximately 484 BCE – 407 BCE) was an Athenian through and through. He was in his mid-thirties, when the Persian Wars ended. We know little of his military career but from a young age he would have seen the war heroes and heard them tell the tale of 'how they saved Athens'. He grew up seeing Athens as the centre of the world, the heart of civic virtue. His town was a winner. And he was a part of it.

In 431, aged just over 50, everything changed for Euripides. Suddenly, Athens was at war again, this time against Sparta. Euripides was to live for the rest of his life in the middle of a crippling conflict. As he eventually came towards the end of his life, he fortunately saw his beloved Athens win a few small strategic battles.

But he was never to know that in the end, they lost the war.

> **Birds of a feather stick together.**[9]
>
> (ἀεὶ κολοιὸς παρὰ κολοιόν)
>
> Aristotle. Rhetoric 1.11.25

THEME: **HUMAN RESOURCES**

CHECKPOINT: Creating good teams with the right mix of talent is a skilful art that pays off big time when done well. Getting the right mix means matching personalities, as well as talent.

Good friends in business don't necessarily make good workmates. And often close-knit relationships of people spending too much time together may not always lead to fresh thinking or complementary skills. They can often devote more time to being good friends than to working as good colleagues.

Friends like to stay together, but look beyond existing group structures to create teams that need to think beyond the day-to-day, habit-forming routines of business life.

WANT TO KNOW MORE? Rhetoric was an essential part of both Greek and Roman education. Plato defined Rhetoric as "using words to win over men's minds." Often it wasn't just the core subject to learn, it was the only subject to learn.

Aristotle was one of the most important text books on rhetoric and young privileged Romans would aim to finish their education at Athens where both rhetoric and philosophy would be taught.

Roman education started at elementary school at age seven. Pupils would learn reading, writing and calculating.

At age 12 they went on to the 'grammar school' ('*grammaticus*') where Greek literature would be taught, followed by Latin literature. Learning poetry was a big part of education. At around age 15, depending on how you were doing, you might go on to learn basic rhetoric, before going on to university at Athens, hopefully – if not, Rome, or Ephesus, or Rhodes. There were plenty of options.

> **We don't see the baggage we're carrying on our own backs.**
>
> *(sed non videmus manticae quod in tergo est)*
>
> Catullus. Poems 22.21

THEME: PERSONAL DEVELOPMENT

CHECKPOINT: If you don't seek professional help at certain stages of your career you will forever be an amateur at your business game. You may be a highly experienced amateur, and that might be good enough to carry you towards the top, but you remain an amateur.

Many people seek both internal and external help to develop themselves. Experts help you to see parts of yourself that you can't see. You may be behaving in a way that you think is fine, but others think is boorish.

Catullus wrote a line just before today's quote: 'Everybody has their own mistake assigned to them.'

You may carry embarrassments or failures from the past. But these can often be turned into positive learning experiences.

When planning to move to another job (maybe a welcome step-change in your career) the first thing prospective employers will look at is your CV.

Think about your CV as the total representation of your 'professional' self.

Build it, craft it, make it look sexy! Baggage and all.

WANT TO KNOW MORE? Catullus was a poet who was not ashamed to show the intensity of his feelings. Whether he was writing to lovers, friends or enemies, he never held back. His poetry has a power and truth that comes straight from a heart that is burning with passion.

Born in Verona in 84 BCE, Catullus moved to Rome as a young man and before too long started up a stormy relationship with a prominent married woman.

Chew the fat.

(ruminari)

Livius Andronicus. Frag. 7

THEME: STRATEGY

CHECKPOINT: Some sound advice here from an old Roman.

You are planning something. A meeting, next year's sales, new products or services, maybe a five-year plan. You have all the information you need. You are well prepared. You are, in fact, ready to press the button.

Stop.

Just for a moment, and have a good, long, hard think.

Go for a walk, take a long weekend; whatever. Just put a little space in between the planning process and finally pressing the button. Ruminate on the problem. (The literal translation of '*ruminari*' is 'to chew the cud'.)

This is not to delay things. On the contrary, it is to ensure the next steps are the right steps. And it won't take long for you to tell.

Sitting down and thinking is one of the most valuable things you can do.

WANT TO KNOW MORE? Livius Andronicus was the granddaddy of Latin literature. He was born around 284 BCE and died at the respectable old age of 79 in 205 BCE. It looks like (although detail on his life is sketchy) he was brought to Rome as a 12-year-old slave in 272 BCE.

He was clearly a smart boy and at some point he won his freedom. He took up teaching and then went on to translate, amongst other things, Homer's *Odyssey*, from the Greek into Latin.

His work became known by subsequent Roman schoolchildren down the line. The poet Horace remembers an unpleasant association between learning Livius Andronicus and being caned when making a mistake.

> **They say that water droplets, drip by drip,**
> **can hollow out a channel even in stone.**
>
> (Ἐκ θαμινᾶς ῥαθάμιγγος, ὅπως λόγος,
> αἰὲς ἰοίσας χἀ λίθος ἐς ῥωχμὸν κοιλαίνεται)
>
> Bion. Frag. 4

THEME: STRATEGY

CHECKPOINT: There are different ways to achieve your end goal. It's human nature to want things to happen as quickly as possible – you need a quick sales turnaround or a sudden influx of customers; usually both. It's rare that business goes like this.

Sometimes a long-term, consistent approach is what is needed. In this situation, your success comes slowly and incrementally but can suddenly lift towards the end. Don't change a strategy because things are going well but slowly, unless obvious market forces tell you to.

IKEA, which started selling furniture in 1948, has never deviated from its core strategy, slowly but surely opening new stores as circumstances dictate.

From humble beginnings, the journey from a small store to a giant global super-retailer took well over 50 years.

WANT TO KNOW MORE? Bion whispers to us very faintly from Izmir in Turkey. Little is known of him and little of his work is left. But we do know a couple of things. He was living around 100 BCE and was an influence on Vergil and Ovid.

Bion's situation reminds us of exactly how much Greek and Latin literature has not made its way down to us.

How much is lost, you might ask?

The problem, of course, is that we don't know what we don't know.

Judging by the written and archaeological evidence, there were thousands and thousands of books. We know that many of the authors who have come down to us have written much more than exists. A sensible estimate might be that we have less than 1% of all the literature that was written. But who knows exactly?

> **Grab this day with both hands and squeeze**
> **every single ounce of juice out of it.**
>
> *(carpe diem)*
>
> Horace. Odes 1.11

THEME: PERSONAL DEVELOPMENT

CHECKPOINT: How many times did a parent, teacher or mentor say to you: "Carpe Diem! Seize the day! Go for it!" It's said so many times, it has become a cliché. Which is a shame. I just wanted to add a dimension to the quote. Horace is urging us to make the most of the day ahead of us. Enjoy every part of it. Not just an opportunity that lies ahead.

Open up to what's around you. Appreciating your surroundings allows you to properly connect with everything that is happening around you and adds to a sense of general wellbeing in the workplace. This is a free Leap Year Day; exploit this rare moment!

WANT TO KNOW MORE? The context of the line is all-important. Horace is holed up in a Tuscan villa with a lover.

As in many relationships today, his friend is trying to work out their future together; how long will their relationship last? The poem goes like this:

You can't find out
You can't access that info
No point trying out horoscopes, poppet.
How much better just to take the future as it comes. Whatever it will be.
You never know, we could see out a few more winters yet.
Or not.
This one might be our last.
It's exhausted our Tuscan sea
Banging away at those soft white cliffs.
So pop that cork of yours, you know it makes sense.
Prune your long wish-list down to a manageable size
I mean, look, even now, while we're chatting, time will have slid by.
What a bastard.
Today is ripe for plucking. Grab it with both hands and squeeze every single ounce of juice out of it.
Tomorrow never knows.

> **I've got to find a way of raising my game and becoming a word-of-mouth sensation!**
>
> *(temptanda via est, qua me quoque possim*
> *tollere humo victorque virum volitare per ora)*
>
> Vergil. Georgics 3.8

THEME: PERSONAL DEVELOPMENT

CHECKPOINT: Sometimes you need to wake up in the morning and give yourself a metaphorical slap in the face!

You need to put a spring in your step. And today is the first day of spring, so no time like the present.

Work's good. Life's fine. Everything's OK.

But fine is not fabulous. And good is not great.

Today is a day you can reprimand yourself for being too settled, too self-satisfied.

The truth is that almost everyone has more to give than they like to admit to themselves.

WANT TO KNOW MORE? Vergil pops up just a few times in the pages of his contemporaries. One time is around 37 BCE when he has joined Horace and others on a trip to Brindisi.

As it happens, 'trip' might be a very good description of the journey which can be read both as a real journey with a political/diplomatic motive and as a metaphorical journey into troubled times – a bad dream, an hallucination.

Vergil then disappears until around 29 BCE when he gives a reading of his *Georgics*, a unique work that expresses his feelings on the politics of his day through the device of a farming manual. I said it was unique.

If today you were to watch Vergil at work you'd think he suffered from Obsessive-Compulsive Disorder, OCD. The four books of the *Georgics* took seven years to complete. The construction was so complex that Vergil must have refined the lines he wrote many times.

With 2,188 lines in total, Vergil's writing rate was less than one line a day. He himself described his style as "like licking his lines into shape, the way a mother bear does her cubs."

What makes this slow composition so remarkable is the turbulent times in which his works were written. He clearly remained calm and just carried on.

> **What are the truly vacuous and dangerous things that people ask for?**
>
> *(ergo supervacua aut quae perniciosa petuntur?)*
>
> Juvenal. Satires 10.54

THEME: HUMAN RESOURCES

CHECKPOINT: Employees are unpredictable. You never know what will come up next.

I once employed someone who asked for a company scooter (the non-motorized version) as part of his package.

People asking for things can be read as a sign of ambition, but you need to know when ambition spills over into the danger zone.

Not everyone is able to do what they want to do, or to have what they ask.

If faced with a strange request, it's worth interrogating the motives behind the request.

Often they come down to simply wanting what other people have.

WANT TO KNOW MORE? Juvenal is a very modern satirist. He would be at home on Saturday Night Live.

He lived well into his eighties and was witness to the great fire of Nero's Rome, the Year of the Four Emperors, the building of the Colosseum, the massive extension of the empire under Trajan and was still alive when Hadrian built his wall in the north of Brittania.

Surely being a satirist under, in total, ten emperors, might have been somewhat hazardous? Well, there is a suggestion he was exiled briefly in 92 CE to Egypt, but he was back in the good books, and Rome, by around 97CE.

> **Have a think about whether this will be of any benefit to you.**
>
> *(ὅρα νυν εἴ σοι ταῦτ᾽ ἀρωγὰ φαίνεται)*
>
> Aeschylus. Prometheus Bound 997

THEME: PERSONAL DEVELOPMENT

CHECKPOINT: There will be occasions when you are presented with choices.
You might have a job offer up your sleeve.
You might be on the verge of a promotion.
There could be a post coming up overseas which you think is perfect for you.
You might be asked to move sideways to another team
There are all sorts of options that will come your way.
To assess these, think of only one thing.
Yourself.
When faced with choices to make it's all about you. Be selfish.
Just like on airplanes, put the oxygen mask over your own face before helping others.
That way you can be sure that the beneficial move you make can benefit any others who will be joining you on the next stage of your journey.

WANT TO KNOW MORE? In Aeschylus' lifetime he would have witnessed first hand the concept of 'ostracism'.
We use the term today to denote someone who is deliberately left out.
In ancient Greece, the idea was to protect the community from tyranny.
It worked like this:
Every year the citizens of Athens performed the legal task of scratching onto a piece of clay pottery 'ὄστρακον' (ostrakon) the name of a man who they considered to be a threat to security. The punishment was 10 years in exile. Six thousand citizens had all to agree on the same name.
As a process it was clearly, well, democratic.
How successful it was is more difficult to determine.

> **We find there's a big gap between good people with principles and mass market opinions.**
>
> *(πολὺ διεστώσας εὑρήσομεν τάς τε τῶν σπουδαίων γνώμας καὶ τὰς τῶν φαύλων διανοίας)*
>
> Isocrates. To Demonicus 1.1

THEME: SOCIAL AND ENVIRONMENTAL

CHECKPOINT: Creating a social and environmental programme certainly feeds into the current popular mood, and research highlights that this is a growing trend.

However, businesses need to be careful about how they go about creating such a programme.

There are some laudable and active campaigners belonging to a wide range of organizations who believe in a wide range of things.

Being too specific about your company beliefs can in fact alienate consumers who might not agree wholeheartedly with you.

Make sure there is someone in the Social and Environmental team who understands the broader relationship between what your business sells and what your customers expect. There's a huge gap between focused idealism and mass market consumer appeal.

WANT TO KNOW MORE? On this day in 51 CE (and for the record, about 500 years after Isocrates wrote today's quote!) the young Nero was given a promotion. He was given the title of '*Princeps Iuventutis*', meaning he was head of the order of Roman Knights. In reality it meant he was being prepped for a fast-track rise to the top.

The job title was relatively new, but it came with all sorts of bells and whistles. The *Princeps Iuventutis* was leader of the younger, next generation. Nero was 14 when he received the title. It gave him the right to oversee a spectacular annual display of horsemanship and put him in the public eye.

> **Huge success doesn't come without huge risk.**
>
> *(μεγάλα γὰρ πρήγματα μεγάλοισι κινδύνοισι ἐθέλει καταιρέεσθαι)*
>
> Herodotus. Histories 7.50

THEME: RISK

CHECKPOINT: "Have we done the risk assessment yet?"
You hear this a great deal nowadays.
There are now well-established processes in place to evaluate how risky a proposed action might be.
When it comes to children or personal safety, there is no doubt that you play safe.
But when it comes to business decisions, there is always a moment where you have to make a gut decision.
Giant companies like Google and Twitter were all risks at their inception. At one point, the Google founders nearly gave up, because creating the company was taking up too much of their student study time.
Sometimes risks don't always come off, but if you're smart and you understand your market, your hunches are usually good bets.

WANT TO KNOW MORE? To find out about life in the classical world before Herodotus, we have to rely on vague reconstructions from poets and playwrights, or, more meaningfully, archaeological evidence.
When Herodotus arrived, we suddenly have written history.
In one stroke of a stylus, he provided a framework for what was going on in and around the Persian War, which lasted on and off for 50 years (499 BCE – 449 BCE).
The Persian War pitted a mighty, united and well-organized Persian Empire against a small number of unconnected Greek city states. It was a David versus Goliath story.
The war was started by just one man, who wanted to extend Persian rule to the island of Naxos. His 'plan' was a disaster and fearing he'd get the sack (or worse), he persuaded other islands close to Naxos to join a rebellion against his old boss (Persia). The Athenians were called in to lend support to the islands. The Persians saw this as a significant threat and the rest is (Herodotus') history.

> **(Julius Caesar) could simultaneously read, write, dictate and listen. He could dictate four important letters to his secretaries at a time, seven if he was less busy.**
>
> *(scribere aut legere, simul dictare aut audire solitum accepimus, epistulas vero tantarum rerum quaternas pariter dictare librariis aut, si nihil aliud ageret, septenas)*
>
> Pliny The Elder. Natural History 7.25

THEME: TIME MANAGEMENT

CHECKPOINT: When you are working in a 'startup company' you find you do everything. You can't afford a cleaner, so you do the cleaning yourself. You don't have any personal assistants, so you do the photocopying yourself. You do all this while running the day-to-day business and finding new customers. You discover that you are a serious multi-tasker.

Then the company grows.

You start hiring more people and before you know it you have an organization on your hands. The jobs you used to do now become full-time jobs for other people.

However, don't lose sight of the multi-tasker you once were. If a task needs doing, be ready to step in and just do it. You can almost always do more than one thing at a time.

WANT TO KNOW MORE? Pliny the Elder was born in 23 CE and, as famously and vividly witnessed and recounted by his nephew, died in the eruption of Vesuvius in 79 CE. He was 56 years old.

Pliny the Elder's major claim to fame is a monumental encyclopaedia of the knowledge of his day. He called it *The Natural History* and claimed it contained 20,000 pieces of information and material from 100 authors.

Pliny had a conventional Roman upbringing. He was born near Lake Como and his father took him to Rome to study law and rhetoric.

When he was 23, Pliny went into military service and while fighting in Germany he wrote a booklet on javelin-throwing from horseback.

Pliny the Elder's *The Natural History* is 37 books long and we have the complete works.

> **Things above our station don't concern us.**
>
> *(quod supra nos, nihil ad nos)*
>
> Minucius Felix. Octavius 13.2

THEME: HUMAN RESOURCES

CHECKPOINT: We all want to get the low-down on what's going on at the level above us and at certain times it's valuable to be put in the picture. But most of the time there is no need to know.

The most important concern we should have is for our own business. 'Mind your own business', you might say.

Concentrate on working within your job definition because even if you do pick up something from more senior colleagues, you may not have the context to diagnose how, or if, it will affect you. Raw information can be difficult to digest and can even make you unnecessarily unwell.

Steer clear.

[Note to bosses: If leaks occur, or gossip is rampant, act! Apply as much context as you can. And avoid telling any lies!]

WANT TO KNOW MORE? I'm afraid we know very little about Marcus Minucius Felix, except that he was a lawyer and a Christian, and that at one point in his life he had worked in Carthage. His book, *Octavius*, written around 250 CE, paints a picture of the religious and social conditions in Rome during this time. In another of his works, *Apologeticum*, he fulminates against paganism and takes aim at most of the Greek and Roman poets and philosophers. He called their work a perversion.

Thankfully for us, Minucius Felix wasn't compelling enough to have had all those 'pagan' works destroyed, otherwise he might have single-handedly deprived all future students of the study of Latin and Greek.

Phew.

....

> **Almost no one dances sober unless they are insane.**
>
> *(nemo enim fere saltat sobrius, nisi forte insanit)*
>
> Cicero. Pro Murena 13

THEME: ENTERTAINING

CHECKPOINT: Partying on office time is fundamentally different to partying in your private life.

Yet somehow that rather obvious fact seems easy to forget.

It's worth thinking for a moment about how you want to be remembered by your colleagues the next day you are back at work. What seemed hilarious at the time can be utterly embarrassing the next morning.

(Don't forget, every single person present will have a camera in their hand).

Dancing usually needs a little lubrication to loosen up those awkward inhibitions. But try not to overdo it. Think of it like this: the office party is an extension of work, however fab the music and however free the bar.

WANT TO KNOW MORE? There are many reasons why Cicero is important, but one of the most striking is that he personally witnessed the fall of the Roman Republic. The Republic had been going since 509 BCE, but 450 years later the structure was cracking under the weight of Roman expansion.

What had once been a small but important and powerful city had now become a Roman global superpower.

Courtesy of Cicero, we meet and hear from the key characters first hand. We understand more about their motives. People like Julius Caesar and Mark Antony.

Cicero's life is made crystal clear through his letters, his philosophical works and his court cases. It is no surprise that the author Robert Harris had more than enough material to write his fabulous three-volume story of Cicero's extraordinary life (*Imperium, Lustrum, Dictator*).

....

Watch your expenses.

(δαπανῶν ἄρχου)

Saying of The Seven Sages

THEME: FINANCE

CHECKPOINT: Remember that in law, businesses are treated almost as if they were people, with many of the same protections. One thing you can't do is use business money as if it were your own, unless it is agreed in advance. If it isn't agreed, it could well be theft. So be careful.

Expenses are a common cause of confusion. And the rules around them are often not easy to follow.

For example, be careful how you account for expenses. It is essential that the business confirms that your particular use of them is justified. This is normally called an expenses policy and you should find time to understand it.

WANT TO KNOW MORE? The Seven Sages were early philosophers; they sound mysterious, don't they? Like something you might discover at the end of a *Matrix* movie. We take it that they were real; after all, they are mentioned by Plato.

The magnificent seven are:

Thales of Miletus, Pittacus of Mytilene, Bias of Priene, Solon, Cleobulus of Lindus, Myson of Chenae and Chilon of Sparta.

They all lived roughly between 650 BCE and 550 BCE.

They were ahead of their time. They had a penchant for brief and terse philosophising, with maxims such as: 'everything in moderation', and 'pardon is better than repentance'.

Perfect for the Twitter age.

> **A speech was given to the troops, as the occasion demanded.**
>
> *(κἀνταῦθα παρακαλέσας τὰ πρέποντα τῷ καιρῷ τὰς δυνάμεις)*
>
> Polybius. Histories 1.60.5

THEME: PRESENTATIONS/MEETINGS/DOCUMENTS

CHECKPOINT: Any form of public address is a presentation. And a presentation needs to be prepared. Each presentation will be slightly different from the last one you gave. After all, you're not a robot.

Try the Five 'L's as an easy aide-memoir:

Listeners – Who is the audience? What are their expectations?

Location – Where are you making the presentation? Your office or at another venue? Make sure you have checked the location and are comfortable with it.

Logic – What is the main point of your presentation? Tell people what you are going to say. Say it. Tell them again.

Length – The usual tip here is: keep it as short as possible.

Look – What does your presentation look like? Natural, just you talking? Or with charts? If the latter, one line per chart is the rule. Watch how TV anchors do it.

WANT TO KNOW MORE? Carthage was Rome's oldest foreign enemy. Geographically it's just a short hop over the water from Carthage to the west coast of Sicily and, hey presto, you're in Italy. The Romans fought three wars against the Carthaginians, eventually crushing them in 146 BCE.

Today's quote comes from a Roman commander, and was made to his troops during the first of the three wars in 241 BCE. He had heard that a Carthaginian fleet was heading to some islands just off Sicily's west coast (for those of you who know Sicily, they are the Egadi islands off the coast of Trapani).

The commander had received intelligence of the fleet maneuver, roused his men, and set out to meet the enemy. The Romans inflicted a decisive defeat and ended the first Carthaginian War.

Think before you speak.

(τὴν γλῶτταν μὴ προτρέχειν τοῦ νοῦ)

Chilon. (Quoted by Diogenes Laertes: Lives of Eminent Philosophers 1.3)

THEME: PERSONAL DEVELOPMENT

CHECKPOINT: It is totally within our control to not open our mouths and speak. Yet sometimes the words just seem to pour out by themselves. What you say may not be what you mean, but it is certainly what is heard. (Or it maybe it is what you mean, but it's best it isn't heard!)

Initiating a conversation can be easier than responding to someone else's comment, because you can give yourself a moment to think through what you are saying.

When responding, if you are concerned about what you are about to say, then simply ask someone to give you a couple of moments to think things through.

It's a sign of respect to the other person to say that your response is important, and that you need to really think about it. Things said in haste invariably fall short of their intended meaning.

WANT TO KNOW MORE? Chilon was one of the Seven Sages (see March 8). Their wise sayings were short and to the point. They were like the pithy maxims you see every day on the internet. They were philosophical Tweets.

One reason they were short and pithy may have been because they were meant to be read out loud to an audience, who would then be able to remember and debate the short sentence.

We are talking about very early philosophy here. This is way before Socrates and the other famous Greek philosophers. Chilon lived sometime around 580 BCE, but Socrates came 100 years later.

This early form of philosophizing should not be dismissed just because it was delivered in neat one-liners and read aloud to a crowd. These comments were thoughtful and helpful.

And after all, we still like them today.

....

> **Practise what you preach.**
>
> *(verba rebus proba)*
>
> Seneca. Epistles 20.1

THEME: LEADERSHIP

CHECKPOINT: There is nothing more irritating than being briefed to do something by someone who has absolutely no experience of doing it themselves.

And even more irritating is someone who asks you to behave in a way in which they do not behave themselves.

Leaders in business must lead by example. Not doing this very quickly leads to a corrosion of the character of the company. The company becomes unfocused, with a 'don't care' attitude.

If you are senior to someone in an organization, make sure that you are a role model.

Hypocrisy is a very negative force.

WANT TO KNOW MORE? Seneca had an interesting view on how he started out in life.

It's conventional to describe someone by talking about where and when they were born. If the birth was noteworthy for any particular reason (weight of baby, thunder and lightning on arrival) you might include that. Seneca's view was different.

He thought that being born was actually quite a trivial matter. You might go on to live a good life; alternatively things might not turn out so well for you. In fact, Seneca thought the odds on either were fifty-fifty.

He did concede that being born was the very first step towards what happens in your life.

But that doesn't make the birth itself better than all the other steps in your life.

I wonder how he felt about birthdays?

What does the man in the street think?

(quis populi sermo est?)

Persius. Satires 1.63

THEME: CONSUMER INSIGHTS

CHECKPOINT: Research is the best method that we have to measure what people are thinking about. But it isn't infallible. Things do go wrong (look at general election voting intentions).

And public opinion can change like the wind.

Ideally, the larger the research sample, the better. It would be lovely to get absolutely everyone's personal view, but in most countries that's just not feasible.

Quantitative research measures the number of people who think this or that.

Qualitative research examines the views people hold and is done in small focus groups.

All well and good. But don't dismiss your own hunches; listen to the things you are told and take note of the knowledge you pick up through personal experience.

Importantly, be prepared to be open-minded about research results.

There are many cases of new products launched on the back of expensive research which go on to fail.

And there are cases where no research was undertaken at all, and the product launches with great success.

WANT TO KNOW MORE? Persius was a serious young man who lived a short life. He was born in Tuscany in 34 CE and died aged just 28 in 62 CE from some sort of stomach disorder.

When Persius was six, his father died and his mother remarried, only to lose her second husband a few years later.

Persius was a good-looking lad, gentle, modest and kind to all the women in his family.

When he died, he left a staggeringly huge amount of money and a massive library of books.

We are left with just six of his satirical poems.

Looks like Persius was cut down in his prime!

> **Don't trust that horse, Trojans!**
> **Whatever it is, I fear the Greeks when they're bringing us gifts.**
>
> *(equo ne credite, Teucri. Quidquid id est, timeo Danaos et dona ferentis)*
>
> Vergil. Aeneid 2.48

THEME: RISK

CHECKPOINT: If you hear yourself saying: 'That looks too good to be true', it almost certainly is.

There is a huge risk in buying something (an idea, a product, a service, a person) when you simply cannot get to the bottom of what makes the thing behave the way it does.

Most things that are of good quality, with a proven record and which will genuinely add value to your business, will not be cheap. They certainly won't be free.

And anything that comes with a 'free added bonus' also needs to be considered carefully. Sometimes, but not always, there's a reason why things are being given away for next to nothing.

WANT TO KNOW MORE? This famous quote comes from one of the well-known stories of The Trojan War – The Trojan Horse.

The story marks the beginning of the end of the ten-year war fought over the abduction of the Greek Queen (Helen) by a Trojan Prince (Paris). The wooden horse was left outside Troy ostensibly as a gift from the gods to say that the Greeks had all gone home. Some of the Greek soldiers were in fact hiding in the horse. The horse was let into the walled city of Troy and sometime later the Greeks jumped out and were able to open the gates for the remainder of their army to swarm in and mount a ferocious attack.

In many respects, everything in Greek and Roman literature starts with the Trojan War. Its effect was like the shockwaves of a tsunami. Homer, The Greek Tragedies, Vergil, they all revolve around this massive event which must have happened at around 1200 BCE. Stories were continually told about it. Vergil's Aeneid is a post-war story of the founding of the Roman race.

> **Brains. Judgment. Memory. Culture. Concentration.**
> **Thoughtfulness. Diligence.**
>
> *(ingenium, ratio, memoria, litterae, cura, cogitatio, diligentia)*
>
> Cicero. Philippics 2.116

THEME: PERSONAL DEVELOPMENT

CHECKPOINT: So, seven tools that could get you to the top are:

Brains. Are you smart? Do you keep learning?

Judgment. Are you perceptive and prudent? Are you able to see the full picture?

Memory. Are you training your memory? It's important. Don't rely on others. Or computers.

Culture. Are you aware of what's happening around you? What are people talking about?

Concentration. Can you focus on the task at hand and not be easily distracted?

Thoughtfulness. Can you think about people and projects in a fully rounded and deep way?

Diligence. Do you have good attention to detail?

If so, you have all the qualities of Julius Caesar, according to Cicero. These tools remind us that it was no accident that Caesar was so successful.

WANT TO KNOW MORE? Today is the Ides of March. You know, "Beware the Ides of March!" It refers to one of the most notorious events in history, involving one of the most famous men in history, Julius Caesar.

The story of the 'Ides of March' goes like this. A psychic-mystic warned Julius Caesar to be careful because danger would be coming his way soon, on the day in March the Romans called 'the Ides' (i.e. today, March 15). On the day, Caesar woke early, feeling alive and well. On his way to an important meeting of the Senate he bumped into the mystic again. "Ha!" he says. "Looks like the Ides of March have come!"

"Yes," says the mystic, "but they have not yet gone."

Caesar was stabbed 23 times, even though there were many more assassins. They weren't really trained killers. They were wealthy politicians, intelligent and cultured, not common thugs.

Behave such that you don't turn friends into enemies
but that you do turn enemies into friends.

*(ἀλλήλοις θ' ὁμιλεῖν, ὡς τοὺς μὲν φίλους ἐχθροὺς μὴ ποιῆσαι,
τοὺς δ' ἐχθροὺς φίλους ἐργάσασθαι).*

Diogenes Laertius. Pythagoras 23

THEME: PERSONAL DEVELOPMENT

CHECKPOINT: There is never a situation in business where Positivity does not beat Negativity.

I know that CEOs shouting hysterically can get things done. But I've met more CEOs who get more done by not behaving like this.

At the end of the day, you want everyone to align behind the same strategy or company business plan. This is more easily achieved by emphasizing the positive aspects of what needs to be done.

This is not to say that there is no room for censure. But it is in all sides' interest for the reprimand to turn a negative into a positive; an unmotivated employee into a motivated one; a disruptive person into a team player; even an unpleasant character into a likeable one.

The demands on businesses to perform put huge pressure on employees and managers at all levels. And accentuating the positive is harder than just lashing out verbally.

But it pays off in the long term. It's a real skill.

WANT TO KNOW MORE? We need to be very grateful to Diogenes Laertius. He did us a huge favour by bringing together three centuries of Greek philosophers from Thales to Epicurus in a massive compendium of their lives and thinking. Without this compendium, our knowledge – and indeed, many of the words – of the Greek philosophers would never have been known.

But here's the thing. Despite his contributions, today we know almost nothing about Diogenes himself.

A real mystery man. We don't even know where or when he was born, or where he lived and wrote. (History sleuths guess a birth date of around 250 CE – but that's it.)

Diogenes wasn't a great thinker himself. Or for that matter a great writer. But he did this important job nonetheless.

And for that, we shall be eternally grateful.

> **[Note To Self] Everything is an assumption.**
>
> (Ότι πάνθ᾽ ὑπόληψις)
>
> Marcus Aurelius. Meditations 2.14

THEME: STRATEGY

CHECKPOINT: As the old saying goes: To assume makes an 'ass' out of 'u' and 'me'.

So never say, 'I assume that …' because someone in the office will either get very cross, or worse, they will repeat that annoying old saying to you.

There are many things that you should and could know, depending on your position in the company. Don't worry about not knowing things that you are not meant to know about. If asked, you reply, 'I don't know, because it's information that is not available to me'.

But in some respects, everything that happens in business is an assumption. It's an educated guess. Even if you have all the facts at your fingertips, you have no idea what external forces will change the 'truths' that led to your assumption.

There is famous quote from a guy called Ken Olsen of a company called DEC (Digital Equipment Corp). DEC was perfectly positioned to lead innovation in computers. Olsen's strategists had briefed him carefully on the market, leading him to decide: "The personal computer will fall flat on its face in business." In fact, it was DEC which fell flat on its face. Ken Olsen's strategy may have looked logical, but unfortunately all of the assumptions were wrong.

Assumptions. Difficult. We make big important ones and small unimportant ones all the time.

WANT TO KNOW MORE? Today marks the death of the great Marcus Aurelius, (121 CE – 17 March 180 CE).

Marcus Aurelius was both an emperor and a philosopher. And he had plenty to think about.

His reign was marked by floods, earthquakes, wars and uprisings across the empire.

He needed to be philosophical.

Marcus Aurelius did not call his thoughts 'Meditations'. That's our word for it.

He called them, 'Notes to Self'.

> **It's enough just to have the will to take on a big project.**
>
> *(in magnis et voluisse sat est)*
>
> Propertius. Elegies 2.10.6

THEME: PROJECT MANAGEMENT

CHECKPOINT: So far in this day-by-day almanac, there have been ideas on how to go about tackling projects.

One thing that you cannot learn, or pick up by observation, is how to create the desire to actually take on the project. And sometimes, that's all you need. Call it what you will – Desire, Hunger, Passion – it's a moment where you decide to 'bet on yourself'.

The confidence to do it comes from within yourself.

A good modern summary of this notion would be Nike's 'Just Do It'.

'Νίκη' ('Nike') was the Greek goddess of victory.

Essentially, you motivate yourself to win.

Definitely worth thinking about when that awesome project comes up for grabs.

WANT TO KNOW MORE? Propertius is a superb poet who left home for Rome very young and fell in love very young.

He is the archetypal tortured soul, the sensitive lover caught in the headlights of the barbaric world around him.

Propertius' (50 BCE – 2 BCE) Rome was the Rome of Augustus, Horace and Vergil and, particularly, Ovid, with whom he seemed very close.

While he was still a child, Propertius lost his father and he was brought up by his mother. Then, when he was about nine years old, he would have seen a large part of his family's land confiscated to hand over to troops who needed property to retire to, as part of their 'golden goodbye' and pension package.

In his early twenties Propertius hooked up with a high-class prostitute, whose grandfather was a well-established and respected man. This lady became the inspiration behind much of his earlier poetry.

> **Just pray you have a sound mind housed in a healthy body.**
>
> *(orandum est ut sit mens sana in corpore sano)*
>
> Juvenal. Satires 10.356

THEME: PERSONAL DEVELOPMENT

CHECKPOINT: Many companies give their employees generous health care packages.

Two thousand years ago, they knew how important it was to have not just a healthy body, but also a healthy mind. It seems we are just beginning to realize that all over again, as mental health becomes a more prominent issue.

Life is more complicated to manage than ever.

Our minds are under pressure from both real and virtual life. The internet has created a complete parallel world for us to inhabit and get stressed about. We are expected to be always available and to answer messages or send in reports 24/7.

Get help early to make sure your healthy body is housing an equally healthy mind.

WANT TO KNOW MORE? Juvenal's Rome was a cosmopolitan city of over one million inhabitants. There were big expensive houses, as well as tenement blocks and slums. The rich people would barge their way through the narrow streets protected by bodyguards who would knock you over if you got in the way.

Poor people might retaliate by emptying out their portable latrines over passers-by.

The Romans had strict rules regarding what could be done in Rome on which days. Whether you could conduct business, vote or sell your wares in the marketplace, for example.

Today was classified as one of the *'nefasti publici'*, a kind of public holiday and general day of rest (for the slave workforce too). The streets would have been full of people celebrating today's religious feast, the *Quinquatrus*. This was originally a day to celebrate the god Mars – there would be ritual dances to watch – but later Minerva was also added. Minerva was the goddess of strategy, and kept an eye on arts, crafts and medicines.

> **We put off thinking about those thoughts that we know will harm us.**
>
> *(tarde quae credita laedunt credimus)*
>
> Ovid. Heroides 2.9

THEME: HUMAN RESOURCES

CHECKPOINT: When we get into the habit-forming regimes and routines of the workplace, we can get lost in the 'everyday', in the 'normal'. At some point, we might objectively note that we're just doing the same thing every single day, like a hamster going around in a wheel. But we don't like to think about what it's all doing to our physical and mental welfare. So often it's only when we get seriously damaged that we sit up and take notice.

If you think this might be you, do something about it. Spend a week of vacation time just thinking about what your future could look and feel like with a change. Get friends and family to help you think things through.

Business leaders take note: people who are actively engaged in their work are more productive and therefore more profitable.

WANT TO KNOW MORE? Ovid was born today in 43 BCE, in Sulmo ('*Sulmona*'). If you go there today, you'll find a marvellous bronze statue of him in Piazza XX Settembre.

Ovid is still very much alive in the hearts of many Italians. At the end of 2017, a motion was put forward by the new political party, The Five Star Movement, which said it wanted to "repair the serious wrong" suffered by Ovid by revoking the order with which the emperor sent him into exile in Tomis (modern-day Constanta, on the Black Sea in Romania).

Technically speaking, Ovid wasn't 'exiled' he was 'banished' (it was a '*relegatio*' in Latin). They sound the same, I know, but being 'just' banished meant Ovid could hold onto all his property. I guess he might have expected that he could come home one day. He never did.

> **Seek assistance from everyone, even the juniors.**
>
> *(auxilium petas ab omnibus, etiam ab infumis)*
>
> Sallust. The War With Catiline 44.5

THEME: PROJECT MANAGEMENT

CHECKPOINT: Help!

Maybe you don't know the answer to an important question, or you're stuck on a proposal or are nervous about a meeting. Whatever the situation, when you need help, make sure you ask for it.

And ask anyone. Your senior, your peer or your junior. It doesn't matter.

Failure to ask for help when you need it inevitably leads to a mistake or an underwhelming piece of work.

And think of it like this. You'd like to be the one asked to help someone out, wouldn't you? We all respond well when we find someone coming to us for assistance.

So don't worry that your request will fall on deaf ears. You'll find the support you need.

WANT TO KNOW MORE? Sallust was a Roman historian and politician who lived in a period of great civil strife in Rome (approximately 86 BCE – 35 BCE). He was in the thick of it, up close and personal with the likes of Julius Caesar and Cicero. Being both a politician and historian, his views on history are tinged with a party-political bias. He used his work to bemoan the declining moral standards of his day.

Mind you, that was a bit rich coming from a politician who was not only sleeping with another politician's wife, but who liberally lined his pockets while he was Governor of North Africa. Sallust was at one point expelled from the Senate for various misdemeanours – 'alleged', I'm sure, like the politicians' misdemeanours of today. He was eventually readmitted.

Sallust certainly found politics a handful and at one point writes a line that many politicians today would agree with. Describing his time in politics he dryly comments: "I encountered many setbacks."

....

> **You only have a brief window of opportunity.**
>
> (ὁ γὰρ καιρὸς πρὸς ἀνθρώπων βραχὺ μέτρον ἔχει)
>
> Pindar. Pythian Odes 4.286

THEME: PERSONAL DEVELOPMENT

CHECKPOINT: When you first get into the world of work, you have somewhere between 40 and 50 years of work life ahead of you, depending on when you start and what you do.

I know. It sounds like a long time. It really isn't.

If you want to rise to the top (not everybody does) you have to be in an influential position by your early thirties. Ideally earlier. That doesn't give you much time.

Then if you want to be in charge of teams (again not everyone does), or even a business, you have to have the expertise and training by your late thirties.

Oh, and you might need to find time to start raising a family too.

Suddenly you're middle-aged and you find yourself making plans that maybe you should have made ten years ago.

I don't want to make this sound depressing. It isn't meant to be. It's more like a cautionary tale reminding you to jump at those opportunities when they come, because they get less frequent the older you get.

WANT TO KNOW MORE? Pindar comes from a period of Greek literature, around 518 BCE to 438 BCE, from which we might expect only fragments of material to survive. But we have a large chunk of Pindar. (Well, about 25%, which is large by comparison with other writers of that period.)

Today's quote comes from his set of *Pythian Odes*, written for the Pythian Games, which took place two years after each Olympic Games.

At the Olympic Games in London in 2012, mayor Boris Johnson (a classicist) commissioned a Pindar-like Ode, keeping the 2,500-year-old tradition well and truly alive.

....

> **It is also said that he planned to appoint (his horse) consul.**
>
> *(consulatum quoque traditur destinasse)*
>
> Suetonius. Gaius Caligula 55.3

THEME: HUMAN RESOURCES

CHECKPOINT: Promotions are always a bone of contention. Who gets promoted and why. And who doesn't. Some appointments make sense and, let's be honest, sometimes they seem plain crazy.

If your organization has a good personal review system you should be able to gauge how you're doing and what your prospects for promotion are.

Don't be afraid to ask about promotion and what you need to do to get it. And be prepared to wait. There might not be a vacancy. That's tough, but it's a reality of business.

Think twice before immediately jumping ship when you don't get what you expected. Often its worth waiting it out. Don't forget, loyalty can be rewarded too.

WANT TO KNOW MORE? Around 100 CE Suetonius wrote the kind of stories that sell well nowadays. He went behind the scenes and brought us the celebrity tittle-tattle and gossip.

As with numerous other writers, we unfortunately don't have everything he produced. For example, he wrote a book called *On the Manners and Customs of Rome* which would surely would have lifted the lid on a lot of inside action in the great capital city. We don't have that, sadly. Nor do we have *On Abusive Terms and their Origin*, with categories such as 'busybodies, idiots and slaves'. That would have been fun too.

What we do have is the hugely entertaining *Lives of the Caesars*, a kind of show and tell exposé of the lives of 12 Caesars from Julius Caesar to Vespasian.

Reading Suetonius is like reading a gossip magazine article on some of history's most fascinating leaders. With a sprinkling of naughty bits to keep us hooked.

> **Smart people can learn a great deal from their competitors.**
>
> (ἀλλ᾽ ἀπ᾽ ἐχθρῶν δῆτα πολλὰ μανθάνουσιν οἱ σοφοί)
>
> Aristophanes. Birds 375

THEME: COMPETITORS

CHECKPOINT: It's very easy to get introspective at work and think that your company knows best, has all the answers, is 'better' than others and so on.

But it's one thing to be proud of your company and another to be delusional.

You track your customers all the time. You'll be investing in new ideas. But what about the obvious other players in the marketplace? Your competitors.

You must watch your competitors closely. And regularly.

At least every week someone should be giving the low-down on what competitive activity is happening in the marketplace.

Don't be afraid of imitating your competitors' ideas if you think they could work for you. After all, they'll certainly be trying to steal ideas from you.

WANT TO KNOW MORE? Have you ever heard the term 'you're in cloud cuckoo land'? Of course you have.

But you might not know that the term was coined over 2,400 years ago by the Greek playwright Aristophanes (born about 446 BCE, died around 386 BC).

Aristophanes was the last of the 'old school' comedians and certainly one of the best. His plays drew crowds, won prizes and occasionally got him into trouble for being too near the mark as far as some politicians were concerned.

Aristophanes was a contemporary of Plato and Socrates. Plato's *Symposium* ('σῦμπόσῐον') tells a story of a party attended by some of the good and the great of Athens: an aristocrat, a lawyer, a poet, doctor, an army general, Socrates and Aristophanes.

At one point in the party, Aristophanes is accused of spending all his time either in beds or bars.

His plays certainly reflect the humour of a man living life, shall we say, to the full.

> **Remember that you're the boss. Allow yourself to be treated as such.**
>
> *(Οὐ μεμνήσῃ Καῖσαρ ὤν, οὐδὲ ἀξιώσεις ὡς κρείττονα*
> *θεραπεύεσθαι σεαυτόν)*
>
> Plutarch. Caesar 60.5

THEME: LEADERSHIP

CHECKPOINT: Whether you are promoted from within a team or come new to a leadership role, it helps everyone if you create the right relationship from day one.

Being someone's boss strangely does not mean you boss them around. But on the other hand, being in charge of a team does mean you are 'one of the team'.

You will, though, be assessed on different criteria than the people in your team. Leaders who blur the lines between 'team' and 'team leader' will find it harder to achieve the things they are contracted to achieve.

The best way to establish a healthy working relationship is to let everyone know what your professional expectations or targets are. Then let each member (or department) know exactly what their role is in helping to achieve those targets.

Set up regular informal chats to see how everyone is getting on and, most importantly, make sure you are seen as a mentor who can help them improve.

WANT TO KNOW MORE? Plutarch had three important things to say about Romans.

First, that the Romans were fighters. They were brave, and they never gave up. You can defeat them in a battle maybe, but you'll never win the war.

Second, the Romans were great diplomats. They were fighters, yes, but they were also politicians. They embraced the defeated enemy into their own political system with a big sales pitch about the benefits of being a part of the Roman system.

Third, Plutarch wanted to emphasize the extraordinary way in which the Romans came together to defeat their enemies. Yes, they fought each other but, at the end of the day, the prevailing political instinct was to maintain Rome's importance in the world.

Rome grew from a small village in 753 BCE to a colossal empire, which eventually imploded in 476 CE. An extraordinary journey of over 1,230 years.

....

> ## When in doubt, don't do it.
>
> *(quod dubites, ne feceris)*
>
> Pliny The Younger. Letters 1.18.6

THEME: PERSONAL DEVELOPMENT

CHECKPOINT: There are many occasions throughout this book when the message from the ancients is: stop; pause; think. Just before you press the big red 'Go' button, stand back and reflect for a moment.

Today's advice goes one step further.

If you are in any doubt whatsoever about an action you are about to take, don't do it.

Don't be talked round, don't think 'it won't matter'. It always does matter.

A decision to stop may be the wrong decision. So be it. It is always better to trust your own instincts and, as time goes on, you will learn from your experiences.

At the end of the day, it is much better to say, 'I'm not one 100% sure about this', than to press ahead with doubt.

WANT TO KNOW MORE? Letter writing is not so common nowadays. But we have to be grateful to the few Romans who bothered to do it and to those who preserved their work. Cicero wrote hundreds of letters and he kept many that were sent to him. Marcus Aurelius wrote love letters to his boyfriend.

We have over 350 of the letters that Pliny wrote, and because there is also archaeological evidence of his life, we know a huge amount about Pliny (unlike so many authors of the ancient world).

Letters can sometimes give us the small tidbits about life that formal historians may choose to leave out. What someone had for breakfast; what the weather was like; what illnesses they had – and so on. All wonderful stuff for filling in the fine detail of life 2,000 years ago.

....

Some people are as oblivious to what they're doing when
they're awake as they are when they are fast asleep.

*(τοὺς δὲ ἄλλους ἀνθρώπους λανθάνει ὁκόσα ἐγερθέντες
ποιοῦσιν, ὅκωσπερ ὁκόσα εὕδοντες ἐπιλανθάνονται)*

Heraclitus (Quoted by Sextus Empiricus. Against The Logicians 1.133)

THEME: PERSONAL DEVELOPMENT

CHECKPOINT: Neuroscientists today accept that only a small percentage of our brains is being accessed on a day-to-day basis to perform functional processes.

The remaining percentage may be our subconscious, which drives so much of what we do without us really realizing what's going on.

Understanding the unconscious messages you send out might help you to be clearer about your aims and ambitions and will certainly make communication clearer.

You don't need to seek professional advice, unless you want to; there are many books and websites that discuss this in a plain and simple way.

WANT TO KNOW MORE? Heraclitus was much quoted and much respected long after he lived (about 535 BCE – 475 BCE). Plato was referencing him 100 years after his death and Marcus Aurelius was referring to him over 600 years later.

It is difficult to know how much Heraclitus wrote, but what we do know is that his thinking was coherent, and that it was in book form.

He may have written the first-ever book of philosophy.

Then, completely out of the blue, Heraclitus' book drops out of world literature. His words of wisdom disappear and all that's left behind are a large number of fragments (some of which don't make sense).

These fragments have become legendary, with Heraclitus only hinting at how profound his works are. But they are extremely accessible too.

When we hear Heraclitus speak from his 'fragments from the past' he can at times sound similar to Buddha, or Confucius. Wise sayings made simple, in an understandable and effortless way.

> **Make haste, slowly.**
>
> *(σπεῦδε βραδέως)*
>
> Augustus (Quoted by Suetonius. Lives Of The Caesars 2.25.4)

THEME: PROJECT MANAGEMENT

CHECKPOINT: Planning a project? Or do you have a report to hand in, or a product to be delivered?

Don't rush it.

And the more you can prepare in advance what you're doing, the easier it will be to do it.

Ideally, all tasks should be undertaken by balancing the requirements of their urgency with a steady and diligent work ethic.

We all know the problems that occur when you rush things. Mistakes are made, costs are incurred and the whole assignment takes twice as long.

WANT TO KNOW MORE? Augustus was Rome's first emperor. His rise to the top and ability to stay there until he died aged 75 is one of the most documented narratives of ancient history.

He was born Gaius Octavius Thurinus on September 23, 63 BCE (i.e. 'Octavius').

He was adopted by his mother's uncle, a certain Julius Caesar (who had no son of his own) and was nominated in Caesar's will to be his heir.

The adoption meant he had to change his name to Gaius Julius Caesar Octavianus to reflect his relationship to Caesar while keeping a link to his old family name (i.e. 'Octavianus').

In 27 BCE, after he had become ruler of the 'known world', he changed his name again, to 'Augustus', a name which had gravitas and religious connotations.

Octavius, Octavianus, Augustus. As he evolved, he changed. As he changed, he developed. As he developed, he grew into the most powerful man in the world, who could claim that he brought, at last, peace to Rome.

> **Formulating a plan is the wise man's response to a crisis.**
>
> *(consilium in dubiis remedium prudentis est)*
>
> Publilius Syrus. Sententiae 141

THEME: STRATEGY

CHECKPOINT: Things happen.

Suddenly, in the matter of minutes, a situation occurs that demands focus and attention.

But just because things happen fast does not mean you have to make a knee-jerk response.

The biggest mistake in this kind of scenario is not to remain objective and gather the facts.

It's human nature to diagnose any situation from within the knowledge and preconceptions that we already hold.

Get the facts.

Create a small team – even if it's not the perfect group of people, you can evolve the team later if you need to. Make sure you include wise heads as well as young bloods.

Formulate a plan.

Then respond.

WANT TO KNOW MORE? Publilius Syrus, once a slave, used his wits to gain his freedom. He was intelligent and funny and became quite a celebrity in the Rome of Julius Caesar's day.

He was an acclaimed playwright, but sadly none of his plays have survived.

He was bought to Rome by a junior Roman officer, after the Romans has conquered Syria in 64 BCE. It was common practice for those enslaved to take the name of the land they came from; hence Publilius from Syria was known as Syrus.

Had Publilius always been a slave, or was he a free man when he was picked up by the Romans?

I guess we'll never know, but my bet is that he had always been an educated and literate man with a real gift for words.

> Anyone who has any experience of bad times knows that when hit by a tsunami of trouble you end up being afraid of every single thing.
>
> *(κακῶν μὲν ὅστις ἔμπειρος κυρεῖ, ἐπίσταται βροτοῖσιν ὡς ὅταν κλύδων κακῶν ἐπέλθῃ, πάντα δειμαίνειν φιλεῖ)*
>
> Aeschylus. Persians 598

THEME: PERSONAL DEVELOPMENT

CHECKPOINT: Sayings, sayings, sayings.

'Once bitten, twice shy'. It's a saying that's as old as the hills.

But does it also mean 'twice bitten, four times shy'? And so on?

Let's hope not, because there's another saying. It's known colloquially as 'Murphy's Law', which states: 'If it can go wrong, it will go wrong'.

Managing uncertainty is a large part of management itself. It's amazing how you can read all the books and case histories you like, yet still something crops up that has never happened before, or nobody has an answer to. Don't let disasters make you apprehensive.

Being shy in business just won't work.

You have to sail through the storms, come out the other end and be prepared to go out again. Only that way will you continue to discover, build and grow.

After all, as yet another old saying goes:

'A ship is safe in a harbour, but that's not what ships are made for' (see December 8).

WANT TO KNOW MORE? Aeschylus was a multi-award-winning talent. Today's quote comes from his play *The Persians*, for which he won the top prize at the leading awards show, The Dionysia.

Performed in 472 BCE, this is one of Aeschylus' earliest plays and one very close to his heart.

The play draws on his first-hand experience of fighting the Persians eight years earlier.

The sentiments expressed would be real and raw to both Aeschylus and the audience.

Imagine a play today drawing on the horrors of a war we all know about and are living through or have recently experienced.

We believe Aeschylus wrote at least 90 plays. Only seven have survived.

> **Better late than never.**
>
> *(potius sero quam nunquam)*
>
> Livy. History of Rome 4.2.11

THEME: PERSONAL DEVELOPMENT

CHECKPOINT: If you make an agreement to deliver something, you should stick to that agreement unless genuine reasons force a delay.

Sticking to agreements in business is an essential part of building a picture of yourself as a competent, resourceful and reliable person.

But we know that sometimes things can get in the way that make your agreement difficult to keep within the agreed time frame.

Or it could be that key elements of information that you need are taking longer to track down.

At the first hint that there is going to be a delay, put your hand up and let the problem be known. It's the right and responsible course of action.

It allows the business to work around a revised timetable, almost certainly giving you more time.

It's called 'managing expectations'.

WANT TO KNOW MORE? Let me tell you about Livy. A contemporary of Horace and Vergil, he lived in the Rome of Julius Caesar, Mark Antony and Augustus. Yet he is not as well known as those illustrious others.

He wrote an absolutely colossal history of Rome in 142 volumes, beginning at the very beginning, with Romulus and Remus, and ending in his own lifetime.

From his giant work, only 35 books survive. Finding the others would provide us with an invaluable history of the rise of Rome. Of course, how much of the earlier part of his history is true or not is very debatable. He himself used a kind of 'rule of thumb' when it came to recording 'facts'. If it 'felt' true, he thought, then he'll give it the benefit of the doubt.

> **Look after your data.**
>
> **(*datum serva*)**
>
> Cato. Collectio Distichorum Vulgaris. I.4

THEME: INTERNET

CHECKPOINT: Not an April Fool.

(The Latin translates as 'look after what is given to you'.)

Nowadays you can't simply collect data, it has to be given to you. And even then, you can't just do anything with it.

Data protection laws have inevitably become tighter as data becomes more important, but if you have acquired your data legitimately, then look after it.

What do we mean by data? In the past, it would have comprised name, address, post code and phone number. It might have included purchasing habits and preferences for and against something, or someone.

Today, everything is data. Every smart phone interaction, every shared connection. We ourselves are data.

We live our lives in such a digital way that we are more like smart devices connected to and interacting with other non-human smart devices.

It's no surprise, therefore, that data is king. And that data must be protected and handled responsibly.

WANT TO KNOW MORE? This 'Cato' is almost certainly a pseudonym. The unknown author was pretending to write moral advice like a much more famous Cato, Cato the Elder (234 BCE – 149 BCE).

These two 'Catos' lived 500 years apart.

The mystery Cato who wrote today's quote would have loved the terse, clipped language of the internet and no doubt would have dispensed his one-liners via Twitter or maybe his own YouTube channel or blog.

In the Middle Ages, schoolmasters used Cato's lines for Latin language tuition and there is evidence that his work had a huge fan base, even being referred to by Chaucer.

> ### Road goes up. Road goes down. Same road.
>
> *(ὁδὸς ἄνω κάτα μία καὶ ὠυτή)*
>
> Heraclitus (Quoted by Hippolytus. Refutation Of All The Heresies 9.10.4)

THEME: PROJECT MANAGEMENT

CHECKPOINT: Life at work will always have its ups and downs. There are, of course, people who wish it only went up. Like one wonderful escalator taking you effortlessly from Trainee to Managing Director. Sadly, it doesn't work like that.

Some people enjoy their work. They are able to take the rough with the smooth. Others think that work life is a flat, monotonous, dreary kind of existence, doing the same thing day in, day out.

You have to 'play the game'. It might seem childish and pathetic, but work life has its own rules and procedures. You have to be at the right place at the right time. You must impress the right people. You must catch the opportunities when you see them flying through the air, even if it means stretching yourself to do so.

Work life is the same for everyone. Good days and bad days and, well, just ... days.

WANT TO KNOW MORE? Heraclitus was born in Ephesus. He was a bit of a misanthrope; he disliked other people, including his fellow Ephesians and Athenians, finding them difficult to respect.

As we saw a few days back (March 27), Heraclitus is very possibly the author of the first book of philosophy, now sadly lost to us.

It was a book of three parts: Politics, Theology and the Universe. He was the first to commit serious thoughts to book form.

How, we might wonder, given his anti-social attitude, did he test and sharpen his philosophical thinking? Who could he bounce ideas off, if no one else was ever going to write a book as good as his?

The answer is, he did it by questioning himself. Well, why wouldn't you ask the only 'other' person you respected?

> **I shall stick to the agreement.**
>
> *(legibus utar)*
>
> Propertius. Elegies 4.8.81

THEME: LEGAL

CHECKPOINT: When you sign a contract, you have to stick to what is agreed. You have to 'abide by the terms'. Otherwise you can get into trouble with the lawyers. So be careful what you sign.

But when you make an agreement and it's not legally binding, you should also stick to what you committed to do.

Sticking to agreements is what makes an organization tick. The everyday tasks that people agree to do in a company are like blood coursing through a company's veins, allowing progress to be made.

If you can't agree to what you've been asked, explain why at the moment you are asked, or very shortly afterwards.

Some people compound the problem of not sticking to an agreement by covering up. If this happens, it feels like a blood clot has occurred. The progress of work slows or stops, causing all sorts of damage.

WANT TO KNOW MORE? When he hit Rome as a young man, the young Propertius threw himself into partying. He had many friends, both literary and non-literary, and was well-acquainted with the rising stars of the emerging new regime headed up by Augustus.

Augustus had two right-hand men. One was a general called Agrippa and the other a wealthy and influential man, a patron of the arts called Maecenas.

Maecenas became a patron to Propertius.

Propertius died at some point in his early thirties, but he knew and admired Vergil and had read, or heard, early drafts of Vergil's *Aeneid*. Propertius was astonished by Vergil's work and, in one poem, he hints that something greater than the *Iliad* is about to be born.

Carthage must be destroyed.

(delendam esse Carthaginem)

Cato The Elder (Quoted by Florus. Epitome of Roman History 1.31.5)

THEME: STRATEGY

CHECKPOINT: Today's quote should not be taken literally! In fact, if anything, Carthage should be preserved. Today it's a wonderful archaeological site giving glimpses of what an amazing city it must have once been.

The quote expresses something that every business strategy needs. A strong purpose, or rationale, behind the strategic direction.

Providing a rationale allows a business to understand what is going on. Why, for example, a specific customer segment is being targeted, or why another office is being opened up.

A rationale will also allow the next steps to be understood. 'We are opening a new office, in Rome. All those speaking Italian, please step forward'.

The underlying strategic direction of a company comes with all sorts of debates around the 'pros and cons'. If you are invited to these debates, be clear and decisive and, importantly, be prepared to back up what you are suggesting.

WANT TO KNOW MORE? Cato the Elder, what a guy.

He was born around 234 BCE, lost his father at a young age and inherited the family farm.

He set about a kind of hair-shirt, quasi-masochistic lifestyle, toughening himself up on the land and facing down the natural elements.

He joined the army as soon as he could (of course) and enjoyed an outstanding military career.

Today's quote comes from his later life (he was thought to have lived into his 80s).

Cato had been part of a failed diplomatic mission to Carthage, which had been engaging Rome in decades of weary and expensive war. His rationale for completely destroying Carthage was based on his belief that Carthage should never have the means to antagonize Rome again.

> **Strength of reasoning is not measured by**
> **height or length but by conviction.**
>
> *(λόγου γὰρ μέγεθος οὐ μήκει οὐδ᾽ ὕψει κρίνεται, ἀλλὰ δόγμασιν)*
>
> Epictetus. Discourses 1.12.26

THEME: PERSONAL DEVELOPMENT

CHECKPOINT: If you have ever found yourself in a meeting with an intimidating person, or someone who had joined the business 'before you were born', you'll find today's quote very meaningful.

The conviction you bring to your argument is much more powerful than someone who just disagrees by exerting some kind of implicit power.

Plan the reasons behind what you believe to be right. Order them. Practice them. Then deliver them with passion.

When faced with the mindless opposition of 'god's gift to the office', don't appear frustrated or get offensive, simply explain your rationale again and assert your belief that you are right in what you say.

Then sit back and watch the bully wriggle about.

WANT TO KNOW MORE? Epictetus (approximately 50 CE – 135 CE) became a well-respected teacher and writer of philosophy.

You can put him in the same school of philosophical writing – Stoic – as Seneca and Marcus Aurelius, the famed 'imperial philosopher'. However, he was not in their league socially.

Epictetus was born a slave and brought to Rome, where he earned his freedom.

Then he set himself up as a teacher in Rome, but was forced leave in 89 CE when the Emperor Domitian decided to kick out all philosophers from Rome. Domitian didn't like people thinking too much (particularly about him and his regime).

So, banned from Rome, Epictetus made his way to a place called Victory City (Nicopolis) and set up a school there, which he called a 'healing centre for sick souls'. (Sounds very Californian, doesn't it?)

Thanks to a very diligent student, who copied everything down, Epictetus' writings, or *Discourses*, have been able to come down to us.

> **It's a pleasure to find peace and quiet restored
> to the finance department.**
>
> *(quam iuvat cernere aerarium silens et quietum)*
>
> Pliny the Younger. Panegyricus 36.1

THEME: FINANCE

CHECKPOINT: Finance departments are the one place where you do not normally expect to find disorder and chaos. They are necessarily hierarchical and work to strict protocols about who can do what, sign what, and when. Payments and receipts must be set up in an organized way and any trained accountant will know how to do that.

Some managers can put their finance departments under stress without realizing it. An example is constantly asking for financial information beyond what is given out at management meetings.

At the end of the day, you need order in your finance system or things will go dramatically wrong.

WANT TO KNOW MORE? Roman consuls served for one year only. There were two of them. In Republican days (509 BCE – 27 BCE), this was a clear way of indicating that one-man rule should never happen again.

Consuls were important and powerful, and the year would be named after them.

Even under the emperors, the consular system remained in place to oversee the day-to-day management of the empire.

If a consul died while in office, someone would be appointed to take their place for the remainder of the year.

These consuls were called 'suffect' consuls and Pliny, our famous letter writer, was one such person.

Pliny was offered the job of '*consul suffectus*' by the Emperor Trajan in 100 CE. The custom was for the newly installed consul to deliver a 'thank you' speech ('*gratarium acto*') to the emperor. Today's quote comes from Pliny's official thank you to Trajan.

> **Things are not always as they seem.**
>
> *(non semper ea sunt quae videntur)*
>
> Phaedrus. Fables 4.2.5

THEME: LEADERSHIP

CHECKPOINT: One of the problems with the business world is that you can never really know what's happening at any one moment.

The speed of events sometimes doesn't give you time to consider things properly.

What looks like a small matter could reveal something very important.

The arrival of a new competitor might look like it is threatening your business, but on closer inspection it has many faults which can be exploited.

Then again, a happy employee might be happy, but that's because they've been offered a fabulous job at another company.

A good new business order book might be undone by underdeveloped cash flow.

Caution, particularly when things seem to be going incredibly well, helps you to the read all the market signs carefully and in as many ways as seem appropriate.

WANT TO KNOW MORE? Everyone's heard of Aesop's fables. But did you know that we don't have any of his original writings? 'Aesop' is an oral tradition and what we have are his stories passed down through history and retold.

One such reteller (600 years after Aesop lived) is Phaedrus, a slave from northern Greece. Phaedrus was brought to Rome a slave, educated, demonstrated real ability and was freed. (We've heard similar stories, haven't we?)

Phaedrus is not a well-known Latin author, but in fact he wrote five books of fables, all based on the Aesop stories.

Phaedrus wasn't the only person to undertake the task of writing down the famous fables, but at least he did bother to do it.

So, when you pick up a book of Aesop's fables, you might want to check who actually wrote them. Things are not always as they seem …

> **No lie lives long.**
>
> *(ἀλλ' οὐδὲν ἕρπει ψεῦδος εἰς γῆρας χρόνου)*
>
> Sophocles. Acrisius Frag. 62

THEME: THE WATERCOOLER

CHECKPOINT: Lies and the people who promulgate them always get found out.

Usually it happens quite fast, but every liar is eventually exposed, however long it takes.

Lying is common to all businesses. In fact, you could say there's a very thin line between an outright lie and a persuasive sales pitch!

But here's the odd thing.

Telling the truth is much, much more powerful. You're much more likely to get those sales by being truthful.

Being known to be trustworthy in business is so much better than being known as someone who is deceitful or wildly exaggerates.

WANT TO KNOW MORE? The playwright Sophocles (approximately 497 BCE – 405 BCE) came from a wealthy background and he would have received as good an education as you could get in those times. He repaid the education he received by working hard to maintain the glory of Athens, which was for much of his life at the height of its fame and power.

Sophocles served in the Greek navy and, as an older man, was appointed to a special commission to advise on the catastrophic defeat Athens suffered during an ill-advised attack on Sicily.

Euripides, the other great playwright of the time, died before Sophocles, despite being younger. Sophocles paid a moving tribute to him by dressing his cast in mourning clothes during one of his major dramatic productions.

Sophocles himself died just a few months after Euripides.

It's a foolish man who fails to hold on to small (but certain) profit by going for uncertain profit.

(ὁ μὴ τὰ μικρά, πλὴν βέβαια, τηρήσας μάταιός ἐστιν, ἢν ἄδηλα θηρεύῃ)

Babrius. Fables 6.16

THEME: LEADERSHIP

CHECKPOINT: In business, there is a difference between being ambitious and being a gambler. The former requires a lot of common sense, the latter a huge amount of stupidity.

Profit is the 'advantage card' in business. It demonstrates your success, even if it's slow and steady. It defines how you are seen by important stakeholders such as banks and shareholders. And it can protect you and save you money when there are short-term, day-to-day financial issues to cover.

Using your profit to gamble on the possibility of a bigger profit is unwise.

Building up profit will allow you to have a wider set of conversations with many types of lenders, if what you seek is funds for expansion, for example.

WANT TO KNOW MORE? We met Phaedrus a couple of days ago. He collected and translated Aesop's fables into Latin.

Now meet Babrius, another mystery man who followed in Phaedrus' footsteps about 100 years later.

While Phaedrus presented Aesop in Latin, Babrius did so in Greek, but, in all honesty, we don't really know much about either of these characters.

And we don't know much about Aesop either. Which is quite remarkable since the stories have persevered throughout history and live on even today. These fables were famous and were surely passed down as cautionary tales, or even bedtime stories.

Another problem we have is that any story that looked and felt a little like Aesop would probably have been attributed to him anyway. We do know that Aesop was well known in the time of Plato, Aristophanes and Herodotus, because they all mention him.

So there you have it. Highly visible tales, by highly invisible people.

> **No one likes the person delivering bad news.**
>
> *(στέργει γὰρ οὐδεὶς ἄγγελον κακῶν ἐπῶν)*
>
> Sophocles. Antigone 277

THEME: LEADERSHIP

CHECKPOINT: Being the one to break bad news to a colleague is never easy. Poor sales, the unexpected departure of a key executive to a competitor or notice of planned redundancies – if it's you who has to do the dirty work, you are about as welcome as a fart in a spacesuit (as Aristophanes might have said).

Be factual. Don't embellish. And don't add any personal dimension like: 'this is as upsetting for me as it is for you'. That's very unlikely to be true.

In business, we all play roles. We are all 'in a position'. We all act with titles.

Let the position and title do the talking and then, when appropriate let the 'real person' inside express their view, if circumstances permit.

This isn't being dispassionate. It's being responsible. When you report business news you are serving the business, not yourself.

WANT TO KNOW MORE? By the time he was 16, Sophocles' star was in the ascendant. He was good looking, intelligent and popular. He was head of the choir at a celebration that followed the victory over the Persians at the battle of Salamis in 480 BCE.

This early success was to follow him throughout his illustrious career.

Sophocles won the top prize at the *Dionysia*, the main drama awards festival, at least 18 times, often beating both Aeschylus and Euripides.

> ## If you're going to do it, then do it!
>
> *(age si quid agis)*
>
> Plautus. The Persian 659

THEME: PROJECT MANAGEMENT

CHECKPOINT: Something you hear very often in business is: 'What we could do is …' or, its twin expression: 'We thought of that idea ages ago … but didn't do anything'.

We can all think up ideas in our heads, but vision without action is pure hallucination.

Over the years, I've been shown prototypes that never got off the ground, or speculative pitches that were never presented.

The more they amass in an office, the more they grow as a testament to failure to implement.

Implementation is critical to business. More important than innovation.

So if you have an idea, sit down and map out how you are going to implement it.

Otherwise it will be another forgotten project left on top of another forgotten shelf.

WANT TO KNOW MORE? Ancient writers tell a story about Plautus. He was born in Sarsina, a small town just south of Ravenna in Italy, and went to Rome as a young man to work in the theatre.

He did well, it seems, both as a stage hand and then as an actor, making himself some serious money.

At this point, he sets his ambitions higher and becomes an entrepreneur ploughing his earnings into certain foreign trade deals, all of which go belly-up.

He's now destitute and returns to Rome where to make ends meet he takes a job in a flour mill, grafting away for a pittance.

While toiling in the mill, Plautus starts to write plays – drawing on his experience of the theatre, no doubt. And, slowly but surely, he crawls out of the mill and climbs back into the spotlight.

True story? Who knows. But it would make a great script, wouldn't it?

> **People put more faith in their eyes than their ears.**
>
> *(homines amplius oculis quam auribus credunt)*
>
> Seneca. Epistles 6.5

THEME: PERSONAL DEVELOPMENT

CHECKPOINT: We have come to understand that it is very difficult to believe everything that comes out of the media. Fake news, fake pictures, gossip masquerading as fact, rumours endorsed by experts before they are found to be false.

Sometimes, the only way to verify something is to go and take a look for yourself.

At least you can believe what you see, rather than listen to a reported version.

Problems in the factory? Go and take a look.

Poor quality display of your products in a supermarket? Go and take a look.

There is a serious school of thinking that proposes 'management by walking about'.

It's a great idea. Try it.

If you stay behind your desk looking out of the window, you might see a little of the outside world, but you'll know nothing of the inner workings of your company.

WANT TO KNOW MORE? Today in 65 CE, Seneca the Younger died. He was the master of the short and pithy line that seems pregnant with meaning.

Here are some that still resonate as strongly as they did in Seneca's day.

"Life is like a play; it doesn't matter how long it is, but how good the acting was."

"Success is a restless thing."

"A life is not incomplete if it is honourable."

One of Seneca's skills as a writer was to create a down-to-earth expression that hid a lofty ideal.

> ## What can I say about the endless memos and the innumerable handwritten notes?
>
> *(quid ego de commentariis infinitis,*
> *quid de innumerabilibus chirographis loquar?)*
>
> Cicero. Philippic 2.38

THEME: TIME MANAGEMENT

CHECKPOINT: Very few jobs can be defined as 'sitting down and reading' jobs. Lawyers, perhaps, can claim this since they are required to scrutinize written documentation.

But for most people, there are too many endless memos, emails, yellow stickies, texts, whatever. They clog up the day and prohibit the human interaction that, let's be honest, gets things done.

It isn't easy to cut back on memos and memoranda.

We are more litigious. That means more documents.

We ensure we can evidence our actions; more emails.

We want to look busy; more and more emails and texts.

If you find them annoying and you feel there are too many, then start by reducing your own output. Demonstrate how few memos are actually needed.

If you can do it, everyone can.

WANT TO KNOW MORE? Cicero's name comes from the Latin word, *'cicer'*, meaning chickpea. The theory was that an ancestor of his might have had a dent in the end of his nose in the shape of a chickpea.

This ancestor must have been a man of some reputation, because successive generations kept the name.

It was once suggested to Cicero that he drop the name to give himself a chance of being taken more seriously in politics. Cicero declined the offer. He was proud of his name and ancestry. In fact, he once inscribed a silver dish with his first two names – Marcus Tullius – followed by an engraving of a chickpea, to stand for 'Cicero'.

> **Be a speaker of speeches and a doer of deeds.**
>
> (μύθων τε ῥητῆρ᾽ ἔμεναι πρηκτῆρά τε ἔργων)
>
> Homer. Iliad 9.443

THEME: PERSONAL DEVELOPMENT

CHECKPOINT: To advance in business, you need to be active. It's a good way of getting noticed.

It's no use being very clever while you hide your achievements and talent from everyone. You'll get lost amongst your pushy colleagues vying for attention.

Not that you need to show off. You just need to stand out.

When the opportunity arises, give some internal talks.

Ask to be the one who makes the presentation to the client or customer.

Be the person who is seen to be active around the office doing things, not sitting behind your desk waiting for something to happen.

This kind of proactivity is all about you marketing yourself.

And that's important, because you can't always rely on someone else to do it for you.

WANT TO KNOW MORE? The Trojan War lasted for 10 years. But in telling the tale of the one of the most famous wars of all, Homer doesn't take us through it year by year. That would be boring, because for a lot of the time, not much happened. The Greeks besieged Troy – essentially hoping to starve the weary Trojans into submission. That's about it.

No, Homer does something very clever. He picks just a few weeks towards the end of war and crams into this brief time period everything we might want to know about the characters involved, so that in the end, you don't get a war diary, you get a very up-close and personal description of the devastation of war.

Very clever.

> ### How can I achieve something that is so way beyond my skill set?
>
> *(τί γάρ μοι καὶ μακροῖς αὐλοῖς;)*
>
> Otho (Quoted by Suetonius. Lives Of The Caesars 7.2.)

THEME: PERSONAL DEVELOPMENT

CHECKPOINT: Some things you just cannot do.

You might not be trained enough, experienced enough, old enough, or even young enough.

It's important to know your limits.

Attempting something you are ill-equipped to do will actually set you back in terms of your personal development, and apart from the damage it could do to the business, will mark you out as someone whose enthusiasm is not tempered by self-awareness. And that's dangerous.

Mind you, that's not to say you shouldn't stretch yourself. That's different.

Stretch yourself to reach a goal that is difficult, but attainable.

WANT TO KNOW MORE? Today's quote from Suetonius was actually an old Greek proverb, which says: 'Long flutes? No business of mine'. Which is a bit like someone today saying: 'There's no point buying me a guitar, I'm never going to be able to play it'.

The Romans liked to quote Greek when they wanted to appear well-educated and sophisticated. Cicero is often dropping Greek one-liners into his letters.

It's a bit like today when we drop in a French expression to elevate our speech.

After all, having a 'tête-à-tête' with someone sounds so much more cultured than having a 'one-on-one'.

> **It's better to finish one small assignment first than to do many imperfectly.**
>
> *(κρεῖττον γάρ που σμικρὸν εὖ ἢ πολὺ μὴ ἱκανῶς περᾶναι)*
>
> Socrates (Plato. Theaetetus 187E)

THEME: TIME MANAGEMENT

CHECKPOINT: There's a big difference between multi-tasking and spreading yourself too thin.

Doing too many things can mean you end up doing nothing at all.

No matter how small the task, if you start it, make sure you finish it.

You can guarantee that a part of the task you thought 'didn't really matter' will end up being the one thing you'll be asked to bring to the meeting to present to the CEO!

One tip for fast-track achievement, which is used by many successful people, is to write a list each evening of the tasks that need to be completed by tomorrow's close of play.

Don't make it too long or totally unachievable (see yesterday's advice).

Then the next day do each task, ticking them off one by one until they are all completed.

Sounds ridiculously simple, doesn't it?

Try it and see what happens.

WANT TO KNOW MORE? Socrates, born around 470 BCE, is widely agreed to be one the founders of Western philosophy. His standing is immense and his thinking has been widely debated amongst philosophers, both in his lifetime and in the 2,500 years since his death in 399 BCE.

What is amazing about his achievement is that we don't have one single piece of written work from Socrates himself.

No books, no notes, no musings scratched into a piece of broken pottery.

His thinking comes down to us via other writers who have recorded their conversations with him. Most notably Plato.

> **Those who are action-oriented are more useful to the company than the smooth intelligent types.**
>
> *(strenui nimio plus prosunt populo quam arguti et cati)*
>
> Plautus. Truculentus 493

THEME: HUMAN RESOURCES

CHECKPOINT: A business is a dynamic entity. It is constantly moving. It makes sales, signs deals and processes transactions.

When it is not doing any of these things, a business is not thriving and therefore not acting for its stakeholders.

Smart thinking is incredibly valuable and is needed as part of the process of moving forward.

But be careful of the types who 'talk the talk', but don't 'walk the walk'.

Unless someone has actually experienced running a business, be careful about taking their advice.

Most businesses aren't rocket science. Even rocket scientists will have colleagues who have practical things to do to make the rocket business run. In fact, NASA is a very good example of an enterprise that makes things happen.

And even businesses selling 'intelligence' need people to do the selling.

WANT TO KNOW MORE? Plautus wrote the play *Truculentus* (from which we get today's quote) in his old age, possibly in 186 BCE, two years before he died.

He would have witnessed huge change in his life. It was an exciting time to be in Rome.

The city was consolidating its position as the most powerful force in Italy and establishing itself as a major Mediterranean power. As Rome conquered, so more wealth was drawn into the city.

Rome would have been full of all sorts of characters from all sorts of places.

High life would have met low life on every street corner.

Truculentus revolves around a clever prostitute who is having fun persuading gullible guys to part with their money.

Apparently, Plautus was very pleased with this play. Maybe he based his characters on people he knew, or had observed?

> **Don't trust appearances.**
>
> *(frontis nulla fides)*
>
> Juvenal. Satires 2.8

THEME: PERSONAL DEVELOPMENT

CHECKPOINT: One skill worth developing is the ability to read people. Not in a psychoanalytical sense – that would take too long and probably go too deep for everyday usage – but in a common-sense way.

It's difficult to understand people by first appearances. They don't give out the clues in the way they once used to. There was a time when you could tell a lot about someone by their accent or dress-sense, where they lived and what car they drove. Today that's almost impossible, as conventional status symbols don't work any more. Jeff Bezos, the founder of Amazon, drives a 1996 Honda Accord. (OK, he also owns a $65 million private jet, but you wouldn't know that when he pulls up to the petrol pump.)

The best way to get behind a persona is to talk to the person.

Spend as much time as you can talking with your colleagues and customers.

That way you're less likely to be surprised when they do something that seems completely out of character.

WANT TO KNOW MORE? Juvenal's view of Rome was not a pretty one. He saw corruption and debauchery wherever he looked.

He was careful not to attack any living people through his satires – he valued his life too much – but he makes one exception.

He lays into a guy called Crispinus, who started life as an Egyptian fish merchant and ended up a Roman senator. Juvenal describes him as 'Nile trash' and includes him in a list of people he can't stand, including rich trustafarian girls, gigolos and millionaire barbers.

He thinks the city has gone to the dogs and that there is no room for good, honest, decent folk, like school teachers, who are on minimum wages and get bullied by the students.

> ## How many days have I spent dicking about!
>
> *(quot dies quam frigidis rebus absumpsi!)*
>
> Pliny The Younger. Letters 1.9.3

THEME: TIME MANAGEMENT

CHECKPOINT: There is nothing more frustrating than trying to get something done, only to find you've been running around in circles, led up a blind alley or trapped in a cul-de-sac.

You'll be pleased to know you're not the first person this has happened to. Seems like this has been an eternal problem.

Most likely, you don't realize at first that this is happening to you, but when you do, you end up repeating the behavioural problem, only faster.

Keep focused on what you're doing.

Set a timetable of activity that you should follow.

Best of all, appoint a buddy to keep an eye on what you're doing; someone you can confide in when you're feeling stuck.

As they say, a problem shared is a problem halved.

WANT TO KNOW MORE? Pliny's letters bring you into the world of the Roman in a vivid and illuminating way.

The sheer breadth of 'ordinary' life that he covers means that reading them is like watching archaeological remains spring to life.

He tells us about how much he loves living in the country and what kind of rural pastimes there were; we discover there were legacy-hunters in ancient Rome; he talks about buying art for his house and garden and goes on to describe at some length what his house looked like.

Pliny's list of revelations goes on. There are his views on Christianity; his first-hand account of the eruption of Vesuvius; he tells ghost stories and he brings us into the dining room to hear what a Roman dining experience was like.

In some respects, his letters are like the time-capsules we make today. Small boxes full of the look and feel of today which are eventually revealed to a future audience.

> **Don't despair!**
>
> *(nil desperandum)*
>
> Horace. Odes 1.7.27

THEME: PERSONAL DEVELOPMENT

CHECKPOINT: It is all too easy to let everything at work get on top of you. Life is not easy, and work is not there to make it easier. (Which is a shame, but that's another story.)

Everyone has a 'bad day at the office', which closes down conversation over dinner and kills the kids' bedtime fairytale.

Today's advice is not professionally proven to lift you clear out of the problem zone, but it could just be a reminder that whatever is going on is also going on for thousands of others, so try not to take it personally.

When everything blows up in your face, don't bury it and internalize it.

Talk to whoever you think can help and give you advice, and do it sooner rather than later.

WANT TO KNOW MORE? Horace can often come across as a rather fusty old man, a bit of an old-timer who likes to communicate his venerable words of wisdom.

He never married, seemed unlucky with lovers and enjoyed a glass of wine, or two, with friends.

But Horace is more complicated than that.

He enjoyed embodying different personalities to get his message across. He was complex.

He preferred to hide his meaning in his words, which makes understanding him both difficult and rewarding at the same time.

Sometimes he would write a poem with a clear direction, only to trip you up in the very last lines, or even words.

For Horace, fate is always there to let you fall flat on your face, so take nothing for granted.

Not even his poetry.

> **Inherited brick. Bequeathed marble.**
>
> *(marmoream se relinquere, quam latericiam accepisset)*
>
> Suetonius. The Deified Augustus 28.3

THEME: LEADERSHIP

CHECKPOINT: When you find yourself in a leadership role, think about what you can do that will improve the situation you inherited. What will be your legacy? Augustus inherited a Rome built of brick. One of his improvements was to create a city built of marble.

The obvious improvement to make would be in profitability. All well and good. But what else could you do?

Perhaps you could improve the way the team works. Or bring in some proven HR ideas from other businesses. Maybe it is as simple as making the office a fabulous space to be in.

Whatever you choose, don't forget to take a serious look at the capital asset that is most important.

People.

It's obvious when you think about it, but people are more productive when they are given the opportunity to work in more productive ways.

WANT TO KNOW MORE? Today was a big day in Rome. It was the anniversary of the founding of Rome in 753 BCE. Romulus was the founder and first king of Rome and everything about him is a mixture of history and myth. Think 'King Arthur'; who knows where fact starts and fiction stops. But it's a great story, nevertheless.

Augustus was like a 'second Romulus'. In fact, the name 'Romulus' was offered to Augustus at one point; he was seen to have 'refounded' the city, bigger, stronger and more beautiful than ever.

To add to the festivities, today was also the annual celebration of sheep and shepherds, a very ancient rural festival designed to cleanse the flocks of any bad spirits, and to give them the protection of a rather curious deity, Pales.

The Romans did not know whether Pales was male, female or both.

Romulus, Pales, fact, fiction? Whatever. Rome was in party mood and there would be eating, drinking and revelry all through the night.

> They plunder the world. They exploit the land's resources until
> there is nothing left to give. Now they have started scouring the sea.
>
> *(raptores orbis, postquam cuncta vastantibus defuere terrae,*
> *iam mare scrutantur)*
>
> Tacitus. Agricola 30.4

THEME: SOCIAL AND ENVIRONMENTAL

CHECKPOINT: The purpose of a business is to make a profit, so it can grow and advance. Profit comes from the Latin word *'profectus'*, meaning 'advance, growth, progress'.

Social and environmental goods might be your core products, but it is more likely they are not. So, putting in place social and environmental policies is not part of sales and does not directly lead to profit; it is part of being a good citizen of the planet.

Some firms attract and impress more customers with their 'green' policies and others do just fine without having any. At the end of the day, it becomes a matter of how you view life.

And, remember, how you view things affects how others view you.

WANT TO KNOW MORE? The Greeks and Romans were clever, but they weren't clever enough to devise industries that would deplete the planet of its natural resources.

Their view of the natural world was, by necessity, more sustainable than ours.

Their lives depended on the food they grew. Harvests were nurtured; grain, olives and grapes were treated like life-blood.

For the Romans particularly, religion was based around places that needed protection. The crops, woods, groves, streams, fields – everywhere – had specific deities who had to be properly honoured all the time (in addition to the main gods who ruled from on high).

Many people today are superstitious about odd things – spilled salt or black cats, for example. Imagine that superstition expanded a hundredfold, so that just about everything on the planet had meaning and had to be considered, worshipped and attended to. Welcome to Roman religion.

> **Be nice to foreigners. You may be one yourself someday.**
>
> *(ξένους ξένιζε, μήποτε ξένος γένῃ)*
>
> Menander. Sententiae 554

THEME: ENTERTAINING

CHECKPOINT: When you are working overseas or receiving overseas visitors, it is not just language that can be a barrier.

Other customs and behaviours can be more difficult to understand than language.

Being courteous to people with different attitudes or ways of doing things (*'modi operandi'*) will help meetings flow and create a positive working environment.

To work out what people from other countries might be concerned about, put yourself in their shoes and imagine travelling to their country. What would make you anxious? What help would you need? What would it take to make you feel you are being treated very well?

WANT TO KNOW MORE? If you are the sort of person who gives the house a good clean and sticks a bottle of something cold in the fridge when a guest is due to arrive, then you are performing the ancient Greek custom of 'xenia' (*'ξενία'*), or 'hospitality'.

Xenia was a fundamental apart of life in ancient Greece. The Greeks thought that the gods might be everywhere and anywhere, all the time. A guest might be a god, or accompanied by a god, or be noticed by a god. How you treated the guest could be observed by a god and therefore you didn't want to offend them. You treated them as you would a friend.

Xenia was a system which allowed guests to be welcomed and treated with respect. They were fed and watered (or wined) and allowed to bathe.

You didn't overload them with questions and you might even give them a gift.

In return, the guest would try not to be a burden to the host and might reciprocate with a gift.

> **Are you looking for word-of-mouth street credibility?**
> **Is that the objective?**
> **Do you want to be famous, whatever it takes?**
>
> *(an ut pervenias in ora vulgi? quid vis? qualubet esse notus optas?)*
>
> Catullus. Poems 40

THEME: PERSONAL DEVELOPMENT

CHECKPOINT: There is actually a lot to be said for being a famous business. It can get you talked about and can help reduce your publicity budget. Fame creates its own column inches.

But there's a downside too. Being talked about when things are going well is good, but not so good when things are going downhill.

Use fame as part of a five-point strategy for building your business. Don't, whatever you do, pursue fame as an end in itself. It will make you look shallow.

First, make sure your revenue stream is sound and consistent. That comes before anything else.

Second, understand the contemporary nature and attitudes of your marketplace.

Third, network like mad. Not just virtually, not just via social media, but in real-life situations as well.

Fourth, ensure you are actively connected to the political/regulatory interests that govern your business.

Finally, you will find that you are becoming talked about. At that stage, hire experts to manage your burgeoning fame.

WANT TO KNOW MORE? Some of Catullus' poetry is sexually explicit, and, when I was at school, my Catullus textbook was savagely edited! That was then, this is now...

Nowadays Catullus can be read without so much embarrassment and in so doing we see a much fuller picture of a man who was highly educated, gifted and prepared to put his emotional neck on the line.

Catullus influenced Vergil, Horace and Ovid. He was a trailblazer who carried on regardless, saying and doing what he believed in a Rome that was on political tenterhooks. He died a relatively young man in 54 BCE, aged 30.

> **I have no desire to make a long speech on subjects you all know about.**
>
> *(μακρηγορεῖν ἐν εἰδόσιν οὐ βουλόμενος)*
>
> Thucydides. The Peloponnesian War 2.36.4

THEME: LEADERSHIP

CHECKPOINT: Good managers could begin every speech they give with today's wise words.

Sometimes talks go on far too long.

Sometimes they are hard to hear.

Sometimes they are accompanied by unreadable PowerPoint slides.

Sometimes they contain mystifying in-jokes.

But worst of all is a speech that tells everybody what they already know!

Avoid this at all costs. Listen to colleagues who have 'an ear to the ground' to make sure you don't come across as someone who is totally out of touch.

WANT TO KNOW MORE? Thucydides wrote the *History of the Peloponnesian War.*

The war was really two wars, with a six-year gap in between. Thucydides was in the thick of it and he sought evidence from both sides.

Both wars were started by provocation from Athens, which saw itself as being at the centre of a large and successful empire. After all, only 18 years earlier, the Greeks had epically seen off the mighty Persians.

By the end of the war, in April 404 BCE, Athens was defeated and weakened.

The Peloponnesian War marked the beginning of the end for Athens' claim to superiority.

Fifty years later, another new chapter was to open when the non-Greek Philip of Macedon, the father of Alexander the Great, put large swathes of Greece, including Athens, under his control.

> **There's a snake lurking in the grass.**
>
> *(latet anguis in herba)*
>
> Vergil. Eclogues 3.93

THEME: HUMAN RESOURCES

CHECKPOINT: The bigger the business, the more likely there will be someone who is sneakily trying to undermine things.

We may wonder what the motive is, because it isn't always for personal advancement.

Sometimes it's done just out of jealousy. Other times, well, who knows?

You'll usually find these characters slithering around, hissing at various things in the office without saying why they disapprove or providing any context to their complaint.

If you find someone being sneaky, spreading lies, or generally undermining people, make notes, challenge them and if necessary report them.

Otherwise, stay clear.

Hopefully they'll either stop or slide out of the company and into a new job.

WANT TO KNOW MORE? Vergil was a recluse.

Although famous in his day, if he visited Rome he would have crept in quietly and stayed at friends' houses, rather than be seen hanging around the forum or in bars.

He was a country lover. His descriptions of fields, trees, flowers and grass transport you to a carefree, simple world. He drew on his personal experience of living on his parents' farm, bringing us close to the inner life of bees and the intricacies of growing fruit.

He must have seen his fair share of snakes, too.

> **The more they covered up the red-hot secret,**
> **the more inflamed it became.**
>
> *(quoque magis tegitur, tectus magis aestuat ignis)*
>
> Ovid. Metamorphoses 4.64

THEME: THE WATERCOOLER

CHECKPOINT: Telling a lie is one thing. Covering it up is another. But continually covering up, laying lie on top of lie, just gets you into all sorts of problems.

Your own life becomes a misery as you're trying to remember which lie you told, when and to whom!

It could be that you are part of a team which is trying to cover something up. In some companies, it could be the culture of the company that you behave in a less than honest way when you think a lie can get you off the hook.

It never works.

At the first sign of a mistake or a problem, put your hand up.

WANT TO KNOW MORE? Today's quote from Ovid comes from the story of Pyramus, a guy, and Thisbe, his girl.

These two were lovers and, although neighbours, they were from rival families. Their parents wouldn't let them meet, so they whispered their love for each other through a crack in the wall that divided their houses.

They talked themselves into a heightened state of passion. Meeting became essential! So they decided to meet at an agreed location.

Thisbe got there first, but saw a lion approaching with blood from a kill dripping from its mouth. She ran (obviously) but left her veil on the ground, which the lion tore at and ripped into shreds.

When Pyramus turned up he saw the bloody veil and some lion tracks, put two and two together and made five. Assuming the worst, he committed suicide.

When Thisbe returned soon after, saw her lover's dead body and killed herself too.

It's a powerful story.

Someone should tell Shakespeare about it.

> **Your face is the mirror of your mind and
> your eyes give away your innermost secrets.**
>
> *(speculum mentis est facies et taciti oculi cordis fatentur arcana)*
>
> Jerome. Letters 54.13

THEME: PERSONAL DEVELOPMENT

CHECKPOINT: The unconscious mind plays a central role in business.

We don't spend our business days analysing each other; in any case, we are not trained to do so.

But our motivations, intentions and interests often reveal themselves.

A slip of the tongue can reveal what you really think about someone.

An unintentional quizzical look can very quickly communicate something negative, even though you are verbally expressing positivity.

Be aware that when you are communicating, you may be communicating more than you think!

WANT TO KNOW MORE? Jerome was a highly devout Christian priest and theologian who spent many years traversing the Roman Empire around 400 CE.

He was never short of a view or comment on the way people lived, and he wrote a great deal about how the good citizens of Rome should live their lives.

Amongst his large number of letters, perhaps the most eye-opening are the 18 devoted to the moral behaviour of women.

One feels he was not personally too well acquainted with women, because his most famous letter on the subject vigorously and passionately argues the case for women remaining as virgins.

Don't look down on juniors.

(neu fastidire minores)

Claudian. The Fourth Consulship of the Emperor Honorius 303

THEME: **LEADERSHIP**

CHECKPOINT: One of the worst traits in any person who holds a senior management position is to belittle juniors.

Actually, it's a form of bullying and it reveals a weak and pernicious mindset in those who do it.

If you happen to be on the receiving end of this type of behaviour, you have a few options.

Ignore it. It might eventually stop, particularly when you have proven yourself and you start to rise in the company.

Tell your peers, reporting exactly what happened. This puts the action 'in the public domain'.

If the belittling persists, report the action to another senior member of staff.

Unfortunately, all workplaces will harbour characters who have less than satisfactory personal standards.

If nothing else, use their bad actions as an illustration of how not to behave yourself, and so improve your own management style.

WANT TO KNOW MORE? By the time Honorius became emperor, in 393 BCE, the mighty Roman Empire was beginning to seriously fall apart.

In the far north, the province of Britannia asked him for help against marauding barbarians. He couldn't help. He was defending Rome against different marauding barbarians.

Mind you, he had his eye on the most important matters of the day.

He banned designer boots and trousers from the city.

> **Winners and losers never come together in genuine good faith.**
>
> *(victores victosque numquam solida fide coalescere)*
>
> Tacitus. Histories 2.7

THEME: HUMAN RESOURCES

CHECKPOINT: The difference between winning and losing in business is everything.

They may try, but winners can't conceal a degree of self-satisfaction.

And losers can feign dignity in defeat, but inside they are furious and tearing themselves apart.

If you have to create situations in the office where teams are competing in a winner-takes-all exercise, try to defuse the final result by acknowledging that everyone is contributing to a common goal.

If you meet a competitor who lost out to you at an industry function, remind them that you too know the pain of defeat and that what goes around, comes around.

It won't make everyone feel a whole lot better, but your honesty will not fuel any flames of ill-feeling.

WANT TO KNOW MORE? Tacitus was a historian of Rome of the utmost importance. He tells us a huge amount about the political, psychological, emotional and hysterical nature of life in the early days of the empire.

Tacitus is famous for his style of writing, which allows him to say a great deal in a very few words.

Unfortunately, we know very little about Tacitus himself, not even when he was born or when he died. We have a vague idea. But that's because he was a friend of Pliny the Younger, who, conversely, we know so much about.

> ## It's time for a drink, or two!
>
> *(nunc est bibendum)*
>
> Horace. Odes 1.37.1

THEME: ENTERTAINING

CHECKPOINT: There's a time and a place for everything.

And when it's time to celebrate, celebrate! Don't use the event as an opportunity to sneak in a quick meeting or to pounce on a colleague for an unscheduled, and unrehearsed, performance review.

Celebrations are important. They build team spirit and confidence.

But make sure they truly are special events. An 'event' every Friday at the local bar waters down the effect of a true moment of reward for work well done. A birthday cake every few days can become too routine an experience. (If the celebration is a personal one, make sure it feels personal.)

WANT TO KNOW MORE? It's Ladies' Day in Rome.

Today is Bona Dea, a women-only celebration of the 'Good Goddess' of chastity, fertility and healing.

And it involved drinking. And euphemisms.

Wine would be taken into the temple, but the women would call it 'milk'. And the jug the wine was carried in was called a 'honey-pot'.

The goddess herself was crowned with vine leaves and, due to a myth in which the god of the countryside, Faunus, had beaten his daughter with a myrtle branch, myrtle was banned.

Women did not have many opportunities to exclude men and publicly celebrate together, but when they did, they made the most of it.

No doubt plenty of 'milk' was consumed that day.

> ### It's not our job to settle such a dispute.
>
> *(non nostrum tantas componere lites)*
>
> Macrobius. Saturnalia 5.4

THEME: DISPUTES

CHECKPOINT: Disputes come in all shapes and sizes.

It's important to know whether you should, or should not, get involved.

Even disputes that clearly involve yourself might not be resolved by you, and your absence from the debate could be essential in clarifying matters.

Always get expert advice if you're not sure whether the dispute is down to you to solve. In some cases, it will require legal intervention, and in others, it could be settled by sensible managers or trained HR personnel.

Sometimes the company might be drawn into something that is not company business. Again, take advice.

The less time you spend in any form of conflict resolution, the more time there is to get on with the day-to-day activity of the business.

WANT TO KNOW MORE? Macrobius' *Saturnalia* takes the form of a dialogue at the house of an eminent Roman academic living in Rome.

It was written sometime around 380 CE and the discussion revolves around the genius of Vergil, who had died 400 years earlier.

Imagine a group of academics today sitting around musing about the virtues of Shakespeare. That would have been what it felt like for the Romans of 380 CE.

The *Saturnalia* book is a good example of the strength of Vergil's legacy and of how he was considered an enduring literary giant, even by the Romans.

> **What happens to people who are constantly travelling,**
> **is that they have loads of contacts, but no real friends.**
>
> *(vitam in peregrinatione exigentibus hoc evenit,*
> *ut multa hospitia habeant, nullas amicitias)*
>
> Seneca. Epistles 2.2

THEME: INTERNET

CHECKPOINT: As we travel and meet people, we become interlinked to everyone we are connecting with.

Connectivity drives our lives and along the way many connections become 'contacts'.

We gather contacts in the non-virtual world as well. When we go to meetings or conferences, for example.

But the truth is, for most of us, we have more contacts than we can manage. Check out the famous *Dunbar's Numbers* for one argument that says we can only really handle up to 150 in our life in a meaningful way. (Other theorists have other numbers.) Many people will have many more than 150.

Be careful that you differentiate between a contact and a friend.

Being 'in contact with contacts' is all well and good and might help with new business, global insights or customer satisfaction. But it is not the same as being 'in contact with friends'.

Friends are important, but can be easily pushed aside when work dominates.

Manage your busy life to 'press the pause button' and check in with your friends now and then.

WANT TO KNOW MORE? Seneca was greatly influenced by the big thinkers of his day. One such thinker persuaded Seneca to give up meat and become a vegetarian. Given that it was not unusual for Romans to eat dormice, doves and peacocks, maybe Seneca enjoyed the prospect of a meat-free diet.

But his vegetarian phase only lasted a year, because his father stepped in and put a stop to it, believing that vegetarianism was some kind of foreign fad, or superstition.

Pythagoras, the famous Greek philosopher and mathematician, was thought to be a vegetarian. In fact, not too long ago, vegetarians were referred to as 'Pythagoreans'.

It is hard to speak in a balanced way when, as a speaker,
the accuracy of what you say is difficult to establish.

*(χαλεπὸν γὰρ τὸ μετρίως εἰπεῖν ἐν ᾧ μόλις καὶ ἡ
δόκησις τῆς ἀληθείας βεβαιοῦται)*

Thucydides. The Peloponnesian War 2.35.2

THEME: PRESENTATIONS/MEETINGS/DOCUMENTS

CHECKPOINT: If you are going to make a persuasive presentation, make sure you know your facts and that you can personally vouch for the information you are imparting.

Your presentation should not contain untrue statements. If by accident something false slips in, take responsibility for it. Don't blame someone else – it will make it look as if you asked someone else to write your presentation for you. And even if you did get someone to do that – surely you don't want to let people know!

You'll also need to be able to think around what you say and be prepared for questions.

You can't keep answering 'I don't know', or 'I'll have to ask someone'.

Knowing your facts will ensure that what you say carries weight.

WANT TO KNOW MORE? By all accounts (and there aren't many) Thucydides was a dreary, priggish man, sceptical about everything and someone who liked to keep himself to himself.

Fortunately for us, he was also smart.

He was smart enough, for example, to see that a war that Athens was embarking on would be hugely significant.

So significant that it needed to be documented. He was right. He would not have known precisely what was to unfold, but of course we do; it was the Peloponnesian War.

Without his history, which is an incredible piece of work, we would be scratching our heads about much of the detail of the wars and skirmishes that ultimately greatly diminished the status of Athens.

> **People are often not sure whether something is right or wrong, or even which of the two right things on offer is the better option.**
>
> *(non solum id homines solere dubitare, honestumne an turpe sit, sed etiam duobus propositis honestis utrum honestius sit)*
>
> Cicero. De Officiis 1.45.161

THEME: THE WATERCOOLER

CHECKPOINT: In business life, someone has to make a decision and then bring the rest of the team along.

Even businesses that are co-owned, or have an influential employee council, will have a decision-making hierarchy.

Most employees don't have the time, inclination or skill to put together a consensus opinion. But what they will do is debate a decision made by someone else endlessly during the lunchbreak or over an after-work drink.

Decisions must be made by the decision-maker. Even asking people to choose between two good options can be difficult. How much information do they need? Do you ask people to vote? What percentage of the vote would win? Aaaargh, nightmare.

It is the nature of business that whatever decision is made, there will be someone who doesn't like it.

WANT TO KNOW MORE? The Romans weren't really philosophers. There isn't a Roman Plato, Socrates, Aristotle or Pythagoras. They loved to study philosophy, but they weren't inclined, like the Greeks, to sit around and muse for hours on end.

In fact, at one point in Rome's early history, all philosophy teachers were kicked out of the city. They came back, of course, and duly passed on the enormous philosophical learning of the previous centuries to their pupils.

Cicero might be considered an exception. By the time he wrote the piece that spawned today's quote, he had lost his job and was on the run from the new military junta who had put themselves in charge after Caesar's assassination.

Cicero wrote *De Officiis* for his son, who was studying in Athens, and it is in essence a manual on moral duties.

> **Such innovation. Epic. Marvellous. That was ingenious.**
> **Have never seen such freshness of thought!**
>
> (῏Ω τῆς καινότητος. Ἡράκλεις, τῆς παραδοξολογίας. εὐμήχανος
> ἄνθρωπος. οὐδὲν ἄν τις εἴποι τῆς ἐπινοίας νεαρώτερον.)
>
> Lucian. Zeuxis 1

THEME: INNOVATION

CHECKPOINT: Innovation is the business buzzword of the day. In fact, an entire industry has grown around the term, offering breakthrough thinking, left-field ideas and paradigm shifts.

Innovation should never be a 'department' of the company. It should be integral to every division and function of the business. The whole business should be an innovative business.

Ideas can come from anywhere. And people from everywhere in the company should be encouraged to step forward and offer up their innovative thoughts.

Company-wide innovation should be managed at the very top of an organization and not left to middle management to 'process' the thinking and turn it into a document, or worse, a memo.

Inspirational senior managers can change the fortunes of a company by recognizing and implementing brilliant innovation when they see it.

WANT TO KNOW MORE? The satirist Lucian (approximately 120 CE – 190 CE) was born in the south of modern-day Turkey and started out as an apprentice sculptor. But he soon turned to writing, preferring to create characters out of words rather than stone. He eventually moved to Athens.

Lucian is fun. He likes to poke fun at philosophers. In one sketch, the great philosophers of the past are auctioned off as slaves. One philosopher is being sold off on the basis of having a diverse range of skills. He was a mathematician, astronomer, good at geometry and a musician. Oh, he was also a con-artist, fraudster and all-around psychic mystic!

Any takers?

> **The guy who kindly shows a straggler the right way,**
> **as if he's throwing light on the situation, doesn't**
> **at all diminish his own brilliance.**
>
> *(homó, qui erranti cómiter monstrát viam, Quasi lúmen de suo*
> *lúmine accendát, facit. Nihiló minus ipsi lúcet, cum illi accénderit)*
>
> Ennius. Fragment (Quoted by Cicero. De Officiis 1.16.51)

THEME: LEADERSHIP

CHECKPOINT: Being a mentor to someone improves their chances of doing well at work. It gives them an all-around understanding of what to expect in the workplace and how they need to develop.

But mentoring is also good for the mentor. They say that the best way to learn is to teach. Certainly, mentoring can greatly enhance your own personal satisfaction and can offer the chance to see business from a completely different perspective.

Being a mentor does not have to be a formal role.

Informally helping someone gives equal satisfaction.

If you see someone struggling at work, offer guidance – if not from yourself, then find someone who can offer specific help.

It will reflect well on you.

WANT TO KNOW MORE? If you were a poet in ancient Rome and someone mentioned the name 'Ennius' to you, you'd fall silent in deep reverence.

He was the father of Roman poetry, whose importance is echoed by Vergil and many others.

Ennius was born in Lecce in Puglia, southern Italy, in 239 BCE and wrote an 18-book epic poem, *Annales*, in Latin.

The poem was a history of Rome from the early days of its foundation up to Ennius' own day.

Latin poetry was intended to be performed in front of an audience (at feasts, for example). The audience would be keen to hear the melodic words and experience the drama and excitement. We don't exactly know how it would have sounded, although scholars enjoy giving examples of what it might have sounded like. Maybe it was not unlike listening to a performance of John Betjeman, or John Cooper Clarke or Benjamin Zephaniah today. Whichever you find the most venerable.

> **It's poor to lean on the good reputation of others.**
>
> *(miserum est aliorum incumbere famae)*
>
> Juvenal. Satires 8.76

THEME: PERSONAL DEVELOPMENT

CHECKPOINT: It is never a good idea to lean on someone else's reputation to improve yourself. There are many ways people do this. All of them are irritating.

You try to claim a role in their success. You overclaim your relationship with them. You reference them in their absence to support your position, without their knowledge.

Getting on in business does not mean stealing the limelight, taking the glory or otherwise borrowing from someone else's success.

Despite the brazen and obvious nature of this kind of behaviour, it persists in business.

And it is because of the blatant and obvious nature of this kind of behaviour that it is clear to everyone what you are doing, and it produces the opposite effect of what you intended!

WANT TO KNOW MORE? Because so many writers like Juvenal flocked to Rome to find work and prosper, we have a pretty good understanding of everyday life in ancient Rome.

Rome was noisy. It was difficult to remain sleeping in bed after 7.00am.

The day would start with sacrifices to the gods (the Romans were religious in a superstitious kind of way – they made sacrifices to avoid any type of bad luck.)

Rome had everything. Gambling, prostitutes, horse-racing, butchers, cobblers, ironmongers, bakers, bars, fast-food outlets, pantomimes, spas, you name it.

Rome was multicultural. People from all corners flocked to Rome to find work and education. The streets of Rome were narrow and crowded, with people barging, jostling and shouting. Anyone who has walked through Venice during Carnevale might get a rough idea of what the sheer volume of people squeezing through the narrow streets might have felt like.

> **An audience always likes to hear something new.**
>
> *(τὴν γὰρ ἀοιδὴν μᾶλλον ἐπικλείουσ᾽ ἄνθρωποι,*
> *ἥ τις ἀκουόντεσσι νεωτάτη ἀμφιπέληται)*
>
> Homer. Odyssey 1.351

THEME: PRESENTATIONS/MEETINGS/DOCUMENTS

CHECKPOINT: Whenever you are making a presentation, try to bring in something fresh. Not something tricksy and flashy, but something the audience hadn't heard or thought about before.

New thinking or new takes on an old issue will make your presentation memorable and get you listened to.

I have seen too many presentations that simply represent, albeit in an interesting way, stale information.

I have sometimes heard this called 'reheating yesterday's food'.

Cook up something new and informative. Surprise the audience.

It will show that you have put some thought into what you are saying and that you respect the time the audience is giving to you.

WANT TO KNOW MORE? Just about everybody has heard of Homer's *Odyssey*. If you haven't, you'll at least be familiar with the basic storyline that Homer has handed down to generations ever since the *Odyssey* first sprang into life. You'll recognize these recurring themes from movies and books.

The everyday life of ordinary people shattered by an event. The call for the hero's return. The pitfalls along the way. The hero's super-human or brave exploits. The meeting of a mystical helper. The hero is tested and tempted. The hero goes to a dark place. The hero returns.

The *Odyssey* is the blueprint for every heroic story ever told. Think about *The Lord of the Rings* or the *Harry Potter* stories. You'll find echoes of Homer in both.

As with the *Iliad*, Homer drills deep into the human psyche and makes his tale both epic and intensely personal at the same time.

Because of this, there is always something new to discover and 2,800 years later, the *Odyssey* is still debated and interrogated and reread and retranslated.

> **A lion in charge of an army of deer is more to be feared than a deer in charge of an army of lions.**
>
> *(φοβερώτερόν ἐστιν ἐλάφων στρατόπεδον ἡγουμένου λέοντος ἢ λεόντων ἐλάφου)*
>
> Chabrias (Quoted by Plutarch. Moralia. Sayings of Kings and Commanders 187 D3)

THEME: LEADERSHIP

CHECKPOINT: Leadership is about leading. It is not about 'directing', even though many leaders in business are called director.

The word 'director' comes from the Latin *'dirigere'* meaning 'to arrange in straight lines' and 'to steer'.

So often, directors do just that – draw organograms, send directional memos and stand at the rear of the ship steering a steady path. But remember, the helmsman is rarely the captain.

Leaders should get up from behind their desks and lead from the front. They should rally the troops and lead by example.

Leadership is part experience, and part natural ability.

Finding and nurturing leaders is essential for a business to grow.

As Chabrias advises us, one good leader can transform the fortunes of 100 ordinary people. But 100 brilliant people can be severely let down by an inexperienced, undynamic and overly apprehensive leader.

WANT TO KNOW MORE? Plutarch wrote a brilliant series of essays on all sorts of subjects from, 'How to Educate Children' to 'Advice for Keeping in Good Health'.

One of his essays gave birth to the ever-famous debate: 'Which came first, The Chicken or The Egg?'.

It's not a simple question. (Or maybe you think it is?)

Aristotle asked a version of the same question many years before Plutarch. But Plutarch put the question in the way we understand it today.

I guess you could ask: who came first with the chicken and the egg conundrum?

Aristotle or Plutarch?

> **Nothing can be properly learned or taught without examples.**
>
> *(nihil recte sine exemplo docetur, aut discitur)*
>
> Columella. On Agriculture 11.1.4

THEME: PERSONAL DEVELOPMENT

CHECKPOINT: The world of business likes facts. It likes to be as sure as it can. Academic business theory is difficult to sell to a board, whereas clear examples of how things can be done well are both practical and easy to understand.

Passing on your experience by citing real-life examples is one way to help people learn to be better at their jobs.

The examples can be both good and bad. In fact, sometimes, an example of a business practice that went seriously askew is more vivid and easy to remember.

Many years ago, I was a junior in an important meeting with a big customer. I remember watching one of our senior executives standing up to give his presentation.

"I am very nervous when I give presentations," he said. "So please bear with me."

From that moment on, everyone in the room was on his side.

It was a good, solid example of how, in this case, honesty can be the best policy.

Always give examples to people who are learning, either by setting an example, or showing one.

WANT TO KNOW MORE? Although the majority of what was written by the ancient Greeks and Romans is lost, what does survive is rich and varied.

We have epics, love poetry, letters, history, biography, philosophy and more.

With Columella we get a farming manual.

Columella was from Cadiz, Spain, and was writing in the 1st century CE.

His book, *On Agriculture*, comes to us complete and offers practical guidance on such things as ploughing, manuring, the care of fish ponds and the duties of a farm manager and his wife.

Columella was above all down to earth, which might explain why he also wrote a book (which sadly we don't have) lambasting fortune-tellers.

> **If you aim for what is enough you'll not be troubled by stormy times.**
>
> *(desiderantem quod satis est neque tumultuosum sollicitat mare)*
>
> Horace. Odes 3.1.25

THEME: PERSONAL DEVELOPMENT

CHECKPOINT: In business, as in life, making plans for the future is essential. A three-year plan, a five-year plan and a ten-year plan are the most usual markers in time.

Don't be greedy when you look at profit projections. Work out what is enough for the businesses to thrive and grow steadily and securely.

When I say, 'don't be greedy', I don't mean don't be ambitious. Creating stretch goals is good practice.

A well-managed business, growing steadily, is an attractive proposition to owners, employees and potential investors or purchasers.

A business that is over-harvested for its cash and thinks that it is bigger, or more valuable, than it really is, is a dangerous proposition.

WANT TO KNOW MORE? Your average Roman would almost certainly have been doing some strange things over the past few days.

On May 9, 11 and at midnight tonight (to prepare for tomorrow, May 13) he would be getting up in his bare feet, making weird signs with his fingers and thumbs, spitting out black beans from his mouth, and banging some bronze pans and utensils together.

He has been performing age-old rites for the *Lemuria*, or Festival of the Dead.

Exactly what all these odd activities were supposed to achieve is not clear, but the Romans were superstitious, and if this is what was needed to be done to exorcise the malevolent and fearful ghosts of the dead from their homes, then so be it!

> **Just wondering whether I can leave out
> any part of my presentation.**
>
> *(σκέπτομαι γάρ εἴ τι δύναμαι περιελεῖν ὧν μέλλω λέγειν)*
>
> Phocion (Quoted by Plutarch. Moralia. Sayings of Kings and Commanders 187 F2)

THEME: PRESENTATIONS/MEETINGS/DOCUMENTS

CHECKPOINT: You have to make a presentation. You want it to be as persuasive and interesting as it can be. You have, say, a 30-minute time slot.

Here's how you do it.

Plan out what you want to say in bullet points.

Then write detailed notes under each point.

Now go to PowerPoint, or whichever presentation tool you like to use.

Without referring to your notes, write one sentence per chart until you feel you have covered everything.

For a 30-minute presentation you need no more than 15 charts. One chart for every two minutes.

Your charts are aide-memoirs for the audience, not prompts for you.

So, edit, edit, edit until the charts do no more than back up what you are saying.

If necessary, give handouts to amplify key points.

WANT TO KNOW MORE? Today is the last of the three days of *Lemuria*, Festival of the Dead. They took place on alternate uneven days. Interestingly, the Romans tended to think of even days as more unlucky than odd days.

These days in May were part of an important annual process of exorcism. It was very much focused on the family and the main temples would be closed. Because of this, May was associated with bad luck and couples were discouraged from getting married on any day in the month of May.

> **Our mind, which we often call our psyche, in which is located our understanding and control of everyday life, is a body part, just like a hand, or foot or our eyes; they are all part of a living breathing human being.**
>
> *(animum ... mentem quam saepe vocamus, in quo consilium vitae regimenque locatum est, esse hominis partem nilo minus ac manus et pes atque oculi partes animantis totius extant)*
>
> Lucretius. On the Nature of Things 3.94

THEME: PERSONAL DEVELOPMENT

CHECKPOINT: Business takes its toll. It can create both physical and mental stress. Repetitive strain injury is the curse of our keyboard-driven society. Back pain is the curse of a sedentary life.

But today's quote makes a powerful case for the care of our minds.

We are slowly catching up with the ancients when it comes to care of the whole body. They knew that a mind under stress was a serious matter.

A broken mind can be treated, just like back pain.

But we can sometimes avoid back pain with preventative measures. A better office chair, or exercise, for example.

There are preventative treatments for the mind as well, although they are still not common. Seek advice from experts.

The whole of you needs to be respected.

WANT TO KNOW MORE? Lucretius was a physicist, every bit as important in his day (around 99 BCE – 55 BCE) as Stephen Hawking is in ours. He wrote a book explaining the physics and the science of the world. It was called *De Rerum Natura*, which is translated as 'On the Nature of Things'. Others have translated it as 'On the Nature of the Universe'.

It was a hugely influential work and an extraordinary achievement for someone who did not have the scientific know-how and technology that we have today.

From the moment it was published (maybe posthumously, because it looks unfinished in places towards the end) it has held a central position in discussions about the physics of our material world.

The scientific achievement of Lucretius is extraordinary, but what makes it even more extraordinary is that he wrote it as a poem.

> **That's your average Joe for you; little is judged on whether it's true or not; most things are a matter of personal opinion.**
>
> *(sic est vulgus; ex veritate pauca, ex opinione multa aestimat)*
>
> Cicero. Pro Quinctio Roscio Comoedo 10.29

THEME: THE WATERCOOLER

CHECKPOINT: Despite the clear evidence staring them in the face, some people deliberately take an opposite view of the way things are. Often this is down to ingrained personal beliefs. Fine. If you don't share their views, then just avoid the conversation.

It might be down to a lack of knowledge. If other people's ill-informed views bother you, then find a polite way to re-inform the person.

Sometimes contrary views are down to a strong belief in conspiracy theories. Conspiracy theories and urban myths abound. They are attractive to many people and they stick in the mind.

In business, stick to the facts and keep your own mind.

If you don't know about something but feel you ought to, then find the time to find out.

After all, the world's knowledge is now at your fingertips.

WANT TO KNOW MORE? As we've noted earlier, Cicero's full name was Marcus Tullius Cicero. His father was called Marcus Tullius Cicero. His son was called, you've guessed it, Marcus Tullius Cicero. This was common practice in Roman times. Anyway, the Ciceros were proud of their names.

Cicero was put to death on the orders of Mark Antony.

A few years later, Cicero's son rose to become a consul and was able to announce Mark Antony' death to the Senate. He also had the honour of revoking all of Mark Antony's previous titles, awards and honours and ordered the removal of all of Antony's statues.

Finally, in a final act of sublime retribution, he ordered that no one in Mark Antony's family should carry the name Marcus.

So, Marcus Tullius Cicero, one way or the other, eventually triumphed and restored honour to his own family name.

> **Every tiny bit of everything lasts forever.**
>
> *(aeterno quia constant semine quaeque)*
>
> Lucretius. On the Nature of Things 1.221

THEME: INTERNET

CHECKPOINT: Work on the principle that every video, photo, paragraph, line, word and full stop you write and send to someone in a digital format lasts forever.

Even deleting something you don't send still leaves traces.

It's true that experts can, in some cases, completely eradicate your digital footprint, but it isn't easy and it can be very expensive.

Think twice about what you transmit digitally.

Over your lifetime, the actions of the younger more boisterous You follow the more senior, later version. There will be times when you'll want to laugh with your old friends about your crazy school days, of course. But there will also be times when you'll want to present the best possible picture of yourself as you go for that big job, or promotion.

Just be careful who can see what, when and how.

WANT TO KNOW MORE? Lucretius doesn't tell us very much about himself. He was known to Cicero and Catullus. But they don't tell us much about him either.

It really is a mystery how one man's work should endure for so long without us knowing much about the man himself.

Lucretius understood that our world was made up of small indivisible elements that cannot be destroyed. Although he doesn't use the words 'atom' or 'particle', he is credited with being at the forefront of atomic thinking. Remember, this is a Roman, living over 2,000 years ago.

Lucretius was writing at a time when the Roman world was tearing itself apart in brutal civil war. He saw signs of the decaying state everywhere. But he knew that not everything can be completely destroyed and was able to show his fellow citizens a way forward though rational thinking. Everything that is destroyed remains. His was a message of hope.

> **To think quickly is not to think safely.**
>
> (φϱονεῖν γὰϱ οἱ ταχεῖς οὐϰ ἀσφαλεῖς)
>
> Sophocles. Oedipus Tyrannus 617

THEME: **STRATEGY**

CHECKPOINT: Business planning is an art.

If you're planning a response to a sudden competitive move, then speed will be important.

There's a kind of 'Goldilocks' rule to planning. Not too fast and not too slow. And of these two, the first is the bigger mistake.

Even if you have a critical move to make, a hastily prepared plan can end up costing you money and, in fact, more time.

Spend time planning the planning process itself. What experience do you need to create the plan? Do you have everything you need in-house? What is the most time, including contingency, that you can give the planning process? Do you have a good leader to manage the process?

Snap decisions in business are invariably fatal.

WANT TO KNOW MORE? The story of Oedipus is an ancient myth that was around before Homer wrote his *Odyssey*.

Oedipus' parents asked an oracle for some information about their unborn baby. They got an answer they didn't want or expect. They were told that the unborn baby would be a boy, so far so good, but that he would kill his dad and marry his mum. Oops.

As soon as the baby was born, they got rid of him by leaving him to die far off in the countryside.

Oedipus is found by a kindly shepherd and eventually ends up with the King and Queen of Corinth, who raise him as their own.

Years later a mysterious stranger turns up and tells Oedipus that his adopted parents aren't his real parents. The King and Queen refuse to verify the news. Shocked, Oedipus visits the oracle to see if it's true. The oracle gives Oedipus the same prophesy that his real parents had heard long ago. Upset, he runs away. Unknowingly he heads towards the city where his real parents live. And we all know what's going to happen next ...

> **It's no good expecting gratitude from anyone for anything.**
>
> *(desine de quoquam quicquam bene velle mereri)*
>
> Catullus. Poems 73

THEME: LEADERSHIP

CHECKPOINT: One of the jobs of chairmen, CEOs, directors, managers and leaders by any other name is to encourage the team and give credit where credit is due.

But don't expect it to work the other way around.

The further up an organization you rise, the less likely it is that you'll be thanked.

You will earn more and have greater privileges. That's thanks enough.

I have heard the role of 'senior management' described as a 'thankless' job.

Well, get over it. It is.

That doesn't mean you're not appreciated or liked. It doesn't mean people don't respect you or even admire you.

Appreciation and respect are the rewards you should earn and aim for.

Just don't expect to be thanked by someone for being their boss.

WANT TO KNOW MORE? Catullus is known for his erotic poetry. But he was much more than just a love-struck poet.

Catullus wrote during the period that Julius Caesar was gaining power in Rome. Caesar must have cut a fearsome figure. He was not someone to rub up the wrong way.

Not that this deterred Catullus, who took pot shots at Caesar, lampooning him, ridiculing him and belittling him.

Caesar seemed to take it pretty well. Eventually Catullus apologized to him and Caesar invited him round to dinner that very same day.

> **Often, silence speaks volumes.**
>
> *(saepe tacens vocem verbaque vultus habet)*
>
> Ovid. The Art Of Love 1.574

THEME: PRESENTATIONS/MEETINGS/DOCUMENTS

CHECKPOINT: In every business, there are those who like to talk a lot, those who insist on being heard and those who sit quietly and say very little.

You don't need to say something just for the sake of speaking. Your silence might communicate more than you think. Use this tactic carefully, because it could lead you into tacitly agreeing to something about which you are uncertain.

If asked why you are not being vocal, give the truthful answer. You are thinking through what is being discussed? You don't have all the facts? You are uncertain about everything that is being said?

It's unnerving when people don't speak; it has a powerful effect.

But, then again, maybe that's what you want to communicate?

WANT TO KNOW MORE? Ovid's *Ars Amatoria* was a 'How To Fall In Love Manual'.

Here's some of his advice.

1. Don't expect your true love to fall out of the sky and land at your feet. You have to put some effort in.
2. Know where your intended is likely to hang out. Could be shows, could be shopping centres.
3. Pay attention to personal grooming. A good haircut, clean fingernails and smartly dressed, please.
4. Persistence pays off. Take the lead, don't hang back. Book in the next date as soon as you can (assuming this is the love of your life).
5. Do the 'Daylight Check'. Candlelight and a few drinks tend to make us all look wonderful. But check out your partner under the harsh glare of daylight!
6. Write poetry to your loved one. (Well Ovid would say that, wouldn't he?)

> **We know how to do fake truth. But when we choose to, we also know how to tell the actual truth.**
>
> *(ἴδμεν ψεύδεα πολλὰ λέγειν ἐτύμοισιν ὁμοῖα, ἴδμεν δ᾽ εὖτ᾽ ἐθέλωμεν ἀληθέα γηρύσασθαι.)*
>
> Hesiod. Theogony 27

THEME: PERSONAL DEVELOPMENT

CHECKPOINT: There's a wonderful quote by Mark Twain: "If you tell the truth, you don't have to remember anything."

If there is something you don't feel you should let another person know, don't lie. There are so many other ways to handle the situation. Like, don't say anything to anyone, for example.

Telling 'false truths, news or views' reveal you to be untrustworthy, which in businesses is almost as bad as it gets. (Theft from a business for personal gain is probably one rung further up on the Bad Scale.)

Spinning stories and telling half-truths is just as bad as lying. Businesses rely on as much absolute fact as is possible.

Being a Master Spinner with your colleagues is confusing and time consuming.

WANT TO KNOW MORE? Hesiod's world was a simple world. Comparatively speaking.

It was a world without war in which farming was absolutely the key to wealth and growth.

You could look to trading overseas with your surplus supply, but only if you, your family and the community were properly catered to. Profit from such activity was a secondary concern.

The only thing interrupting Hesiod's charming, idyllic life was his brother, Perses.

When their father died, the two sons, Hesiod and Perses, squabbled over the inheritance. Perses seems to have come out on top. This was clearly upsetting to Hesiod, who makes a big point about the importance of justice, even within his simple rural life.

> **Power is more often destroyed by flattery than by enemies.**
>
> *(opes saepius assentatio quam hostis evertit)*
>
> Quintus Curtius. History of Alexander 8.5.6

THEME: LEADERSHIP

CHECKPOINT: Is there anything more unedifying than watching someone suck up to the boss?

I don't mean agreeing with the boss, I mean overtly pouring on compliments when compliments are not due.

The process of flattering and being flattered plays out every day in some organization somewhere. Whether it comes to anything is really down to the temperament of the boss.

Some people are very susceptible to adulation. It can feel very good. It can go to their heads.

But the sensible leader will spot the motivations behind such actions and keep a balanced mind.

Uncontained, flattery can convince a leader than every action is the right action. Flattery can also diminish the role of key advisors whose job it is to maintain a level-headed decision-making process.

WANT TO KNOW MORE? Alexander the Great occupies a landmark position in Western history.

It is another name from the classical world, like Julius Caesar, that many people instantly recognize.

'Alexander the Great' is also a name that sums up 'impossible achievement'. Here is some of what he did achieve:

1. Aged 16, he ran the country of Macedonia, defeated a nearby warmongering tribe and founded a city, which he named after himself: 'Alexandroupolis'.
2. At the age of 22, he defeated the Persian army, in his first major battle.
3. Two years later, while just 24, he conquered Egypt.
4. When he was 25, he finally defeated the mighty and long-established empire of Persia.
5. Still only 29, he ventured even further and won victories in India.

Alexander died aged 33.

> **It's rare, but it does sometimes happen,**
> **that certain people get to appoint their leader.**
>
> *(raro, sed tamen factum est, ut populus deligeret imperatorem)*
>
> Cicero. In Vatinium 36

THEME: HUMAN RESOURCES

CHECKPOINT: Decision-making in companies is always best left to those responsible for doing it.

But sometimes, when you are putting together a team for a specific one-off purpose, it works well if the team themselves appoint the leader for the project. It can amplify the idea that everyone in the team is important, with an important contribution to make.

Set a process for this, to avoid it becoming simply a popularity contest.

For example, is the leadership for a fixed term? Should the job rotate? What specific skills are you looking for? If the person doesn't work out, should the team be able to appoint a different leader?

The tighter the job description, the more likely you are to choose the right person.

WANT TO KNOW MORE: We know about the big names of ancient history, but there were plenty of more ordinary citizens, Vatinius being an example. Publius Vatinius was a big supporter of Julius Caesar, helping to get him the key commands that would later put Caesar in such a dominant position. He was once verbally attacked by Cicero in court, but a few years later, Cicero was his defense attorney.

We know about Vatinius' outstanding military career. He received the top honours for campaigns in Illyricum, a province that lay across the Adriatic from Italy.

But we also know some small details. Vatinius suffered from glandular tumours. His whole body, but particularly his neck and face, were covered in large bumps. Although often laughed at, his disability never held him back.

> **Not everyone who has a guitar is a great guitarist.**
>
> *(non omnes qui habent citharam sunt citharoedi)*
>
> Varro. On Agriculture 2.1.3

THEME: HUMAN RESOURCES

CHECKPOINT: Just because someone has the tools to do something doesn't mean they automatically know how to put the tools to the best use. For example, everyone has Excel, or similar, on their computer. But that doesn't mean that everyone is an Excel wizard. In my experience, far from it.

Different people are suited to different things. Some people can write a good presentation. Others will be able to turn it into a visual masterpiece.

To find out how to get the best out of people, you have to understand them as much as you possibly can, because what you see is not always what you get.

Investing time with people is almost always rewarding.

Not only do you find out what people are good at and not so good at, but you'll often be surprised when you discover they have a skill set you never ever imagined of them.

WANT TO KNOW MORE? Varro was greatly respected by the big writers of the Roman world. Cicero called him a "prolific writer". He certainly was.

Varro, we are told, wrote around 500 books, including books of satire, text books on the Latin language and an agricultural handbook.

His life spanned the old Roman Republic to the new 'imperial' regime established by Augustus.

Varro witnessed first-hand the biggest change of political order the Roman world had seen for half a millenium. He held political office, yet his output during that time was so great that he must have spent every spare moment he had writing.

Busy as he was, he was able to remain a grounded family man. Varro dedicated the first part of his agricultural handbook to his wife, Fundania.

> **Everything unknown is automatically assumed to be magnificent.**
>
> *(omne ignotum pro magnifico est)*
>
> Tacitus. Agricola 30.3

THEME: INNOVATION

CHECKPOINT: Real innovators have a lust for the discovery of the new product or service that will make a difference.

To compete effectively today, every business should enshrine professional innovation at the heart of the business.

But be careful. As Tacitus cautions us, not everything unknown is necessarily magnificent. There are many blind alleys and dead-ends in the quest for the new.

As said earlier, innovation should never be a specific department. It should be embedded within all departments and it should be driven by people who have a real lust for the process of invention and the experience to deliver it.

WANT TO KNOW MORE? The historian Tacitus wrote a biography of his father-in-law, Gnaeus Julius Agricola. His name is not well known to many Brits, but it was the Roman soldier Agricola who conquered much of the island of Brittania.

Britain was only 'investigated' by Julius Caesar, who didn't pursue his enquiries. It was 100 years later, under the Emperor Claudius, that the real invasion took place. Agricola spent a serious amount of time in Britain, first as a junior in the early days of the Roman invasion, then again as a commander of a legion, and finally as Governor.

We can add archaeological evidence to Tacitus' account and build up a reasonable picture of Agricola's life in Britain.

He was a well-organized military man who subdued Wales and northern England, before establishing forts in Scotland.

Agricola knew a lot about Ireland too. He entertained key Irish leaders and realized its strategic potential, but decided not to invade.

....

> ## The unexamined life is not worth living.
>
> *(ὁ δὲ ἀνεξέταστος βίος οὐ βιωτὸς ἀνθρώπῳ)*
>
> Socrates. Quoted in Plato's Apology 38a

THEME: INNOVATION AND PERSONAL DEVELOPMENT

CHECKPOINT: We spend roughly one third of our lives asleep and, up until retirement, one third of our lives at work. Thank goodness for the weekends and evenings. Without them, we'd all be wandering around in a zombie-like trance.

Think about what you are doing with the time allocation you have. Obviously there's not much we can do about the time we spend asleep – but while we are awake, there is plenty of time to do more of the things that can stimulate us.

You might say, 'I haven't got any time left to do anything, I live a full and busy life'.

That is unlikely. If you want it, time will expand to allow you to do it.

Make yourself interesting. Life is for the living.

WANT TO KNOW MORE? In ancient Greece, men and women lived segregated lives. The men met with other men at the marketplace or the gymnasium and the women stayed at home looking after the house. Women did go out for funerals and festivals and may also have visited the theatre.

Even in the home, there were separate rooms for men and women.

Women stayed with women and men with men.

All of which makes a couple things Socrates says about his life quite interesting.

He appears to have had two female friends. Both of whom he says taught him many things.

One of these girls actually slaps him on the wrist in a 'lesson'. That's pretty close contact, I would say. The other girl instructs him on love. Some say these girls are the same person.

Socrates eventually married a woman called Xanthippe and they had three children. She was almost certainly much younger than Socrates and was described as a very strong-willed woman.

....

> **What happens to someone can happen to anyone.**
>
> *(cunctis potest accidere quod cuivis potest)*
>
> Publilius Syrus. Sententiae 133

THEME: PERSONAL DEVELOPMENT

CHECKPOINT: The German expression '*schadenfreude*' is used to describe someone getting joy from another's misfortune.

But be careful, there's another expression. 'He who laughs last, laughs longest'.

Taking delight in others' misfortunes might be an immediate instinctive response, but it's not good practice.

As we've seen many times, 'what goes around comes around'.

Better to rise above the petty joy of another's bad luck and see the big picture. What caused the situation in the first place and what can you learn?

Clever of the Germans to come up with such a neat phrase. But, of course, they didn't.

The ancient Greeks said it first: '*ἐπιχαιρεκακία*' (epikhairekakos), means 'joy at the misfortune of another'.

WANT TO KNOW MORE? Theatrical productions in ancient Rome were very common and were very popular. They were also big business. Winning was essential.

Corruption was endemic both at the level of the local politicians and the general public. Rigging the system by bribing actors to lose was one common tactic.

If outright bribery proved difficult to arrange, then gangs of professional applauders could be recruited to wave and clap when their chosen candidate appeared on stage.

Publilius Syrus, an ex-slave, turned his ready wit and repartee into an income. He toured the country towns, successfully turning his mime show into a professional act. He was a theatre professional. When Julius Caesar invited him to perform in a contest in Rome in 46 BCE, he knew his moment had come. It was a head-to-head contest featuring a series of contenders. Despite being the outsider and no doubt being up against some local rigging, Publilius beat them all and won the competition.

> **And now, which expenses currently being incurred can we strip out without causing any harm?**
>
> *(ἢ τῶν ἀναλωμάτων τῶν νῦν ἀναλουμένων, τίνα τε καὶ πόσα περιαιρεθέντα τὰ ὅλα μηθὲν βλάψει)*
>
> Aristotle. Economics 2.1346a

THEME: FINANCE

CHECKPOINT: It's often called the 'orange juice' moment.

Finances get tight. Income is slowing, and the competitive scene is looking tougher.

Out of the blue a memo goes around saying the company is cutting back – the free orange juice has to go. Well, savings need to be made.

Harmless enough isn't it?

Actually, it sends a devastating message. It alerts the workforce to a downturn without any real attempt to address the problem at the fundamental level.

When there is a need to cut outgoings, cut once, and cut deep.

The cuts need to resculpt the business into a lean, mean, fighting machine.

Employees would rather keep their jobs than keep their benefits and risk redundancies.

Engaging the staff in the process can also be helpful. This allows everyone to voice what they would cut, without causing any harm to the business.

WANT TO KNOW MORE? Today's quote comes from Aristotle the economist. But there was also Aristotle the psychologist and Aristotle the biologist. In fact, Aristotle was phenomenally talented and turned his hand to many routes of enquiry.

Aristotle the zoologist demonstrated his enthusiasm for fact-finding.

For a while he was tutor to Alexander the Great, who gave him a research team to look into animal life. Alexander arranged for all sorts of animal experts to be at Aristotle's disposal: beekeepers, shepherds, farmers, fishermen, you name it. If there was an animal expert out there, they were brought in to assist Aristotle.

Aristotle knew that these experts would bring a different perspective to his studies.

From his team's research, Aristotle was able to dispel some myths of the natural world, such as: fish don't have sex. They do, said Aristotle, and his experts could prove it.

> **What job did you do? What was your life like?**
>
> *(ἔργον μεριμνῶν ποῖον ἢ βίον τίνα;)*
>
> Sophocles. Oedipus Tyrannus 1124

THEME: PERSONAL DEVELOPMENT

CHECKPOINT: There are new companies springing up all the time, doing things we simply don't understand.

Of course the 'conventional' jobs are still there: lawyer, doctor, teacher; but even those titles conceal a whole range of different specialisms.

The world of work has in many respects never been so diverse and so exciting.

Make sure you know what is going on out there. Find time to discover what jobs there actually are.

Don't assume that just because you have worked only in one industry, you don't have any transferable skills.

The most important thing is to make sure you are doing a job you enjoy doing. Whatever it is, there is delight in every job.

One day you'll be looking back at your life and mulling over how it all went. You have the chance to make it a positive memory.

WANT TO KNOW MORE? We have seen how clever the ancient Greeks were in mathematics, physics, philosophy and the arts. But today in 585 BCE is a serious marker in terms of ancient scientific know-how.

In fact, the great science fiction writer Isaac Asimov called this day "the birth of science".

Thales, a philosopher living in the years around 600 BCE, predicted a solar eclipse on this day.

And he was absolutely right. No one knows how he did it, but he did.

The eclipse was written up by the Greek historian Herodotus because it happened slap-bang in the middle of a battle (between the Medes and the Lydians) taking place in Turkey on May 28, 585 BCE.

Thales' prediction was so accurate that historians make the claim that this was the first battle in history that can be accurately pinned down to a specific day.

> **Advice is what you give to someone who is in the process of planning something.**
>
> *(consiliarium est quod cogitanti factum est)*
>
> Seneca. Natural Questions 2.39.4

THEME: LEADERSHIP

CHECKPOINT: You might think that giving advice to colleagues in the workplace is always a good thing.

Well, it isn't always.

It's not a good idea to dispense advice casually, as if people are always in need of it. It can be seen to be condescending and, at worst, highly irritating. There's always someone in the office saying, 'I wouldn't do that if I were you', or 'Why are you doing it that way?'.

Irritating indeed.

Recommendations and guidance are, however, most helpful when you are in the process of planning or doing something and when it clearly helps you to advance your work.

Give advice on the best way to tackle a project but then leave some space and let people ask for specific help as and when they need it.

WANT TO KNOW MORE? Seneca was known as Seneca the Younger to distinguish him from his father (Seneca the Elder).

He was born in Spain but lived in Rome and worked closely with the unpredictable Emperor Nero.

As well as philosophy and drama, Seneca wrote a number of letters that open a window for us onto daily life in ancient Rome.

He talks about the brutality of the gladiatorial shows (not all Romans revelled in blood and gore). He mentions going to the seaside and he recalls the boats bringing the post to Rome from Alexandria in Egypt.

He also tells us about himself, about his asthma and other troubling illnesses such as fever attacks and travel sickness.

> **When a debt has been acknowledged, or a judgement given, the legal due date will be 30 days.**
>
> *(aeris confessi rebusque iure iudicatis XXX dies iusti sunto)*
>
> Twelve Tables. Table 3 (Quoted by Gellius. Attic Nights 20.1.42)

THEME: LEGAL

CHECKPOINT: Every day, all around the world, there are millions of interactions, big and small, which represent the heartbeats of business. Buying, selling, dealing, inventing, employing – all these are interactions that drive a business forward. And all of these are bound by agreements. Mostly legal ones.

Make sure your valuable interactions are properly covered by contracts which have been written by a professional.

Templates for many day-to-day contracts can be found online; even so, make sure you are one hundred percent happy that they are robust enough. These contracts bind the interactions together.

Once signed, keep on top of them. There will be details that must be adhered to. If you persistently neglect to enforce the contractual arrangements you made to protect your own business, you might be demonstrating that you don't really care about the contract. This can be dangerous for the business because your behaviour can set a precedent.

WANT TO NOW MORE? The legal history of Rome started with the Twelve Tables. These were a written code, a legal charter, drawn up in 445 BCE. The idea was to stop squabbles between the ordinary people and the richer ruling classes. It was a great achievement for a small rural community (as Rome then was) to agree to something in writing and, in a sense, it marked the transition from uncivilized community to civilized regime. It was a major step in social organization that would facilitate Rome's rise to super-stardom.

The Twelve Tables lasted a long time. Cicero tells us that in his youth, every schoolboy would learn them by heart. The suggestion was that they were learned by rote and were chanted in the way pupils today often learn the 'twelve times table'.

> **Loyalty is rare.**
>
> *(rara est fides)*
>
> Phaedrus. Fables 3.9.1

THEME: LEADERSHIP

CHECKPOINT: No matter how benign the company is, or how wonderful the working environment is, most people will always put themselves first.

Even so, senior management can get misty-eyed about the issue of loyalty, citing a low churn rate and long-serving employees.

Good managers, in well-run companies, should expect consistency from employees, but don't take it for granted.

Everybody in the company will have their own individual level of tolerance. Each will be unique. And if you don't take note of it, you will wake up one morning with the surprise resignation letter that you least expected.

Don't assume loyalty, but aim to build it. When you have it, nurture it.

WANT TO KNOW MORE? Phaedrus would have remained in dark obscurity were it not for a certain Frenchman called Peter Pithou. Monsieur Pithou discovered Phaedrus' Latin translations of Aesop's Fables in the library of the Abbey of St. Remi, in Reims.

Without this discovery, we would have very little of Aesop's Fables because we don't have the original work, which, if written (it was orally transmitted) would have been written in Greek.

Discoveries of this kind are rare today, but still happen.

In 2014, two new poems by the female erotic poet Sappho were unearthed.

Nowadays, we rely less on ancient libraries to reveal new Greek or Latin texts.

Classics has moved into the 21st century and new digital imaging methods allow the experts to start peering into a wet rolled up papyrus that would fall apart if opened by hand.

This is exciting. Given that we have so little of what was written, the discovery of a new text is a landmark moment in the world of classics!

> **One swallow does not a spring make.**
>
> *(μία γὰρ χελιδὼν ἔαρ οὐ ποιεῖ)*
>
> Aristotle. Nicomachean Ethics 1098a

THEME: STRATEGY

CHECKPOINT: A cardinal sin in business is to take one solitary piece of evidence and turn it into just the trend you were hoping for or the strategic result you had planned.

Yet it happens all the time.

It's a kind of corporate self-delusion. You are desperate to see signs of improvement, or the first shoots of recovery, and you leap on the first positive fact you can find.

Experience tells us that life doesn't work like that. In order to see if things are going your way, you need to see that the change has been sustained over a long period of time.

The competitive nature of business puts uncertainty into everything. You might see a genuine positive trend, but your competitors might see the same trend and react faster than you.

When building strategy, don't rely on hope.

WANT TO KNOW MORE? The great philosopher Aristotle was thought to be somewhat idle and debauched in his early years. He helped himself liberally to his father's wealth, funding a dissolute lifestyle which included, amongst other things, dealing in drugs. (Allegedly).

But in his later teens, after his father's death, he headed to Athens to hear the famous Plato giving lectures at his Academy. He was hooked, and everything changed.

Inspired, he knuckled down and focused.

After spending some 20 years with Plato, who was by then coming to the end of his life, he got the entrepreneurial itch and left to pursue zoology and botany on the island of Lesbos.

Aristotle ate in moderation and slept very little. To ensure he never slept too long, he invented an early form of 'alarm clock'. He slept with one arm permanently out of his bed holding a lead plug in his fist which hung over a metal bowl. When eventually his fist loosened, the lead dropped into the bowl with a clang and woke Aristotle from his slumber.

> **We don't address this. We ignore the fact that we're under threat from a serious and growing danger.**
>
> *(ὧν οὐδεμίαν ποιούμεθα πρόνοιαν, ἀλλ᾽ ἀγνοοῦμεν κοινὸν φόβον καὶ κίνδυνον ἅπασιν ἡμῖν αὐξανόμενον)*
>
> Isocrates. Discourses 5 To Philip 121

THEME: COMPETITORS

CHECKPOINT: Most organizations will have the obvious departments. Sales, marketing, new product development, finance and so on.

But how many have the 'competitor' department?

None that I've heard of.

And yet competitor activity has never been more sudden, or immediate or threatening than it is now.

Even if a Department of the Competition is going a bit far, it is worth assembling a team who take a regular look.

There is always an enormous amount of information about competitor activity.

Check it out and act upon it. Before it's too late.

WANT TO KNOW MORE? The Romans had many competitors. In the early days, it was the tribes of Italy who resisted Rome's advances. Then, as Rome grew, it was conquest outside of the Italian peninsula that created, understandably, many more enemies.

But today marks the first day of a two-week period in 455 CE that saw an eastern Germanic tribe, called the Vandals, come right down into Rome and loot and pillage – hence, our word 'vandalism'.

Known by historians as 'The Sack of Rome', the fourteen-day event stripped Rome of much of her priceless art, but the Vandals agreed not to destroy buildings – one of the reasons they are still there to be seen today.

> **Disagreements go hand in hand with shared leadership.**
>
> *(sociisque comes discordia regnis)*
>
> Statius. Thebaid 1.130

THEME: LEADERSHIP

CHECKPOINT: Are two heads better than one? Of course they are, when you're trying to solve a problem.

But when it comes to decision-making, you need to be, well, decisive. And that means you need the final decision to be taken by one person.

Most organizations are pyramidical in structure, with all roads leading to one person, the CEO.

Having more than one final decision-maker is a recipe for disaster and should be avoided.

Each of us holds different views, sees different outcomes. When you have two leaders, there will always be some degree of disagreement which can easily spiral out of control.

Such situations lead to a slowing down of progress and an over-politicization of normal business practice.

WANT TO KNOW MORE? This day in Rome was a day for paying due respects to the goddess Bellona, the goddess of war. The Romans paid great attention to Bellona, which is not surprising, since war was the engine of economic, social and cultural growth for Rome.

Bellona was the sister of Mars, the god of war, although others think she might have been his daughter, or even his wife. Her temple was outside of the walls of Rome.

The priests of this goddess put on a good show. They cut themselves, creating large incisions, often on their legs. They rubbed their hands in the blood and offered the blood to the goddess as a sacrifice.

Just outside the temple was 'the column of war' against which the priest, when war was declared, hurled a spear. It was a symbolic act, and one which aimed to recruit Bellona into the Roman military campaign of the moment.

> **One shouldn't speak in a way that the audience can
> understand us, but in a way that it is impossible
> for them to misunderstand us.**
>
> *(quare non ut intellegere possit sed ne omnino possit non intellegere curandum)*
>
> Quintilian. Institutio Oratoria 8.3.24

THEME: PRESENTATIONS/MEETINGS/DOCUMENTS

CHECKPOINT: Make sure what you are saying cannot be misunderstood!

A long-standing expression used for many years is KISS: Keep It Simple, Stupid.

As soon as you use long words, you've lost most of the audience.

If you put up an unreadable chart and then say: 'You probably won't be able to read this chart', what do you think people are thinking about you? (Clue: It's not very positive.)

Meetings that get mired in too much technical speak or complex finance data become a waste of time very quickly.

Just ask yourself, 'can what I've written be, in any way, misunderstood?'. If so, rewrite it.

WANT TO KNOW MORE? Quintilian (about 35 CE to about 100 CE) was the foremost teacher of rhetoric in Imperial Rome and the greatest Latin authority on education.

Here are some of his firm beliefs about education:

1. Early learning should be fun.
2. Schools are better than home-learning.
3. Teachers of any subject and at any level should be of the highest calibre.
4. Greek should be taught at the earliest possible age.
5. Grammar is essential. It's the superstructure that supports all language and literature.
6. Don't hurry an education. It's better to learn thoroughly than to learn quickly.
7. All pupils must read Homer and Vergil.
8. Also important are geometry, music, astronomy and philosophy.
9. Teaching many different subjects concurrently is good. It stimulates the pupil's brain.
10. The time for learning rhetoric is dependent on ability, not age.

> I strongly advise you to think carefully. Sure,
> the sum of money we are talking about is not massive.
> But it's the mindset it creates which is the serious point.
>
> (παραινῶ μέντοι σκοπεῖν καὶ λογίζεσθαι πρὸς ὑμᾶς αὐτοὺς
> ὅτι τἀργύριον μέν ἐστι τοῦθ᾽, ὑπὲρ οὗ βουλεύεσθε, μικρόν,
> τὸ δ᾽ ἔθος μέγα, ὃ γίγνεται μετὰ τούτου)
>
> Demosthenes. On Organization 2

THEME: FINANCE

CHECKPOINT: At some point in each year, a group of people in the office will sit down and start working out next year's budget. Budgets create action and therefore each sum of money allocated defines a purpose and resculpts the company.

Budgets also create mindsets. Is the company in 'saving' or 'spending' mode? Does the company believe in innovation? Does the company value its employees?

It is not the absolute amounts of money that resculpt the character of the company; it is more about emphasis. Even a small allocation to something experimental, for example, can receive both negative and positive reviews.

Once the budget has been set, it needs to be appropriately presented to the right people and explained so that it can motivate and inspire the organization.

WANT TO KNOW MORE? We live today in a global village. We can see trading opportunities at the same time as we can see threats from hostile nations.

In the ancient Greece of Demosthenes (born 384 BCE , died on October 11, 322 BCE) people faced opportunities and threats of no less intensity, though obviously less 'global' than ours.

The threat to Athens, at the time of Demosthenes' quote, came from the north, from a place called Macedonia.

Philip II of Macedon was expanding his empire and Athens was in his sights. Many Athenians wanted to make peace with Philip, but Demosthenes was a vocal force for resistance. He launched scathing speeches against Philip. Demosthenes did not win his arguments. Politics triumphed over oratory and Athens submitted to both the powerful force of Philip and, later, to Philip's son, Alexander the Great.

....

> **Adequate provision of basic resources must be made to those who require them.**
>
> *(τούς τε ἐν ἀπορίᾳ ὄντας τῶν ἀναγκαίων εἰς εὐπορίαν καθιστάναι)*
>
> Aeneas Tacticus. On The Defence Of Fortified Positions 14.2

THEME: LEADERSHIP

CHECKPOINT: When you hire someone, you must also buy in the resources that the person needs to do the job. If you don't, you are not hiring the 'complete person'.

For many desk jobs, this resource will be a computer and/or laptop. It might also mean a mobile phone. All these items have costs attached to them, maybe as much as $5,000.

You might need to set up a task force to look into a new opportunity or investigate an internal issue. Again, plan ahead and look at what extra resources will be required to facilitate the process.

The employees themselves might not ask for what they need because, as they say, 'they don't know what they don't know'.

Remember, a fully functional employee is a person, plus the resources to do the job.

WANT TO KNOW MORE? Aeneas Tacticus (who lived around the year 350 BCE) was the inventor of the first long-distance messaging machine.

Long before morse code, telegram or radio he invented the hydraulic semaphore system.

It was an ingenious system involving identical 'communicators' placed on hilltops, each filled with water. Using fire torches to signal STOP/GO, the water would be released simultaneously from each communicator and stopped at exactly the same point. That allowed one communicator to let the other know what level of water it was signalling. Each level of water denoted a different message. So, if the water on both units stopped at 'ADVANCE', you knew what you had to do. Ingenious.

Aeneas invented this because he was a military man. He wrote several military textbooks but the only one that survives is one on the defence tactics you need if you find yourself under siege.

....

> **People naturally apply themselves when they get together
> and brainstorm innovative actions and ideas.**
>
> *(sic homines, natura congregati adhibent agendi cogitandique sollertiam)*
>
> Cicero. De Officiis 1.44.157

THEME: INNOVATION

CHECKPOINT: Every company has a brainstorm at some point in the year. Mini-brainstorms happen quite regularly, but it's the big formal brainstorms that yield the most value … if done properly.

I have managed brainstorms all around the world and at every level of an organization. I have even conducted them at The World Economic Forum in Davos, with global CEOs and politicians.

I say all this not to brag, but to make the point that all brainstorms follow the same basic guidelines, wherever they are and whoever they are with. These guidelines are:

1. One person must chair the meeting and must be in charge of events!
2. Everyone in the meeting must be inspired to create a true step change. Otherwise it's not a brainstorm – it's a meeting.
3. All contributions are equally valid.
4. If the purpose is to change company direction, you need a minimum of two days.
5. Important brainstorms cannot be held 'on-site'(in the workplace) .
6. The brainstorm must be sanctioned at the highest level and have senior management backing and involvement.
7. The recommendations from the brainstorm (in total or in part) must be seen to be actioned. A brainstorm that goes nowhere deflates the team and creates animosity.

WANT TO KNOW MORE? Fun times in Rome today. It is the '*Ludi Piscatorii*', The Fishermen's Games, held on the Campus Martius in Rome.

The games were overseen by a local Roman politician on behalf of the fishermen of Rome, who played their important part in feeding the citizens of the big city.

One ritual was to throw the live catch of the day into a fire, possibly as a symbolic reference to ancient human sacrifice. The fish came from the River Tiber, which had been sacred to Rome from the city's very earliest days.

> It's true isn't it that 'thought' and 'speech' are the same?
> It's just that the former is a silent internal conversation
> which is specifically named 'thought'.
>
> *(Οὐκοῦν διάνοια μὲν καὶ λόγος ταὐτόν· πλὴν ὁ μὲν ἐντὸς*
> *τῆς ψυχῆς πρὸς αὐτὴν διάλογος ἄνευ φωνῆς γιγνόμενος*
> *τοῦτ᾽ αὐτὸ ἡμῖν ἐπωνομάσθη, διάνοια;)*
>
> Plato. Sophist 263E

THEME: PERSONAL DEVELOPMENT

CHECKPOINT: Psychologists know that our thoughts and speech are completely related and connected. We might try to hide our thoughts, but very often they appear in our speech without us even realizing they are there.

Sometimes our thoughts very clearly tumble out when we least expect them to.

We all use the expression 'Freudian slip' when someone says something that exposes something they hadn't intended to reveal. It might just be a gesture or tone of voice that accompanies what you say, but it will signal something that you consciously hadn't intended.

Think very carefully about what you say. You might not be an expert in deciphering the meaning of what is being said, but other people may well be.

Words are important. What you verbalize has an effect.

Mind what you say!

WANT TO KNOW MORE? While we are on the subject of thoughts and mind, today was a day that Romans decided to keep in mind.

It all goes back to the Battle of Trasimene, in 217 BCE, where Hannibal (he of the Alps and elephants) decisively, unquestionably and categorically defeated the Roman army.

The Romans decided to remember this day and dedicate a temple to the goddess *Mens Bona* (Goddess of The Mind, or Right Thinking).

You might think it odd that the Romans wanted to remember such a humiliating defeat, but the logic goes like this:

Even in times of crisis you must remember the goddess of good thinking, i.e. learn from experience!

> **Luck loves her brutal business. Persistently, wantonly toying with us. She shifts her fickle favours, being kind to me one minute and kind to someone else the next.**
>
> *(fortuna saevo laeta negotio et ludum insolentem ludere pertinax transmutat incertos honores, nunc mihi, nunc alii benigna)*
>
> Horace. Odes 3.29.49

THEME: PERSONAL DEVELOPMENT

CHECKPOINT: Luck has no role to play in business. It is not an active agent. It cannot turn your business around.

If you get a lucky break (a celebrity suddenly endorses your product for no explicable reason whatsoever) then accept it as just that – a lucky break.

Saying things like, 'we could do with a bit of luck' exposes a lot of shortcomings in the business.

Poor sales? Then look at the sales process.

Aggressive competitor? Then look at your product propositions.

If you are desperate for luck you may have run out of ideas, in which case, get in some outside help quickly.

WANT TO MORE? On this day in 68 CE, the Emperor Nero committed suicide the Roman way, by falling on his sword.

Nero's reign had started well. Well, he may have murdered his half-brother – who was also his brother-in-law. (It's complicated.)

Nero had the power-mum to beat all power-mums. Agrippina was the architect of her little boy's success and she played the Roman political game to perfection.

For the first five years, Nero was a benign dictator, taking advice from both his domineering and manipulative mother and his tutor, Seneca the Younger.

In his late twenties, Nero started to cut the apron strings and enjoyed the company of a wider circle of women, including an ex-slave called Acte. His mother did not approve.

Things started to go wrong for Nero at this point. Eventually, he decided to kill his mother – well, that's one way of cutting the strings.

Nero contrived an over-elaborate boating accident that would have made it looked like his mother died by accident. It failed, and, in the end, he made sure she was assassinated.

> **While it's 'on hold', life is speeding by.**
>
> *(dum differtur, vita transcurrit)*
>
> Seneca. Epistles 1.2

THEME: **STRATEGY**

CHECKPOINT: You've had the idea. You've initiated the brainstorm. You've conceived the strategy. You've doubled-checked everything. You've consulted widely. Everything is in place.

The team is ready to go, and then … you press the pause button.

Sometimes it makes good sense to do that. Finance under pressure? Competitive activity?

Other times it simply represents a nervousness about taking a bold decision.

You need to judge the effect of not taking action when it's due or has been announced.

Things can get left on the shelf very easily. What's hot becomes luke-warm in a matter of days.

Meanwhile, the pre-existing status continues.

The reasons why you took the initiatives are still there; life just carries on.

Putting things 'on hold' usually means ditching them.

It's a business euphemism for 'we're not going to do this'.

Better to say what you really mean about a shelved idea, than to pretend it has a future.

WANT TO KNOW MORE? Seneca was wise and his sayings have filled many a book of quotations. But he was also a satirist and he wrote (well, it's thought he wrote) a book lampooning the Emperor Claudius, called *The Pumpkinification of Claudius*. In brief, it goes like this:

Claudius, having died, ascends to heaven, asks to be one of the gods, is judged, loses and descends to Hades.

(Well, I did say 'in brief'.)

Claudius had banished Seneca to Corsica, but Seneca returned to Rome once Claudius had died.

The political situation changed, and Seneca was back in favour.

The *Pumpkinification* is a skilfully written piece. It is fresh and lively, and it has all the energy you would expect from a satirical sketch aimed at such a high-profile figure as Claudius.

> **Bankers keep a record of outstanding loans, the use of the funds loaned and the repayment schedule so that they have the debit and credit facts at their fingertips for accounting purposes.**
>
> *(οἱ γὰρ τραπεζῖται εἰώθασιν ὑπομνήματα γράφεσθαι ὧν τε διδόασι χρημάτων, καὶ εἰς ὅ τι, καὶ ὧν ἄν τις τιθῆται, ἵν᾽ ᾖ αὐτοῖς γνώριμα τά τε ληφθέντα καὶ τὰ τεθέντα πρὸς τοὺς λογισμούς)*
>
> Demosthenes. Against Timotheus 5

THEME: FINANCE

CHECKPOINT: Your business is not floating in a universe of its own.

All businesses have stakeholders.

As discussed, stakeholders are all those communities, organizations and individuals who are directly affected by what the company does.

One stakeholder you should keep very close to the business at all times is your bank.

Regularly engage the bank in what you are doing.

Be proactive with your updates.

Explain the market you are in; how it works; the seasonality, if any.

Larger companies will have a finance director who is in contact with the bank for many practical reasons (e.g. payroll), but that is no reason for other senior managers to avoid meeting the bank personnel.

The more your bank can understand your business, the better support to your business it will be.

WANT TO KNOW MORE? June was a month full of festivals and religious affairs in ancient Rome.

On this day there was a female-only festival, the *Mater Matuta*, a kind of mother earth figure who was linked to the dawn, to the seas and, less romantically maybe, to ports and harbours.

The rites and rituals surrounding the worship of this goddess required that only a 'first-time' wife could decorate the statue of the goddess. Then these 'first-timers' and any single women would enter the temple with one female slave who was slapped around the head and repeatedly hit about the body. Not nice.

Exactly why they did this is not entirely certain. Was it a warning to other excluded women not to try and join in the adoration of *Mater Matuta*?

> ## Who's going to read that?
>
> ### *(quis leget haec?)*
>
> Persius. Satires 1.2

THEME: PRESENTATIONS/MEETINGS/DOCUMENTS

CHECKPOINT: We live in a visual age. Every second, a million minutes of video content will run through the internet.

Video is easy and can communicate complex ideas swiftly.

But every now and then, we have to write something down. With no video content at all.

Writing is actually only the half of it. What you write has to be read.

It might be a finance report, a status report. It could be a strategic recommendation.

There is an art to making something readable.

Before you start, sit down and think, 'what would I feel like if I had to read a report?'.

You'd probably feel it would be heavy going. So make it easy going.

Use short sentences. Read back what you have written after every paragraph (put in lots of paragraphs).

Keep the language simple and straightforward. No long mysterious words, unless it's necessary.

Get someone else to read what you've written before you submit it. Ask them to assess its ease of reading, understandability and persuasiveness.

WANT TO KNOW MORE? Persius, who lived in the time of Nero, wrote less than 700 lines of poetry. He seems not to have had the customary military career and was not a sailor, entrepreneur or adventurer. His poems do not disclose a rampant erotic love affair.

He was a good-looking, clean-living young man.

Comes across a bit boring, doesn't he?

Well, he lived in dangerous times amongst dangerous people. He was part of the political elite, the 'chatterati', the 'politicos'. He was born into wealth and lived a comfortable upper-class life.

Some of his close friends were more active politically and got themselves into trouble.

Perhaps this pleasant, quiet chap just kept his sensible head down?

> **There's always something new coming out of Africa.**
>
> *(semper aliquid novi Africam adferre)*
>
> Pliny The Elder. Natural History 8.17

THEME: INNOVATION

CHECKPOINT: No matter what size of business you are, or what you make or provide, you must make sure you are aware of what's happening in other places around the world.

Every time I landed back in London after a trip (particularly to Asia) I would feel the pace of life slow right down. Business here seemed lethargic, less hungry, less innovative.

This is not to suggest that all businesses need to emulate Asian standards, but they should recognize who the pacesetters are.

Being aware of what's happening is brain food. Knowing where the new thinking is coming from is stimulating.

There will be so much more innovation to consider if you take a look around the world. Emerging markets are forced to think differently, established markets have the weight of experience behind them. Both have the expertise.

WANT TO KNOW MORE? As described earlier, Pliny the Elder wrote a gigantic encyclopaedia called *The Natural History*.

It's groaning with facts.

He writes about the island that lies to the northwest of Germany (and the north of France).

How accurate was he about Britain?

He tells us that the length of Britain is 800 miles, based on calculations made by the military commander Agricola (see May 24).

Converting Roman miles to modern miles, we get approximately 736 miles.

Now, we know it to be 874 miles. But come on, be fair, that's not a bad estimate by the Roman of 2,000 years ago.

He gets better. He estimates the width of Britain to be 300 Roman miles, which converts to 276 modern miles. Today, we measure it to be 271 miles.

He was five miles out.

Again, not bad.

> **An arrow doesn't always hit its target.**
>
> *(nec semper feriet quodcumque minabitur arcus)*
>
> Horace. Ars Poetica 350

THEME: **STRATEGY**

CHECKPOINT: All businesses like certainty. You like to know that if you are going to invest in something, you'll get a return. You want to know that the superstar you have hired is going to deliver.

But then business, despite all the many years of case histories, the proven expertise and the famous business books, is not an exact science.

If anything, it's an art. An art that relies on certain scientific truisms to keep it afloat. Just as a sculptor must know the realities of how certain materials respond, so in business you need to know the basic rules and then create a unique enterprise.

If there is one rule which is proven a thousand times over it is this: 'Not everything goes according to plan'.

Just knowing that is half the battle to overcoming such frustrations!

WANT TO KNOW MORE? Another interesting festival in Rome today. June is full of them.

Today marked the middle of the three-day *Lesser Quinquatrus*. It was a festival of the guild of flute-players. For three days, the esteemed flute-players would wander through the streets of Rome in their fine, ornate robes (possibly women's clothes). They would wear masks and play their instruments and thoroughly enjoy themselves. They might even be seen interrupting important events and bringing some levity to serious occasions.

Why flute-players, we might wonder?

Well, they were important participants at religious festivals, sometimes drowning out unpleasant noises that might cast a bad spell over events.

They attended funerals too, and were present at big feasts, where they would provide the entertainment and liven things up a little.

> **Once you've begun, you've half the job done.**
>
> *(dimidium facti qui coepit habet)*
>
> Horace. Epistles 1.2.40

THEME: PROJECT MANAGEMENT

CHECKPOINT: Some projects seem daunting, don't they?

A project that has a wide scope could look like a mountain to climb.

A project which requires masses of research analysis could make you go weak at the knees.

A project which has been given the green light by the board and is of the highest importance might cause you to lose sleep at night just thinking about it.

The solution to all these is simple.

Just start.

Make sure you have everything you need and the right environment to do it in, and then start.

Suddenly the work will start flowing.

WANT TO KNOW MORE? Horace is a world-class poet. His work rewards repeated reading. He is subtle, and clever. He can be guarded and closed at times, but he'll let you in if you persevere.

What sort of man was he?

He enjoyed his food and wine and he describes himself as short and fat, and prematurely grey. He liked the sun, so we assume he was always tanned.

He could flare up quickly with some people or over certain situations and was not an easy man to get to know or befriend.

Rumour had it that his appetite for sex was as great as that for the food and wine. Scurrilous tittle-tattle suggested that one room in his house had walls lined with mirrors, and prostitutes were so arranged that wherever he looked, he could see his sexual appetite at work first hand.

Tittle-tattle of course.

Maybe.

> ## He who has faith in his strategy is fair-minded, even to the competition.
>
> ### *(etiam hosti est aequus qui habet in consilio fidem)*
>
> Publilius Syrus. Sententiae 188

THEME: STRATEGY

CHECKPOINT: Every business needs a strategic direction and it is essential that you get behind it with all the passion and enthusiasm you can muster.

Of course, spend as much time as you need to do your analyses and research, but when you have devised your strategy, believe in it one hundred percent.

There is something very powerful about conviction. It sets a clear agenda and focuses everyone's minds.

If you totally believe in what you are doing, you are less bedevilled by the competition.

Don't ignore them. And don't stop studying their every move.

But with confidence in your own strategy, you will not be spooked by the competition, or fear them.

You will even find yourself complimenting them on their market strategies, because they present no threat to yours.

WANT TO KNOW MORE? Publilius Syrus, who gives us our quote for today, knew Julius Caesar. It's doubtful that they were best friends, but they knew each other. Caesar invited Publilius to give a performance of his work on stage in a fun competition, which Publilius won.

Given that Publilius was at one point in his life at the epicentre of Roman life, one wonders who else he might have been rubbing shoulders with.

Active in Rome at this time were: the famous Cicero; the famous academic, Varro; the historians Sallust and Livy; the risqué female poet Sulpicia; the architect and civil engineer Vitruvius; the great poets of the day – Vergil, Horace and a poet whose work we know about, but don't have, Gaius Cornelius Gallus ... the list goes on.

An afternoon in the *'taberna'* (bar) with just two or three of these characters would have been a highlight of Publilius' life, if it had ever happened.

We shall never know!

Don't re-order stock at the point of it running dangerously low.
Plan your future needs ahead when you have a good supply of
what you need.

*(μηδέποτε ἀναμένειν τὸ πορίζεσθαι τἀπιτήδεια ἔστ᾽ ἂν ἡ χρεία σε
ἀναγκάσῃ· ἀλλ᾽ ὅταν μάλιστα εὐπορῇς, τότε πρὸ τῆς ἀπορίας μηχανῶ)*

Xenophon. Cyropaedia 1.6.10

THEME: PROJECT MANAGEMENT

CHECKPOINT: Stock inventory and cash flow are critical factors in
many businesses and they need to be managed carefully and by people
who have experience.

The process needs to be fluid and highly organized.

It's not a sexy part of business, but don't let that fool you, or make you
take your eye off it.

In fact, any type of re-order process needs to be well-managed.

Something as simple as photocopier/printer supplies, for example.

Watch this important aspect of your business. It may seem insignificant
in the greater scheme of things, but when the supply chain does not work
properly, it's one disaster than you'll know about immediately.

WANT TO KNOW MORE? Xenophon's personal story is so vivid and
exciting that it's not surprising he has been the inspiration behind numerous books and movies.

Born around 430 BCE, he was a wealthy Athenian citizen and a friend
of the philosopher Socrates.

In 401 BCE, aged 29, he left his comfortable life in Athens and joined
an expedition against the Persian king Artaxerxes II, who was based in
Babylon. The expedition was led by the king's brother Cyrus, who was the
governor of Persia. It was brother against brother, and to bolster his troops,
Cyrus had recruited a mercenary force that included 10,000 Greeks.

Xenophon was one of those Greek soldiers.

The expedition was a disaster. Artaxerxes prevailed, and Cyrus was killed.

Now the real story begins. Xenophon starts a journey back home. It
soon becomes an epic tale of one man leading thousands of bedraggled
troops through thick and thin and over hundreds of miles of enemy ground
to eventually get back home.

> ### Entertain rarely.
>
> *(convivare raro)*
>
> Cato. Collectio Distichorum Vulgaris. I.19

THEME: ENTERTAINMENT

CHECKPOINT: Entertaining customers or clients has been a long-standing part of business life.

Over time, both the rules and the accepted way of doing it have changed (for the better).

In a workplace it is important to establish some ground rules about entertaining. Purpose, budget, frequency, venue and numbers of personnel is a good start.

This needn't be a formal list, (although it could be); it is more like a set of guidelines.

You might be a customer of a supplier and you in turn will have customers. Entertaining can make communication easier and build the relationships.

But don't do it too often, or the value of it will start rapidly decreasing and you'll have to start increasing the cost and style of the event.

WANT TO KNOW MORE? Entertaining Roman style is often represented in a clichéd way, with multiple courses of food and wine being brought to reclining diners who eat and eat until they can eat no more.

I'm afraid it's true! Well, obviously, not every single day, and not every single person, but there is plenty of evidence that attests to the excesses of the upper-class Roman diner.

We would recognize of lot of what was being eaten. Lobster, asparagus, goose liver, wild boar, truffles and mushrooms.

Other food we might pass on. Flamingo tongues and giraffe, for example.

There are other interesting nuances of Roman dining.

The Romans had no forks, just knives and spoons. This is because they ate with their fingers. Hence there was plenty of handwashing going on throughout the dinner.

Romans often brought their own napkins to dinner, in which, afterwards, they used to take home any of the left-over food that took their fancy.

It is thought that the mark of someone who has practical wisdom is the ability to really think about what might be good and helpful. Not in specific terms, like health and fitness, but generally, in terms of what might lead to a good life.

(δοκεῖ δὴ φρονίμου εἶναι τὸ δύνασθαι καλῶς βουλεύσασθαι περὶ τὰ αὑτῷ ἀγαθὰ καὶ συμφέροντα, οὐ κατὰ μέρος, οἷον ποῖα πρὸς ὑγίειαν ἢ πρὸς ἰσχύν, ἀλλὰ ποῖα πρὸς τὸ εὖ ζῆν ὅλως)

Aristotle. Nicomachean Ethics 1140a

THEME: **PERSONAL DEVELOPMENT**

CHECKPOINT: Should business be a force for good? That's a big question, but we're coming up to the longest day of the year, so plenty of time to think about it.

Research conducted over the years by reputable companies will tell you that being socially responsible works (i.e. your business benefits). So why doesn't every business step up to the challenge?

Well, it can be expensive to implement. To do it properly, you need to be audited to validate externally the responsible actions you are taking.

Also, to be realistic, the concept of being a 'good' company comes in and out of fashion. It can be a difficult position to sustain. Maybe you need to make cutbacks that don't damage your core business. Social and environmental causes might seem an easy target.

The truth is that beyond doing what the law requires you to do, how much you want to be an 'ethical' business is down to the owners and/or the management. This kind of positioning only makes sense if it chimes with the attitudes of those who run the company.

WANT TO KNOW MORE? Aristotle was the most highly regarded and most educated of all philosophers, according to King Philip II of Macedon, who asked Aristotle to be his son's private tutor.

Aristotle accepted the offer and in 343 BCE, aged 41, left Athens to go and tutor the king's son in Macedonia, which is in northern Greece.

As noted earlier, this son happened to be Alexander the Great.

It was said that Aristotle was paid extremely well and he stayed in Macedonia for eight years. Alexander was taught ethics, politics and medicine, plus various other subjects close to Aristotle's heart. Aristotle also took Alexander through one of the classic Greek texts of his time, Homer's *Iliad*.

> **He stirred up a storm in a teacup, as they say.**
>
> *(excitabat enim fluctus in simpulo, ut dicitur)*
>
> Cicero. De Legibus 3.16

THEME: THE WATERCOOLER

CHECKPOINT: Things can blow up quickly in a work environment. A misunderstanding, an unintended slight, a misplaced joke. And things can blow up quickly in a market environment too. An unexpected rate rise, derogatory social media, or some bad PR. Never respond to any of this using your first instincts. If you're annoyed, explode in private. If you're worried, worry with a few close colleagues and then stop worrying as soon as you can.

Keeping a cool head when there's a storm in the air settles things very quickly.

Sure, there may well be things that have to be properly and formally attended to.

Then again, maybe not.

Occasionally, things fizzle out of their own accord.

WANT TO KNOW MORE? Over 300 years after Plato (the big Greek thinker) wrote his famous books, *The Republic* and *The Laws*, Cicero (the big Roman thinker) wrote two books: *The Republic* and *The Laws*. They are different, you'll be pleased to know.

Cicero idolized Plato. He considered him to be Greece's greatest thinker.

Cicero deviated from Plato in a number of places. Plato was trying to create the perfect city, whereas Cicero thought that Rome was already the greatest city, but that the politicians and ruling classes of the day were making the city less perfect than it used to be.

Cicero wanted a return to 'the good old days'.

It was on a summer's day around 51 BCE that Cicero, his brother Quintus and his best friend Atticus began a discussion that would lead to his book *De Legibus* (*The Laws*). They took a long walk at one point, visiting some local, tranquil places, where they could converse to their hearts' content.

All the places they visited on that day are still there, just outside Rome.

> **For fear of failure he didn't go for it.**
>
> *(sedit qui timuit ne non succederet)*
>
> Horace. Epistles 1.17.37

THEME: PERSONAL DEVELOPMENT

CHECKPOINT: There are three ways to look at what happens when you are asked to go the extra mile.

1. Sometimes you are asked to stretch yourself just that little bit further than you feel might be comfortable, and you might be apprehensive about that. Stretching to improve is a good thing.
2. Sometimes you want to take on the task, but just know that it is beyond you. Maybe you've tried before; maybe you don't yet have the skill sets. That's fine. You should express your enthusiasm whilst defining your limits.
3. Sometimes you don't even want to think about what's on offer. You are petrified about the prospect of the task ahead. This situation is different from the other two.

You need to think about what is causing the fear and focus on addressing it.

You'll be asked many times in your career to push yourself or put yourself in an untried situation. It's a sure sign that your colleagues think you can improve and go further.

Just make sure you have the confidence to match their faith.

WANT TO KNOW MORE? Horace never married. Nor did his very close friend Vergil.

Nor did the erotic poet Catullus.

Martial almost certainly never married.

So, was marriage a bit of a no-no in ancient Rome?

Actually, marriage was encouraged, not least as a means of producing legitimate Roman heirs.

To produce legal heirs, you had to have a legal marriage and that meant that the happy couple were both Roman citizens, that they were the right age (i.e. both had reached puberty) and that they weren't closely related.

This was called a *'matrimonium iustum'*.

> **When making an entrance, exercise caution:**
> **don't hold back, but don't be over keen either.**
>
> *(cautus adito: neu desis operae neve immoderatus abundes)*
>
> Horace. Satires 2.5.88

THEME: PERSONAL DEVELOPMENT

CHECKPOINT: You're late for a meeting. Or you are being ushered into a customer meeting full of people you don't know.

It's unnerving.

Avoid making a big statement when you arrive. You are not the point of the meeting – the agenda is.

On the other hand, don't slide in like a shrinking violet, looking apologetic. That could very easily establish you as someone not worthy of making a contribution.

Be businesslike. Nod to whomever is leading the meeting, take your seat and, at the appropriate time, immediately address the agenda.

If you just 'get on with the job' you'll find you are far less criticized, if at all.

WANT TO KNOW MORE? Today marks an important chapter in the history of Greece and Rome.

The Romans had been operational in Greece for a long time, but had been happy to let the Greeks live in a kind of 'assumed independence' or 'protectorate'.

On this day, in 168 BCE, (we know it was June 22, because Roman historians note that there was an eclipse of the sun on that day), the Romans, antagonized by a local ruler, fought and beat an army in Greece. It was the last battle the Romans would fight against another civilized state, as opposed to uprisings and invasions of barbarian hordes. They crushed Greece on this day and brought the entire 'civilized' world under Roman control. That changed things.

The Romans had always worked on a simple rule. They would not establish garrisons in foreign countries; it was too complicated and expensive.

Then, 22 years later, when further conflicts broke out, the rules were rewritten. They converted Greece into a Province (which they called Macedonia) and established a permanent garrison. Their foreign policy changed forever. Rome was now knee-deep in the detail of running a 'multi-national state'.

> **A bell doesn't ring by chance:**
> **unless someone gives it a push or a pull, it stays completely silent.**
>
> *(numquam edepol temere tinnit tintinnabulum: nisi qui illud*
> *tractat aut mouet, mutum est, tacet)*
>
> Plautus. Trinummus 1004

THEME: SELLING

CHECKPOINT: Many years ago, I worked for an irascible old American boss. "The only reason anyone has poor sales," he would bellow, "is because they have poor salesmen."

He had a point.

Why is it that some companies sell more of their goods than others, in the same marketplace, with the same products?

In the sales process, you have to have something to sell and someone who can sell it.

Is the salesforce up to date on the benefits of the product or service? This should be a continuous process of reinforcement.

Is the salesforce fully aware of which customers it has to focus on?

Is the salesforce properly trained?

And finally, is the salesforce in active engagement in the marketplace with customers and potential customers?

There's never a wrong time to review the strength of the salesforce.

WANT TO KNOW MORE? When Plautus was writing his comedies, Rome was only really in command of Italy and Sicily. In his lifetime, he would see the islands of Sardinia and Corsica come under Roman control, but there was no 'empire' beyond Italian waters at this stage.

Plautus wrote for the theatre. His language was that of ordinary people.

He lets us know what lovers, real-life boyfriends and girlfriends, called each other.

Here are some examples. You might like to try them out yourself!

meus ocellus, meaning 'my eye'. (We might say 'apple of my eye'.)
mea rosa, meaning 'my rose'.
mi anime meaning 'oh my heart!'.
mea voluptas meaning 'my darling'.

> **Victory hops from one to another.**
>
> *(νίκη δ' ἐπαμείβεται ἄνδρας)*
>
> Homer. Iliad 6.339

THEME: PERSONAL DEVELOPMENT

CHECKPOINT: Some you win and some you lose.

In the great game of business, one day you are masters of the universe, unbeatable. And the next, well, you're not.

In fact, most of the time you are hovering somewhere in between the two. You are trying to win, and you are avoiding loss.

The feeling of winning is a good feeling. It can mobilize a company to go from strength to strength. And winning is attractive. People like to be with winners. Winning new business attracts even more new business.

It's tougher to lose. But the important thing is to lose business without losing heart.

Keep an eye on the things that made you winners and you should start losing a little less.

WANT TO NOW MORE? Rome's feared enemy Hannibal crossed the Alps and started his attack on Italy from the north. In terms of military achievement, it was an astonishing feat.

At first, the Romans met him at the Alps and he simply swept them aside. He seemed unstoppable.

He marched down through northern Italy. The Romans regrouped and on June 24 met him again, this time at Lake Trasimene. Again, the Romans were utterly defeated.

Hannibal was to march further south and the following year he defeated the Romans again at Cannae. Hannibal's army killed approximately one-fifth of the entire population of male citizens over 17 years of age.

He was invincible. But he didn't take the fight to Rome itself and he left Italy. Could it be his supply-chain was too weak? Or was besieging Rome dangerous, as his army would have stagnated outside the walls for weeks, allowing for reinforcements to come to Rome's aid? Scholars still debate the reasons why Hannibal didn't 'finish the job'.

> **Treat those who are junior to you**
> **as you wish to be treated by your superiors.**
>
> *(sic cum inferiore vivas, quemadmodum tecum superiorem velis vivere)*
>
> Seneca. Epistles 47.11

THEME: LEADERSHIP

CHECKPOINT: Do you moan about your superiors? Do you sometimes think they don't really know you?

Do they give you too much work without enough support? Do they ask you to do things which are plainly unnecessary?

When you are reviewed by your superiors, have they properly prepared?

Are they rude? Do they tell uncomfortable jokes? Do they make inappropriate comments?

Are they always late for meetings? Do they steal the limelight and take all the credit for work you've done yourself?

If you experience behaviour like this from your superior, make sure you don't behave the exact same way when working with your juniors.

WANT TO KNOW MORE? For such a thoughtful, academic kind of chap, Seneca twice got himself into serious trouble. Both times were over women.

In 41 CE, he was banished to Corsica. The story making the rounds was that he was having an affair with Caligula's married sister, Julia Livilla. Whether he was guilty of this or not, we may never know. He was pardoned in 49 CE and returned to Rome.

Nine years later it happened all over again. This time he was accused of sleeping with Nero's mother.

It has to be said that if these rumours were true, Seneca certainly made interesting choices when it came to women. He was playing with fire.

Another reason for these accusations might have been that many people thought Seneca a hypocrite and wanted to bring him down.

Seneca was very successful, immensely rich and famously well connected. Yet his philosophical work encouraged a simple, honest life. Seneca found no contradiction there.

Philosophers, he said, didn't always practice what they preach. Clearly.

Job done, my conscience is clear!

(tum facta omnia, sum circumlatus)

Lucilius. Satires 2.75

THEME: PROJECT MANAGEMENT

CHECKPOINT: There are times when you struggle to complete a task. Then there are those projects which you put some serious effort into. You give them one hundred percent.

You research more than you should. You go over your conclusions again and again, interrogating them to make sure they hold true. You go through the project with a colleague to see if what you've done is clear.

We all know that a job well done gives us a real sense of satisfaction. Maintaining this level of personal attention is not easy. Here's one way of keeping the standard high:

At the beginning, make sure the project has the right resources behind it. Next, plan what the finished product will look like – how it's presented, how detailed it will be.

Now that you have something that you can potentially feel proud of, how you conduct the middle portion will be a matter of personal self-discipline.

WANT TO KNOW MORE? Lucilius is one of those writers who is always held in high esteem. He is considered 'important', he was influential.

And the reason is this: Lucilius wrote satire. Unlike epic poetry, philosophy, love poetry, history, tragedy, comedy and speeches, which all came from Greece, satire was uniquely Roman. It was about Romans, created by Romans, written for Romans. It was something they could call their own.

Lucilius, who was born around 180 BCE and died in approximately 102 BCE, wrote 30 books of satire, but what we have left to read today is just over 1,300 lines of fragments.

Lucilius spent time living in Rome and was a contemporary of the Roman playwright Terence.

> **Imagination requires laborious detail and focus in getting the perfect idea. Innovation on the other hand is finding solutions to obscure problems and using laser-sharp minds to find something completely new.**
>
> *(cogitatio est cura studii plena et industriae vigilantiaeque effectus propositi cum voluptate. Inventio autem est quaestionum obscurarum explicatio ratioque novae rei vigore mobili reperta)*
>
> Vitruvius. On Architecture 1.2.2

THEME: **INNOVATION**

CHECKPOINT: At some stage a company needs to catch up or keep up. Many need to keep ahead and stay ahead. It is important to know what you want out of an exercise that is about giving birth to something new. If you are not absolutely clear up front, you will waste a lot of time and money.

First of all, define exactly what it is you need. Write a dream outcome.

Then decide exactly what the outcome would look like. Something totally new? A product extension? Something to take on a competitive product or service?

Ask yourself if the project can be fulfilled with internal resources or whether it requires external input.

If the latter is the case, narrow down the input you need and make sure the company you use has had proven experience and success.

WANT TO KNOW MORE? You may have heard the term 'Vitruvian Man'?

It is the drawing of the proportions of a man by Leonardo da Vinci – legs and arms outstretched and defined within a circle.

Da Vinci based his drawing on the work of the Roman architect and engineer Vitruvius.

Vitruvius wrote about architecture.

Rome had grown from a village, to a small town of brick buildings, to a capital city built of marble. Architecture was, and still is, the visible monument to the rise of Roman power.

Vitruvius didn't have aspirations to be a poet like Horace or Vergil. He was a practical man and his book, *De Architectura* (*About Architecture*), is a practical book that gives us a fascinating insight into the building methods behind Rome's houses, aqueducts, towns and baths.

> **I've taken on a challenging task. But what motivates me is the ultimate achievement. Easy success isn't satisfying.**
>
> *(magnum iter ascendo, sed dat mihi gloria vires:*
> *non iuvat e facili lecta corona iugo)*
>
> Propertius. Elegies 4.10.3

THEME: PROJECT MANAGEMENT

CHECKPOINT: If you are the sort of person who enjoys a challenge, make sure you are challenged at work.

By definition, a challenge is hard. But the payoff comes at the end.

If the work you are doing doesn't naturally present a challenge, then go and look for one, otherwise you will get bored very quickly.

Accepting and completing a challenge is one way of driving a business forward.

You might consider the 'ultimate work challenge' – setting up your own business.

There are many good examples of people who have decided to create a small business that challenges a big established one.

Define what success looks like and then go for it.

As a rule of thumb, if it's all going too easily, then there's something wrong!

WANT TO KNOW MORE? Propertius the passionate love poet set himself an interesting challenge.

After writing three books of classic love poetry to his girlfriend Cynthia, he suddenly changed course and decided to write a fourth book of 'serious poetry'. He wanted to write about the great Roman nation, about its religions and about its history.

In the course of writing his book of 'national poetry', Propertius slipped back into his old world. Cynthia reappears, taunting him, haunting him.

Did he succeed in his challenge? The experts still debate this. But one thing is certain. Propertius was indisputably a great poet and the more time scholars spend delving into the subtleties of his work, the more they discover.

Competition is good for us.

(ἀγαθὴ δ᾽ Ἔρις ἥδε βροτοῖσιν)

Hesiod. Works And Days 24

THEME: COMPETITORS

CHECKPOINT: Competition is good. It drives down prices, it offers choice, it promotes customer loyalty.

Use your competitors to challenge yourself. Every so often, you should do a competitor analysis.

Are you bigger than your competitor? Is that good?

Are you better? How do you know?

Should you be your own competitor, by creating alternative products that challenge your existing product lineup?

Treat your competitors with respect and never undervalue them.

What might look like a small insignificant company today could end up changing the market dynamics tomorrow.

WANT TO KNOW MORE? Hesiod is one of the earliest European writers we have.

He demonstrated a great deal to us about how his world lived and thought 100 years before the earliest known philosophers started to pronounce on the meaning of life.

His work is full of all sorts of ideas. Instead of classic philosophy, he tells us the classic proverbs and sayings of his day.

There's a suggestion that Hesiod had a wide knowledge and appreciation of other cultures, including those of Egypt and India.

Hesiod was writing as Greece was entering a new and exciting phase in its history (around 700 BCE), one in which philosophy, as we understand it, was not in existence.

However, the simple world of Hesiod gave him plenty of food for thought and his is some of the earliest European thinking we have on how we humans learn to live with each other.

> **Stress and anxiety make it impossible for workers to get any sleep.**
>
> *(οὐδὲ γὰρ εὕδειν ἀνδράσιν ἐργατίναισι κακαὶ παρέχοντι μέριμναι)*
>
> Theocritus. Idylls 21.2

THEME: HUMAN RESOURCES

CHECKPOINT: The UK government has calculated that over 11 million business days are lost a year because of stress at work.

Stress is not to be taken lightly. Stress and anxiety are killers. We know more about how this works than ever before.

We have all become accustomed to the various ways we can look after our physical health through diet and exercise. But what about our mental health?

Fortunately, the discussion about looking after ourselves is gaining in importance.

Make sure you read up on workplace stress and how to mitigate and manage it. There's plenty of officially endorsed information on the internet.

If you are not looking after your mind as much as you are looking after your body, you are not looking after yourself.

WANT TO KNOW MORE? Theocritus was a pastoral poet. He wrote about the simple life of shepherds, animals and the countryside. He was born around 300 BCE in Syracuse, Sicily.

Sicily today is Italian, but because of its prominent position in the Mediterranean it has seen a lot of action and, over the centuries, boatloads of different people have come and gone. Roughly from the time of Homer and Hesiod (around 750 BCE), the Greeks started to settle in Sicily; from the get-go, Syracuse was an important settlement.

From 750 BCE to around 400 BCE, Sicily was part of Greece, as was a large part of southern Italy.

If you go to Sicily, you will still see many Greek temples and ruins. Sicily was called *Magna Graecia* (Great Greece) for many years.

> **Given that it's common sense and analysis that takes away anxieties and not staring at some stunning sea view, it's just a change of climate you get when you go overseas, not a change of character.**
>
> *(nam si ratio et prudentia curas, non locus effusi late maris arbiter aufert, caelum, non animum, mutant, qui trans mare currunt.)*
>
> Horace. Epistles 1.11.25

THEME: HUMAN RESOURCES

CHECKPOINT: Today is the first of July and the holiday season is coming upon us. Wherever you go, remember that your holidays are well-deserved and should be taken in full.

People who don't take their full holiday allowance do themselves no favours. Rest and relaxation are important. Being ever-present in the office isn't clever. It can be damaging to you and your colleagues.

But don't confuse what a simple vacation can do. It's nothing more than time away from work to do what you most like doing.

If you need a substantial change in your life, a holiday is unlikely to be helpful. Having a break to 're-evaluate your life' is an ambitious thought. Usually, you'll need to carve out some specific time and get some outside help to achieve that.

WANT TO KNOW MORE? You could think that the Romans spent a lot of time on holiday, because in the yearly calendar, so many days were given over to religious festivals. Even slaves were given time off to participate in some of the special ceremonies. But then, the Romans didn't have weekends.

The Roman holidays were more like extended 'days off' rather than what we might think of as a holiday, so they would have experienced occasional breaks over an irregular period of time.

Wealthy Romans certainly liked to travel and, under the emperors, a relatively more peaceful empire and an extensive road network afforded a certain level of safe travel. To travel overseas, Romans would hire a merchant ship and even book a cabin.

Catullus the love poet, for example, tells us that he looks forward to sightseeing in the cities and resorts of Asia Minor.

....

> **Whenever a person sets a bad example he does not feel good about it.**
>
> *(exemplo quodcumque malo committitur, ipsi displicet auctori.)*
>
> Juvenal. Satires 13.1

THEME: LEADERSHIP

CHECKPOINT: Being in a leadership position means that many eyes are on you all the time.

Not everything you do will always be right. After all, you're not a robot. But there is one thing you can do that will establish you as a good leader and one who is always trying to do the best for the company.

You should set a good example. Maintain high standards of professionalism and behaviour.

Managers who fall short of this often end up blaming everyone else for breakdowns in company standards. But in reality, they know they are the perpetrators themselves.

Any projection of your poor example onto someone else will inevitably bounce back onto you. In the end, you will feel bad about yourself, however much you seek to pass the buck onto someone else.

WANT TO KNOW MORE? Juvenal's *Satire 13* was written sometime around 127 CE under the reign of the Emperor Hadrian, who was just putting the finishes touches to his famous wall.

The empire was absolutely massive, and the social and economic institutions that ran the empire were huge and well-established.

The Romans now had experience of large-scale government. It was complex, but it was organized.

This satire lets us peek into one moment in the life and times of one Roman, a certain Calvinus. He has been defrauded of a small sum of money.

Calvinus was around 60 years old when this injustice was done to him and he is ranting and raving about what happened. Juvenal has little time for Calvinus. At his age and with his experience in the capital city, he should know better. Calvinus' behaviour is childish. Very unbecoming for an elderly Roman!

Money alone rules.

(sola pecunia regnat)

Petronius. Satyricon 14

THEME: FINANCE

CHECKPOINT: A quote like 'Money alone rules' doesn't sound very life-affirming does it?

It needs some context.

What actually happens is that businesses make a product or service that then makes money.

But the cornerstone of a successful business is money-management. You have to have the economic capital to get started and you have to have the cash flow to keep going. You can only make decisions on growth or downsizing based on the figures. So in a sense money does rule, because it governs every aspect of the commercial operation.

However ...

Henry Ford, founder of the Ford Motor Company, once wisely said: "A business that makes nothing but money is a poor business."

It is pride in the quality of your work that provides both the emotional and financial payback. Money becomes the servant under wise managers who understand that business is a fundamental part of people's lives and not a money-making machine that exists in a vacuum.

WANT TO KNOW MORE? Petronius' *Satyricon* is a book full of controversy.

What we have today is just a small part of what is believed to be a much longer novel. We are thrown into some part of a book and then ejected, without knowing either the beginning, middle, or the end.

Petronius uses words that we don't understand, such as: '*oclopeta*' and '*tangomenas*'. How many other strange words were there? Was he writing a local dialect? Were these slang words?

Petronius' novel is full of sex. Of every type and inclination. Modern readers today might find it less surprising than readers of even a generation ago. For many years, the short segment that we have of Petronius' long novel was made even shorter by the censors' cuts.

....

> **When enquiring of the enemy, the Spartans don't ask 'how many?',**
>
> **they ask, 'where are they?'.**
>
> *(τοὺς Λακεδαιμονίους ἐρωτᾶν πόσοι εἰσὶν οἱ πολέμιοι, ἀλλὰ ποῦ εἰσίν)*
>
> Plutarch. Moralia. Sayings Of The Spartans 215

THEME: INTERNET

CHECKPOINT: The internet has changed the way we think about companies. It is not how big they are, but where they are, that matters today.

The internet has the capability to put your competitor right under the eyes and fingertips of your customer.

Size is less important than reach.

The internet allows the small guys to outgun the big hitters, by occupying their habitats and offering a better, cooler, faster, cheaper alternative.

Your internet strategy is now the most important weapon in your arsenal. Make sure it's fully up to date.

WANT TO KNOW MORE? The Spartans were bred to be tough. Seriously tough.

It all started with a somewhat mythical figure called Lycurgus, who imposed a discipline on his society based on Austerity, Military-Grade Fitness and Citizen Equality. In essence, he instilled a nationwide programme of genetic engineering.

To breed a nation based on those attributes, you have to start at the beginning, with mothers.

Motherhood was deemed to be the most important thing and the role of women was elevated in Spartan society. They were looked after and trained to be physically fit, just as the men were. Lycurgus believed that if both parents were strong, the child was likely to be strong. He was breeding a race of superhumans.

His next plan was to limit intercourse between husband and wife, so that sexual desire would increase, and this too would lead to stronger babies.

We learn all this from a Greek writer called Xenophon, whose book on Spartan society contains a breathtaking and eye-watering number of similar ideas for engineering a super race.

....

> **Do your important thinking at night time.**
> **People's minds are sharper at night.**
> **The quiet is good for anyone seeking to do their best work.**
>
> *(νυκτὸς βουλεύειν, νυκτὸς δέ τοι ὀξυτέρη φρὴν ἀνδράσιν·*
> *ἡσυχίη δ᾽ ἀρετὴν διζημένῳ ἐσθλή.)*
>
> Phocylides. Fragments 8

THEME: PERSONAL DEVELOPMENT

CHECKPOINT: Thinking is not a luxury in business. It is vitally important.

And thinking is not simply the process of coming up with thoughts.

It is employing your mind rationally to address the past, present and future concerns of your enterprise. It's about making your mind an employee, and putting it to work.

Find a time and place that works for you (Phocylides recommends the night time), then sit down and just think about your business.

And do it regularly. You'll be surprised how beneficial it can be.

WANT TO KNOW MORE? We are told that Phocylides flourished as a poet 647 years after the Trojan War. That's nice and precise, but it doesn't help because we don't know when the Trojan War finished. So we settle for a time around 550 BCE, and that puts him into a period of history that's full of estimated dates!

Every now and then, we get an ancient Greek writer referring to a lunar eclipse or a comet, so we can start to date things with some certainty.

For example, scientists have used a reference to an 'eclipse' in Homer's *Odyssey* ("the sun is blotted out of the sky") to pinpoint the year in which The Trojan Horse entered Troy, thus bringing the war to a brutal end. The scientists claim it was 1188 BCE.

OK then. So Phocylides was flourishing around 541 BCE. Unfortunately, we still know little more than that because we have only fragments of what he wrote. Such is the difficulty of early Greek history!

....

> **There is no sex discrimination in leadership roles.**
>
> *(neque enim sexum in imperiis discernunt)*
>
> Tacitus. Agricola 16.1

THEME: LEADERSHIP

CHECKPOINT: Any form of prejudice and discrimination is rooted in a fear of 'otherness'. Other people who are not like you can feel threatening. You have to work harder to bridge the differences that 'people who are not like you' can bring to the party. Weak leaders see 'others' as a threat to their own narcissistic view of the world.

Strong leaders recognize that diversity can bring new dimensions to a company. It is human capital that grows a company and the more you invest in quality human capital – no matter where it comes from – the more successful your company will be.

'Others' now includes a wide spectrum of people across race, age, gender and sexuality.

The workplace should always offer an equal opportunity to all who can benefit the company.

WANT TO KNOW MORE? The Romans thought of Britains as 'others'. Britain was a long way from Rome, it was not easy to get there, and the people were different.

When Cornelius Tacitus wrote today's quote, in about 98 CE, Britain was not an identifiable entity. Different tribes ruled over different parts of the land.

Tacitus would have shocked his readers by writing today's quote. Women as leaders? Talk about a threat to the rampant narcissism of the Roman male.

The leader Tacitus is writing about is the famous Boudicca, the widow of the king of one of the big tribes and the leader of a celebrated uprising against Rome.

Boudicca's story stands for 'British Rebellion'. She certainly gave Rome a punch in the face. She stormed through Colchester, St. Albans and London, razing all three to the ground.

There is no archaeological evidence that Boudicca existed, but Tacitus was writing just 30 years after the events he highlights, so his story is generally believed.

....

> **A rare bird in this world and most like a black swan.**
>
> *(rara avis in terris nigroque simillima cycno)*
>
> Juvenal. Satires 6.165

THEME: STRATEGY

CHECKPOINT: Nassim Nicholas Taleb's influential book *The Black Swan: The Impact of the Highly Improbable*, has become an integral part of looking at unanticipated change in business. The book concerns our blind spots when it comes to big deviations from the norm.

Most businesses aren't big enough to hire clever (expensive) consultants to guide them through the tricky decision-making processes needed to navigate Big Change.

But all businesses can learn to 'look for the signs'. Think back to the big changes you have already experienced. Was it one a year? Three every five years? Then look at how some companies capitalized on the change, and others didn't.

Project the same number of changes going forward.

They will happen. You won't know what they will be. But you can be ready to absorb them when the time comes.

WANT TO KNOW MORE? Today in Rome was the feast day *Nonae Capritonae*, held in honour of female slaves – *'ancillarum feriae'*. It was an ancient ceremony, and over time, the Romans themselves were a little unsure about what lay behind it.

One story is that way back, dastardly Latins nearby threatened Rome and demanded their womenfolk. A slave girl disguised herself in the fancy clothes of a Roman lady and went over to the Latin camp. When the Latins were asleep, she climbed a fig tree and sent a signal to the Romans to come and attack, which they successfully did.

The holiday is remarkable for an insight into the relationship between freeborn Romans and slaves.

There was much frolicking about and mock fighting on this day, and, not surprisingly, much use made of fig trees and fig branches.

....

> ## The leader must inspire positivity in the troops by use of facial expressions rather than words.
>
> *(διὸ χρὴ πλέον τῷ σχήματι τοῦ προσώπου στρατηγεῖν τὴν τοῦ πλήθους εὐθυμίαν ἢ τοῖς λόγοις παρηγορεῖν·)*
>
> Onasander. The General 13.3

THEME: LEADERSHIP

CHECKPOINT: Words alone never communicate the full story.

When you have to 'speak to the troops', your body language and facial expressions will give a lot away.

If you are saying something you don't mean, 'the troops' will pick up on it immediately.

Often you think you are 'getting away with it'. You speak confidently, you have been well briefed, you have rehearsed a question and answer session. But trust me, you're unlikely to hide what you really feel.

It is often confidentiality and the discussion of sensitive issues that lead people to say one thing while revealing another.

The best thing is to go with the flow. Begin by saying how you are feeling about the matter. You can end by talking about positive next steps.

Being a real person, rather than a robotic performer, will always win you more credibility.

WANT TO KNOW MORE? Onasander's book, *The General*, is a little gem.

Written sometime around 56 CE, it is a handbook on the duties of an army general.

Its 42 chapters cover various aspects of 'generalship', but what makes it stand out for the modern reader is its emphasis on ethical considerations.

Onasander (of whom we know practically nothing) was keen to remind the senior strata of the army that troop morale was important.

He emphasizes the importance of a general's character, and his behaviour and attitude towards the troops.

And in a fascinating link with yesterday's quote about black swans, Onasander stresses the importance of taking note of things that cannot at first be obviously understood.

....

> ## A façade deceives many people.
>
> *(decipit frons prima multos)*
>
> Phaedrus. Fables 4.2.5

THEME: HUMAN RESOURCES

CHECKPOINT: Sometimes in business, you can meet real tricksters who go out of their way to create a complete and believable façade.

The most obvious place to find such people is during the recruitment process.

You can be easily duped by being told what you want to hear, and by being flattered by someone who has done their in-depth homework on you or the company.

Sometimes in business you'll come across people who are way out of their depth and who successfully bluff their way through. In the worst cases you find out too late – when they have committed the company to something that is not real.

There are more people in business like this than you might think.

Make sure you professionally interview people. Don't go on 'gut instinct' over a coffee, or worse, a glass of wine.

If you suspect something, do some subtle checks.

WANT TO KNOW MORE? Phaedrus was writing in the first half of the 1st century CE.

There is a suggestion that he was a slave freed by the Emperor Augustus. He would have witnessed the death of Augustus and the accession of Tiberius.

Those would have been interesting times. The succession of Tiberius to the title of emperor was the first real act that defined the long-term power of the imperial family.

Political intrigue was rife. But Tiberius, an experienced politican and military man, kept it all together.

Tiberius was already an old man when Augustus died, but he hired people to do the tough work. One such person was the head of the powerful imperial guard, the infamous Sejanus. Phaedrus appears to have crossed Sejanus, but like some characters in his fables, he managed to wriggle his way out of trouble.

JULY 10

> ## In each situation he wanted to know the reason why and all the ins and outs.
>
> *(ἑκάστου δὲ τὴν αἰτίαν ἀπαιτεῖν καὶ τὸ διὰ τί πυνθάνεσθαι)*
>
> Plutarch. Cato The Younger 1.5

THEME: THE WATERCOOLER

CHECKPOINT: There are only 24 hours in a day. And hopefully you don't spend all of them in the office.

In the time you are actually working, be careful what you ask for.

It's always seductive to want to know the whys and wherefores of actions and decisions.

But using your judgement about what you need to know is a better use of your time.

Just knowing things that don't really drive the business forward might be interesting, but they are better saved for an idle chat on a train journey or around the infamous watercooler.

It is just not possible to process feedback on everything.

Work out what to focus on and what to leave behind.

WANT TO KNOW MORE? If you sliced through Cato the Younger, you'd find Roman Roman Roman written through him like the writing through a stick of seaside rock candy.

He was the embodiment of old school Republican Rome.

No surprise, then, that he should have strongly resisted the rampant rise of Julius Caesar.

The sort of descriptions you will find of Cato include words like 'steadfast,' 'earnest' and 'honourable'.

Yes. He was a bit boring.

But he stood his ground and never for one moment did he give up his opposition to the one-man tornado that was Caesar.

Cato was born in Rome and no doubt he would have loved to have been buried in his beloved Rome, but that was not to be.

He fought Caesar on the battlefield, fled to North Africa after losing, and committed suicide when Caesar marched into Africa to finish off the remnants of his opposition (and enjoy his much frowned upon affair with Cleopatra).

> **Mix with those who will make you a better person.**
>
> *(cum his versare, qui te meliorem facturi sunt)*
>
> Seneca. Epistles 7.8

THEME: PERSONAL DEVELOPMENT

CHECKPOINT: As you develop in your working life, follow this simple rule: Associate with those who can improve you.

Ask for advice on issues you are struggling with. Some might even be prepared to mentor you.

Most people like to know that they are valued and usually are only too pleased to offer advice.

In general, try to hang around with the people who are going places as opposed to the ones who are just in it for a nine-to-five paycheck.

It sounds very strategic, doesn't it? That's because it is. You have to work hard at improving your working life.

Be careful how you go about this. Good people are usually busy people and the last thing you want is a reputation for being a pest.

WANT TO KNOW MORE? There is an interesting link between Boudicca the warrior queen of the Iceni tribe and the philosopher and playwright Seneca, living 1,200 miles away in Rome and working in the court of the Emperor Nero.

Seneca was a financier and had been part of a consortium of lenders who had lent money to Boudicca's husband Prasutagus. When Prasutagus died, he left half his estate to his daughters, and half to Nero. Seneca and his money-lending colleagues decided to call in their loans, an act that would have certainly impoverished vast numbers of the Iceni as well as Boudicca and her children.

They called the money in using serious strong-arm tactics and this may have been one of the reasons that Boudicca flared up and rebelled.

Seneca writes that you need to be careful and considerate when loaning money or giving gifts.

In this case, he appeared highly hypocritical, to say the least.

> **There's nothing so hard that can't be solved by a good search.**
>
> *(nil tam difficilest quin quaerendo investigari possiet)*
>
> Terence. The Self Tormentor 675

THEME: PERSONAL DEVELOPMENT

CHECKPOINT: Just about everything you need to know can be found on the internet. 'Searching' has become second nature.

Everyone has access to the same amount of information. What separates the discerning from the dumb is how assiduous you are in your search.

When putting together any analyses – competitive, trend, strategic, etc. – make sure you know where to look.

Search engines offer the obvious route to information, but there is still information worth buying and there are still sites worth subscribing to.

If your job is to keep ahead of the game, make sure you ask for the resources to be logged into, and alerted to, the best possible sources of information.

WANT TO KNOW MORE? The city of Rome had no permanent stone theatre until 55 BCE.

Up to that point, putting on a play meant using the same space as other entertainments (gladiatorial, dancing or racing, for example) and waiting until there was free time to quickly erect a wooden structure and perform. In some cases, plays were put on in front of temples, the temple steps providing useful seating.

Plays were put on during public holidays, of which there were a lot.

The funding for these plays seems to have been as knockabout as the erection of the wooden stages. The Senate, local magistrates and local impressarios all contributed one way or another.

Today's quote comes from Terence's play *The Self Tormentor* (great title!).

It was a complicated play involving two sets of fathers, two sets of sons, two love affairs and two slaves. It was based on a play of the Greek playwright Menander with the same title.

> **Don't you think it's painfully sad that at my age Alexander was already king of such a vast empire, while I've achieved so very little.**
>
> *(Οὐ δοκεῖ ὑμῖν ἄξιον εἶναι λύπης, εἰ τηλικοῦτος μὲν ὢν Ἀλέξανδρος ἤδη τοσούτ ἐβασίλευεν, ἐμοὶ δὲ λαμπρὸν οὐδὲν οὔπω πέπρακται)*
>
> Plutarch. Caesar 11.3

THEME: PERSONAL DEVELOPMENT

CHECKPOINT: Wanting to achieve early success is a noble ambition and being an entrepreneur is a great way to earn a living.

Wanting to earn loads of money is understandable. Life's for the living, right?

A good way to start is to ask yourself some hard questions. Have you got what it takes to work all hours of the day? Do you have the stamina to weather the inevitable storms?

The most important attribute for early success is the ability to be realistic about the skills you have. You may have a great idea, but not have the ability to execute it.

Keeping realistic will allow you to grow by adding in the resource you don't have.

It's better to be a small part of something large, than a large part of something small.

WANT TO KNOW MORE? Julius Caesar was born today in 100 BCE.

His name tells us that he was a part of the clan of the Julii, the oldest aristocratic family in Rome. He was class.

He was also a winner.

Caesar's life was a period of almost non-stop bloody warfare. Hundreds of thousands of people were butchered across Italy and the provinces of Greece, Gaul and Spain. There was both murderous civil war and brutal military expansion. Caesar himself is said to have committed mass killing in Gaul on a scale that today we would call genocide.

He did it to win. All his opponents lost.

Even after he himself was mown down in a bloodbath, his killers and his opponents lost.

His heir and successor, Augustus, took his classy name and background and continued the winning streak.

> In the middle of our chat we found ourselves in the market;
> all the stallholders were thrilled to see me; snacks, tuna fish,
> meat, hot food, chicken, seafood! They'd made money out of me
> in good and bad times and often still do now. They all greeted me.
>
> *(dum haec loquimur, interea loci ad macellum ubi adventamus, concurrunt
> laeti mi obviam cuppedenarii omnes, cetarii, lanii, coqui, fartores, piscatores,
> quibus et re salva et perdita profueram et prosum saepe. Salutant)*
>
> Terence. The Eunuch 255

THEME: STRATEGY

CHECKPOINT: I once worked on a project for a famous UK high street retailer. I spent time in the stores watching the customers and the staff interact. Often customers would just come in (maybe from the rain or the cold) and just sit around, or move slowly through the aisles, not really intending to spend anything. The staff were as attentive to these customers as they were to the ones spending money.

The management of the retailer told me that the store operated on an '80/20' basis. This meant that 80% of the customers accounted for only 20% of the sales. But the stores recognized the need to maintain customer satisfaction at the highest possible level, at all times and with all customers.

The retailer has been one of the UK's most profitable stores for many years.

Make sure you keep making your customers feel that you love them, even when they are spending little, or not shopping with you at all.

WANT TO KNOW MORE? In ancient Rome, starting today, six days were set aside for markets and fairs. It was like one huge commercial trade show. Traders would pour in from the countryside. Everyone was welcome.

The six-day period was called *Mercatus* and it was timed to start after the *Ludi Apollinares*, important games in honour of the god Apollo. The games would have drawn in big crowds, so holding *Mercatus* immediately afterwards made sound commercial sense.

Trade fairs are common today, as are all kinds of food and fun fairs, particularly during the holiday season.

Interestingly, the word 'fair' comes from the Latin '*feria*', meaning 'holiday'.

I'm not looking to buy fish;
I need to have a conversation with you.

(non edepol piscis expeto quam tui sermonis sum indigens)

Plautus. The Rope 943

THEME: INTERNET

CHECKPOINT: The internet is about connectivity. Before anything else, think about the connectivity you can get with your customers.

Even before trying to sell them something, or enticing them with the fastest-possible delivery times, or the lowest-possible prices.

Connectivity means you can engage with a huge number of your customers at the same time, whilst offering a personal service.

When you walk into the fishmongers, does the conversation go like this?

Fishmonger: "Want fish?"

You: "Yes"

Fishmonger: "Buy this"

You: "OK"

Or, is there a much more of a discussion about what type of fish, why, and what for?

Make sure your internet strategy expresses the personality you want to communicate, not just the product or service.

WANT TO KNOW MORE? You can't talk about fish, fishmongers and fish markets without mentioning the famous fish sauce 'garum'. Everyone in ancient Rome ate it, as an ingredient and condiment, when they could.

'Garum' was made from fermented fish intestines and is not dissimilar to the modern fish sauce you can find today in, say, Asian cooking.

'Garum' production was a huge industry that produced an incredible number of trade routes throughout the Mediterranean to ensure that the product got to the tables that demanded it. It came in many grades, from basic to extra-fine. The best 'garum' sold for astronomical sums.

....

> **Contracts are only as credible as the signatories and their backers.**
>
> *(ὁποῖοι γὰρ ἄν τινες ὦσιν οἱ ἐπιγεγραμμένοι ἢ φυλάττοντες,*
> *τούτοις αἱ συνθῆκαι πισταί εἰσιν.)*
>
> Aristotle. Rhetoric 1.15.21

THEME: LEGAL

CHECKPOINT: Anyone can sign a contract.

If you are going to make a deal with someone, the trick is to know who they are, what history they have, and whether they can provide an honest third party to vouch for them. In many cases, when a contract is signed, it is signed on behalf of another entity.

The problem is that so often contracts are not worth the paper they are written on.

If the person signing has no liability, then the contract won't mean much.

The simple answer is to get legal advice on all contracts.

All businesses need to be protected. Contracts are formal links to the world outside of the business and as such are potential doorways in and out of the business.

A poor contract can allow information to flow out and let a competitor in.

Be careful when writing and signing any contracts, and always get advice.

WANT TO KNOW MORE? Every now and then, the ancient world of the Greeks and Romans throws up some wonderful relationships. The poets Horace and Vergil, Anthony and Cleopatra, Seneca and Nero, for example.

Here's one relationship that was truly fascinating.

One of the world's greatest ever philosophers, Aristotle, was tutor to one of the world's greatest ever military commanders, Alexander the Great.

These two weren't friends or lovers. It was a master/pupil relationship that lasted for as long as the education was needed.

Aristotle's father was both a friend of, and the doctor to, Alexander's grandfather. Keeping things in the family, Aristotle was asked to tutor the young Alexander.

> Someone who has specialist knowledge will always do very well.
> Whereas the person who just has an opinion will sometimes
> do well and sometimes not.
>
> *(ὅτι ὁ μὲν τὴν ἐπιστήμην ἔχων ἀεὶ ἂν ἐπιτυγχάνοι,*
> *ὁ δὲ τὴν ὀρθὴν δόξαν τοτὲ μὲν ἂν τυγχάνοι, τοτὲ δ᾽ οὔ.)*
>
> Plato. Meno 97c

THEME: HUMAN RESOURCES

CHECKPOINT: We live and work in an age of technology and there is no doubt that skilled specialists are needed to build and maintain the tech that now makes the world go around. Specialists are trained in specific areas. The clever ones keep retraining to keep up. This makes them valuable.

But business will always consist of humans selling to humans, no matter how much tech is involved.

Knowing as much as you can about all the aspects of the business you are in can only be a good thing. Your customers are unlikely to be specialists, so make sure you communicate to them in a clear and simple way.

But make sure you turn to the specialists when there is something very specific to be done.

WANT TO KNOW MORE? If you want to 'get into' Plato, *Meno*, written around 402 BCE, is not a bad place to start, for two reasons. One is intellectual, and one practical.

The intellectual reason to read Plato's *Meno* is that it is accessible, interesting and entertaining and it is a great introduction to the study of his thinking.

The practical reason is that, compared with many other of his works, it's very short.

The book opens with a big question. Is virtue something that can be taught?

The fact that such subjects were discussed in 402 BCE is a reminder of the cornerstone contribution of the Greek philosophers.

They taught us to ask questions, and in a rational process of finding answers, we learn about ourselves and each other.

> **Keep in with the boss.**
>
> *(ad praetorium stato)*
>
> Cato. Collectio Distichorum Vulgaris 1.33

THEME: PERSONAL DEVELOPMENT

CHECKPOINT: From the earliest time in your business life, you will have a boss. Few people escape having one.

Even when you are the boss, you might find you have big influential investors, or large financial institutions, that you have to report to. The increasing number of checks and balances in business mean that you might have more than one boss to answer to.

You should see those more senior to you as part of an inevitable process of integrated management.

Kicking against someone who has line responsibility for you, or who can adversely affect your career, is never a good idea.

Keep close to your boss. If they are good, you should learn something. And if they are bad, you will also learn something.

Honest disputes with your boss should be handled objectively.

Never make your boss a personal issue.

WANT TO KNOW MORE? Today in Rome was a Black Day, a '*dies ater*'.

Mind you, your average Roman would need to know his Roman history pretty well to understand why today was so dark. The day recalled two humiliating military disasters, one in 477 BCE and the other in 390 BCE, but both on the same day – July 18.

The day was cursed. Almost any form of activity was not a good idea. And the Romans were superstitious, so they kept their heads down. Discretion in all matters was the name of the game.

It's funny how things work out. I bet everyone was super careful on July 18, 64 CE.

But the very next day, the Great Fire of Rome ripped through the city. Three of Rome's fourteen districts were completely devastated, and seven more were reduced to a few charred ruins.

> **You can pick up a great deal through diligent study.**
> **But you know, there's a lot to be learned from the University of Life.**
>
> *(cum tibi contigerit studio cognoscere multa,*
> *fac discas multa a vita te scire doceri)*
>
> Cato. Distichs 4.48

THEME: PERSONAL DEVELOPMENT

CHECKPOINT: Make the best of school. If you are offered the opportunity to study, take it.

If you have the ability to learn, you should feed that ability. Keep studying as an adult. The older you get, the more you'll want to learn.

There is nothing a prospective employer likes more than someone who has taken up all the opportunities put their way.

Once you start working, you'll realize that there's no educational establishment in the world that can train you for everything that happens day-to-day.

You need to learn the practical, on-the-job skills of worklife, however well versed you are in your particular trade.

You'll need to understand the habits and behaviours of people who are nothing like you.

You'll discover new skills that no one ever told you you'd need.

Some people bail out of education and still reach business superstardom.

But such characters are not common. Most successful businessmen have studied hard and then learned on the job.

WANT TO KNOW MORE? Most children in ancient Rome were taught at home. But like everything in Rome, things changed when you were monied and had status.

If you were wealthy, you could hire a Greek nanny to get your child's Greek note-perfect. A private tutor would be brought in to make sure that little Julius' or Julia's reading of Latin was up to scratch. Not unlike today.

There were schools for the super-rich (seven days a week, when not interrupted by the numerous holidays and festivals) to learn rhetoric, poetry and writing.

For the privileged few, there was further education at one of the Greek universities, ideally Athens, where you would learn philosophy.

....

> ## The completion validates the job.
>
> *(exitus acta probat)*
>
> Ovid. Heroides 2.85

THEME: PROJECT MANAGEMENT

CHECKPOINT: You often hear people say 'the end justifies the means'.

There has to be an end result to a project, and for most businesses, that's what really matters.

Keep the end in sight.

Make sure you are delivering on brief and on time.

Your work will be judged on its completed state. How you got there will be a journey for you and your colleagues to muse over later.

History always remembers the end point, and only sometimes does it recall the journey to get there.

WANT TO KNOW MORE? Alexander the Great was born today (some think tomorrow) in 356 BCE.

We call him 'the Great', but there are equally those who would call him 'the Terrible'.

It depends on how you evaluate his achievement.

Many in the West see his exploits as truly heroic – a great visionary warrior spreading the culture of the civilized Greek world. A real hero with a sword in his hand and a copy of Homer's *Iliad* under his pillow.

Then again, if you were on the receiving end as he swept down through Greece, into the Middle East and on into India, you might have witnessed a brutal dictator, murdering anyone who stood against him (including his own people). He razed whole cities to the ground, he held little regard for conventional justice and he slayed so many people that today we would call it genocide.

Whatever your view, one thing is certain. He wasn't 'Great' at succession planning. When asked on his death bed who should take over, he replied "the strongest". Surprise, surprise – that led to internal fighting and the inevitable undoing of everything he had achieved.

....

It takes an age to establish a community, but just one hour to destroy it; It takes forever to make a forest, but it can become ash in the blink of an eye; A great number of safety checks can be in place with things going from strength to strength, but quickly and suddenly, everything can fall apart.

(urbes constituit aetas, hora dissolvit; momento fit cinis, diu silva; magna tutela stant ac vigent omnia, cito ac repente dissiliunt)

Seneca. Natural Questions 3.27

THEME: LEADERSHIP

CHECKPOINT: You need optimism, day in, day out, to keep going in business. Optimism opens you up to new ideas and provides the much-needed energy to power through the ups and the downs and the routines of life.

But sometimes disaster can strike.

A fire in the warehouse destroys your stock, which is inadequately insured. A sudden departure of key staff members leads to competitive dangers. Persistent bad weather keeps shoppers away.

There are all sorts of things that can cause serious damage.

Such damage, lasting sometimes only a few days, can undo work that took years to build. Make sure you are properly insured. Make sure your contracts are watertight. Make sure your company is agile enough to swiftly react to unforeseen problems.

This isn't being pessimistic. This is being realistic.

And yes, stay optimistic. But while your head is in the clouds, make sure your feet are firmly rooted to the ground.

WANT TO KNOW MORE? While Alexander the Great was being born (see yesterday) the Temple of Artemis was being destroyed by an arsonist called Herostratus. As punishment, he was sentenced to death and his name was damned and could never be used again. (That second part didn't really work since his dastardly act was mentioned many times. I mean, I'm mentioning him now...)

The Temple had suffered misfortune before. In the 7th century BCE, it was destroyed by flooding. But the temple stood as symbol of great hope and determination, and by 140 BCE it had become one of the seven wonders of the world. A poet at the time urged his contemporaries to see it. It was better than the Pyramids, he said, and better than the hanging gardens of Babylon.

Sadly, it was finally destroyed in 401 CE.

> **Consensus develops small ideas,
> lack of consensus destroys big plans.**
>
> *(nam concordia parvae res crescunt,
> discordia maxumae dilabuntur)*
>
> Sallust. Jugurthine War 10.6

THEME: LEADERSHIP

CHECKPOINT: In any aspect of life – domestic, political, commercial – getting consensus can be difficult.

Oftentimes, you'll experience a lack of consensus about the way things are going, or, worse, about decisions being taken by the company's leadership.

A company that is more united in its direction will operate more productively than one that isn't. A small plan can become a big deal when everyone is behind it.

It's worth making time to create consensus in your team, department or company as a whole.

One way of doing this is to make sure that everyone understands what is going on. It sounds simple and obvious, doesn't it?

But actually, in many companies, employees can drift along happily, blissfully unaware of the overall direction. That's not good. Try to get total engagement behind what the company is doing. That way, you can be sure to get the maximum input when you need to increase, or adapt, what you're doing.

WANT TO KNOW MORE? Happy birthday to the great Temple of Concord, the remains of which lie in the Forum in Rome, at the foot of the Capitoline Hill. You can still visit its site today. Just click on Google maps and punch in 'Temple of Concord, Rome'.

The temple was built, possibly in 367 BCE, to help to create some harmony amongst the ruling and working classes.

As time went on, the temple would have served as a focal point to bring all sorts of different factions together. Rich and poor; politicians and military; ruling classes and entrepreneurs.

The original temple was destroyed and rebuilt by the Emperor Tiberius in 7 CE and, over its long, illustrious history, it was refurbished or rebuilt a number of times.

> This is the best idea for what to do next. Painful as is it,
> as long as the framework doesn't fall apart I shall stay where
> I am. And if things get stormy and everything falls apart,
> I'll start swimming. I can't see there are many other choices.
>
> *(ἀλλὰ μάλ᾿ ὧδ᾿ ἔρξω, δοκέει δέ μοι εἶναι ἄριστον· ὄφρ᾿ ἂν μέν κεν*
> *δούρατ᾿ ἐν ἁρμονίῃσιν ἀρήρῃ, τόφρ᾿ αὐτοῦ μενέω καὶ τλήσομαι*
> *ἄλγεα πάσχων· αὐτὰρ ἐπὴν δή μοι σχεδίην διὰ κῦμα τινάξῃ,*
> *νήξομ᾿, ἐπεὶ οὐ μέν τι πάρα προνοῆσαι ἄμεινον)*
>
> Homer. Odyssey 5.360

THEME: PERSONAL DEVELOPMENT

CHECKPOINT: At various points in your working career, you get itchy feet. You feel you're not going anywhere. You've been passed over for promotion too many times. The work is getting repetitive.

Sometimes, your internal 'body clock' just says: 'Time's up. It's time for a change.' In many cases, your general unease points to a need to make a change. But don't act too suddenly.

Talk things through with people you trust – and people who don't have a vested interest in whatever decision you make.

Sometimes sticking where you are can look like a better option for you when you lay out all the benefits rationally.

Set yourself some indicators for when you need to rethink your situation. It could be your fear for the company's future, or your worry that you won't get any further.

Practice 'swimming to safety'. What I mean is, make subtle enquiries about what else might be on offer. Talk to experienced recruitment professionals (make sure you talk to more than one). That way, if you finally decide to jump ship, you will know exactly where (and why), you are going next.

WANT TO KNOW MORE? Homer's *Odyssey* is an exceptional tale.

It's a sequel to his *Iliad*, which lifts the lid on 50 or so days in a 10-year siege of the city of Troy.

Eventually (and after the *Iliad* finishes) the Greeks break into Troy (cue: Wooden Horse), lay waste to the city, reclaim the notorious Helen and return home. There were few Trojan survivors. Victory to the Greeks!

Well, not quite. Odysseus spends 10 years getting home (the story of the *Odyssey*) and many of the leading Greeks suffer tragic ends (cue: Greek Tragedy).

> **Don't take any notice of what's said in hushed tones:**
> **Only self-conscious people think they're being talked about.**
>
> *(ne cures, si quis tacito sermone loquatur:*
> *conscius ipse sibi de se putat omnia dici)*
>
> Cato. Distichs 1.17

THEME: THE WATERCOOLER

CHECKPOINT: Sideways glances, tittle-tattle, giggling in corners, sudden silences. Added together, they all amount to a serious chunk of time in office life.

Be careful not to get paranoid.

Unless you know that something you have done is the subject of rampant gossip, what people are talking amount almost certainly won't concern you.

I won't deny that it's not easy to ignore whispering voices. Most of us like to be 'in the know' and in an office environment FOMO ('fear of missing out') can pander to latent paranoia.

You might notice that it is often the same crowd who are gossiping together, and this might give you a clue to help you navigate their gossip-mongering.

Certain people love to gossip, whinge and generally pour their heart out at one another's expense.

Try to rise above it and just focus on the job you are doing. You'll go home each night much less panicked, I promise you!

WANT TO KNOW MORE? The *Couplets* of Cato present modern-day readers with a bit of a mystery.

Who exactly was this 'Cato'?

There were some famous Catos in Roman times, such as the ultra-conservative Cato the Elder and his great-grandson Cato the Younger (see July 10).

The *Couplets* ('*distichs*') endured through Roman times and were often quoted. Later, they were found and used as teaching material in practical ethics in the Middle Ages.

The mystery writer remains a mystery.

> **Ah. Shopping bag. Bit of a useless accessory to carry around.**
>
> *(ἀνόνητον ἄρ᾽ ὦ θυλάκιόν σ᾽ εἶχον ἄγαλμα)*
>
> Aristophanes. Wasps 314

THEME: INTERNET

CHECKPOINT: Diagnosing the effect of the internet is a complicated issue. It is dangerous to make assertions one way or the other, because things are not always what they seem.

E-commerce, for example, remains a much smaller percentage of shopping than was first predicted. Not everyone wants everything delivered to their door.

Shopping bags have gone from redundant to required. And because supermarkets are urged, rightly, to cut back on plastic bags, old fashioned bags are now seen more often.

Take, for example, the case the of the holiday firm Inspiring Travel Company (ITC).

ITC does not accept online bookings, something we are all used to and take for granted. Yet it enjoys an annual turnover of almost £100 million and employs over 200 people.

ITC offers a tailor-made, personal service and they want to engage personally with their customers.

Understand your customer. And only then will you be able to understand how the internet can be of service to you.

WANT TO KNOW MORE? We can pretty much go to theatre whenever we want. Plays run for long seasons and if we book in advance we'll get good seats for a play we really want to see.

Spare a thought, then, for the poor Athenians, for whom plays were performed in just two seasons a year, in January and March. These plays were performed during the two festivals of *Dionysia* (during which much wine was consumed).

One *Dionysia* (in March) saw plays performed in the theatre of Dionysus, which is still there today at the foot of the Acropolis.

The January plays were performed during the festival of *Dionysian Lenaia*.

The plays were put on in competition with each other, and the name of the game was to win!

Aristophanes won several times.

Fear subsides when your mind is made up.

(tamen obfirmato animo mitescit metus)

Pacuvius. Periboea Frag. 316

THEME: PERSONAL DEVELOPMENT

CHECKPOINT: There will be occasions during your career when you are extremely nervous, or even terrified.

It might be that you've been selected to make a big and important presentation or that you've been asked to submit a report on a key aspect of your business. Maybe it's just a meeting you have been asked to attend with people you don't regularly meet.

Everyone has their own threshold of anxiety, but whatever it is, the fear is real and should be taken seriously.

My advice is to tell people how you feel. You can pretty much guarantee that just about everyone has experienced the same jitters over something.

Talking to people will remind you that although the matter is stressful, it is achievable.

It can also confirm your resolve to get on and do it.

Trust me, few people will notice you are nervous once you start the task at hand.

WANT TO KNOW MORE? Pacuvius (born around 220 BCE) had two careers in his life.

He started out as an artist. He was well respected, and his work was still being viewed almost 200 years later.

At some point, he decided to pursue his second career – writing tragedies.

Roman tragedy was highly regarded, with the playwrights Ennius, Lucius Accius and Pacuvius being the leading writers that we know about.

Unbelievably, not one single play from these three survives.

In fact, very little Roman tragedy survives at all. Two hundred years after Pacuvius, our old friend Seneca wrote plays based on Greek tragedies. An unknown playwright wrote a tragedy called *Octavia*, which focuses on three days during the reign of the Emperor Nero. And as far as Roman tragedies are concerned, that's about it.

> **Out of the frying pan and into the fire (as the old saying goes).**
>
> *(de fumo, ut proverbium loquitur vetus, ad flammam)*
>
> Ammianus Marcellinus. History 14.11.12

THEME: PERSONAL DEVELOPMENT

CHECKPOINT: Sometimes things go from bad to worse.

You don't just have a bad day, you have a bad week.

You try to rid yourself of one problem only to find that by doing so you created another.

Get help!

I don't mean find a shrink. (Although therapy might work for you over a longer period!)

I mean seek the help of others to help damp the flames of whatever fire you are trapped in.

Often, problems start to compound once you try and cover up a mistake. Don't do that.

Everyone makes mistakes; just put your hand up and let others help you sort it.

Everyone at every level makes mistakes. Just accept it as part and parcel of everyday life.

WANT TO KNOW MORE? Ammianus Marcellinus (around 330 CE – 400 CE) was an officer who had an ambitious plan.

He would write a 31-volume history of Rome, starting where Tacitus had left off, in the year 96 CE, and ending it with the death of the Emperor Valens in 378 CE.

The 18 books that we have cover the last 25 years of his chosen period.

Now, admittedly, Ammianus would have known a lot about the life and times he was in, but his history was seriously unbalanced. The first 13 books covered 250 years, from 96 CE to 353 CE, and the last 18 books covered just 25 years!

However, since we don't have the first 13 books, we'll just have to make do with what we do have.

Ammianus, an ex-military man, included many economic and social aspects of his life and times, and was considered to be fair-minded in his treatment of non-Roman peoples.

> **Avoid asking what tomorrow will bring.**
> **Whatever kind of day Fortune donates, enter it in as profit.**
>
> *(quid sit futurum cras fuge quaerere et quem*
> *Fors dierum cumque dabit lucro appone)*
>
> Horace. Odes 1.9.13

THEME: PERSONAL DEVELOPMENT

CHECKPOINT: Living in the future is a dangerous pastime.

All the income you earn is made doing today's work and you need the past to see exactly how it accumulates.

Don't gamble on futurology.

Use forecasts intelligently (I'm writing this in pouring rain, according to my weather app, even though it's hot with blue skies outside).

These days we are probably more attuned than ever to the whimsical nature of news reports and predictions.

Capitalize on what you can achieve today and hopefully bank the benefits at the end of the month.

WANT TO KNOW MORE? For the poet Horace, 'living in the moment' and not 'fretting about tomorrow' were recurring themes.

Horace repeatedly advises us to make sure we cash in on everything that today can offer.

He would be telling us today to drink that expensive bottle of wine we were gifted, instead of keeping it for some special occasion.

He would urge couples to love their hearts out today. What's the point in leaving something so utterly wonderful until tomorrow?

Today's quote comes from one of Horace's greatest poems. It is known as *The Soracte Poem*.

Oozing with suggestive imagery, alive with sexual possibility and pregnant with nostalgia, regret and loss, this poem is a masterpiece.

Horace uses brevity and suggestibility to a magical level, teasing, taunting and telling us that soon old age will kick in, denying us of many of the pleasures of youth.

Grab it all while you can.

> **We're only human; there's a percentage chance that
> things could go completely the opposite way,
> particularly when launching a big offensive.**
>
> *(νέμειν δὲ μερίδα τῷ παραδόξῳ πανταχῇ μὲν ἀνθρώπους
> ὄντας, μάλιστα δ᾿ ἐν τοῖς πολεμικοῖς.)*
>
> Polybius. Histories 2.4.5

THEME: PROJECT MANAGEMENT

CHECKPOINT: Just be aware that things don't always go according to plan, and if they don't, try not to explode. This is easier said than done, I guess. Especially when something big and important goes wrong.

Human error is the one thing that is extremely difficult to anticipate. It doesn't matter what size or type of company you are, at the end of the day business comes down to humans interacting with other humans.

The most important thing to do when something goes wrong is not to overreact.

Gather all the facts.

Work out what to learn from the experience.

Make sure the people involved are properly retrained or advised.

Instantly firing people for making a mistake is usually unwise. Immediate dismissals can cause increased workplace anxiety and lead to even more problems.

WANT TO KNOW MORE? The Greeks were extraordinary. They were the master-philosophers. They boasted the first major literature of our modern 'Western World'. The artistry of their sculpture and pottery was widely admired. They introduced formal political thinking and administration, when Rome was still a group of wooden huts.

Yet eventually Rome came to conquer Greece and commandeered so much of all this Greek culture, absorbing it into their own developing society.

For a close-up perspective on how this process of absorption took place, look no further than the brilliant Polybius.

His history, from 220 BCE to the famous date of 146 BCE (when Rome finally consolidated Greece and North Africa), sets out to explain how it happened that Rome was able to conquer the birthplace of democracy.

> ## Good ideas may fail but they don't die completely.
>
> *(bene cogitata si excidunt non occident)*
>
> Publilius Syrus. Sententiae 83

THEME: INNOVATION

CHECKPOINT: There's a great deal of wastage in the process of creating new ideas.

More often than one might think, companies want to change direction, create new products or services, or re-invent substantial parts of themselves.

There are many ways to do this. Some companies are sophisticated enough to do it by themselves, but the majority will hire outside help.

During the process of invention, many ideas will be generated.

Make sure you save these ideas. They, or versions of them, might be useful to you later.

WANT TO KNOW MORE? Today is Good Luck Day. Here's why.

The progress of the Roman domination of the Mediterranean and their growing empire to the north was littered with huge, momentous and decisive battles. One such battle took place in the north of Italy, on this very day in 101 BCE, against an invading tribe called the Cimbri. The numbers relating to this battle are huge.

The Romans won an overwhelming victory and claimed to have killed almost 160,000 of the enemy and captured 60,000 more, including women and children.

It was usual in those times to big up the numbers, but, even allowing for this, the battle was clearly an impressive win for the Romans.

To celebrate the enormous success (and delivery from the barbaric hordes) a temple was consecrated to 'The Fortune of this Day'.

Given the superstitious nature of the Roman religion, it is not surprising that 'good fortune' should be integral to their lives.

Consequently, the deity Fortuna presided over any happy events on any day of the year.

> **Futurologists who have studied, over a long period of time, the interconnectivity between facts and events understand what's coming next. Well, they know in the majority of cases. OK, they only sometimes know.**
>
> *(qui cursum rerum eventorumque consequentiam diuturnitate pertractata notaverunt, aut semper aut, si id difficile est, plerumque, quodsi ne id quidem conceditur, non numquam certe, quid futurum sit, intellegunt)*
>
> Cicero. De Divinatione 1.128

THEME: STRATEGY

CHECKPOINT: Futurology is now an established part of the business world.

Trendwatchers use clever algorithms to plot what consumers will buy next.

Forecasters predict the economy. Pundits tell us what the world will look like in 20 years time.

A few books have been truly visionary. H. G. Wells' *World Brain*, Marshall McLuhan's *Understanding Media* and Alvin Toffler's *Future Shock* are great books that predicted the future with alarming accuracy.

When thinking about the future, look back at the past.

Take a look at how 'new things' changed the commercial history of your business. You'll find that many things are obvious extrapolations from what has already happened.

Even if you don't see things coming, don't worry. In almost every case it can be valuable to learn how the market assimilates new ideas, giving you time to adapt your business accordingly.

WANT TO KNOW MORE? You cannot mention Cicero without giving a courteous nod to his assistant Tiro.

Cicero was a prodigious writer. He wrote many books of rhetoric, several books of philosophy, and a number of books on politics. Over 80 of his (long) speeches in the law courts were recorded, and we have 37 books of his letters (there are over 30 more yet to be unearthed).

Tiro was on hand to help Cicero manage his writing process. He developed a shorthand technique to write as fast as his boss dictated. Tiro was Cicero's executive assistant and he also helped in the management of the household and with the finances of Cicero's large estates.

Tiro started life as a slave but was freed in 56 BCE. He managed to buy a house and live a long life, possibly into his nineties.

....

> **While there's life there's hope. When dead, there's none.**
>
> (ἐλπίδες ἐν ζωοῖσιν, ἀνέλπιστοι δὲ θανόντες)
>
> Theocritus. Idylls 4.42

THEME: PERSONAL DEVELOPMENT

CHECKPOINT: If there's one thing that pays dividends in business, it's tenacity.

You have to keep at, even when things look boring, or gloomy.

I'm afraid it's the old bicycle maxim. If you stop peddling, you fall off.

If you fall off your bike when you're young, what do they tell you?

'Get right back on and start peddling again.'

To keep being tenacious, you have to keep being optimistic.

Accept that there will be downs as well as ups, and keep going.

Eventually you might even find that work life is as easy as riding a bike.

WANT TO KNOW MORE? Romulus, the legendary founder of Rome, divided the year into 10 months and started the year with March, named after the god of war (that's why December, named after the Latin for ten ('*decem*'), is the tenth month).

That made August ('*Sextilis*') the sixth month and September the seventh – '*septem*' is seven in Latin. August was called '*Sextilis*' for hundreds of years.

An ancient Roman king added in January and February to bring the calendar into line with the lunar year.

In 8 BCE, the Roman Senate (no doubt with a with a little firm prodding) decreed that the month '*Sextilis*' should be renamed '*Augustus*' in honour of, you guessed it, the Emperor Augustus.

And so the sixth month became the eighth month and then became August. (Still with me?)

There was a precedent for this. The 'fifth' month '*Quinctilis*' was renamed '*Julius*', after Julius Caesar.

If you think any of that is confusing, wait until you hear about the ancient Greek calendar.

....

> **I came. I saw. I conquered.**
>
> *(VENI. VIDI. VICI)*
>
> Suetonius. The Deified Julius 37.2

THEME: STRATEGY

CHECKPOINT: A great deal of business strategy uses military terminology. In fact, the word strategy itself comes from the Greek word *'στρᾶτηγός'* ('strategos') meaning a leader or military commander.

We use 'intelligence' and 'deploy' people. We refer to employees often as 'the troops'. We run marketing 'campaigns'.

Often the Romans would seek a *'casus belli'* before going to war. It would be the reason for war, or the case made for the war.

This is not a bad way to look at bold initiatives you are making.

What is the fundamental reason behind your proactive move, or your deployment of funds? This can often provide a 'mission' statement to 'rally the troops'.

The mission statement of Juul, the company behind e-cigarettes is: "To eliminate cigarettes from the face of the earth." I feel Julius Caesar would have approved of the tone of that message, given his ability to neatly summarize!

WANT TO KNOW MORE? Contrary to popular opinion, these are not the words Caesar spoke before invading Britain (which he never really did, but that's a different story).

In fact, let's set the record straight over a few matters pertaining to those three little words.

They were not spoken. They were written, rather in the manner of an advertising hording (*'titulus'*), at one of Caesar's triumphs, possibly on the side of a chariot.

The statement was nothing to do with Britain. In fact, it proclaimed Caesar's victory on this day, August 2, 47 BCE at the Battle of Zela (now called Zile, and in Turkey).

The battle marked a high point in Caesar's military career, demonstrating his speed, skill and ruthless thoroughness.

His celebrations in Rome the following year were a five-star spectacular that cemented his position as leader of the world.

> **A great deal of damage is done by someone holding you back.**
> **Life's too short for that.**
>
> *(multum autem nocet etiam qui moratur, utique in tanta brevitate vitae)*
>
> Seneca. Epistles 32.2

THEME: PERSONAL DEVELOPMENT

CHECKPOINT: You can go to business school. You can study marketing. You can go on training courses. But it's very hard to teach someone not to behave like a complete buffoon.

The biggest problem a business has to contend with is the people it employs.

You know the kind I'm talking about. The Jealous One who constantly snipes at you. The Snake who constantly undermines you. The Paranoid One who constantly keeps you in the dark. The Unproductive One who steals all your ideas.

You should try all the formal methods to remove these blockages from your path.

Don't stoop to personal tactics, though, as they bring you as low as they are.

As a last resort, if you don't get satisfaction, move on.

WANT TO KNOW MORE? What actually happens in the seats of power is always fascinating.

Behind the closed doors of No. 10 Downing Street, inside the deepest recesses of the Kremlin and within the heart of the White House, discussions and decisions take place that are often only fully disclosed some decades later.

There are leaks and rumours of course, and there are official pronouncements. But what really goes on?

The same questions can be applied to the inner councils of the Roman emperors. The emperors had a private guard and a secretive advisory council.

Seneca was in Nero's inner circle, and to confuse matters further, he himself was a complicated character.

He was a sober philosopher, who became a multi-millionaire. He was a moral crusader who worked at the heart of Nero's corrupt government.

The workings of the inner council were never fully recorded and Seneca himself remained restrained in his writings about what went on. Perhaps he never wanted to implicate himself?

> **Everybody wants the information; no one wants to pay for it.**
>
> *(nosse volunt omnes, mercedem solvere nemo)*
>
> Juvenal. Satires 7.157

THEME: INTERNET

CHECKPOINT: It was H G Wells who first thought seriously about the value of searching for information. In the late 1930s, he gave a series of lectures which he gathered together in a small book entitled *World Brain*. The book accurately predicts Wikipedia, (amongst many other extraordinary predictions). He recognized the importance of fast access to "all human knowledge".

Today we have Google and Wikipedia amongst other free information sources.

What's free is an enormous amount of general knowledge. But to be sure you have the information you need, and that it is in-depth and unbiased, you still have to pay for it.

Make sure your business is accessing accurate market intelligence and not just the information that every other business can collect.

WANT TO KNOW MORE? So much of Roman history is not known to us. Legend has it that Rome was founded on April 21, 753 BCE.

From 320 BCE onward, an annual record of magistrates and memorable events was logged, but Roman literature properly began, to the best of our knowledge, 80 years later in 240 BCE. Therefore, the actual recording of history did not happen until a good half a century after this extraordinary civilization had taken root on that spring day in April.

Historians in ancient Rome would know the legends and the stories passed down orally from parent to child. There would have been some written treaties and laws and maybe archives in priestly colleges. We are left with archaeology, and our fingers crossed, to find out much more.

> **Ha! I guess we are striving for either a job title or a role.**
>
> *(ita, credo, de honore aut de dignitate contendimus)*
>
> Cicero. Tusculan Disputations 3. 21

THEME: HUMAN RESOURCES

CHECKPOINT: Everyone likes a job title. It affirms one's position in the organization. There are other rewards too as you progress upwards through the company, perks that define you and set you apart.

It is important to recognize that there is a big difference between a job title and a role.

You can call people almost anything you like.

You can call a sales assistant a Customer Experience Consultant, if you like, but it won't change the actual job.

A title that is often misused is 'director'. Anyone can be called a director. A Client Management Director could be a receptionist, for example.

Job roles are a better indication of what people really do and they can help define a specific scope of work. Keep the description tight, but understandable.

WANT TO KNOW MORE? Cicero was married for over 30 years to an extremely wealthy woman, Terentia, who came from an old, upper-class Roman family.

They had two children: a daughter called Tullia who was born in 78 BCE, and a son, Marcus, born in 65 BCE.

Tullia supported her husband financially, strategically, commercially and emotionally. They seemed to work as a team, although Terentia would not tolerate any involvement by her husband in the management of the household. There are a handful of letters in which Cicero writes about his wife. As we read them, we see that over time their relationship begins to break down.

They eventually divorced around 46 BCE.

After Cicero's death in December 43 BCE Terentia lived on, with only some speculation about whether or not she remarried.

She outlived her husband by many, many years, dying in 6AD at the age of over 100.

Cyrus centralized the admin functions. That enabled him to manage every part of his organization by communicating with just a few line managers. In this way, he had more spare leisure time than someone who's only got a house, or a boat, to look after.

(οὕτω καὶ ὁ Κῦρος συνεκεφαλαιώσατο τὰς οἰκονομικὰς πράξεις· ὥστε καὶ τῷ Κύρῳ ἐγένετο ὀλίγοις διαλεγομένῳ μηδὲν τῶν οἰκείων· ἀτημελήτως ἔχειν· καὶ ἐκ τούτου ἤδη σχολὴν ἦγε πλείω ἢ ἄλλος μιᾶς οἰκίας καὶ μιᾶς νεὼς ἐπιμελόμενος)

Xenophon. Cyropaedia 8.1.15

THEME: LEADERSHIP

CHECKPOINT: In a large company, most CEOs will create a number of direct reports to keep management and decision-making nimble, efficient and fast.

One question that CEOs need to ask is what it is that they *personally* need to do. Just being someone 'who people report to' isn't enough.

Decision-making requirements will change according to ownership structure, and companies come in all shapes, sizes and sectors.

One thing that leaders must do is buy themselves time to think.

Organize your company to facilitate this.

High-quality thinking is best done by people who have the widest possible experience and the best possible managers.

WANT TO KNOW MORE? Xenophon, the historian and mercenary, became a pupil of the philosopher Socrates.

They first met in a narrow alley in Athens.

Xenophon was walking along the alley when Socrates – an old man now – stuck out his walking stick and barred his way.

What could have been a mild scuffle (Xenophon was a country boy and would have had no problem manhandling Socrates) turned into a philosophical discourse.

Socrates kept asking Xenophon where you could obtain all sorts of items, such as general commodities. Xenophon answered each time.

Eventually Socrates asked: "Where do people acquire Virtue?"

Xenophon was stumped and not a little puzzled.

"Well," said Socrates, "you'd better follow me then, and learn."

So began Xenophon's education in philosophy, at the feet of the one of the greatest philosophers of all time.

....

> **Speed gives it its force. This speed does not resemble anything like speed as we know it. This speed is many many times faster than anything we humans have seen before.**
>
> *(βίην δὲ ἡ ταχυτὴς ποιεῖ, ἡ δὲ ταχυτὴς αὐτῶν οὐδενὶ ἔοικε χρήματι τὴν ταχυτῆτα τῶν νῦν ἐόντων χρημάτων ἐν ἀνθρώποις, ἀλλὰ πάντως πολλαπλασίως ταχύ ἐστι.)*
>
> Anaxagoras. Testimonia 2. D14

THEME: INTERNET

CHECKPOINT: The speed of the internet has an effect.

Yes, you like the idea of a customer ordering from you online. You get paid instantly and the customer gets their purchase delivered into their hands at home, lickety split.

Download speeds are accelerating.

When you order your Netflix movie, you expect it to be right here, right now.

Customers, of course, are growing used to the speed of delivery.

But press the pause button for a moment. The speed of the internet takes away the element of desire. Desire is a process that builds commitment to a product or service.

In the face of ever-increasing speeds, have a think about how you might replace the all-important 'longing-for' – the desire for – your product.

WANT TO KNOW MORE? Anaxagoras.

Another Greek name.

What happens when you delve into 1,200 years of Graeco-Roman history is that you meet a lot of names.

And many sound very similar to each other. (Anaxagoras, Anaximander, Anaxarchus, Anaximenes of Miletus, oh, and Anaximenes of Lampsacus.) Had enough? I know I have.

Anaxagoras was a philosopher.

Here's a simple way to think about Greek philosophers.

If, like Anaxagoras, they lived before Socrates we call them 'pre-Socratic'.

As for those who followed Socrates, remember this.

Socrates taught Plato, and Plato, in turn, taught Aristotle.

....

> **Don't think there's any distinction between perfume and cheap leather wrist bands: profit smells sweet, whatever its source.**
>
> *(neu credas ponendum aliquid discriminis inter unguenta et corium: lucri bonus est odor ex re qualibet)*
>
> Juvenal. Satires 14.203

THEME: SELLING

CHECKPOINT: The word 'margin' comes from the Romans. Its Latin root *'margo'* means an edge or a border.

The wider your border, the safer you are from harm.

Each of your products will have different profit margins. For example, products that sell in huge volumes may have low margins.

You'd be surprised at which common items have enormous margins.

In 2014, a company called Dealhack made some calculations.

Restaurant wine was on average marked up 400%. Better have a soda then. Well, soda is marked up 1,150%, said Dealhack.

Your pricing strategy is of critical importance. You are seeking profit, not vanity. Cut out the lines that are loss-making, or re-engineer them to come into profit. If necessary, seek outside help from experts.

At the end of the day, it's not about what you sell, it's about how much you sell it for that counts.

WANT TO KNOW MORE? Today's quote is another great quote from the satirist Juvenal.

In his 14th satire, he takes aim at all the bad habits children can learn from their parents and grandparents.

Gambling was one. An early taste for haute cuisine was another.

Juvenal gives us a peek at some of the richer delicacies of the day that spoilt kids of the rich might indulge in.

Peeled truffles, a refined sauce for mushrooms, quails and other small birds. Too much for a child, thinks Juvenal. These bad habits are an affliction that affect generation after generation, asserts Juvenal.

Apart from gambling and gluttony, other 'inherited diseases' are cruelty and promiscuity.

Today, expert psychologists tell us that bad habits like hoarding can be inherited.

Maybe Juvenal was onto something.

....

> **Personally, I love the truth.**
> **I want to be told the truth. I hate a liar.**
>
> *(ego uerum amo, uerum uolo dici mi: mendacem odi)*
>
> Plautus. The Ghost 181

THEME: LEADERSHIP

CHECKPOINT: It was *The Godfather*, Don Corleone, who liked to be told bad news immediately.

It's important to encourage everyone in an organization to report any news quickly and truthfully. We all like to be the bearer of good news. But bad news is not so nice.

We often don't tell the whole truth because we might fear a negative response, or awkward consequences.

Yet telling the truth has real power.

It positively helps the company to assess situations fully and react positively.

A person who 'tells it as it is' demonstrates confidence and strength. These are good qualities.

When telling the truth be aware of your audience and choose your words carefully. The truth can be hard to hear and in such cases you might find that diplomacy is the best policy.

WANT TO KNOW MORE? Some days really are decisive. This is one of them.

Today in 48 BCE, Julius Caesar, who was significantly outnumbered, won a battle that in effect ended 500 years of Republican Rome and started 500 years of one-man rule.

The battle was the Battle of Pharsalus and it was fought between Caesar and his arch-rival Pompey.

Pompey, a great and distinguished Roman general, was outclassed and he fled the battlefield ignominiously, disguised as a civilian.

Pompey made his way to Egypt, where the local ruler promptly beheaded him in a show of support for Caesar.

Bad move.

Caesar was appalled that a Roman citizen as renowned as Pompey should have ended his life in such a brutal way. In any case, he had every intention of pardoning Pompey.

....

> **If your heartfelt passion is to get rich, do this:**
> **work, work and work some more.**
>
> *(σοὶ δ᾽ εἰ πλούτου θυμὸς ἐέλδεται ἐν φρεσὶν ᾗσιν,*
> *ὧδ᾽ ἔρδειν, καὶ ἔργον ἐπ᾽ ἔργῳ ἐργάζεσθαι)*
>
> Hesiod. Works And Days 381

THEME: PERSONAL DEVELOPMENT

CHECKPOINT: '99% Perspiration, 1% Inspiration.'

You might have heard this common business expression.

It reflects the fact that few things happen in business because of luck.

Ask any successful entrepreneur and they will tell you that things happen because of hard work, persistence and commitment.

Working hard does not mean staying at work 12 hours a day or slavishly executing every task you've been given to a level that is not required.

Be sensible. Work out exactly what needs to be achieved, by when and, if necessary, with whom.

Working hard is more about being organized and efficient than anything else.

One thing that all successful people in business say is that you need to be dedicated to the task.

And, of course, dedication requires commitment.

WANT TO KNOW MORE? Hesiod holds an important role in all of our Greek and Roman literature.

He is the first writer to have to written under his own name.

His book *Works and Days* can be divided into three parts.

Part 1: Hesiod explains why we mere mortals have to work hard. If we don't, it means we are living off other people, and that's not right.

Part 2: He sets out a calendar of the farming year and explains the right way to work. He drops in information about the sailing seasons too – after all, you might want to sell your produce overseas.

Part 3: The final section is full of good advice about sowing and ploughing, and so on.

As Author Number One in the history of Western literature, Hesiod does a good job of introducing us to a world that is usually discovered through archaeology.

> OK team, let's take a look at what the issue actually is;
> I'm aware that sometimes things have a tendency to get
> befuddled by terminology.
>
> *(rem potius videamus, patres conscripti, quam quidem*
> *intellego verbo fieri interdum deteriorem solere)*
>
> Cicero. Philippic 8.4

THEME: LEADERSHIP

CHECKPOINT: Encourage your team to speak in a simple and easily understood way.

There is the classic business jargon like: 'let's touch base tomorrow' or 'this project will wash its own face'. But there's also a deluge of acronyms.

The point is that you should not assume that everyone knows every acronym.

ROI, YTD, SOW, CTA and UI all stand for straight-forward business expressions. Yet, Return on Investment, Year to Date, Scope of Work, Call To Action and User Interface are all much easier understood when written out in full.

When you avoid calling a spade a spade, and call it an HHTMI (Hand-Held Terrain Moving Implement), it can be difficult to get to the root of an issue quickly.

Every language has good words for everything. Only when you are absolutely certain there can be no confusion should you start to use business slang, jargon or abbreviations.

WANT TO KNOW MORE? A Roman education for the ruling classes always included rhetoric. This discipline forced you to order your thoughts coherently. Rhetoric was based on messages of intent which were often used as part of power-moves.

Your education might then take you into the military. Cicero's military career was almost non-existent. In fact, he made a deliberate choice to avoid any military service and was just involved briefly enough to know he didn't like it.

The pen is mightier than the sword, they say, and in Cicero's case, the pen was his chosen weapon, and his voice his method of attack.

Cicero attacked Mark Antony in a series of stinging speeches. Today's quote comes from one of them. Cicero successfully turned the Senate against Mark Antony.

But in the end, the sword was mightier than the stylus, and Cicero was eventually executed on Antony's orders.

> 'Don't judge until you've heard both versions of the story.'
> Whoever said that was very wise!
>
> *(ἦ που σοφὸς ἦν ὅστις ἔφασκεν· "πρὶν ἂν ἀμφοῖν*
> *μῦθον ἀκούσῃς, οὐκ ἂν δικάσαις")*
>
> Aristophanes. Wasps 725

THEME: LEADERSHIP

CHECKPOINT: It's so easy to jump to conclusions. Time isn't on your side, and you rush to judgement. Your preconceptions get the better of you, and you've heard enough when you've heard what you want to believe. There are always two sides to every story, and you owe it to the business to hear all the evidence.

It doesn't matter if it's an internal dispute or a contentious investment strategy – if people have gone to the effort to put forward a case, then you should reciprocate and listen to all the parties involved.

There is an expectation that senior management will be fair and balanced. When these are lacking, the business as a whole can lose confidence and it can become harder to motivate the team and move the business forward.

WANT TO KNOW MORE? Sometime around this time, in August of 30 BCE, the infamous Cleopatra died.

She was Queen of Egypt and had an open affair with Julius Caesar, with whom she had a son, Caesarion. She actually lived with Caesar for a while in Rome, much to the shock and disgust of many prominent Romans, including Cicero.

When Caesar was assassinated, she stayed in Rome for a few weeks, hoping her son would be recognized as Caesar's heir. He wasn't, and she hot-footed it back to Egypt.

A few years later, Cleopatra started the now-famous relationship with Mark Antony.

She was clearly some woman, but it was not so much her beauty that ensnared these mighty Roman leaders as her intellect. She was super-smart.

She could speak Greek, ancient Egyptian (written in hieroglyphics), Persian, Arabic, Hebrew and Latin. She was educated in (amongst other subjects) geography, history, astronomy, mathematics, medicine, zoology and economics.

> **Come on then, let's get the party started with vino and some nice banter.**
>
> *(age ergo, hoc agitemus conuiuium uino ut sermone suaui)*
>
> Plautus. The Comedy of Asses 834

THEME: ENTERTAINING

CHECKPOINT: There are many genuine reasons to get the vino out and have a party with your colleagues at work.

You may want to entertain your customers. Fair enough.

A new, large customer order? Well, that deserves a celebration. But make sure you are inviting everyone involved and not just the heroes who made the successful pitch.

There may a reason for a departmental party. It's a straightforward bonding session. The budget, if any, will be smaller and you might need to ask for personal contributions.

Is it someone's birthday? Keep it simple. The bigger the company, the crazier this becomes if there is a celebration at least every week.

Christmas? That's usually the big one. Make sure it is properly organized and has a clear end point.

Friday night? These are end-of-week gossip sessions. Avoid, or dip in and out judiciously.

WANT TO KNOW MORE? Talk about entertaining.

Half the Roman year was spent on holiday. And August, as in modern times, had all sorts of feasts, festivals and fun.

None more so than today.

Women whose prayers had been answered could join the torchlight procession to Aricia, 16 miles southeast of Rome. At a grove, sacred to Diana, they might leave models of reproductive organs or infants to give thanks.

Or you could choose instead to celebrate an Etruscan God, or the goddess Fortuna, or Hercules, or Castor and Pollux, or the deities of spring … the list goes on.

Most of all, this was a great day for all slaves.

They too could have the day off and enjoy a holiday.

> **Mountains will go into labour only to produce a ludicrous mouse.**
>
> *(parturient montes, nascetur ridiculus mus)*
>
> Horace. Ars Poetica 139

THEME: PROJECT MANAGEMENT

CHECKPOINT: Never use a sledgehammer to crack a nut.

Don't boil the ocean.

Don't sweat the small stuff.

We all have our versions of Horace's advice for today.

You can over-think what you need to do if you don't take one minute just to think about the delivery requirements.

And you can labour for weeks to produce something of little consequence.

Most businesses now analyse the time spent on a project and the value of the project itself.

Spending less time on a high-return project is very good news.

Spending time on low-return projects is an early indicator that something isn't working.

WANT TO KNOW MORE? In the *Ars Poetica*, the poet Horace gives advice on how to write. Poetry and drama were the principle avenues for writers, the novel not yet being à la mode.

Here's a little of what he suggests.

1. When writing poetry keep in mind unity and simplicity. Always write about what you know and have experienced – this will allow your work to flow.
2. Give a fresh tone of voice to familiar words and expressions.
3. It's very important for drama to feed into the feelings of an audience. Prick and stimulate feelings that might be latent.
4. Make sure you keep characterization consistent.
5. Keep the beginning simple and then flesh-out and elaborate.
6. Study the curious and eventful history of human life.
7. And finally, look to the Greeks. They were so much more eloquent and sophisticated.

> Time is flying by. While I'm talking I'm using it up.
> What are you going to do then? You're pulled apart by
> conflicting agendas. Are you going to do this, or that?
>
> *(fugit hora hoc quod loquor inde est en quid agis? duplici*
> *in diversum scinderis hamo. huncine an hunc sequeris?)*
>
> Persius. Satires 5.153

THEME: TIME MANAGEMENT

CHECKPOINT: Today's message is: Organize Yourself!!

Getting organized takes much less time than you think and saves much more time than you might imagine.

Organize tomorrow's work today.

Make sure you are focused on the key agendas or projects and don't be tempted to get sidetracked unless it's absolutely imperative that you do so.

If you have an ongoing project, break it down into component parts.

Over the years, I have seen as many systems as there are individuals, but if you're looking for ways to get organized, just search online or, better still, ask that super-organized person sitting next to you!

WANT TO KNOW MORE? We all remember our schoolteachers. Some of them stick in our minds more than others.

One of my teachers was known as 'Basher', but his bark, thankfully, was worse than his bite!

The poet Horace was taught by a certain Lucius Orbilius Pupillus, whose nickname was 'Flogger'. Nice.

Poor old Persius was taught by Remmius Palaemon, an ex-slave so infamous that both the Emperors Tiberius and Claudius declared him unfit to work with children.

Palaemon was certainly a colourful character. He liked to visit the baths several times a day and was very fond of the ladies, –often, it was whispered, going way too far and being accused regularly of indecency.

Palaemon also had the very annoying habit of kissing everyone he met (male or female) to such a degree that it earnt him a seriously bad reputation.

Be that as it may, his teaching was considered to be good, and young Persius clearly benefitted from being taught by this eccentric man.

> **It's so much better to brainstorm than blamestorm.**
>
> *(quanto satius est quid faciendum sit quam quid factum quaerere)*
>
> Seneca. Natural Questions Preface 3.7

THEME: LEADERSHIP

CHECKPOINT: In business, you cannot tolerate mistakes that inflict serious damage.

But remember, saying goodbye to someone takes just a few minutes, while hiring a new person takes a long time and can be expensive.

Clever businesses use mistakes as part of an ongoing learning process.

A company that runs under a blame culture will find people passing the blame around as in 'pass the parcel'. Time is wasted and often witchhunts prove to be fruitless. Morale, too, can be seriously dented.

A company that understands mistakes will be made, but then chooses to learn from them, encourages a more open attitude, leading to faster generation of new ideas, higher morale and greater efficiency.

WANT TO KNOW MORE? Seneca was implicated in an attempted assassination of the Emperor Nero in 65 CE. A certain Gaius Calpurnius Piso was the leader of the plot. There were a number of conspirators involved.

One story goes that the plot was uncovered when the appointed assassin, on his way to the theatre the night before the assassination, spotted a prisoner about to be led in front of Nero.

"Just hope and pray that you can get to the end of this day, my friend," the assassin said to the prisoner. "Tomorrow you will be very grateful to me."

The prisoner realized there was a plot and tipped off Nero, no doubt expecting a sizeable favour in return.

Nero used the discovery of the plot to conduct a major purge of all his enemies.

Seneca was probably not a conspirator, but he almost certainly knew about it. For this, he was ordered to commit suicide, which he duly did.

....

> **There are ups and there are downs in life.**
>
> *(modo sic, modo sic)*
>
> Petronius. Satyricon 45

THEME: LEADERSHIP

CHECKPOINT: Stock markets go up and go down.

Sales have upturns and downturns.

Fashions come and go.

Life in the world of work is indeed a roller-coaster experience.

The best resource you could have to manage the turbulence is experience.

Usually that means some older and wiser heads around the table.

It's easy to think that each new problem you have is completely new.

It's even easier to cite new technology as a reason for older executives being unable to contribute.

But most business problems are not new. They are the same old problems disguised in a contemporary set of clothes.

WANT TO KNOW MORE? Yesterday we heard about Piso's conspiracy against the Emperor Nero, which led to Seneca's suicide.

In another, separate, case of treason, Petronius, author of today's quote, was arrested and also chose to commit suicide before he was sentenced to (almost certain) death.

Petronius and Seneca must have known each other well, although there is no record of this.

Seneca was not only Nero's personal tutor, he was a member of Nero's 'inner sanctum' (*'amici principis'*). He was an imperial speech-writer and 'head of communications', working hard to represent the emperor and his views in a positive light.

Petronius was also close to Nero, becoming the emperor's *'arbiter elegantiarum'* (a kind of fashion and taste advisor). Petronius rose to become consul and must have known Seneca.

....

> **Often wisdom can be found behind the scruffy jeans and a t-shirt.**
>
> *(saepe est etiam sub palliolo sordido sapientia)*
>
> Caecilius Statius. (Quoted by Cicero. Tusculan Disputations. 3.23.56)

THEME: HUMAN RESOURCES

CHECKPOINT: Be careful not to impose your own sense of taste and decorum onto others, or to judge people by what they look like or are wearing.

Nowadays there is much more acceptance of difference.

When I first entered the workplace, it was expected that men wore a suit.

Today, what you wear is such a matter of personal taste that jeans and a t-shirt are as acceptable as anything else.

Nowadays, it is almost impossible to tell what someone is like by the clothes they wear.

It's only by sitting down and engaging with the person in conversation that you can get a clearer understanding of the person's true character.

WANT TO KNOW MORE? Today's quote comes from a fragment we have (courtesy of Cicero) of Caecilius Statius, a comic dramatist who lived roughly between 220 BCE and 166 BCE.

Caecilius was probably a prisoner of war, taken during the Roman conflicts in the region of Alpine Italy, in around 200 BCE.

He was enslaved and taken to Rome, but eventually won his freedom.

He was clearly well known by later writers because his plays are often mentioned.

Caecilius wrote at least 40 pieces, but all we have today is some 300 lines.

As is so often the case, we hope that one day full texts of some of his works will be unearthed (probably literally).

As far as how respected he was, the ancient Romans held mixed views, with Cicero less positive and Horace less critical.

In case you wondered, the Romans did not wear jeans and t-shirts. That's just my loose translation of *'palliolo sordido'*, which actually means 'scruffy little cloak'.

> **It's of no consequence. Neither here nor there.**
>
> *(susque deque)*
>
> Cicero. Letters to Atticus 14.6

THEME: STRATEGY

CHECKPOINT: How many times have we wished we could go back into the past and undo something we did or said? Hindsight is such a wonderful thing.

Although we don't have hindsight, we do have foresight.

Never rush to judgement. Give yourself thinking time.

For as long as you can, try not to 'rule anything in, or rule anything out'.

No one can predict the future, but with careful planning and consultation you can reassure yourself that you gave those all-important matters your due consideration.

WANT TO KNOW MORE? These two little words, quoted here today for us by Cicero, are, in this context, amongst my favourites in all Latin literature. They are an expression of indifference.

Cicero uses the expression in a letter to his close friend Atticus:

Dear Atticus,

I was at Fundi when I received your letter of the 12th. I was having dinner. Well, first off, I learn that you are feeling better and secondly that you have some more encouraging news.

That report about the legions marching was disquieting, to say the least; (by the way, regarding Octavian, he's neither here nor there) …

Unluckily for Cicero, his comment revealed one of the biggest underestimations in global history.

Octavian was the heir to Julius Caesar's estate. In true Roman tradition, he was also heir to his name. Cicero was executed 18 months later under the orders of Antony, operating in collusion with Octavian. Cicero would never see Octavian grow to become Augustus, the first (and longest-reigning ever) emperor of Rome, and one of the most famous people in history.

Augustus died this day in 14 CE, just a few weeks before his seventy-sixth birthday.

> **The light at the end of the tunnel is in our own hands.**
> **You don't win by being idle.**
>
> *(τῷ ἐν χερσὶ φόως, οὐ μειλιχίῃ πολέμοιο)*
>
> Homer. Iliad 15.741

THEME: PERSONAL DEVELOPMENT

CHECKPOINT: One of the skills you need to get you through your working day is tenacity. This is easier said than done.

One trick I have used is to think back to a past assignment that I was able to complete with a sense of pride.

I was the junior, and so I was given a job no one wanted to do. I decided up front that I would not just do the work, but I would make it a thing of beauty. I would make everyone else wish they had taken the assignment.

It was hard – at one stage it involved me driving through London riots to reach a specialist print company. But I did it and I was handsomely rewarded by the client for whom this 'boring' job was, for him, of the utmost importance.

If you have a difficult task ahead, elevate it. Say to yourself, 'I'm going to make this the best piece of work I have done in a long time'.

Sometimes self-motivation is all you need.

WANT TO KNOW MORE? Today in 480 BCE, the Battle of Thermopylae was fought.

You simply cannot overestimate the importance of this battle. The battle was between the Greeks and the Persians. Xerxes, the Persian leader, had put together the biggest army the world had ever seen.

We don't know the numbers exactly, but estimates suggest it was up to 300,000 strong.

The Greeks scraped together about 7,000 soldiers from a ramshackle collection of small cities. The Greeks held out against all odds. The invading Persians retreated.

Greece was free. If it had gone the other way, the history of Western philosophy, democracy, art and literature may well have taken a completely different course.

> **He asked his friends about what the next steps should be.**
>
> *(περὶ δὲ τῶν ἑξῆς ἐβουλεύετο μετὰ τῶν φίλων)*
>
> Polybius. Histories 5.4.13

THEME: PERSONAL DEVELOPMENT

CHECKPOINT: When you are unsure which way to go, your friends are usually a good source of honest objectivity.

They are close enough to want to help, but distant enough not to be embroiled in your own confusion.

At work, you might have a few close co-workers who you can turn to.

You're looking for dispassionate, non-partisan guidance. It could be an issue at work or a career move or even a personal matter.

Over time, people build up just a small handful of close friends and many acquaintances.

It's the friends, not the acquaintances, who can usually give the most appropriate advice.

WANT TO KNOW MORE? Polybius was a very important historian.

He looked at the rise of Rome and how it became the dominant Mediterranean force from 264 BCE to 146 BCE.

Polybius was at pains to represent the reasons and the causes for events.

He tells us that he wants to discover facts, root out stories and explain exactly what was going on.

Very professional, you might think.

But then he also tells us about two forms of chance that occur and make things inexplicable!

One form of chance is unpredictable disaster (earthquakes, storms, droughts and floods, for example).

The other is human unpredictability. Inexplicably men (it's always the men) have sudden bouts of aberrant behaviour, either massively over-achieving, or pathetically falling far short of their own standards.

> **Hand in hand with debt and litigation comes misery.**
>
> *(comitemque aeris alieni atque litis esse miseriam)*
>
> Pliny The Elder. Natural History 7.32

THEME: LEGAL

CHECKPOINT: The word 'profit' comes from the Latin *'profectus'*, meaning 'advantage'. But the word 'loss' comes from an Old Germanic word *'Los'*, meaning 'utter destruction' or 'ruin'.

As soon as your business starts losing money, you end up working twice as hard to avoid utter destruction. You have to work twice as hard just to stand still.

Your investors start sweating and demand you churn out more management information and turn up for meetings to explain what's going on.

You are no longer building and creating – you are firefighting and keeping creditors at bay.

Cash management is the primary task of any business, yet it is the least visible.

Grow your business carefully. Slowly, if necessary.

Always remain profitable and only borrow if you absolutely know that you can pay it back.

WANT TO KNOW MORE? One extraordinary thing we learn from Pliny the Elder is that Rome traded with India and Ceylon (today called Sri Lanka).

More than that. The Romans met with the peoples of southern India and Sri Lanka.

This is truly extraordinary.

Today Sri Lanka is a 15-hour flight away from Rome. It's over 6,000 miles away.

Yet archaeological finds in Arikamedu in Southeast India attest to a lively and strong trade, so Pliny is backed up by some evidence.

The story goes that an employee of a Roman tax collector on the Red Sea was carried by gales down the coast and a fortnight later he ended up in Hippuri, a harbour in Sri Lanka.

This employee was well treated, learnt the local language and briefed the local king on the Romans and their emperor.

Pliny also tells us that a trade delegation from Ceylon reciprocated and visited the Emperor Claudius.

> **Don't charge ahead when you're hot-tempered.**
> **Give yourself a moment; press the pause button.**
> **Being impetuous always does you a disservice.**
>
> *(ne frena animo permitte calenti, da spatium*
> *tenuemque moram, male cuncta ministrat impetus)*
>
> Statius. Thebaid 10.703

THEME: PERSONAL DEVELOPMENT

CHECKPOINT: We all get angry at work. Sometimes our colleagues drive us mad and we go home seething.

For example, the office buffoon has been given a ridiculous promotion. 'What's that all about?', you scream to yourself.

Or you lose that 50-page proposal that you were sure you saved on your computer. Aaaarghh.

Work can be maddening.

The most important thing to do when you find yourself in a hot-tempered mood is to try not to react immediately.

No! Don't call your boss and tell her she made a mistake promoting that idiot instead of you.

Go for a walk. 'Talk it out' of your system with friends.

Sure, at some point, react if you feel it will benefit you (but only if it benefits you).

A sober, sensible response is much more likely to be listened to.

WANT TO KNOW MORE? Statius was born and died in Naples, but spent much of his life in Rome.

He was married to a lady called Claudia who was unable to have children, and so they adopted a son, who sadly died at a young age.

Child mortality rates would have been high in ancient Rome, with some scholars suggesting a rate as high as one in three.

Children who died before the age of one were not mourned.

After they reached the age of one, they were considered to have made it through an important benchmark.

Mourning for children was progressively extended the longer they survived, until they reached the age of 10, when the mourning period lasted as long as that for adults.

> ### Fortune favours the brave.
>
> *(fortes fortuna iuvat)*
>
> Pliny The Younger. Letters 6.16.12

THEME: PERSONAL DEVELOPMENT

CHECKPOINT: Sometimes at work, you need to make a brave move or a brave decision. I don't mean a rash move, I mean a brave one.

You need to muster up the courage and keep your nerves or apprehensions under control. These moments come every so often, and they come for everyone. They are part of the inevitable process of growing in your workplace.

Like so many things in life, once you've jumped that hurdle you will look back and think 'that wasn't so hard'.

The more you can progress at work, the more rewarding it will be. Emotionally and financially. But be sure of one thing. Those hurdles?

They keep coming. Even when you've reached the top.

WANT TO KNOW MORE? One place not to have been on August 24, 79 CE was Pompeii. On this morning, at around 8.00, you'd have felt more of the tremors you'd been feeling for the past few days.

As Pliny tells us, the locals were used to it.

At lunchtime, Mount Vesuvius suddenly erupts with huge force. A huge volcanic umbrella-shaped cloud fills and darkens the sky.

By mid-afternoon hardened lava stones start raining down on the townspeople and Pliny relates that people start running, taking cover and putting pillows over their heads to protect themselves.

Suddenly, the sea gets sucked away from the sea shore, leaving behind all manner of stranded sea life.

It was horrific.

Pliny's account tells how his uncle (Pliny the Elder) tried in vain to help, but was struck down by the sheer size of what has become one of the most famous volcanic eruptions in history.

> ## You know how to say it more appropriately than that.
>
> *(οἶσθα καὶ ἄλλον μῦθον ἀμείνονα τοῦδε νοῆσαι)*
>
> Homer. Iliad 7.358

THEME: THE WATERCOOLER

CHECKPOINT: It's just laziness that makes people say things inappropriately.

Laziness due to tiredness, or lack of consideration.

Saying things to people in a way that causes unnecessary unpleasantness can take just a moment's lack of thought, but the impression you leave can last for a very long time.

A lifetime even.

It's amazing how just one minute of thought can re-assemble your words and phrases into something much more appropriate.

So just be thoughtful, and the workplace will hum along much more pleasantly.

WANT TO KNOW MORE? Homer's *Iliad* takes 50 or so days towards the end of the Trojan War and uses them to describe people and emotions. It's not a war story, as such, it's more a snapshot of the human cost of brutal fighting. It's about people.

The war was between the Greeks and the Trojans, but the book doesn't go there immediately.

Its first word is the clue to whole bloody mess that ensues.

Anger.

The book starts with a fight between two of the key Greeks leaders, King Agamemnon, leader of the Greek coalition, and Achilles, the number one soldier.

The fight is over the abduction of a woman. She was from a family allied to the Trojan cause and was captured by Achilles.

Achilles is angry, because Agamemnon is now claiming the woman.

Women and children, brothers and sisters, husbands and wives, rich and poor. They're all people caught up in this ghastly, bloody, brutal mess.

The Trojans don't want the war. The Greeks want to go home.

Everyone is tired, angry and upset.

> **[Note To Self] Mustn't unnecessarily, or indeed often, say or write in a note, 'I'm too busy'.**
>
> *(τὸ μὴ πολλάκις μηδὲ χωρὶς ἀνάγκης λέγειν πρός τινα ἢ ἐν ἐπιστολῇ γράφειν, ὅτι ἄσχολός εἰμι)*
>
> Marcus Aurelius. Meditations 1.12

THEME: LEADERSHIP

CHECKPOINT: All businesses are made up of people. I don't know of a single business that has no people involved. Even companies building robots employ people.

Managers have to manage people. That's why they are called managers. And they must find the time to do the job properly.

The most important part of managerial duties is being available to the people who report to you.

You need to encourage them, inspire them. You need to motivate them on the difficult days and congratulate them on the wonderful days.

You need to make sure they are trained and properly rewarded.

You need to stand up for them.

You can never be too be busy for people if you are a manager.

WANT TO KNOW MORE? Marcus Aurelius' *Notes to Self* (as he called them) are regularly plundered to find quotes for books on inspiration or meditation.

He was a gentle man, who became known as the last of the five good emperors (Nerva, Trajan, Hadrian, Antoninus Pius and his good self, Marcus Aurelius).

His second book of *Notes to Self* starts with a cracker of a thought, but one that might make you think that this nice chap had, if not a 'dark' side, then maybe a 'light grey' one.

Every morning, say to yourself: "I shall come across a meddlesome busybody, someone who is unappreciative, a bully, another who is very deceitful, a disparager and someone who is antisocial. They are like this because they don't know good from bad."

Now there's a thought.

> **People (particularly those in business) who readily believe whatever they are told never do well.**
>
> *(nunquam autem recte faciet, qui cito credit, utique homo negotians)*
>
> Petronius. Satyricon 43

THEME: LEADERSHIP

CHECKPOINT: It's one thing to be open to advice, it's another to know how to act on it.

Advice can come from inside or outside an organization. Often, it's not asked for.

There is always the urban myth of the chairman's wife choosing the advertising campaign.

Whoever gives you advice, mull it over. If necessary, get a second opinion.

People are full of their own ideas and there's always someone prepared to seed a thought into someone at the top.

Even if the person giving the advice is your closest companion or colleague, you must retain some healthy scepticism, rather than race to agreement just because you know them.

The higher up the company you go, the more you are being rewarded for your own brainpower. Use it!

WANT TO KNOW MORE? One of the most (in)famous moments in Latin literature was written by Petronius in his book, *Satyricon*. It's 'The Feast of Trimalchio'.

Trimalchio was an ex-slave who became a brash millionaire. So brash that he tells us how he did it. By shrewd investments and deals … oh, and by sleeping with the right women.

As soon as the guests arrived at his house for dinner, they were aware they were in the presence of serious money, off-the-scale bling and a bizarre host.

They were first greeted in the hallway by a magpie in a golden cage. Before they sat down, they were treated to an ice-cold hand wash and a pedicure.

Hors d'oeuvres included dormice dipped in honey and poppy seeds, and sausages with damsons and pomegranates. Included in the next course were bull's eyes, testicles and a young sow's udder. Yum. Then came the live birds sewn into a pig . . . you get the idea.

All this was served with a very expensive vintage wine, and the feast descended into a drunken orgy.

> **It's said that truth is often beset by problems, but it never dies.**
>
> *(veritatem laborare nimis saepe aiunt, exstingui nunquam)*
>
> Livy. History Of Rome 22.39.19

THEME: THE WATERCOOLER

CHECKPOINT: The thing is, you can't hide, or keep the lid on, the truth.

It will eventually pop out from wherever is it supressed.

Or, as Shakespeare so eloquently put it: "Truth will out."

Sometimes the truth is hard to swallow. So you sit on it.

Not a good idea.

Pretending something didn't happen won't make it go away.

Businesses that can manage an open, tolerant culture, where telling the truth is encouraged, are happy places to work in.

Happy places find it easier to recruit good people and good people are the principle assets that will grow a company.

WANT TO KNOW MORE? Titus Livius (known to us as Livy) was born in 59 BCE and died in 17 CE, making him a contemporary of the Emperor Augustus and the poets Horace, Tibullus, Propertius and Ovid.

He wrote a monumental history of Rome, starting right back at beginning of it all, with Romulus and Remus.

The word 'monumental' is often used loosely, to generally suggest something quite big and fairly important.

But in Livy's case it's hard to imagine how else you could describe his work.

Coming in at 142 volumes (we have just 35), Livy's work was immense.

No other prose writer of the time could come close to Livy, whose clarity and factual balance provides a lively and thorough history of Rome's long road to social, economic and military success.

....

> **Let them say we were worthy of what we acheived together.**
>
> *(cum digno digna fuisse ferar)*
>
> Sulpicia. Poems 1

THEME: HUMAN RESOURCES

CHECKPOINT: Nothing beats compatibility when you want things to move fast and with fluidity.

Matching people to companies, or teams to individuals, is not an easy task. Well-matched people add to each other's worth. When it's done well, and that usually means it's been done professionally, you reap the rewards very quickly.

There are all sorts of ways to make sure the matching process goes well.

Some are semi-scientific, others are pseudo-psychological. Don't knock them.

They are usually based on sound methodology and, in some cases, many years of experience.

If you need to match someone up in your company, put some thought and effort into it, and get outside professional help if necessary.

WANT TO KNOW MORE? Shock! A female Roman poet! Such a shock, in fact, that still today experts argue about whether 'Sulpicia' was a woman or a man.

Arguing for a man are those who say the writing is too risqué. A woman would never have written such poetry.

Weirdly, arguing for a woman are others who contend that the poetry is not well written.

Over the years, this gender speculation has given way to a more acute reading of the poetry (a mere six poems, I'm afraid) and a more accurate attempt to understand the writer – an educated woman from a wealthy and literary background, networked in the highest echelons of Roman society.

The shockwave is subsiding, although it may never disappear.

We have very little of the Latin literature that was written, and we know that the majority was written by men.

It cannot be suprising that what has come to us from women writers remains a very small percentage of the total.

> **Think small, get little.**
>
> *(parvum parva decent)*
>
> Horace. Epistles 1.7.44

THEME: LEADERSHIP

CHECKPOINT: One expression in the workplace that is often used to define future planning is 'strategic intent'. The word strategy comes from the Greek word '*στραταγός*' (strategos) – meaning a leader or army commander. The word intent comes from the Latin '*intendere*' meaning to stretch out.

A company that has a strategic intent is one that is reaching for a stretch goal.

Leaders should always think big.

Thinking big can provide energy and enthusiasm. It can define the kind of people you need, and it can encapsulate the ambition of the company.

Thinking big does not mean thinking dangerously.

Your ambition has to be achievable and actionable. Don't forget, vision without action is hallucination.

WANT TO KNOW MORE? Horace wrote his *Epistles* (letters) around 21 BCE. He's approaching his mid forties and he's going all philosophical. He likes philosophy. It works like magic on upset souls.

He's been rereading his Homer, who he thinks is the wisest of all philosophers.

The *Iliad*, says Horace, looks at the disastrous decision-making of leaders and the terrible suffering it can bring to people. The *Odyssey*, he believes, has life lessons for us all, showing the value of courage and self-control.

In another letter, Horace asks after the newer, younger set – the up-and-coming litterati. "Don't forget yer philosophy," he finger-wags.

In 33 BCE, a patron of the arts bought Horace a farm in the countryside, supposedly near Licenza, just outside Rome. Contemplating life in the countryside versus life in the big city became a pastime for Horace.

> **Self-reliance and an unwavering intent not to leave anything to chance. And not for one moment to rely on anything other than common sense.**
>
> *(τὸ ἐλεύθερον καὶ ἀναμφιβόλως ἀκύβευτον· καὶ πρὸς μηδὲν ἄλλο ἀποβλέπειν μηδὲ ἐπ᾽ ὀλίγον ἢ πρὸς τὸν λόγον)*
>
> Marcus Aurelius. Meditations 1.8

THEME: PERSONAL DEVELOPMENT

CHECKPOINT: This book very often implores you to seek a variety of ways of developing your skills.

But, never forget the one person you have to rely on day in, day out. Yourself.

You will carry the burden of managing yourself for most of the time you are at work.

Marcus Aurelius has three pieces of advice that might help:

1. Rely on your own ability and the resources you bring to the workplace, rather than on others.
2. Focus hard on not leaving anything to chance. If it can go wrong, it will go wrong.
3. Use your common sense! As they say: if it looks like a duck, walks like a duck and quacks like a duck, then it is a duck.

Finally, consider a proposition called 'Occam's Razor': the simplest solution tends to be the right solution.

WANT TO KNOW MORE? Today in 12 CE, Caligula was born. He joins the ranks of just a very few Romans that the general public have heard of, along with Julius Caesar and, maybe, Cicero.

Caligula was a nickname, meaning 'little boots' – a name given to him by the soldiers he was brought up with while he was with his father, who was stationed in Germany. His real name was Gaius.

Seneca tells us that he was a hideously ugly man, with a pale, wan face and wild eyes that made him look insane.

Caligula was clearly unbalanced. He was accused of being a murderous sociopath, of committing incest with his sisters, of turning the imperial palace into a bordello and threatening to appoint his horse to the position of Consul. (He didn't, he made his horse a 'priest' instead.)

He was assassinated aged 28, after less than four years as emperor.

The love of habit is a mighty force.

(consuetudinis amor magnus est)

Symmachus. Relationes 3.4

THEME: PERSONAL DEVELOPMENT

CHECKPOINT: The biggest barrier to personal development, business development and innovation is habit-forming routine. We all do it.

We have our morning routines. We take the same route into work. We grab coffee from the same place, same time. We set out our workstations the way we like them.

Routines are comfortable. They de-stress the start of the day. You don't have to switch on the old brainbox yet.

In fact, any change is disruptive, right?

All understood.

But the key to originality and creative thinking – indeed, the absorption of anything new – is to break the routine.

Only you know how to do this. And once you start to shake things up a little, you'll find you're starting to jump-start that all-important, under-utilized brain of yours.

WANT TO KNOW MORE? If August provided an abundance of feast days and holidays, then September is the month for Games. The *'Ludi Romani'* ('Roman Games') were a big affair. They were the major Roman festivities of the year and their roots went way back into early Roman history.

September was a good month to build in a bit of 'down time'.

The military campaigning season was over, the harvest was in and there were still a few weeks before the grapes were ready.

The Games were held between the 5th and the 19th of this month. Yes, that's right, a whole two weeks of fun. They were held in honour of the chief Roman god, Jupiter (equivalent to Zeus for the Greeks). Citizens could expect theatre, formal processions, chariot races, boxing matches, dancing and much more.

Fun times!

> **What you see is not always what you get.**
>
> *(fallaces enim sunt rerum species)*
>
> Seneca. De Beneficiis 4.34.1

THEME: HUMAN RESOURCES

CHECKPOINT: We have all become professional '*curriculum vitae*' builders.

Some people have had to 'present' themselves from a very early age to make the right impression, to get into college or gain an apprenticeship.

We can go online and get free advice on what to say and what not to say.

We can look at other people we admire and see how they have presented their qualifications and experience.

So looking beyond first impressions is very important if you want to be doubly sure that the person sitting in front of you is who they claim to be.

The most important thing to do when hiring is always to seek professional advice.

Then get the candidate to meet two or three of your colleagues so you can get a full 360-degree picture.

WANT TO KNOW MORE? There are just a handful of dates in the vast span of Greek and Roman history that have produced clear and undeniable change.

Among them were the Battle of Thermopylae in the August of 480 BCE. There was the assassination of Julius Caesar on the Ides of March (March 15, 44 BCE). Another falls today, September 2, 31 BCE.

Today the battle of Actium took place. The battle took place at sea off the coast of Greece, just to the south of modern-day Corfu.

The forces of Julius Caesar's heir, Octavian, met those of Antony and Cleopatra in a fight to decide who should be master of the world.

The battle was won by Octavian, who changed his name to Augustus and became the first emperor of Rome.

It ended decades of bloody infighting between various Roman factions.

And it heralded the end of the Roman Republic that had lasted for almost 500 years.

> **Be guided by fairness when you steer the team.**
>
> *(νώμα δικαίῳ πηδαλίῳ στρατόν)*
>
> Pindar. Pythian Odes 1.86

THEME: LEADERSHIP

CHECKPOINT: Being a leader of a team of any size means that you have to demonstrate equanimity.

Your own experience might tell you that something doesn't feel right and that maybe you should favour one person's opinion over another. If so, be sure you are right.

You might know in your heart of hearts that someone else needs an opportunity, but you're just not that drawn to them.

It's important to understand that your workplace comprises different people, from different backgrounds, abilities and ages.

These inner views you hold immediately become public knowledge once you demonstrate unfairness in the workplace.

It's an unfortunate fact of life that everyone takes notice of managers who are unfair, or who have favourites. You have to make sure that everyone gets the same chances.

WANT TO KNOW MORE? Pindar (approximately 520 BCE - 438 BCE) lived through extraordinary times. His life spanned the series of military conflicts that would destabilize and define Greece forever – The Persian Wars.

Dear old Pindar seems to have hardly noticed them. Born into an aristocratic family, he contented himself with writing odes for the great 'Pan-Hellenic' games of ancient Greece: The Pythian Games, the Nemean Games, the Isthmian Games and, of course, the Olympic Games.

What took his mind off the great conflicts of the day?

Maybe it was the athletic prowess shown at the games.

Pindar could have sat by and watched any of the following:

The 200 and 400 meter sprint; a three-mile race; or a race in full armour. Wrestling, boxing and, um, a flute competition.

Much more interesting than a 50-year conflict that defined Western civilization.

....

> **Many people say the 'right' thing but do the wrong thing.**
>
> *(δίκαια μὲν γὰρ λέγοντες πολλοὶ ἄδικα ποιοῦσι)*
>
> Xenophon. Memorabilia 4.4.10

THEME: HUMAN RESOURCES

CHECKPOINT: Inconsistency of character is difficult to process and understand.

One day your colleague is extolling the virtues of saving the planet and the next you notice his complete misuse of the recycling bin.

Adhering to moral, ethical and sustainable beliefs is difficult. Our views and opinions change as we grow older and we experience the consequences of our actions with the benefit of hindsight.

Some issues (to do with race, sexuality, age and gender, for example) have become enshrined in law. There are some things that it's just not right (or legal) to denigrate in public. 'Political correctness' has become a minefield.

What you say, your beliefs and how you act are now three completely separate modes of behaviour which you merge at your peril.

Although it is difficult at times to separate your private life (and views) from your work life – given that we spend so much of our time at work – try to maintain a professional work persona.

Consistency of character at work does not prohibit the development of a fascinating and unique character in private!

WANT TO KNOW MORE? Every now and then, life throws up some wonderful coincidences that seem so unbelievable as to be almost untrue. Just take a look at this:

Romulus was the founder of Rome in 753 BCE. Augustus was the first emperor of Rome. And Romulus Augustus was the last emperor of Rome. I bet his parents could not have imagined his destiny when they christened him Flavius Romulus Augustus.

On September 4, 476 CE, Romulus Augustus (often known in a derisory way as 'Augustulus' – little Augustus) died and the Roman Empire in the West came to an end.

....

> **Internal strife is an opportunity for your competitors.**
>
> *(seditio civium hostium est occasio)*
>
> Publilius Syrus. Sententiae 680

THEME: COMPETITORS

CHECKPOINT: So many companies suffer damaging internal conflict. Disagreements over strategy and overall direction can lead to boardroom battles. Office politics can lead to sudden power moves that disrupt employees.The truth is that businesses squabble as much as people do. Internal strife is an own goal and very often leaves the business weaker.

Sometimes the wounds heal quickly, other times simmering resentment stays warm enough to boil over at any moment.

Such internal wars are often a golden opportunity for competitors. They start poaching your key staff and customers. They capitalize on the inevitable delays caused by such strife.

Internal conflict is actually an inevitable byproduct of the competitive nature of business.

But the companies that deal with it quickly and efficiently (sometimes with external arbitration) bounce back faster and stronger.

WANT TO KNOW MORE? Today in Rome marks the start of the oldest and most famous of all the Roman Games, the Ludi Romani.

The two-week event would start with a procession from the Capitol, through the Forum to the Circus Maximus.

The procession would be led by the chief magistrates, followed by young men on foot or horseback. Then came chariots, athletes and dancers accompanied by musicians playing the flute and lyre (a kind of small, hand-held harp). Next up would be men dressed in goatskins pretending to be satyrs.

More musicians would follow. Then came incense burners. They were followed by displays of gold and silver vessels, some holy. Finally came the images of the gods carried on wooden pallets. That was the morning of Day One.

> **You were the only one talking sense at that meeting a while ago.**
>
> *(concilio antiquo sapiens vir solus fuisti)*
>
> Lucilius. Satires 1.23

THEME: LEADERSHIP

CHECKPOINT: It's so difficult being the only sensible person in a workplace full of fools!

Ah! How often have we caught ourselves wondering why everyone is so stupid?

If only they had listened to meeeee!!

Sometimes it is true that you have nailed the issue and you are so on top of things that you are head and shoulders ahead of your colleagues.

But are you like that all the time?

It's unlikely. You'll have good days and bad days.

Sure, make as much mileage as you can out of the good times. It's important that your abilities take you as high as they can.

But try not to be too arrogant about your success.

No one likes a smarty pants.

WANT TO KNOW MORE? Lucilius, the satirist, was born in Sessa Arunca, about 45 miles north of Naples.

He was not a Roman citizen and so took no part in politics, but he moved to Rome and befriended many who were.

He was an outsider, if you like, but he was inside the heart of the action, where the movers and shakers were.

He observed. He took notes.

He witnessed the early signs of a growing, changing and more 'Greek' Rome. There was social and political discontent.

There were a lot of people with an awful lot of money and privilege – and even more who had neither.

Lucilius used his satirical wit to start documenting those changes, but in a unique Roman style.

> **Faultless and intelligent. A speech such as never heard before!**
>
> *(οὐπώποθ᾽ οὕτω καθαρῶς οὐδενὸς ἠκούσαμεν οὐδὲ ξυνετῶς λέγοντος.)*
>
> Aristophanes. Wasps 631

THEME: PRESENTATIONS/MEETINGS/DOCUMENTS

CHECKPOINT: Have you ever been asked up to give a presentation at work? Daunting, isn't it? And it doesn't matter what the subject is.

Whether it's 'What I did On My Holidays' or 'The Effects of Artificial Intelligence on the Workplace Of The Future', it makes no difference. You are in front of people and you have to deliver your message in a clear and competent way.

Hopefully you can be fun and engaging too.

Presentations are theatre. You want your audience to applaud.

Just remember, the audience does not know what you are going to say. It's not a test! Be natural and use as little technology as you possibly can.

I have manged to never use technology; if the presentation is a disaster, I only have myself to blame!

Finally, enjoy it. Present as if you really love what you're talking about.

WANT TO KNOW MORE? Aristophanes (born around 446 BCE and died around 386 BCE) was the great comedy writer of ancient Greece. He was known as The Father of Comedy.

His play *Wasps*, from which today's quote is taken, tells us something about the workings of the Athenian courts. It really was a 'trial by jury'.

Every year, 6,000 citizens were chosen to join the candidate list for jury service, all sourced from volunteers who were over the age of 35.

Each case to be tried drew jurors from this list and the size of the jury depended on the type of case. The number of jurors was never less than 200, but in extreme cases it could be as many as 1,000.

The jurors would hear the case, make their decision and cast their vote – no summing up by the judge.

....

The greater the fellow, the greater the fall.

(τοῖσι δὲ μεγίστοισι αὐτῶν μέγιστα)

Herodotus. Histories 7.203

THEME: PERSONAL DEVELOPMENT

CHECKPOINT: Climbing up the greasy pole to success is not everyone's idea of a happy and fruitful career, but for many it is.

Remember, all organizations are pyramidical in structure. The higher you go, the less opportunities there are and the more people there are competing for the same jobs.

Aiming high is a laudable ambition. 'Going for gold' is more desirable than 'settling for bronze' for many people, and it's only in the striving that we can measure ourselves and our abilities.

As you ascend the rungs of the business, be prepared for what might happen when things don't go according to plan.

Falling from a top job is not a disaster if you know how to handle it.

After all, you will have gained experience and expertise, both of which are transferable skills.

WANT TO KNOW MORE? Before Herodotus, history was myth, song, legend, hand-me-down stories and fairytales woven together into a vision of a heroic age of gods and men.

Herodotus changed all that with his *Histories*, written in 440 BCE.

Herodotus kicks off his history with an immediate statement of intent.

He intends to put real research into his work and he wants events, and their causes, recorded so that they won't be forgotten.

Herodotus was writing about the rise of the Persian Empire and the roots of the (unsuccessful) Persian invasion of Greece.

Herodotus writes about the confrontation of East and West and sets about travelling to all points of the compass to gather evidence.

Pessimistically, he concludes that the differences between the peoples of the East and West are such that they could never live in harmony.

....

> **Honour and glory shall go to the victors!**
>
> *(at victoribus decus, gloriam)*
>
> Tacitus. Annals 1.67

THEME: COMPETITORS

CHECKPOINT: All businesses have people in them.

All businesses are in competition with other businesses.

Therefore, at any one point, thousands of people are in competition with thousands of others, even if they are not at the forefront of 'the battle'.

No wonder Sun Tzu's 6th century BCE book *The Art of War* has been adopted and revised by business gurus as a textbook for how win battles in the field of commerce.

Winning is a wonderful feeling. Experts say that winning increases testosterone, which in turn increases dopamine. Dopamine is wonderful for motivation!

The same effect is seen virtually, in online gaming.

Enjoy your business successes. Ensure you celebrate your wins and include everyone who has been involved in the win in your celebrations.

WANT TO KNOW MORE? September 9, 9 CE was a day Rome never forgot.

A Roman general by the name of Publius Quintilius Varus was ambushed by Germanic tribes in the Teutoberg Forest and three whole legions were mown down.

The legionary standards were taken by the enemy as spoils of war.

Augustus was famously claimed to have been found banging his head against doors and wailing aloud, *"Quintili Vare, legiones redde!"* ("Quintilius Varus, give me back my legions!").

Varus couldn't do that. He committed suicide and died without seeing the return of the legionary standards.

Five years later, enter Germanicus, the dashing nephew of the new Emperor Tiberius.

With decisive victories, he takes back the land lost to the Germanic tribe and wins back two of the standards.

Germanicus. Winner!

....

> **Does it all seem so wonderful just because it was done back in 'the good old days'?**
>
> *(mirum videtur quod sit factum iam diu?)*
>
> Livius Andronicus. Ajax The Whip Bearer. Frag. 15

THEME: **STRATEGY**

CHECKPOINT: You won't be surprised to learn that the word nostalgia is made up from the ancient Greek words; '*νόστος*' – ('nostos') – meaning a homecoming and '*ἄλγος*' – ('algos') – meaning an ache or pain.

Nostalgia is an aching for the home you want to return to. It's a yearning to get back to something that you remember with warmth and fondness.

You'll often hear people yearning for 'the good old days', when everything was better and simpler. I don't personally believe that life was better, say, 'pre-internet'. And I remember it well. But, like everything in life, there is an element of truth in people's desire to look back fondly.

Not everything we do today is perfect. There are lessons to be learned from the past.

Next time you hear someone say, 'it was so much better then', ask them why, and open up your mind to the possibility that the past can still offer relevance.

I mean, look. What's this book all about?

WANT TO KNOW MORE? Livius Andronicus (born about 284 BCE, died around 204 BCE) was the first Roman to start writing Latin literature. He translated Homer's *Odyssey* from Greek to Latin and he wrote a number of tragedies with titles like *Ajax* (a Greek warrior who fought against Troy) and *Achilles* (the principal Greek fighter at Troy).

He liked writing plays about the heroes of the Trojan War. But then, in his time, Rome was feeling pretty heroic.

When Livius Andronicus was 20, the Romans delivered a thumping defeat on their first real foreign enemy – Carthage (on the coast of modern-day Tunisia). The Romans were feeling good about themselves. Their confidence started to breed a heroic Roman 'culture'.

....

> **A lobster will give birth to an elephant before that happens.**
>
> *(atque prius pariet lucusta Lucam boevem)*
>
> Naevius. The Punic War. Frag. 65-66

THEME: STRATEGY

CHECKPOINT: There's no point banging your head against a brick wall.

Some things will never ever happen.

It is important to be utterly realistic in business.

Thinking you will double in size by the end of the year just because you had one recent success may not be achievable.

But thinking that you might incrementally grow is sensible.

The difference between outlandish forecasts for the future and a measured approach is enormous.

The former encourages rash expenditure and delivers dashed hopes.

The latter brings a steadiness to the business that both employees and outsiders will admire.

WANT TO KNOW MORE? Naevius was born around 270 BCE and died about 199 BCE.

Naevius was a Roman, with a capital 'R'.

Yes, he too (like yesterday's author, Livius Andronicus) wrote plays based on Greek dramas, and yes, he too had a predominant interest in the Trojan War.

But he was innovative as well.

Naevius was the first Roman to write 'Roman Plays'.

Drawing on both Roman history and contemporary events, Naevius brought the heroics of true Romans to the stage.

Interestingly, this type of play never really became popular with the Roman dramatists who were to follow Naevius. Instead of Naevius' 'lobster and elephant', today we say, 'Pigs might fly!'.

> **Why go chasing after the one that's run off?**
>
> *(τί τὸν φεύγοντα διώκεις;)*
>
> Theocritus. Idylls 11.75

THEME: LEADERSHIP

CHECKPOINT: Sometimes, you've just got to let it go.

A key employee leaves. They're happy in their new job; why keep pestering them to come back? Presumably they found something more to their liking in the new company. And if you try to tempt them back by matching the offer they received, you will almost certainly get the response: "Why didn't you offer that before I left?"

Concentrating on what you already have and recognizing want you do not want to lose are priorities in business.

It's so much harder to retrieve something than to retain something.

So look after your customers and your employees.

Make sure they don't leave by reminding yourself of what you would lose if they left.

WANT TO KNOW MORE? Today, September 12, 490 BCE, is held by some to be the traditional date for the Battle of Marathon. It's a good guestimate, shall we say.

The Battle of Marathon took place during the first attempt by the Persians to invade Greece.

The famous Greek playwright Aeschylus fought in this battle but frustratingly does not give us a first-hand account. (Or if he did, we don't have it).

The Greek army of (mainly) Athenian citizens numbered around 10,000.

The Persian force numbered around 200,000.

The Persians were defeated, losing some 6,500 men, while the Greeks, using clever strategy, lost just 200.

The battle is remembered as the first in a number of unsuccessful assaults by the mighty Persians. Greece was to withstand each attack with great cunning and bravery.

> ### Each of us is the architect of our own fortune.
>
> *(fabrum esse suae quemque fortunae)*
>
> Appius Claudius Caecus. Sententiae (Quoted by Sallust. Letters to Caesar 1.1.2)

THEME: PERSONAL DEVELOPMENT

CHECKPOINT: Well. I think today's quote should be copied and pasted onto every bathroom mirror in the land. In a sense it's the perfect summary of all motivational sayings.

Personal development is the only way you can be the architect of your own fortunes.

A combination of ongoing training, education and experience is an improvement process that will make you a more competent and interesting person in the world of work.

Make sure both your training and experience are not too narrowly defined.

Experience can be working abroad, training can be learning a new language.

Make sure your place of work offers you the opportunity and time to make yourself the best you can be.

WANT TO KNOW MORE? It's the names of today's author that tell the story.

Appius Claudius Caecus (and his nickname *'Centimanus'*, meaning 'hundred-handed') was born around 340 BCE and died about 273 BCE.

He was responsible for the construction of the Appian Way (named after him, obviously), a long road that led from the Forum in Rome to Brindisi on the heel of Italy. Brindisi was as important to the ancient Romans as it is to modern Italians, being the jumping off point for Greece.

His second name tells us he was from an old and respected noble family (*'gens Claudia'*), which immediately fast-tracked him to responsible positions and ensured he would reach high office.

The name Caecus refers to the blindness he contracted in old age.

His nickname *'Centimanus'* was given to him because of his prodigious multi-tasking skills.

He turned his hand to law and finance, road and aqueduct construction, and literature, focusing on grammar and poetry.

> **Let's notice the mistakes that we are most prone to making. (Different people will make different errors). These will be pretty obvious. Some things we do are pleasurable, others painful.**
>
> *(σκοπεῖν δὲ δεῖ πρὸς ἃ καὶ αὐτοὶ εὐκατάφοροί ἐσμεν - ἄλλοι γὰρ πρὸς ἄλλα πεφύκαμεν - τοῦτο δ' ἔσται γνώριμον ἐκ τῆς ἡδονῆς καὶ τῆς λύπης τῆς γινομένης περὶ ἡμᾶς)*
>
> Aristotle. Nicomachean Ethics 1109b

THEME: PERSONAL DEVELOPMENT

CHECKPOINT: We looked yesterday at the importance of training, education and experience.

There is another dimension to this. We need to notice what things we are doing less well and focus on improving those things.

This is not meant to be a message that we should strive for 100% perfection in all things.

Obviously, some things that we aren't very good at can be done by others. We can't all do everything (as Vergil himself once said; see January 20).

But in those cases, where we need others to fill in our gaps, we need to make sure that we are able to delegate properly. Are we properly resourced to manage all our tasks in an optimal way?

Be your own manager. Watch what you're doing. Look out for strengths and weaknesses. That way you can maximize the former and minimize the latter.

WANT TO KNOW MORE? You might have heard of the expression, 'Management By Walking About'.

It's the idea that managers get up from behind their desks and walk around the workplace, meeting people and getting first-hand experience of what is going on.

There is some evidence that the philosopher Aristotle (384 BCE – 322 BCE) did the same thing in his school of philosophy.

He would walk and talk with students, who would follow him and hang on his every word.

Plato also sometimes liked to stroll around chatting, so maybe Aristotle borrowed the idea from him.

This walking and talking would provide plenty of material for the comedy writers of the time, who, like today, enjoyed taking potshots at celebrities.

> **Unless you speak more clearly, we can't understand you.**
>
> *(non intelligimus, nisi si aperte dixeris)*
>
> Pacuvius. Antiopa Frag. 7-10

THEME: **PRESENTATIONS/MEETINGS/DOCUMENTS**

CHECKPOINT: Don't mumble! Don't look at floor while you're speaking!! Maintain eye contact!!!

I can hear the schoolteachers of my day barking instructions at me as I stood before the class to deliver my talk on 'whatever'.

We aren't trained to speak. Oratory is not an A Level.

Yet it is something that many of us will be called to do at some point in our working lives.

Some people are naturals at this. Others go weak at the knees at the mere thought of having to stand up in front of a group of people.

Speak slowly and clearly and avoid using long words.

And talk as if you're addressing a single person right at the back.

That way, everyone will think you're addressing them personally.

WANT TO KNOW MORE? The nearest land mass to ancient Rome was the North African coast of modern-day Tunisia. And the biggest city there was Carthage.

The city was at the centre of a huge trading empire and was Rome's most obvious enemy.

Rome fought Carthage three times in the course of 120 years, between 264 BCE and 146 BCE.

It was all about control of power in the Mediterranean.

Today's quote comes from Pacuvius, who was born right in the middle of these wars.

So many of the early Roman writers who we have already heard about (such as Plautus, Terence, Lucilius, Ennius and Livius Andronicus) were writing against a backdrop of real or threatened war.

The Romans never forgot their first 'proper' enemy and anti-Carthaginian propaganda would still be around many years after Rome burnt Carthage to the ground.

> **Everyone seeks knowledge. It's in our DNA.**
>
> (*πάντες ἄνθρωποι τοῦ εἰδέναι ὀρέγονται φύσει*)
>
> Aristotle. Metaphysics 980a.22

THEME: THE WATERCOOLER

CHECKPOINT: Do you want to hear something amazing?

Fancy some juicy gossip?

Do you want to know what I know?

Would you like to know more about the job?

Would you like to know more about your boss?

Of course!

We all want to be in the know. It's human nature (as Aristotle reminds us today).

But be careful.

Make sure you can differentiate between the knowledge that will definitely help you and the knowledge that is just tittle-tattle.

Filling your head with useless information is not a good use of your brain.

WANT TO KNOW MORE? You might have heard of physics.

But what on earth is metaphysics?

Aristotle's book, *Metaphysics*, written well over 2,000 years ago, is today regarded as one of THE greatest books of philosophy ever written.

So, what's it all about then, eh?

Answer this one question and you'll get close to an answer:

What is existence?

And if you get the right answer you go on to understand The Meaning of Life.

Simple.

Actions speak louder than words

(ἀξιοτεκμαρτότερον τοῦ λόγου τὸ ἔργον εἶναι)

Xenophon. Memorabilia 4.4.10

THEME: **PERSONAL DEVELOPMENT**

CHECKPOINT: There is nothing more irritating than people who talk a good talk, but don't deliver.

The number of times I've heard:

"We thought of that idea ages ago. We just didn't execute it."

Or, "I've got a brilliant idea, why don't we do this?"

The dreaded 'we' in that last sentence denotes a nameless and faceless group of people, none of whom think it's their responsibility to actually do anything.

At the end of the day, business is all about action.

As I've written in these pages before, Vision without Action is Hallucination.

History only records the achievements of business, not the wish lists.

WANT TO KNOW MORE? In 399 BCE, the great philosopher Socrates was put on trial for corrupting the minds of the young people of Athens. He was also accused of not believing in the gods of the city state.

He was found guilty and sentenced to death.

This is what happens when you keep asking the question 'What is it?'. You get to challenge anything and everything. Athens at that time was in a fragile state, with many citizens questioning whether democracy itself was the right form of government.

In this atmosphere, Socrates could easily have been seen as undermining the state.

Socrates committed suicide by drinking hemlock, a highly poisonous plant.

Xenophon's *Memorabilia*, from which today's quote comes, is a defence of Socrates and a reminder that everyone who came into contact with him actually benefitted from the philosophical discussions they had.

....

> **He was unable to say, "Everything's OK."**
> **Instead he said: "It *will* be OK."**
>
> *("Est bene" non potuit dicere, dixit: "Erit.")*
>
> Suetonius. Domitian 23.2

THEME: LEADERSHIP

CHECKPOINT: Be careful choosing your words.

People hang on to every syllable when there is something difficult to report.

Employees will listen acutely for versions of the expression 'cutbacks'. It will sound awfully like 'redundancies' to some.

Investors and analysts will pore over every word of a company report looking for clues to the company's current state of health.

In personal reviews, both managers and employees will want to be exact with their wording. A slip of the tongue could mean the difference between a good review and a bad one.

If your message is particularly sensitive, get one or two people to read the words carefully and give you some feedback.

Sometimes, someone from outside the business can see or hear things which you might not have at first intended.

WANT TO KNOW MORE? Today was a big 'transition' day in the ancient Rome of 96 CE.

After much scheming, told to us in some detail by the Roman historian Suetonius, the Emperor Domitian was assassinated.

Domitian was somewhat of an enigma. Some writers at the time portray him as a sadistic tyrant. The longer historical view suggests he was certainly authoritarian and maybe more 'king-like' than he should have been.

The 'transition' was from a string of 'bad' emperors to a string of 'good' ones.

Domitian was succeeded by Nerva, who is known as the first of 'the good emperors'.

As it happens, today is the birthday of the second of 'the good emperors', Trajan, born in 53CE. He won't wait long to be emperor.

Just 15 months after Nerva, in fact.

....

I hardly ever see my husband at home. He is often away overseas on important global business. He takes his job very seriously.

(ἀλλὰ πόσιν μὲν ὁρῶ παῦρον χρόνον ὀφθαλμοῖσιν οἴκῳ ἐν ἡμετέρῳ, πολέων γάρ οἱ ἔργον ἑτοῖμον μόχθων, τοὺς ἐπὶ γαῖαν ἀλώμενος ἠδὲ θάλασσαν μοχθίζει πέτρης ὄγ' ἔχων νόον ἠὲ σιδήρου καρτερὸν ἐν στήθεσσι)

Moschus. Megara 41

THEME: TIME MANAGEMENT

CHECKPOINT: Even with the benefit of the internet, Skype, WhatsApp, Facetime and all the other many modes of connectivity, we still need to travel. In fact, air travel is still increasing year-on-year. Air travel is time-consuming and tiring. If your job entails a lot of travel overseas, make sure everyone knows your schedule.

It's much easier to understand the complexities of such travel if you can map out the chunks of time when you are not available.

Finding the right time to stay in contact will avoid rushing round airports with your mobile phone wedged between your ear and your shoulder, your passport and boarding card clamped in one hand and the other wheeling your suitcase.

That's the scene you see most often in airports and that's the scene that causes most stress, in my experience. (Along with loss of passport and boarding card.)

WANT TO KNOW MORE? Although there are precious few women writers from the world of ancient Greece and Rome, women play key roles in a great deal of the literature. The characters of Andromache, Cassandra, Helen, Penelope and Dido, for example, are intrinsic to so many of the plots.

Sometime around 150 BCE, Moschus, from Syracuse, Sicily, wrote a poem in which Hercules' wife and mother bemoan the absence of Hercules, labouring, as he did, the world over.

It's a soft poem making a hard point. The first word is 'mother' and we are brought immediately into a private, domestic scene, full of tears and unhappiness – at one point, Hercules' wife, Megara, is crying tears 'as big as apples'.

The domestic scene is rocked by the reminder that Hercules, driven insane by the goddess Hera, has slaughtered his own children.

Strong stuff.

> **Oh, how so very often bad times give rise to good things!**
>
> *(o, quam saepe malis generatur origo bonorum!)*
>
> Rutilius Namatianus. De Reditu Suo 491

THEME: PERSONAL DEVELOPMENT

CHECKPOINT: We are used to thinking that bad times can herald good ones.

'Every cloud has a silver lining', we hear ourselves chirpily say.

'Something good will come of this', we might say on more solemn occasions.

The truth is that misadventures can indeed lead to good adventures, but only if you take time to learn from them.

Learning from any type of mistake is important, from cock-up to catastrophe.

If the learning process is positive, then you will get the most out of it.

Storming through the workplace trying to find 'culprits' is not a positive process.

Unless the mistake marks persistent bad behaviour or wrongdoing by an individual, firing someone or finding someone to blame is not the answer.

Examine what happened.

Is it possible to avoid such mistakes? Can the experience be turned into a positive benefit?

WANT TO KNOW MORE? Rutilius Namatianus was from Toulouse, France. He had been brought up a Roman, as had generations before him ever since Julius Caesar conquered that region some 450 years earlier, in 58 BCE.

Rutilius Namatianus is the last of classical Latin poets, ending a period of 700 years since Livius Andronicus started writing epic poetry around 250 BCE.

Rutilius Namatianus' book *Going Home* was written about his journey from Rome to his hometown between September 22 and November 21 416 CE. He was writing at a time when Rome's decline was leading fast to its inevitable fall. Rome had suffered three days of brutal onslaught at the hands of Alaric, King of the Visigoths.

As is so often the case, we don't have the whole book, but what we do have is entertaining and important.

> **It's a fortunate person who can understand
> how anything and everything works.**
>
> *(felix qui potuit rerum cognoscere causas)*
>
> Vergil. Georgics 2.490

THEME: PERSONAL DEVELOPMENT

CHECKPOINT: The world of business has a complex set of rules, regulations, guidelines, '*modus operandi*', systems, protocols and procedures.

Each business is different from the next, which is surprising, but it evidences the fact that once you get different combinations of humans involved, you get any number of different outcomes.

It takes time to understand how a workplace system operates. Recognizing how complex and differentiated organizations can be, look out for the new people coming into the workplace for the first time.

Lend a helping hand and an attentive ear when you think they might be floundering.

WANT TO KNOW MORE? On September 21, 19 BCE, the greatest poet of them all, Vergil, died in Brindisi.

He had set out earlier that year to travel through Greece and Asia, no doubt to research further and deeper into themes for his masterwork, the *Aeneid*.

We know that he was devoting a lot of time to what he called 'valuable learning'.

He reached Athens, where he met with the Emperor Augustus, who persuaded Vergil to abandon his trip. We are not quite sure why. Maybe Augustus could tell that Vergil was frail.

On their way back from Athens to Italy, they stopped in Megara, where Vergil became seriously ill. It was summer. The heat was intense. That would not have helped.

They carried on and made it to a port where a ship carried them to Brindisi.

Knowing he was at death's door, Vergil asked two friends to destroy the *Aeneid* because it was unfinished to his satisfaction.

Working on instructions from the Emperor Augustus, the friends ignored Vergil's request. They all knew that the book was 99.99% finished and was a masterpiece.

> **A good reputation shines brightly in dark times.**
>
> *(bona fama in tenebris proprium splendorem tenet)*
>
> Publilius Syrus. Sententiae 83

THEME: PERSONAL DEVELOPMENT

CHECKPOINT: Word gets out, as they say.

If you are someone whose (good) reputation preceded them, things go very smoothly indeed.

You get headhunted. You get promoted. You get listened to.

Same goes for companies as a whole.

You are talked about. You are liked by customers. You are attractive to investors. You gain a good reputation by having good values and sticking to them through thick and thin. It's the measure of a company that it can stay consistent through the difficult times.

When the going gets tough, a good reputation is one of the strongest assets you can have.

WANT TO KNOW MORE? The *Ludi Romani games* ended on September 19, and it was customary to follow such games with three days of market fairs. What sort of foods might we find in a Roman market?

Well, almost exactly the same as you can find in any farmer's market today.

Apples	Figs	Mutton
Asparagus	Fish (watch sell-by dates)	Olives
Bread	Geese	Onions
Carrots	Grapes	Oysters
Cheese	Honey	Pears
Chicken	Lamb	Pomegranates
Chickpeas	Leeks	Sausages
Duck	Melons	Strawberries
Eggs	Milk	Wild boar

> **The job's been done quickly enough when it's been done well enough.**
>
> *(sat celeriter fieri quidquid fiat satis bene)*
>
> Augustus (Quoted in Suetonius. The Deified Augustus 25.4)

THEME: TIME MANAGEMENT

CHECKPOINT: 'We need it ASAP.' 'I needed it yesterday.'

There is no doubt that the speed of operations has increased. Everything is wanted as soon as it's asked for.

It would be very rare to hear: 'Please take as much time as you need.'

But you should insist that you are given the right time to do the job properly. Every task in the workplace takes time to accomplish. Even the mundane jobs are prescribed by time.

If you are rushing out of the office and you need a document copied quickly, the photocopier won't speed up just because you're the boss.

When you are tasked to do a piece of work, make sure you have the time to do it to your satisfaction. You might even need an hour or so to plan out how long it will take.

Managing your time is an important part of being professional in the workplace.

WANT TO KNOW MORE? Augustus, born today in 63 BCE in the city of Rome, holds immense status in Roman history. Not just because he became the first emperor of Rome, after half a millennium of Republicanism, but because he is considered to be one of the most significant leaders in all history.

Inevitably there have been plenty of biographies written about Augustus, but one thing that has never excited historians is his personality.

You could think at first glance that he was a bit dull.

He was born into a pretty nondescript family. He lucked out by being named Julius Caesar's heir. He was a bit 'old school', eating modestly, living modestly and dressing modestly.

But with cold, calculated, precision engineering he step-by-step set about a strategy that made him the first ruler of the Roman Empire.

> **Many people are just bent on contradicting every point made. But they go about it in the wrong way. These people would do well to look to the old saying: 'Let that be your opinion and let this be mine.'**
>
> *(ἔθος περὶ παντὸς ὁμοίως, ὀρθῶς δ᾽ ἀντιλέγειν, οὐκέτι τοῦτ᾽ ἐν ἔθει. καὶ πρὸς μὲν τούτους ἀρκεῖ λόγος εἷς ὁ παλαιός· "σοὶ μὲν ταῦτα δοκοῦντ᾽ ἔστω, ἐμοὶ δὲ τάδε.")*
>
> Euenus. Fragments 1

THEME: THE WATERCOOLER

CHECKPOINT: Petty squabbles or tiffs at work are invariably pointless and often painful. And there's always one person who seems set on stirring things up, isn't there?

The best thing you can do is not let yourself be drawn into silly debates.

It's a fact of life that some people love to recruit others into their own view of the world. These might be tempting – it could be an interesting debate, or a trivial one, but how you feel about the world is a matter for you, and no one else.

These gossip sessions can become dangerous liaisons.

You might casually agree with someone because you can't be bothered to debate the point or because you are busy. But then you might find yourself unwittingly recruited as a witness in a follow-up debate on something you don't really subscribe to.

Keep clear of gossip and tittle-tattle before it engulfs you and starts following you around!

WANT TO KNOW MORE? So much literature of the ancient Greeks and Romans is lost to us. Many manuscripts have made difficult journeys through the years and end up as fragments. Some great works are known to us because they are referred to by other important writers.

Many individuals are referred to, and some of them we can cross-reference in various works and pull together a partial scrapbook of their lives. One such character is the Greek philosopher Euenus, who lived approximately at the same time as Socrates.

He appears almost ghostlike to us, so little do we know. He was, however, mentioned by both Plato and Aristotle and was respected in his day.

He left us just a few lines out of what, we assume, might have been a much larger body of work.

> ## Seize the opportunity, go on!
> ## And a make a virtue out of necessity.
>
> *(arripe, quaeso, occasionem et fac de necessitate virtutem)*
>
> Jerome Letters 54.6

THEME: PERSONAL DEVELOPMENT

CHECKPOINT: An opportunity arises.

It's one you are perfectly positioned to take up.

Go for it!

It's rare that these chances come in your working life.

It could be an opportunity to do something that the boss personally witnesses.

Or to lead something that will stretch you and test your managerial skills.

Go for it!

You'll soon realize that those who succeed in business are not those who are slow in coming forward.

And look at it this way. If you don't take the chance while it's staring you in the face, somebody else will.

And it could be months, or years, before the next opportunity arises.

WANT TO KNOW MORE? Jerome (born about 345 CE, died around 420 CE) liked to travel.

He was born in the Roman province of Dalmatia, which today covers the countries along the east coast of the Adriatic (Croatia, Bosnia and Herzegovina, Montenegro and Albania).

Exactly where he was born is not certain, but he wasn't too bothered by his birthplace either because from a young age he started to travel.

In his twenties, Jerome visited Gaul (France) and then the eastern Mediterranean.

He spent six years (373 CE – 379 CE) as a kind of monk in Syria.

He then went north to Istanbul, before heading off to Rome.

Three years later he was off to Palestine and then to Egypt.

Finally he settled in Bethlehem and stayed there until his death.

What did the Romans ever do for us? Well, built good transport links, clearly.

> In truth, very many people aim for the highest yield as soon as is possible, making no provision for the future, as if they are living from one day to the next.
>
> *(fructum vero plerique quam uberrimum praesentem consectantur, nec provident futuro tempori, sed quasi plane in diem vivant)*
>
> Columella. On Agriculture 3.3.6

THEME: FINANCE

CHECKPOINT: The most important imperative for any business is to stay in business. Whilst there are some businesses that have successfully traded non-stop for hundreds of years, others barely make it through a decade. The biggest mistake businesses can make is racing to make quick profit. Slow and steady is much more attractive than crash and burn.

It is also important that you set aside cash for a rainy day. At some point there could be a cash flow crisis – lending yourself money is much easier, and far cheaper, than going cap-in-hand to a bank.

You might see an opportunity to expand into something. If you've milked your businesses, expansion is always hard to do. Just make sure you have the resources to 'fix the barn roof while the sun is shining'.

WANT TO KNOW MORE? Columella lived roughly between 4 CE and 70 CE. The chapters of his book look like episodes of a TV farming show:
1. How to choose your land, select your staff and secure access to water.
2. How to look after your land, plough, add manure and grow various types of crops.
3. & 4. How to create a vineyard and look after vines.
5. How to measure out the land. The growing of elms and olive trees.
6. Looking after livestock – cattle, horses and mules.
7. Looking after sheep, goats, pigs and dogs. Cheesemaking.
8. Poultry and fishponds.
9. Cattle and bees.
10. Garden management.
11. Month-by-month responsibilities of the farm manager.
12. Duties of the farm manager's wife: pickling, preserving fruit, making wine and salting pigs.

> **You see the threats, abuse and insults to which we are exposed?**
>
> *(vides quot periculis quot contumeliis quot ludibriis simus obnoxii)*
>
> Pliny The Younger. Letters 3.14.5

THEME: INTERNET

CHECKPOINT: I remember once receiving a letter at my office with child-like writing on the envelope.

When I opened it, it was a death threat. It was traced, fairly quickly in fact, to a disgruntled ex-employee who had suffered a severe breakdown.

Although I was advised he was not a threat, I must confess to having looked over my shoulder for a good few months afterwards.

In my career I only ever received one other 'hate letter', but curiously, whilst specifically addressed to me, it was not for or about me. Odd.

The police investigated both these, as they should any threats, abuse or insults you receive in the workplace.

The internet has ramped up the 'insult' game. Ask anyone in public life. Receiving just two threatening letters might be considered trivial today.

Trolling and defaming online is widespread. Report it and talk about it.

Don't keep it bottled up.

WANT TO KNOW MORE? Next to Cicero stands Pliny in terms of what we know about a roman author.

His letters tell us so much about himself, his connections, how he lived and the people around him.

He had the standard Roman upbringing – a full private education followed by military service in Syria. On his return to Rome he rose through the famous '*cursus honorum*', which was the official way to rise through the ranks of the Roman civil service.

He navigated himself through the choppy waters of the Emperor Domitian's reign, eventually becoming chair of the Senate.

He was married three times but had no children.

To be continued . . .

> **One can surely hope that everyone will get behind
> a project which will be profitable to all.**
>
> *(certaque spes omnes libentissime adgressuros
> opus omnibus fructuosum)*
>
> Pliny The Younger. Letters 10.41.2

THEME: PROJECT MANAGEMENT

CHECKPOINT: There are many times in business when it's a case of 'all hands on deck'. You need everyone in the team, or department, or even the entire company, to get behind something.

Don't assume that everyone will pull their weight.

People bring to work all sorts of beliefs about who they are and what can be expected of them.

Some people will hear the cry for 100% participation and assume it does not include them – even though the combined effort will benefit everyone involved.

Sometimes you need to spell it out.

If you need full participation, make sure everyone is spoken to personally about it, either through line management or, if possible, by going around to everyone yourself. Explain what is needed and why it needs each and every individual to help. That way every single person can feel the value of participation.

WANT TO KNOW MORE? Pliny was considered to be an excellent manager. After Domitian died, he managed to work successfully with the aged and short-reigned Emperor Nerva.

He was appointed to the position of head of all state documentation.

Two years later, in 100 CE, he was appointed to be one of the consuls.

By now, Trajan was emperor.

Pliny was then given the job of overseeing the vitally important River Tiber, which involved the management and maintenance of the river banks, the river channel and the drainage of the city.

His final post was to be the emperor's special and personal representative in the province of Bithynia.

His was a prestigious and well-managed career. To be continued . . .

> **It is situated where the whole world connects, even the most remote places, as if it were the marketplace of one single global cosmopolitan city, introducing everyone to each other and, in so far as is possible, creating one race of people.**
>
> *(κεῖται γὰρ ἐν συνδέσμῳ τινὶ τῆς ὅλης γῆς καὶ τῶν πλεῖστον ἀπῳκισμένων ἐθνῶν, ὥσπερ ἀγορὰ μιᾶς πόλεως εἰς ταὐτὸ ξυνάγουσα πάντας καὶ δεικνύουσά τε ἀλλήλοις καὶ καθ᾽ ὅσον οἷόν τε ὁμοφύλους ποιοῦσα.)*

Dio Chrysostom. Discourses 32.36

THEME: **INTERNET**

CHECKPOINT: In my other books[10] I have argued that the internet has brought about an advancement in human capability comparable to our development of the opposable thumb some two million years ago. Our ability to communicate and learn and connect is now limitless. This advancement puts everyone at the centre of their own universe. A universe which contains everybody else. The internet is combining with three other forces that together rewrite how business is done:

Data – do you have a data plan in place?

Automation – are you automating as much of your business as you can, while developing the human touch?

New technology – are you constantly on the lookout for what technologies are available to help your business compete?

WANT TO KNOW MORE? Pliny the Younger (who we have been hearing about these last couple of days) bumped into the author of today's quote, Dio Chrysostom.

Towards the end of his life, Dio began legal proceedings against people who were accusing him of some wrongdoing. He asked Pliny to oversee the hearing of the case.

It's always good when characters who lived separate lives cross paths and provide us with a more three-dimensional view of history.

Dio was a philosopher and historian. He gives us his perspective on the province of Bithynia, which we can add to that of Pliny and gain a fuller picture of life in that part of the world under Roman rule.

Dio's quote is a description of Alexandria, a city so cosmopolitan and interconnected it was like a 'human internet' of its day.

> **Mmmm. Fidgeting. Obviously worried about something.**
>
> *(ὥσθ᾽ οὗτος ἤδη σκορδινᾶται κἄστιν οὐκ ἐν αὑτοῦ)*
>
> Aristophanes. Wasps 642

THEME: THE WATERCOOLER

CHECKPOINT: Body language.

We all know about it, superficially. Few of us bother to look into it in more detail. If you have time, you should. It's very revealing. It is non-verbal communication.

For example:

Crossing your arms tightly across your chest: you are putting up a barrier.

Drumming your fingers: you are bored and/or impatient.

Raising your eyebrows at someone: reveals you know and like that person.

Slumped shoulders: you are feeling insecure, lazy or unhappy.

Lack of eye contact: you are trying to deceive the other person.

This is a properly recognized science.

Why not get an expert into your workplace and find out more about it?

WANT TO KNOW MORE? Aristophanes, who lived approximately between 446 BCE and 386 BCE, wrote what is commonly called 'Old Comedy'.

Maybe one way of understanding Old Comedy is to contrast it with Greek Tragedy.

Greek Tragedy was about great, famous, serious, heroic celebrities falling apart, sinking fast and often meeting a terrible end.

Old Comedy was about little, unknown, insignificant, ordinary, unimportant people suddenly rising up and becoming important.

Comedy was as popular in Athens as it is today. It poked fun at famous people and lifted the spirits of Athenians when times were tough.

It is thought that during the Peloponnesian War, which lasted 27 years, there were up to 10 new comedies a year.

We only have nine and they are all by Aristophanes.

> **What is the most important thing?**
>
> *(quid est praecipuum?)*
>
> Seneca. Natural Questions 3. 11

THEME: PERSONAL DEVELOPMENT

CHECKPOINT: Prioritizing what you do is essential if you are to efficiently manage your workload.

Juggling projects and keeping many things permanently on the go is being like the performer who keeps multiple plates spinning at the same time.

The trick to prioritization is to make sure you give yourself 10 minutes at the end of each day to plan tomorrow.

What is the most important thing to achieve?

There can only be one.

Then what should be achieved next, once 'the important thing' is done? There might be a few.

Finally, what can you leave out, or ask someone to do, if you are unexpectedly asked to do something?

You can't replace 'the important thing' with another 'important thing' without ensuring that both can be achieved within an agreed timeframe.

WANT TO KNOW MORE? Seneca asks us this question today.

He asks: "What is the principal thing in our life?"

He answers his own question like this:

"The principal thing for us humans is to endure adversity with a happy heart. It is to put up with whatever happens as if it were something we wished to have happened."

This is called Stoicism.

When someone today 'grins and bears it' we say the person is being stoical.

Stoicism was appealing to many Romans.

For some, it helped endure the mad behaviour of some of the emperors, including Nero, under whom Seneca was to serve in an important capacity.

> **If it starts badly, it'll end badly.**
>
> *(κακῆς ἀπ' ἀρχῆς γίγνεται τέλος κακόν.)*
>
> Euripides. Aeolus 32

THEME: PROJECT MANAGEMENT

CHECKPOINT: Preparation is essential before you embark on any project. Enthusiasm is to be applauded, but throwing yourself head first into any task without thinking it through is a recipe for disaster.

You can easily end up producing work that is not what was required.

I've seen it happen many times. A customer contacts you with a request. You jump straight onto it and work furiously to fulfill what was asked for. Only much later do you realize that it wasn't needed for at least two weeks, because you'll need data that someone else has to supply.

As they say in all exams: Read the question!

Twice.

Prepare carefully.

Start well, and you can be certain the project will end well.

WANT TO KNOW MORE? Euripides was an activist. His plays are outspoken statements about his society.

Audiences came to the theatre for more than entertainment. They wanted guidance. They looked to writers like Aristophanes and Euripides to speak out. Sometimes they wanted their confusion to be encapsulated neatly into a sharp argument.

Euripides examined the ethics of war (he wrote during the time of the Peloponnesian War).

He looked at how war affected both public and private life. He also noted how family life was deteriorating due to the subjugation of women. Women were told to accept a servile life because it was nature's way. Often women had to buy into marriages to secure a prominent husband.

Euripides had plenty to say about this degrading attitude. In his brilliant play *Medea*, the star says: "We have to buy husbands with our money and serve them with our bodies." Powerful stuff.

> **It was just not possible that all these events could have happened by chance or without being pre-planned.**
>
> *(non haec omnia fortuito aut sine consilio accidere potuisse)*
>
> Caesar. The Gallic Wars 7.20

THEME: COMPETITORS

CHECKPOINT: You wake up one morning and say to yourself:

"Hang on. How did we suddenly lose all those customers? How come that upstart company with no experience in our sector has suddenly captured a huge market share?"

The answer is, you were caught sleeping.

In business, things don't happen mysteriously, or by chance.

The attack on your customer based was planned. And obviously it was executed very efficiently.

You need to keep your ears and your eyes open.

Watching the competition is essential.

Look for the early signs of strong competitive messaging.

If you were a customer, would you be attracted to this new company?

You have to be Aware, Agile and Action-oriented to give your emerging competitors the slip.

WANT TO KNOW MORE? On October 3, 52 BCE, the great leader of the Gauls Vercingetorix surrendered to Julius Caesar. Caesar had effectively now conquered Gaul (modern-day France).

Vercingetorix had pulled together and mobilized all the tribes of Gaul.

His army was immense, and Caesar was beaten a number of times, making the success of Caesar's invasion of Gaul far from certain.

Eventually Caesar cornered Vercingetorix, who was holed up at a place called Alesia.

With astonishing speed, Caesar surrounded Alesia with not one but two sets of fortifications in what became a famous 'doughnut' shaped arrangement. This kept Vercingetorix cooped up and it also blocked the reinforcements he needed to relieve him.

Vercingetorix was taken to Rome, imprisoned for eight years and eventually executed.

He is as heroic a figure to the French as Boudicca is to the British.

> **Thinking through the most useful thing you can do
> is the safest form of delay.**
>
> *(deliberare utilia mora tutissima est)*
>
> Publilius Syrus. Sententiae 151

THEME: STRATEGY

CHECKPOINT: Analysis of your own business can often be a revelation.

Do you know which products are more profitable than others, and why?

What actions should you be taking to improve profitability overall?

Have you got teams of people working on projects that are just using up time and resources without getting anywhere?

Is everybody fully employed?

What is the one thing you could do tomorrow that would be truly useful to the company?

Focusing on well-defined strategic action and acting on it is what drives businesses forward.

But take time to think it through carefully.

WANT TO KNOW MORE? Augustus liked old Roman tradition.

He was a little old-fashioned in many of the ideas he supported, particularly religious ones.

Bringing the Romans of his day back into touch with the traditions of the Roman Republic was one way to soften the obvious blow that the Republic was no more and that an emperor was now in charge.

One tradition he brought back was 'The Fast of Ceres'.

Way back in 191 BCE, the Sybilline books (the fount of all sacred knowledge) were consulted and it was determined that every five years, a fast was observed.

Nice idea, thought Augustus.

But instead of every five years, he ordained that it should happen every year, today, October 4.

> **Many fearful anxieties, brought by turbulent dreams at night, dissolve in the dawn.**
>
> (τὰ πολλὰ τῶν δεινῶν, ὄναρ πνεύσαντα νυκτός, ἡμέρας μαλάσσεται)
>
> Sophocles. Acrisius Frag. 65

THEME: PERSONAL DEVELOPMENT

CHECKPOINT: Stress. Between 2016 and 2017 in the UK, 12.5 million days were lost to work related stress, depression or anxiety.

I'm not an expert so I'm not going to give you any remedies. You should seek professional advice for this if you are suffering from these kinds of problems.

But we can sometimes easily magnify small events so that they grow out of all proportion. And what I can tell you is that sometimes problems seem less serious the next morning, particularly if you've had time to work them through with a partner, or a colleague at work.

Don't shoulder the burden of a worry all by yourself.

Go to bed knowing that you have determined to talk to someone.

Some problems, not all, are smaller than you think.

WANT TO KNOW MORE? Sophocles knew about war. His long life encompassed the two great, defining wars of the ancient Greek world. He was born into the 50-year struggle against Persia and as an old man he witnessed Greece tearing itself apart in its homegrown fight – the Peloponnesian War.

His father, Sophillus, was an arms manufacturer and clearly wealthy enough to make sure his son was well educated.

Sophocles became an outstanding and highly awarded playwright, writing over 120 plays – although only seven have survived intact.

A story of Sophocles in his own age has survived.

One of his sons, Iophon (also a playwright), accused him being insane.

It was a ruse to get his hands on his father's money.

Sophocles proved he was not mad by reciting a number of lines from one of his plays by heart.

That proved he wasn't mad? Families!

There's that force that prevents great success from being
the pure and unadulterated enjoyment that is should be.
This force blends together the good times, lending a kind
of ambiguity to human life.

*(Ἡ δὲ μηθὲν ἐῶσα τῶν μεγάλων εὐτυχημάτων ἄκρατον εἰς ἡδονὴν καὶ
καθαρόν, ἀλλὰ μίξει κακῶν καὶ ἀγαθῶν ποικίλλουσα τὸν ἀνθρώπινον βίον)*

Plutarch. Marius 23.1

THEME: **PERSONAL DEVELOPMENT**

CHECKPOINT: You might be in a job interview, or just reminiscing with
family and friends. Someone asks you for your greatest achievements and
suddenly your mind goes blank. Everything's a bit of a blur. It's weird,
isn't it?

You will have big wins in your career. You'll get well deserved promotions. There will be big celebrations. But as time goes on, they begin to
merge together into a haze.

Sounds a tad gloomy, doesn't it?

The point is, try to remember the good times. Try to remember your
achievements.

You are your best PR agent. Write your career up on a sheet of paper
and highlight every single personal win.

It's not being big-headed. It's just an assessment of your natural talents!

And let's be honest, it's unlikely anyone else is going to do it for you.

WANT TO KNOW MORE? On this day in 105 BCE, the Romans suffered a huge defeat.

They'd been stupid. They'd been disorganized.

Their enemy, tribes from southern France and Germany who were
working together, took advantage of two legionary commanders who were
not working together as a team.

Rome had been expanding out from the city itself for many years.

To be so thoroughly beaten (they say over 80,000 Romans were slaughtered) was a big setback. Rome needed to sort itself out. And, of course, it
did. Rome appointed a new general, Marius. Plutarch is writing about him
in today's quote. Marius set about overhauling and reforming the army.

This fundamental restructuring played an invaluable part in enabling
Rome's rise to domination.

> **The amount of life we actually live, is actually very small.**
>
> *(exigua pars est vitae, qua vivimus)*
>
> Seneca. De Brevitate Vitae 2.2

THEME: PERSONAL DEVELOPMENT

CHECKPOINT: Work hard.

Yes, but play hard too.

Too much time spent at work is a sign that there is something not working properly.

Of course, there will be occasions when you'll have to put in some extra time, but not every single day.

There's an official term for being in the workplace more than you should.

It's called 'presenteeism'. It's the polar opposite of absenteeism.

You work better if you find time to relax, look after yourself and have outside hobbies or pursuits.

You have to organize your life while you are at work.

Work is a big slug of time. Don't let it squeeze out Your Life.

WANT TO KNOW MORE? Today we hear again from Seneca and from his book *On The Shortness Of Life*.

As you might expect, it's a short book.

Seneca's book has an unnervingly contemporary feel to it.

It is a real reminder that people living 2,000 ago were troubled by exactly the same things we are today.

You hear writers talking about how time flies.

And here Seneca develops that thought even further.

He says that time rushes by so fast that almost all us find that our lives are drawing to a close just at the point when we are getting ready to live!

We all know of people who have worked hard all their lives and look forward to retirement, but then fall prey to some affliction just when they have time on their hands.

Make sure your life is conducted with Profit, Pleasure and Personal Progress, advises Seneca.

OCTOBER 8

> **With friends, make sure any remuneration is a fixed agreement.**
> **The same goes for your own brother. Put a smile on your face…**
> **and get a witness!**
>
> *(μισθὸς δ᾽ ἀνδρὶ φίλῳ εἰρημένος ἄρκιος ἔστω· καί*
> *τε κασιγνήτῳ γελάσας ἐπὶ μάρτυρα θέσθαι)*
>
> Hesiod. Works And Days 370

THEME: LEGAL

CHECKPOINT: Trust no one!

If you are going to hire a friend to do something (and be careful, it can often lead to all sorts of problems down the line), make sure you have everything in writing.

Even if you are hiring family members (an even worse idea, under most circumstances), make sure a proper contract is signed. And get it witnessed.

Business is business and trust is all well and good, but it's no substitute for a proper, clear, unequivocal, wriggle-free contract.

WANT TO KNOW MORE? Today's quote is one of my favourites. There's such humanity to it.

And the fact that it was written just under 3,000 years ago somehow gives it even greater zest.

Hesiod's world was one in which two great commodities were grown: corn and grapes.

These two would remain at the centre of the ancient Greek and Roman economies for centuries.

Olives, pears, figs and oranges were important too.

The people of Hesiod's time would have been natural stock-breeders, with lessons on breeding bulls, oxen, cows, lambs and horses passed down from father to son.

Cornfields and vineyards would keep your household sustainable.

Good stock-breeding could make you wealthy.

Hunting, fishing and beekeeping were also important activities in this simple but also, it appears, humorous and thoughtful world.

> **There is no journey if it doesn't have an endpoint.**
>
> *(nullum sine exitu iter est)*
>
> Seneca. Epistles 77.13

THEME: PROJECT MANAGEMENT

CHECKPOINT: Before you start any project, take time to map it out.
Treat it like a journey.
When is it due to start?
What colleagues do you need with you to accomplish your task?
What information will you need along the route, and when?
What resources do you need to accomplish the whole task?
And when will the project be completed?
No project should be without a completion date.

WANT TO KNOW MORE? There were four ways you could get from A to B in Roman times.
By boat, by animal (horse, donkey, camel), by cart or by foot.
None of them was comfortable, and all of them took a long time.
There is an expression, 'All roads lead to Rome', and this was in fact true.
The main arterial road system of Roman Italy spread out like tentacles from the centre. Wherever the Romans went, they either built roads or greatly improved the existing road network.
The routes all contained milestones so you knew exactly where you were, and how far you had to go; there were even private stop-overs and state-sponsored hostels.
Sea travel was highly seasonal and consisted of both long journeys across the Mediterranean as well shorter 'coastal hops'.
When you landed in a port, a road network would be ready and waiting to take you straight on to your next destination. It was extremely well organized.

> **How often the best brains lie hidden away!**
>
> (*ut saepe summa ingenia in occulto latent!*)
>
> Plautus. The Captives 165

THEME: HUMAN RESOURCES

CHECKPOINT: It is a wonderful feeling when you suddenly discover that hidden amongst the talent pool of the company are gifts you hadn't expected to find.

To find the hidden talent, you have to look for it.

When recruiting, we quite rightly want to know that the person has the correct skills for the job in question.

That should be the primary role of the interview.

But don't be afraid to enquire further, maybe after they've been hired.

What other skills do people have? What amazing hobbies? What unusual interests?

You never know, you might have someone in your business who is just the right person for a project, but who has come from completely the 'wrong' part of the business.

Get to know as much as you can about as many people as you can, and you might find you have more skills within the workforce than you realized.

WANT TO KNOW MORE? The characters in Plautus' plays are just like the audience.

They are ordinary people living ordinary lives.

They are real people using language the audience would readily understand.

Nothing of what the actors is saying is meant to be deeply philosophical, or highbrow.

Given that Plautus is one of the earliest Roman writers we have, this is quite a treat.

We get a glimpse into ordinary life some 200 years before people like Julius Caesar or Vergil.

The Latin is much looser than that of later, more formal and well-educated writers like Cicero.

Words elide together, and grammar goes awol; dialects slip in; foreign terms appear.

Just as they do today on TV and in the movies.

> **As they say, '*in vino veritas*'.**
>
> *(volgoque veritas iam attributa vino est)*
>
> Pliny The Elder. Natural History 14.142.

THEME: THE WATERCOOLER

CHECKPOINT: Oh dear.

You know what it's like.

You go for a quick drink after work with colleagues – 'just the one drink then I'm off home' – and before you know it two hours have slipped by and you're having a merry old time.

And why not? You work hard, you deserve a moment of relaxation.

Then a colleague comes up close and whispers to you a secret about someone else in the company.

Oops!

Now the cat is well and truly out of the bag.

The gossip mill is operating at full capacity and work tomorrow morning is going to be interesting. To say the least.

This is almost certainly what you might call the collateral damage of working 'up close and personal' with colleagues day in, day out.

The best advice is not to spread any gossip and keep an open mind.

Often stories told '*in vino veritas*' can be vastly exaggerated.

WANT TO KNOW MORE? Versions of the expression '*in vino veritas*' appear regularly in ancient literature.

Herodotus reports that if the Persians decided on something while drunk, they made a rule to reconsider it when sober.

Others have added that if the Persians came to a decision while sober, they made a rule to reconsider it when they were drunk.

And today in Rome is a day to celebrate all that wine can bring.

It is the festival of '*Meditrinalia*', an important day when wine tasting was not only strictly permitted, but widely encouraged!

....

> ### What is done cannot be undone.
>
> *(Τὰ μὲν δὴ τότε πραχθέντ᾽ οὐκ ἂν ἄλλως ἔχοι)*
>
> Demosthenes. Third Olynthiac 6

THEME: PERSONAL DEVELOPMENT

CHECKPOINT: It is always difficult to go back on something you have said, or to retract a document.

It's even harder to call back an email, undo a text, or erase a tweet.

There's a story in the media almost every day about someone being admonished for an online message sent many years ago which is now utterly regrettable.

One of the effects of our internet age is unfettered rapidity.

We see what we want, and we get it immediately. There is very little delay.

Yet delay is the one process that gives us time to engage our brain. What are we about to say? What are we about to write?

If there is the slightest doubt in your mind, don't do what you were going to do.

Time is cruel. It moves on very quickly and puts past actions beyond our grasp almost before we have realized it.

WANT TO KNOW MORE? On October 12 in 322 BCE, the professional speechwriter and orator Demosthenes committed suicide on the Greek island of Poros as he was being hunted down for execution.

Demosthenes was a true Athenian. He loved his city and everything it stood for. When it came under threat, first from Alexander the Great, and then Alexander's successor, Demosthenes stood up for his hometown. He knew Alexander would undo much of the political and cultural life of the city.

Many Athenians wanted to make peace with Alexander's regime, but for Demosthenes that would have been a sellout.

Demosthenes has been considered by many experts to be the greatest of all the ancient orators.

Amongst those experts is Cicero, an orator who also died for the city he loved.

....

Not everyone can come out on top every time. When you've
reached the top step on the ladder of fame you'll find it's tough
and you'll fall faster than it took you to get there.

(non possunt primi esse omnes omni in tempore.
summum ad gradum cum claritatis veneris,
consistes aegre et citius quam ascendas cades)

Decimus Laberius. (Quoted by Macrobius. Saturnalia 2.7.9)

THEME: **PERSONAL DEVELOPMENT**

CHECKPOINT: Businesses are pyramid shaped. The closer you get to
the top, the fewer jobs there are to be had and the more people there are
after them.

Even when you've got a top job, life doesn't get any easier. There will
be others trying to get the job you fought hard for and earned. You can't
blame them. They are only doing what you did.

This Darwinian 'survival of the fittest' in the workplace has been in
place ever since industrialization turned businesses into military-like
machines with 'direct reports' and the 'power of command' being situated
at key points throughout the hierarchy.

If you are ambitious, you have to keep striving to get 'higher'.

But make sure it's what you want.

WANT TO KNOW MORE? Decimus Laberius (born about 105 BCE,
died in 43 BCE) is a fascinating Roman character who lived in Rome at
the time of Julius Caesar's great rise to power.

He was a mime artist.

Now, when I write 'mime artist', you're immediately thinking of
Marcel Marceau.

Roman mime was nothing like that.

It was a form of theatre that very specifically was not about great tragedy, or about hilarious comedy. It was popular theatre for the masses and
it was about low-life situations. It was the kind of theatrical event that
your average Roman man-in-the-street would have gone to see for a right
rollicking night (or day) out.

Decimus knew Caesar well enough to lampoon him, even predicting he
was soon due for a great fall because he had reached as high a position as it
was possible for anyone to reach.

> **All good times are unstable and uncertain.**
>
> *(omnis instabilis et incerta felicitas es)*
>
> Seneca The Elder. Controversiae 1.1.3

THEME: LEADERSHIP

CHECKPOINT: Let's not get over-pessimistic, but we all know that life isn't one long holiday. There are good times. And there are bad times. Businesses often use the metaphor of sailing a ship.

Sometimes it will be plain sailing. Other times, you'll hit choppy waters.

The metaphor is useful because the environment in which businesses operate is as moveable and unpredictable as the sea.

We say, 'with a fair wind we should get everything done by next week.'

Again, as at sea, some winds are fair, and some winds are so against you the ship can fall apart. Keep the 'sea metaphor' in your mind.

When times are good, it's not being pessimistic to expect more turbulent times, it's just being realistic.

WANT TO KNOW MORE? If you had enjoyed a good and proper education in ancient Rome, you would be learning oratory and the law in secondary education.

To do this properly you would have needed textbooks with example speeches. They could be real or made up.

For example, it could have been an imaginary speech by Caesar deliberating on why he should or shouldn't cross the Rubicon.

Seneca the Elder (you might have guessed, correctly, he was Seneca the Younger's father) wrote such books for students.

By all accounts, he lived a very long life of 92 years (from around 54 BCE through to about 39 CE).

Given that his life spanned one the most exciting periods of history ever, he no doubt had plenty of speech material to work with!

> **Don't give in to misfortunes, but be bold, and face them head on!**
>
> *(tu ne cede malis, sed contra audentior ito)*
>
> Vergil. Aeneid 6.95

THEME: **LEADERSHIP**

CHECKPOINT: It isn't always plain sailing. It is when you hit tough times that leadership qualities come most to the fore. There are some things you can do to steady the ship.

First, just like when you are on airplane, it's helpful to hear from the captain about what is happening. Give out as much information as you can.

Second, a call for 'all hands on deck' can provide the right kind of rallying cry. Get people involved and busy. If you get buy-in to the possibility that everyone pulling together might solve many problems, you are likely to energize the workforce.

Finally, don't make wishy-washy speeches to 'the troops'. People can see through waffle, and in any case your body language is very likely to give things away.

WANT TO KNOW MORE? The truly magnificent and perennially influential poet Vergil was born on this day on 70 BCE.

He wrote three major works (the *Eclogues*, the *Georgics* and the *Aeneid*) and possibly a few minor pieces. If he had just written the *Eclogues* – ten neat and interconnected pastoral poems in a style developed by a Greek poet some 250 years earlier – Vergil would be highly acclaimed.

He next wrote the *Georgics*, which looks very much like a farming manual, but you soon realize Vergil has written one long, deep metaphor about the care and survival of humans in political times.

Then he wrote the *Aeneid*, a thrilling, fast-paced, action-packed story of the foundation of Italy. The book is laden with symbolism, clever wordplay and characterization, and the whole piece is so interconnected it feels like you are reading a finely embroidered tapestry.

It is a work of literary genius.

....

> **Wait until you have heard everything before you pass judgment.**
>
> *(ἐπειδὰν ἅπαντ᾽ ἀκούσητε, κρίνατε, μὴ πρότερον προλαμβάνετε)*
>
> Demosthenes. First Philippic 14

THEME: **THE WATERCOOLER**

CHECKPOINT: You're having a coffee break and someone collars you with a negative story about a fellow employee or rumour about a management decision.

It's human nature to be very engaged. We humans are hard-wired to hear and process worrying news as a matter of priority. So hear it. And process it. But don't overreact.

It is highly likely that what you are listening to is either not the full story, or is the story, but massively exaggerated. And, importantly, try to avoid criticizing anyone involved.

The point is, you won't have the full picture.

If you feel you need more information, go to the person whose job it is to keep you informed, rather than another colleague who might just give you an even more twisted version of the original story.

WANT TO KNOW MORE? The time between the Athens of Socrates and the Rome of Seneca was some 500 years.

In modern history, 500 years is a very long time. It's the span of time that separates us from characters like Leonardo da Vinci and Henry VIII in our European history, people who dressed very differently from us.

But the changes that took place in these ancient times were much more moderate.

Buildings, roads, ships and weaponry would have made gradual improvements for sure, but how you dressed remained remarkably consistent.

The ancient Greeks wore a '*himation*' which looks very much like a Roman '*toga*'.

They wore sandals like the Romans did; and they both had similar-looking pins, combs, nail files, razors and so on.

But the Greeks did modernize thinking in a way that would have astounded their ancestors.

And the Romans modernized multinational management, in a way that Alexander the Great would have envied.

....

> **It's hard to find good people.**
>
> *(rari quippe boni)*
>
> Juvenal. Satires 13.26

THEME: HUMAN RESOURCES

CHECKPOINT: If you ask any CEO what his top business priorities are, 'finding good talent' will be right up there. There are plenty of good people around. But very good people are rare.

It is essential you find a system to manage and retain the best people you have.

Clawing people back from the brink of leaving to go to another company is difficult; it reflects badly on an organization if it doesn't try to take preventative action in the first place.

A company's human capital is an invaluable asset, and to be able to retain good people you need them to know that you are taking an interest in them and giving them opportunities that will stretch them. You need to be able to offer training that will improve them. And you need to reward them. Salary is important, but once you know your person well you might find that other benefits count as well.

WANT TO KNOW MORE? It took time for the city of Rome to grow into the heaving mass of over one million people at the time Juvenal was writing. A combination of making treaties with neighbours, an expansionist programme into Italy and a slow but steady domination of the Mediterranean trade routes turned Rome into a truly cosmopolitan city.

Rome at its height was a city at the heart of an empire of over 45 million people.

Anyone who was able to get to Rome did so.

If you wanted to succeed, it was the only place in the world to go.

Rome was like London, New York and Shanghai all rolled into one.

Juvenal had plenty of characters to assassinate (in a literary way!) and plenty of cross-cultural clashes to record.

> **Nothing great is created suddenly.**
>
> *(Οὐδέν τῶν μεγάλων ἄφνω γίνεται)*
>
> Epictetus. Discourses 1.15.7

THEME: TIME MANAGEMENT

CHECKPOINT: If you ever attempt to start your own company don't be tempted to run before you can walk.

Things take time.

Most start-ups will make a loss in the first year, maybe even the first two years. There are one-off set-up costs that you'll need to fund (website, office, etc.) and you'll need to spend on promotional material to start attracting customers.

You will hope to break even in year two – this might take an extra year to achieve. But by the third or fourth year, you should be aiming to make modest profits.

Don't plan to make your enterprise an instant success; for most start-ups, this just doesn't happen. Give yourself time to learn how your business is growing. That way, you'll know what levers to pull when the time comes to put on a growth spurt.

WANT TO KNOW MORE? If you decide one day to sit down and read Epictetus, be prepared to be challenged.

Our modern day standards of success (good job, good promotion prospects and good salary) didn't really wash with Epictetus.

In fact, he thought they were trivial.

What you need to think about, he says, is whether you are living a happy life and whether you are a good person.

Everything else is incidental.

Central to this thinking and to achieving the status of 'good person' is to reconcile yourself to the fact that some things are in your power to control, and some things are not.

Maybe a quick list in two columns on one side of a blank sheet of paper is a way for you to start thinking like Epictetus.

One column is headed, 'Things I Can Control'. The other column, 'Things I Can't Control'.

> **He'll either find a way or make one.**
>
> *(inveniet viam aut faciet)*
>
> Seneca. Hercules 276

THEME: LEADERSHIP

CHECKPOINT: The purpose of leadership is to lead.

It is not a skill that everyone has. The idea that in a business there is natural leadership succession is nonsense. Just because you have been the deputy CEO does not mean you are automatically eligible to be the CEO once there is a vacancy. The two jobs are not the same.

Determination, smart tactics, shrewd expenditure, clever cost-cutting, skilful '360-degree' people management and an ability to keep an eye permanently on the endgame without flinching are the kind of skills you need.

These leaders will always have reserve strategies up their sleeves for when they need to break through obstinate barriers. These could be strong links to outside investors, or an ability to work wonders with the company's finances.

WANT TO KNOW MORE? Today's quote is attributed to the great Carthaginian general Hannibal, who was defeated at Zama in modern day Tunisia on this day in 202 BCE. Hannibal fled the battle scene and raced to Carthage to advise the city elders to make a peace deal with the Romans. Thirty city elders prostrated themselves in front of the triumphant Roman general Scipio and begged for peace.

The deal they got reduced Carthage to a small trading city. Rome refused them the right to fight without permission. As part of the peace deal, huge amounts of money, ships, weapons and, of course, the famous elephants, were handed over to the victorious Romans.

Hannibal eventually became leader of the city of Carthage and, in a somewhat ignominious end, died from an infection from a self-inflicted sword cut a few years later.

> **Why go into a pitch with the odds stacked against you?**
>
> **(*quid dispar certamen inis?*)**
>
> Ovid. Amores 2.61

THEME: LEADERSHIP

CHECKPOINT: Sales pitches are the routine competitive battles every business has to make.

It feels good to be invited to make a pitch. You have the opportunity to grow your business and make new connections. And often there is valuable PR to be had from a successful win.

Before you go into the pitch, do as much background work as you can.

Why have you been asked to pitch (is there a real chance of winning, or is it a long shot?).

What benefit is to be gained from pitching? Is there a good profit margin in the business if you win?

In short, not every pitch is worth going for. Commit your resources shrewdly.

WANT TO KNOW MORE? The poet Catullus is known for his heart-achingly passionate poetry written to a lady with a pseudonym. Catullus' girl 'Lesbia' was almost certainly a wealthy lady, from a highly respected Roman family, called Clodia Metelli, whose esteemed ancestor constructed the Appian Way (see September 13).

Catullus was followed by Cornelius Gallus (approximately 70 BCE – 26 BCE), an associate of Vergil, who committed suicide after apparently offending Octavian (soon to be Augustus). Nine lines of his work survives. His girl, possibly an ex-slave called Cytheris, was code-named 'Lycori'.

Next up was Tibullus, who wrote to 'Delia' (real name Plania). Propertius follows Tibullus. His lady was 'Cynthia', who might have been a prostitute called Hostia, who also wrote poetry.

Finally, we have Ovid. He has a lady called 'Corinna' in mind. But Ovid plays games. 'Corinna' might just be a pun on a Greek word for maiden. Ovid might have had many girls in mind. Or none.

> ## Three laid. Two hatched. One fed.
>
> *(Τρία μὲν τίκτει, δύο δ᾽ ἐκλέπει, ἓν δ᾽ ἀλεγίζει)*
>
> Musaeus. (Quoted by Aristotle. History of Animals 563a)

THEME: INNOVATION

CHECKPOINT: Many times in these pages I've stressed the importance of innovation.

We live in a time when original ideas are flourishing and there is a real appetite amongst consumers to try new things.

Innovation should be built in to your business, not bolted on.

Ideally there will be employees in all departments who are charged to look for new ways of doing things.

Many firms seek outside, professional help. If you go down this route, make sure the innovation company has strong case histories and reliable references.

Whichever route you go down, hedge your bets. Have more than one iron in the fire.

Innovation is a process, not a guaranteed instant delivery mechanism.

Through the process of innovation you will discover concepts that had never occurred to you previously.

Eventually you will have to whittle down your routes and at some point you will start heavily investing in just one.

WANT TO KNOW MORE? Musaeus was a bit of a legend. He was cited a number of times by the most eminent Greeks.

Euripides refers to him as being highly educated. Plato mentions him in the same breath as Homer. Socrates lists him amongst the people he would love to have conversed with – a kind of 'which people would you most like to have come around to dinner?' thought.

And we know that Aristotle refers to him, not just in today's quote, but elsewhere too.

Heck, even Vergil mentions him, saying he is one the people the favoured heroes of the past would surely be looking up to!

What do we know of Musaeus?

Sadly, very little, I'm afraid. Such is the passage of time.

....

> **Stand by your opinion.**
>
> (*in sententia permaneto*)
>
> Cicero. Pro Murena 65

THEME: PERSONAL DEVELOPMENT

CHECKPOINT: Everybody has an opinion, don't they? Even if they know zilch about the subject they are talking about they'll still offer a point of view.

And then there's the argumentative type. Sometimes you feel they are just arguing for the sake of it. If you have a point of view that you believe in, stick to your guns.

If you know you are going to be put on the spot and asked to defend your views, then spend time beforehand making a list of the reasons why you believe in your opinion. This will help to jog your memory when the time comes.

Hold on to your view for as long as you feel it is right. Sometimes you find that eventually people will come around to your way of thinking days, or even weeks, later.

Knowing you are not easily swayed gives you credibility in the workplace.

WANT TO KNOW MORE? If there was one person in Roman history who stuck to his guns, it was Marcus Tullius Cicero.

Cicero believed in the Roman Republic and would use great oratorical force to face down individuals he thought were undermining it.

His first big moment came in 63 BCE, when he convinced the Senate that a rogue senator was acting like a terrorist. By condemning the man, he in one fell swoop saved the Republic from ruin. Well that was *his* story.

He took on the big boys of his day. Pompey the Great, the enormously capable soldier whose power made him a permanent threat. Julius Caesar, whose power Cicero despised. And Mark Antony, whose claims to power after the assassination of Caesar must have made him look as terrifying as both Caesar and Pompey put together.

Cicero stood by the beliefs he held. And died for them too, executed by Antony's hitmen.

....

> **I'm just praying that you accomplish what you have in mind and urge you not to drag your feet. People are already talking about it.**
>
> *(Συνεύχομαι, ὑμῖν ἐκτελεῖν ἃ κατὰ νοῦν ἔχετε καὶ παρακελεύομαι μὴ βραδύνειν· οὐ γὰρ σιωπᾶται τὸ πρᾶγμα)*
>
> Popilius Laenas. (Quoted by Plutarch. Brutus 15.4)

THEME: PROJECT MANAGEMENT

CHECKPOINT: There's nothing worse than being in the middle of a project only to find everyone is talking about it, raising expectations and even interfering every now and then.

You really want to be left alone to get on with it!

So take control. You might choose to speed things up a little. You might need to work out of the office. You might decide it's time to manage expectations. This is always a good thing to do when you think others might have formed unrealistic ideas of what the scope and ambition of the project is.

Whatever you do, do something.

Falling into an annoyed silence will only aggravate the situation and get everyone asking even more questions.

WANT TO KNOW MORE? Julius Caesar was stabbed 23 times by his assassins. Only one of the wounds actually killed him.

The nervousness of the conspirators, led by Brutus (who died today in 42 BCE, in a battle against pro-Caesar forces) and Cassius, was evident in the panic and muddle of the attack itself, but also in the jittery actions of the wider group of conspirators involved.

A number of times, the conspirators thought they had been rumbled. Almost anything anyone said to them was taken as an example that their plans had been leaked.

Popilius Laenas, who gives us today's quote, unnerved the conspirators twice.

First he cornered Brutus and Cassius and told them to get on with the job. People are beginning to talk, he said. Soon after, he was seen to approach Julius Caesar as he arrived at the Theatre of Pompey, where the Senate was meeting that day. The conspirators stopped and held their breath. Surely Popilius wasn't going to tell Caesar about the plot?

Nope. It was just an innocent chat. Phew.

....

> ### Play, so you can focus on work.
>
> (παίζειν δ᾽ ὅπως σπουδάζῃ)
>
> Anacharsis. (Quoted by Aristotle. Nicomachean Ethics 1176b.)

THEME: THE WATERCOOLER

CHECKPOINT: All work and no play makes Jack a dull boy – as they say. Actually, they've been saying it for a long time. The phrase goes back to the mid-1600s.

It is utterly essential that you find time to both relax and actively do something other than work. Not only will it be good for you in general, improving your overall well-being, it will also help you to unwind, give you perspective and will rest parts of your brain that have been constantly used.

Your brain is like a muscle. If you only use it for one type of activity – work – you are not as mentally fit as you can be.

Physical exercise is essential, obviously, but so are reading, watching movies, listening to music, attending concerts and so on.

WANT TO KNOW MORE? Anacharsis, who provides today's quote, was a bilingual philosopher.

He spoke Greek (from his mother) and one of the early eastern Iranian languages spoken by a people called the Scythians (from his father).

At some time between 591 BCE and 588 BCE, he came to Athens from his home far away on the shores of the Black Sea.

He loved Athens and all things Greek. He had the language skills to converse widely.

The story goes that he decided to take back to his homeland everything he had discovered about the Greeks – language, customs, habits, etc.

It didn't go down well. His Scythian community felt he was undermining the culture and habits of their own society.

One day, his brother went out hunting with him and took the opportunity to murder him.

And that was the end of Anacharsis.

....

> **Many people can come up with a strategy,**
> **but it takes experience to deliver it.**
>
> *(consilium inveniunt multi sed docti explicant)*
>
> Publilius Syrus. Sententiae 124

THEME: STRATEGY

CHECKPOINT: Developing a strategy is not an easy thing to do. A strategy is not 'an idea', as in 'I've got an idea, why don't we start selling saucepans!'.

A strategy is a fully developed proactive move. It encompasses vision, planning, targets and measurements.

Many people are trained to develop strategies and companies usually have no problem coming up with number of options. What businesses often lack, however, is the ability to deliver the strategy. Sitting behind a desk and putting together a brilliant strategy is only 50% of what actually needs to be done. Implementation is the other 50%.

How easy is the strategy to fulfil? How much time and resources will it take? Do you have the people with the skills and experience to deliver it?

A strategy without an implementation plan is just another 'idea'.

WANT TO KNOW MORE? Many of the quotes in this book have come from Publilius Syrus. His name suggests he originated from Syria, a province of Rome since 64 BCE.

The Romans were pretty dismissive of native Syrians because they were not natural warriors.

A number of Roman military men and some writers too had over the years put Syrians in a simple box labelled 'servile'.

Syrians were the descendants of the great trading race, The Phoenicians.

The Phoenicians preferred to do business than to wage war.

When Publilius arrived in Rome as a slave, sometime around 60 BCE, he would have been met with racist slurs and disdain.

It is to his credit that he rose above all this, gained his freedom and enjoyed a good career in the theatre.

> ## What better time or place than the present?
>
> *(τίνα γὰρ χρόνον ἢ τίνα καιρόν τοῦ παρόντος βελτίω ζητεῖτε)*
>
> Demosthenes. Third Olynthiac 16

THEME: LEADERSHIP

CHECKPOINT: As a team leader, or manager, you will have to make decisions, press buttons, establish time frames. Knowing when to act on certain matters is of critical importance.

Very often, if you have thought things through and you have something in mind, acting sooner rather than later is the wisest choice.

Business moves forward with each decision taken. It moves slowly when you persist in delaying. People know when there is 'a decision in the air', or a special meeting to be had.

If you are resolved in your mind to act, then there is no time like the present.

Don't leave things. They have a habit of being talked about and the fabric of the matter in hand can start to deteriorate.

Strike while the iron's hot!

WANT TO KNOW MORE? The Peloponnesian War between Athens and Sparta (and their respective allies) ended in 404 BCE with the surrender of Athens.

Their naval power had been wiped out with the loss of their fleet the previous year.

The famed democracy of Athens was dismantled and a political junta of 30 'tyrants' was put in charge, with a Spartan garrison to keep control and supply military backup.

Things looked bleak.

But in just a year Athens was able to start bouncing back as Sparta came under attack from a different enemy.

By the time Alexander the Great's father was threatening the city, Athens had staged a remarkable social and economic comeback, even re-installing its democratic institutions.

Demosthenes was born into this resurgent and reinvigorated city.

He was to stand up for his city, speaking out against those who intended to take it back to the dark days.

> **The route from the ground to the stars is not a smooth one.**
>
> *(non est ad astra mollis e terris via)*
>
> Seneca. Hercules 437

THEME: PERSONAL DEVELOPMENT

CHECKPOINT: So you've decided to start up a new venture. You have the seed money to get going. And importantly, you have boundless energy.

Here's a way of helping you think about what you need to consider.

Think of horse racing. Think of yourself as a jockey, your business as the horse, your competitors as the other horses and the marketplace you wish to operate in as the racecourse.

What experience do you have? What skills don't you have that you need to bring on board?

How strong is your business? What could make it fall at the first fence?

What is the competition like? What do they have that you don't? How many are there?

What's the marketplace like? Tough going? What storms could come up to make the going even tougher?

And finally. Good luck!

WANT TO KNOW MORE? Seneca once wrote that it takes your entire life to know how to live – and your entire life to learn how to die.

The historian Tacitus wrote about the death of Seneca and it has to be said that, as in some other contradictory aspects of Seneca, he surely fell short of his own advice.

His death, a suicide, was a bit disorganized.

He first tried the time-honoured method of slitting his wrists. He was an elderly man at this stage – in his late sixties – and he was thin and wiry, having lived on a frugal diet. The wrists weren't doing the trick, so he starts cutting his legs. No luck there either.

Next he tried poison – Tacitus tells us it was 'Athenian'– i.e. hemlock. Still no luck.

Eventually he was carried into a hot steaming bath. The steam overpowered him and he finally died.

....

> **A clear distinction was made between office hours and 'off duty' relaxation.**
>
> *(iam vero tempora curarum remissionumque divisa)*
>
> Tacitus. Agricola 9.3

THEME: HUMAN RESOURCES

CHECKPOINT: It is very easy to get totally absorbed by work. Work becomes your life.

Your friends are work colleagues. You eat at your desk ('al desko'). You work late.

You talk about your work all the time.

Just reading this list makes you realize that it's not a healthy way to run your life.

I have worked with entrepreneurs who do live and breathe their work like this.

But even the self-made millionaires, who built their business up from scratch, take time out.

If necessary, diarize your breaks. Holidays, evenings out, family.

You'll still work hard and be absorbed by your business, but you'll also be able to accommodate important times of relaxation.

WANT TO KNOW MORE? Tacitus has been described as the greatest historian of the 'Silver Age' of Latin (18 CE to 133 CE). He gives us invaluable information about the Roman political scene from 14 CE – 96 CE (albeit with many gaps from missing books). His histories contain plenty of detail and salacious insights about Tiberius, Caligula, Claudius and Nero, as well as the famous (and very chaotic) Year of the Four Emperors (69 CE).

He tells us about Britain, about its geography and peoples.

He tells us about the tribes of Germany.

But as for the life of Tacitus himself, we have much less information.

We don't know where or when he was born (a date of 55 CE is guessed), or where and when he died.

> **Our past experiences are one inheritance we all have.**
>
> *(αἱ μὲν γὰρ πράξεις αἱ προγεγενημέναι κοιναὶ*
> *πᾶσιν ἡμῖν κατελείφθησαν)*
>
> Isocrates. Panegyricus 9

THEME: PERSONAL DEVELOPMENT

CHECKPOINT: When you go for a job interview, you – every version of you since your data first went into the public domain – goes with you. Today, you are everything you have ever been.

So be careful.

That drunken tweet.

That embarrassing photo.

That comment by a disgruntled ex-colleague.

Your friends.

Your family.

Your political views.

The places you have visited.

The people you have met.

Learn to separate the 'private you' from the 'public you' as much as you can.

You want the right version of you to be going for that job.

WANT TO KNOW MORE? Oratory was held in high regard in ancient Greece, from the earliest times.

Homer tells us that the great soldier Achilles was also an excellent orator.

Isocrates (approximately 436 BCE –338 BCE) is one of a handful of orators who was considered to be at the top of his game.

But he saw himself as more of a philosopher and educator and, sometime around 390 BCE, he set up the first-ever academy of rhetoric in a placed called Clius, in modern northwest Turkey.

Earlier in his career, Isocrates wrote speeches for other people to give in the Athenian law courts, but his heart was in education and later he wrote material which was designed to be discussed more like textbooks, rather than to be delivered as real speeches.

> **She was thirty-seven years old, an age when, if you have any common sense left, you begin to slip into an older mindset.**
>
> *(annum agebat tricesimum et octavum, tempus aetatis, si mens sana superesset, vergentis in senium)*
>
> Macrobius. Saturnalia 2.5

THEME: **PERSONAL DEVELOPMENT**

CHECKPOINT: A little bit of wisdom here about acting your age. But this is not a straightforward subject.

When are you considered 'too adult' to behave like a young person?

When are you 'old'? What does 'being mature' mean nowadays?

One way to look at this is in terms of responsibility, rather than age.

In the workplace, if you do well and are promoted you are progressively given more responsibility. With the responsibility come more rights – rights to work in a way that suits you, for example. You cannot blur the lines of your level of workplace freedoms with those of others who might have fewer.

By definition, the longer your career at work, the more chances there are of greater responsibility, and therefore the older you are.

Acting as if you are a graduate trainee when you have some standing in the company diminishes your position and makes it less easy for people to respect you.

WANT TO KNOW MORE? On October 30, 39 BCE, the Emperor Augustus' only child Julia was born. Today's quote is about her. Women in ancient Rome were not given full citizenship rights. They couldn't vote and they couldn't pursue military careers (although they could have business interests).

Julia was a member of the imperial household and she was expected to fulfil certain roles. One role was to make a strategic marriage. But she was a rebel.

She was having affairs as soon as she was strategically married off to her father's friend, the great military commander Agrippa.

The numbers of boyfriends increased and eventually her father, desperately trying to encourage a more moral and sober society, exiled her to the island of Pandateria.

> **You don't make many mistakes ... but you do make some.**
>
> *(non multa peccas ... sed peccas)*
>
> Cicero. Pro Murena 60

THEME: PERSONAL DEVELOPMENT

CHECKPOINT: Everyone makes mistakes. Even the most perfect of us. And even the people you would never imagine making a mistake – like the boss of your company, for example.

'To err is human', they say.

Never say that you don't make mistakes. It will only hold you hostage to a future moment when you inevitably make the biggest blunder of your career!

Most mistakes are benign. Just simple errors made through lack of experience or the need to work too quickly.

If you lapse and commit some terrible gaffe, the first thing you should do is own up. It relieves the pressure on the situation in an instant.

Ideally own up and say what you plan to do about it.

That way the problem is resolved and, usually, erased from the collective memory!

WANT TO KNOW MORE? Cicero's life (January 3, 106 BCE – December 7, 43 BCE) spans a period of Roman history that witnessed the rise of dictators, bloody civil war and the end of the 500-year-old Roman Republic.

Cicero was there. He lived through it. He reports it to us first-hand.

We are lucky that not only do we have work of this quality, but that we have so much.

But then these two facts became a self-fulfilling prophecy.

Because he wrote so much, there has been a much greater chance of a reasonable amount surviving (still, a great deal of what he wrote is lost).

Secondly, because he wrote so well, his literature was used as an educational tool down the ages, thus preserving many manuscripts which were copied many times over for students.

....

> ## Love conquers all!
>
> **(omnia vincit Amor)**
>
> Vergil. Eclogues 10.69

THEME: PROJECT MANAGEMENT

CHECKPOINT: You've gotta love what you do. Or at least try to. Thinking that one day you will win the lottery and retire to the Bahamas is wishing your life away.

Work might not always be enjoyable. But it can be rewarding, life-affirming, uplifting and educational. Work takes up so much of our waking hours. If you are unable to find anything positive about what you do, then you might be in the wrong job.

Or you might be in the wrong frame of mind.

Look to colleagues to provide some lighter moments when days seem interminably long.

Look at what else is happening in the workplace.

Is there something that inspires you?

Look hard to find the enjoyable aspects of what you do.

WANT TO KNOW MORE? Homer's *Iliad* is about the devasting human cost of war. His *Odyssey* is about finding home after the war.

Vergil's *Aeneid* is both, but in reverse. It's about finding Rome. And it's about the devastating war that follows to secure it.

Now that the Emperor Augustus had brought peace to the world, a long and bloody chapter in Rome's history had come to an end.

There was a sense of a settlement. The Romans now had an identity, forged in battle, which could allow them to glorify their achievements.

Vergil gave them the epic story of Rome in an epic poem.

Whereas Homer tells of the Greek Odysseus who leaves the fires of Troy to find home, Vergil tells the story of the Trojan Aeneas who leaves the fires of Troy to find Rome.

Vergil assumed his audience knew Homer's *Iliad* and *Odyssey* backwards. Homer was his Greek springboard to a truly epic Roman tale.

....

> **Don't be gloomy before you need to be.**
>
> *(ne sis miser ante tempus)*
>
> Seneca. Epistles 13.4

THEME: PERSONAL DEVELOPMENT

CHECKPOINT: They say you're either an optimist or a pessimist. That you see your glass as either half full, or half empty. Some say that optimists live longer. Pessimists say they're just being realistic.

Who knows? Except that I'm sure, like me, you must find the company of pessimists exhausting, if not draining!

At work, things have a habit of never quite turning out how you expect them to.

You think you have a meeting clash – then the next day there's more diary changes and suddenly you're no longer double-booked.

You expect a bad meeting, but it turns out to be not so bad after all.

There's me being all optimistic. The reverse happens as well, of course.

The point is, try to worry about things at the right time.

If the meeting next month is a worry for you, worry about it in three weeks at the earliest.

WANT TO KNOW MORE? If you feel that tomorrow might hold some difficult challenges at work, you might want to invoke the Roman goddess of Good Luck, *'Fortuna'*. But make sure you get the right one.

There was *'Fortuna Equestris'*, who looked after the commercial and entrepreneurial classes of Rome. (Not a bad choice.)

There was *'Fortuna Muliebris'*, who had special jurisdiction over women.

There was *'Fortuna Primigenia'*, an ancient goddess, who was concerned with the well-being of first-born children.

Don't forget *'Fortuna Virilis'*, whose job it was to make sure that boys grew into strong, virile men.

You might be forgiven for thinking that there was a Fortune Goddess for just about everyone; there just about was. Roman religion was nothing if not about superstition, and everybody needed their special good luck charm.

> **Enough of this combative and shrill discussion. Perhaps we might now enter into discussion and reach a compromise?**
>
> *(ἔσθ᾽ ὅπως ἄνευ μάχης καὶ τῆς κατοξείας βοῆς ἐς λόγους ἔλθοιμεν ἀλλήλοισι καὶ διαλλαγάς;)*
>
> Aristophanes. Wasps 471

THEME: HUMAN RESOURCES

CHECKPOINT: Employees can get very fractious with each other. When tension builds and opinions collide, temperatures will rise and you can be sure of some vociferous outbursts in the workplace.

Everyone stands back. But it needs to be sorted.

Equally you can find yourself in the middle of an unintentional verbal fracas with a supplier or even a customer. Maybe over a misunderstanding – an invoice or a breach of contract.

Letting off steam is one thing, not allowing things to settle down is another.

Mediation in these situations is not a clear-cut issue because it really depends on the nature of the altercation.

Judge as quickly as you can whether this can be sorted 'locally' – i.e. by the people involved.

Otherwise, suggest to everyone that a third party will have to be brought in.

(That suggestion alone can sometimes very quickly calm things right down!)

WANT TO KNOW MORE? Aristophanes was a multi-award-winning playwright. We don't know exactly how many plays he wrote, but it looks like around 40 were staged.

Of these, we have 11.

In the biggest Athenian award ceremonies, he won at least six top prizes, and he garnered silver and bronze medals in many others.

One of his most celebrated plays is *Frogs*.

Aristophanes had just turned 40 when this won the first prize at one of the two major award shows, The Lenaia. It was so well-received that it enjoyed the unusual honour of being staged a second time the following year.

In the same year, Euripides, the distinguished writer of tragedies, also won first prize, for his play *The Bacchae* at The Dionysia, the other big show.

Both plays survived the passage of years and are still staged today.

> **'Trust yourself.' That is one hell of a good point:**
> **It's the raison d'etre and the bedrock of a Happy Life.**
>
> *(unum bonum est, quod beatae vitae causa et firmamentum est, sibi fidere)*
>
> Seneca. Epistles 31.3

THEME: PERSONAL DEVELOPMENT

CHEKPOINT: Self-doubt must be one of the biggest anchors on our personal development.

The odd thing is that almost everyone worries about looking bad or silly.

An old boss of mine, a very successful American who had made millions of dollars over the years and who was lauded in his business circles, once wouldn't leave his hotel room in London because he didn't have a smart jacket.

He feared he'd be laughed at by the other guests.

We can so easily get it into our heads that we are not good enough.

Picture everyone in the workplace with the same hang-ups, and business looks like one huge sea of ships all dragging their anchors as they move cautiously around one another!

I'm no psychologist, but it's a safe bet to say that you are much better than you think you are.

Trust yourself.

Honestly, you don't need to worry that everyone is looking at you, wondering why you're so slow to come forward.

They are too busy dragging their own anchors around!

WANT TO KNOW MORE? The *Ludi Romani* (5-19 September) were the biggest games in Rome, but the *Ludi Plebeii* came in a close second.

They kicked off today and lasted for two weeks, and were followed immediately by market days, as was the custom.

Games were a big part of Roman life, with half a dozen public events held during the year.

The chariot races were extremely popular.

There were always four chariot teams competing, distinguished by the colours blue, green, red and white. Each colour represented company sponsorship. The companies were called '*factiones*', giving us our politically charged term 'faction'.

....

> **From this point onwards, the night kicked in,**
> **decorated with brightly burning stars.**
>
> *(hinc nox processit stellis ardentibus apta)*
>
> Ennius. Annals 10.348

THEME: TIME MANAGEMENT

CHECKPOINT: There is nothing more irritating than meetings that run over. Particularly if you have somewhere else to be, like at a Fireworks Party.

It should only happen in the most extraordinary of circumstances. I once sat through the night negotiating a business deal because the parties involved had to conclude the meeting by the next day for regulatory purposes.

But when regular day-to-day meetings overrun, it simply means that they have been badly managed.

When you are in a meeting, follow this etiquette:

1. The chairperson must keep to time.
2. Make sure there is an agenda that is previously agreed and then adhered to.
3. Have the right people in the room. (As a general rule, there are often too many people in meetings!)

Importantly, make sure when it's your turn to contribute that you stick to the time allotted.

WANT TO KNOW MORE? Ennius claimed to have descended from royalty, which would have added to the venerable status he held amongst the good and the great of the Roman literary world.

He came from the bottom of the heel of Italy, an area colonized by people known as the Salentinoi. Today, the area is still known as the Salento.

Ennius was proud to have royal connections from this part of Italy, an area that spoke Greek as readily as it spoke Latin. Ennius was the perfect bridge from the world of Greek literature to the new world of Latin literature.

The Romans colonized the Salento in 266 BCE as they began their long, slow push outwards from Rome. This was less than 30 years before Ennius was born, so memories of a free and independent Salento would have still been fresh in his community.

....

....

> ## The way things fall due to fate cannot be calculated in advance.
>
> *(τὰς προσπιπτούσας τύχας οὐ λόγῳ διαιρετάς)*
>
> Thucydides. The Peloponnesian War 1.84.3

THEME: STRATEGY

CHECKPOINT: When expert strategists put together a strategy, they normally include an allowance for both positive and negative unforeseen future activity. You don't know which way it will go.

For example, fluctuating exchange rates, or a change in national trade policy, are unpredictable.

On a smaller scale, you might consider the arrival of unexpected sudden competitive activity, or a change in raw material costs. They are all possibilities. That's all.

These factors must not change a strategy, but they might suggest what changes in strategic direction are needed if trading conditions change.

Such calculations of change can only be guestimates based on past performance or previously seen market changes. But in truth, no one knows what the future holds.

When you put your strategy together, pay most attention to what is happening right now and less to what fate might throw at you tomorrow.

WANT TO KNOW MORE? Thucydides' history covers the war between Sparta and Athens that continued for almost 30 years, between 431 BCE and 404 BCE.

Athens lost the war, but like so many conflicts that lasted so long and tore so many communities apart, there was no real winner.

Thucydides shows real skill in drawing out the human aspect of war.

Human fear drove much of the strategy of both sides.

Both Sparta and Athens had pride in their long histories and it was a matter of honour not to give way.

Thucydides is referenced today by many political and military leaders who seek to understand the causes of war. Thucydides gives some key pointers, such as how rising economies begin to threaten established ones and how uncontrolled growth becomes difficult to contain.

....

....

> **We will deal with all of this later.**
>
> (ἀλλ᾽ ἤ τοι μὲν ταῦτα μεταφρασόμεσθα καὶ αὖτις)
>
> Homer. Iliad 1.141

THEME: TIME MANAGEMENT

CHECKPOINT: Every day at work you will be hit with new, and sometimes different, things to do.

You can end up firefighting short-term issues and never get to grips with the bigger things.

And, let's be honest, sometimes you can be overloaded with things to do.

So, prioritizing is the obvious way to tackle this problem. Online there are many tools and tricks to help with prioritizing.

One trick is so simple it seems almost childlike. But I have found it to work extremely well.

Write a list of everything you have to do in the order they come to you.

If you can, group some things together, so they turn into mini-projects.

The list is prioritized by the time at which you receive them, not by the size of the project.

Now, go through the list ticking off each job done in order.

If the list regularly outruns the length of your working day, then, quite simply, you are overworked.

WANT TO KNOW MORE? Homer's *Iliad* does not tell us many of the famous tales of the Trojan War.

That's because it's not a history of the conflict, it's a peek into the ferocious fighting to report to us the horror of war and its human costs.

The *Iliad* can be said to stand for all wars.

The hostilities began because of the abduction (or was it an elopement?) of Helen, a Greek queen.

Her brother-in-law, the leading Greek king, is then forced, by religious observance, to sacrifice his own daughter to ensure a fair wind and successful outcome.

The war ends with the same king murdered by his wife and/or her lover on his return home.

The *Iliad* is a snapshot of a conflict born of horror and which ended with horror as well.

....

> **You promise the world when you've been drinking all night.
> Then the next day you fail to deliver.**
>
> *(omnia promittis cum tota nocte bibisti; mane nihil praestas)*
>
> Martial. Epigrams 12.12

THEME: THE WATERCOOLER

CHECKPOINT: Have you ever asked out a junior colleague for an after-work chat and a drink?

You get chatting. It's pitched as a casual session.

After a couple of drinks, the alcohol starts to subtly do its job.

Tongues are loosened. Inhibitions are relaxed.

You want to be the kind of person who is upbeat about the company.

Soon you end up dropping hints and intimating all sorts of possibilities.

Your colleague only hears one thing: 'I'm doing well, I'm advancing through the company.'

But the reality is a little more mundane than that.

Your colleague is doing fine and is at the level they should be. You cannot offer anything more.

No people-management of any kind should be handled in an 'off-duty' kind of way.

Leave socializing to free time and let a professional review process handle the official duties of the workplace.

WANT TO KNOW MORE? Three days a year – on August 24, October 5 and today, November 8 – a mysterious, ghoulish ceremonial ritual was performed in Rome.

A lid was lifted on a vaulted pit called the *'mundus'*. The *'mundus'* was an entry point to the underworld, and on these three days the spirits of the dead would wander around the streets of Rome.

No public business whatsoever could be done on this day. No battles could be fought.

No ships could sail and no marriages could take place.

This was a day for the dead.

Or was it? It might have started that way, but like Halloween, its true roots and meaning are difficult to determine and the attention to ritual loosened over time.

....

> ### Control anger.
>
> *(θυμοῦ κρατεῖν)*
>
> Chilon (in Diogenes Laertes: Lives of Eminent Philosophers 1.3. Chilon 70)

THEME: PERSONAL DEVELOPMENT

CHECKPOINT: Split anger in two types. Irrational Anger and Rational Anger.

Irrational anger is often no more than excessive irritability and can be born of complex emotions, tiredness and frustrations. Not good. It reflects badly on you and suggests you are somewhat out of control. Go for a walk, go to the gym, go to the doctor. Whatever. Keep it out of the workplace.

Rational anger, however, can have a value. An outburst of annoyance at yourself or at the unintended consequences of certain actions can present a powerful moment.

It can cause the workplace to pause for a moment and to reflect on the issue.

It can expose a human side to a senior manager.

It can harness a collective opinion on an unfairness or misadventure.

If you think you're going to boil over, control yourself. What value will it have?

Nine times out of ten (and that's a lot of times to be angry!) you'll be pleased that you did.

WANT TO KNOW MORE? The philosopher Chilon of Sparta lived in the period around 560 BCE.

He had a number of pithy one-liners to provide guidance for his fellow Greeks.

For example:
- Don't talk too much over dinner
- Don't be rude to your neighbours
- Never threaten anyone
- Visit friends in need
- Don't speak ill of the dead
- It's better to make a loss than take a dishonest gain
- Never laugh at another's misfortune
- Respect the elderly

....

> **Even an injured sheep can turn angrily when pushed.**
>
> *(verum etiam instanti laesa repugnat ovis)*
>
> Propertius. Elegies 2.5.20

THEME: HUMAN RESOURCES

CHECKPOINT: The world of work is populated by different beasts.

The cheeky monkeys.

The sharks.

The nervous shrewish types.

The super-cool cats.

The bulls-in-a-china-shop.

And, of course, the 800-pound gorillas.

This jungle is not as dangerous as it sounds.

Aggressive people can be brought to their senses by the softest of techniques.

When you find someone being particularly aggressive, immediately challenge them.

To ask the question, 'why are you being so aggressive?', is often enough to demonstrate that when you need to be, you can be a wolf in sheep's clothing.

WANT TO KNOW MORE? The period between Vergil's birth and Augustus' death (70 BCE – 14 CE) was a period of extraordinary creative output in ancient Rome.

The poets Catullus, Vergil, Horace, Tibullus and Ovid were all famous and fertile writers. Other writers that we know about, while having precious little of their work, include Gallus and the intriguing lady known as Sulpicia.

Into this unbelievably talented pool of people we must throw the wonderful Propertius.

This crowd obviously knew each other (Rome was big, but not that big) and they were often connected by the same literary agents and sponsors.

The Emperor Augustus encouraged the arts and famous patrons of the arts were amongst his closest friends.

Propertius' work clearly at times shows the influences of Vergil, Tibullus and the young Ovid.

> ### For each individual, cash reserves become either
> ### your master or your servant.
>
> *(imperat aut servit collecta pecunia cuique)*
>
> Horace. Epistles 1.10.47

THEME: FINANCE

CHECKPOINT: Building up cash reserves in business is hard. To save, you need to avoid spending.

Sounds rather obvious, doesn't it? But then, the old maxim 'you have to speculate to accumulate' lies at the heart of every business' need to put its money to work.

Keeping money in the bank seems an odd thing to do when you hope that your trading performance will deliver double-digit returns – something savings rates in banks in the UK haven't done since 1991.

For some, cash reserves can be profitably put to use in a way that will not jeopardize the business.

For others, a cash mountain can just grow and grow without a strategy.

Put your cash to good use the moment you feel secure about cash flow.

Remember what the automobile manufacturer Henry Ford once said, "A business that makes only money is a poor business."

WANT TO KNOW MORE? Horace was born in 65 BCE and died aged 57 in 8 BCE.

He was very close friends with the poet Vergil and was hugely admired by the Emperor Augustus.

Horace was the country boy who went to Rome and whose status grew so much that he could afford to turn down a job offer from the emperor.

He was the coward who fled the field of battle, yet grew into the affections of the big shots who were pulling the levers of power in Rome.

Horace generates controversy. There is no aspect of his life that is clear-cut. He toys with us and deliberately deceives. He can be difficult. Does he occasionally deposit a truth amongst his obscure, obvious or misleading lines? Maybe.

It naturally follows that a person who is dedicated to
a highly specialized line of work is bound to do it
to the highest possible standards.

*(ἀνάγκη οὖν τὸν ἐν βραχυτάτῳ διατρίβοντα ἔργῳ
τοῦτον καὶ ἄριστα δὴ ἠναγκάσθαι τοῦτο ποιεῖν)*

Xenophon. Cyropaedia 8.2.5

THEME: TIME MANAGEMENT

CHECKPOINT: It is customary to divide roles in the workplace into two
types: specialists and generalists.

As businesses seek to maximize profits, the trend is to get more out of
people and specialists start to take on more managerial roles. This breeds a
hybrid 'Generalist-Specialist'.

That seems to cover all options, then. Well, not really.

Today we are seeing the rise of the Super-Specialist, particularly in the
area of internet-related software. Coders are coming out of the basement
and into the boardroom.

Similarly, in AI (Artificial Intelligence) and the booming fields of VR
(Virtual Reality) and AR (Augmented Reality), real experts are called for.

If you need to bring these skills into your business, be prepared to
rework your timing plans. These guys operate within the tiniest margin
of error. Your timing plans have to adapt to a workflow that is all about
100% perfection.

WANT TO KNOW MORE? Xenophon, the Greek historian, does not give
us full dates, names and addresses of everyone he mentions.

In his day (430 BCE – 354 BCE), the most accurate way of attributing
actions to dates would have been to have witnessed them yourself.

Even if he'd wanted to get very accurate, he'd have had a problem. Dates
were often set in relation to the four Olympiads that were established first
in 776 BCE.

How about the Greek calendar? Would that have helped him?

Not really. Each city had its own calendar. Some regions used the cycle
of the moon. Others used the stars. Every now and then, a comet would
be recorded, allowing a later generation of scientists to pinpoint an event
with greater accuracy.

> **One's memory is uncertain and unreliable.**
>
> *(dubitat anceps memoria)*
>
> Seneca. Oedipus 847

THEME: PERSONAL DEVELOPMENT

CHECKPOINT: Make notes. Do you think you've got a photographic memory? Well, it's unlikely.

And in any case, the recording of meetings, however brief, however long, is as much for the benefit of others as for yourself.

Agreements made between you and others can nowadays be followed up with a quick email.

If it's an important agreement, get the recipient to reply as quickly as they can, approving the notes you sent.

There is nothing more frustrating in businesses than the 'he said, she said, I said, you said' biopsy of the confusion caused by lack of proper recording.

Make notes!

WANT TO KNOW MORE? One way of understanding Roman religion is to go right back to the earliest days of Rome.

The early settlers worked the land. It was a subsistence economy. You ate what you produced.

Farming can be tough. You can be hit by floods, or droughts. An untimely frost could bring disaster, an early warm spring could produce a windfall.

These ancient societies would have experienced things they couldn't explain, so they assumed spirits were at work – '*numina*'. You had to make sure these spirits were happy, or you might not make it through the year. If things went badly for you, you needed to search your soul – was there some spirit that maybe had not been honoured? These spirits grew in number as the society grew. They would look after anything and everything.

On this day in the Roman towns and villages the goddess Feronia would have been worshipped. Initially she may have been honoured with the first fruits of the season to ensure continued bountiful years ahead.

Over time, she increased her scope and became associated with the granting of freedom to slaves.

I am in the habit of saying what I mean.

(ἃ μὴ φρονῶ γὰρ οὐ φιλῶ λέγειν μάτην)

Sophocles. Oedipus Tyrannus 1521

THEME: **LEADERSHIP**

CHECKPOINT: "Oh, he doesn't really mean that, he's just saying that."

Disaster! If this is how you are described, you are really not helping anyone; least of all yourself.

What you say to people at work is very important.

If you are asking someone to do something and it needs to be done by a certain time, then be very clear and very specific.

If you are reprimanding someone, don't try to disguise what you really mean in a vain attempt not to hurt their feelings.

Words matter.

Be known as someone who means what they say, as opposed the sort of person who waffles on vaguely.

WANT TO KNOW MORE? Sophocles loved creating characters. He once said that he created the sort of characters one ought to create, while he felt that Euripides portrayed people as they actually are.

Two of Sophocles' female leads are extraordinary characters.

One was Antigone, the daughter of the famous Oedipus. Antigone's mother, Jocasta, was also her grandmother. Her name can be translated as 'against my parents'. Families! If only Oedipus had had therapy in his day.

The other character was Electra, the daughter of Agamemnon, king of the Greek forces that went to fight in the Trojan War.

Agamemnon sacrificed his other daughter, Electra's sister, before he sailed to Troy.

Then his wife, Electra's mother, murdered him on his return.

As I said …

Families!

> **This invention will engender memory loss in those who have learned to use it. Memory skills will no longer be required.**
>
> *(τοῦτο γὰρ τῶν μαθόντων λήθην μὲν ἐν ψυχαῖς παρέξει μνήμης ἀμελετησίᾳ)*
>
> Plato. Phaedrus 275a

THEME: INNOVATION

CHECKPOINT: You can find just about anything you want on the internet. (I'm saying 'just about' to cover myself against the one-in-a-trillion chance there's something you can't find.)

And don't worry if you can't be bothered to find it on the billion-plus websites out there – just ask Siri, or Alexa, etc.

When we visit new places, or see new things (museums, cultures, thoughts), we take a picture and store it on our 'external memory hard drive'.

There are an increasing number of studies which look at the effect of the internet on our memory. But there is one obvious one.

If we delegate machines to record and memorize things, we are remembering less ourselves – making us unable to immediately call up and cross-correlate what we have experienced.

But imaginative people are persuasive and attractive. Their ideas are quickly compelling. They can quickly draw on a reservoir of interesting thoughts.

Try to really remember what you have experienced.

It will make you a more impressive person!

WANT TO KNOW MORE? Today's quote comes from Plato's *Phaedrus*.

Socrates here is arguing against the invention of writing. By writing things down, we use our memory less, thus weakening our capacity to remember things.

All of Socrates' thinking is to be found written up by others. Maybe he followed his own advice?

Socrates singled out writing from a list of new developments as an innovation that would have a long-term negative effect. On the other hand, innovations that he considered to be acceptable were: the idea of numbers and the arithmetic they caused; geometry and astronomy; and, (I think rather hilariously) draughts and dice.

> **People are innately smooth operators.**
> **They create all sorts of stories. Their talk is as broad as it is long.**
> **You end up hearing what you wanted to hear.**
>
> *(στρεπτὴ δὲ γλῶσσ' ἐστὶ βροτῶν, πολέες δ' ἔνι μῦθοι παντοῖοι, ἐπέων δὲ πολὺς νομὸς ἔνθα καὶ ἔνθα. ὁπποῖόν κ' εἴπησθα ἔπος, τοῖόν κ' ἐπακούσαις)*
>
> Homer. Iliad 20.248

THEME: THE WATERCOOLER

CHECKPOINT: Often we realize that we've been taken advantage of, and we kick ourselves.

Like the online quiz that leads us to pages of ads (the clickbait on social media).

Or the smooth-talking waiter who talks us into that dessert we never wanted. It happens all the time.

You'll be surprised at how clever some people can be.

Being good at any form of selling requires an ability to understand what other people want and then deploying the right tactics to sell it to them.

Often these 'wants' are emotional. That's why a good salesperson will sell you something you think you've always wanted.

Try to keep your own council on stories or messages that require 'buy-in'.

Keep a little emotional distance. The last thing you need is to be suckered into anything at work that you would rather avoid.

WANT TO KNOW MORE? The *Iliad* is Homer's story about a few days during the 10 year-long Trojan War.

What Homer doesn't mention in the book is the Trojan Horse, the device that allowed the Greeks to eventually get inside the huge walls of Troy. Once inside, they set about slaughtering the Trojans and burnt the city down from the inside out.

But twice Homer mentions the Trojan Horse in the 'sequel' to the *Iliad*, the *Odyssey*.

The story is told to Odysseus' son, who meets with one of the Greek generals to find out more about his father's whereabouts. And Odysseus himself hears the tale told by a blind storyteller named Demodocus.

The story has been told many, many times since. It is a story of an ingenious idea. Ingenuity in the face of struggle and loss regularly occurs through both of Homer's epics.

> **Every dispute has arguments on both sides.**
>
> *(utrimque omni negotio disseratur)*
>
> Minucius Felix. Octavius 14.7

THEME: HUMAN RESOURCES

CHECKPOINT: HR.

Very few arguments or disagreements are one-sided. The power of an argument comes from a vociferous defence of both sides of the dispute.

When you are drawn into such a debate, the temptation is to take one side over the other. But try to avoid this. Try to listen carefully to both points of view.

The great American writer F. Scott Fitzgerald once said: "The test of a first-rate intelligence is the ability to hold two opposed ideas in mind at the same time and still retain the ability to function."

Both views will hold some truths.

The skill is to fathom out what those truths are and to give them both equal value in your mind.

If you are really clever, you might be able to communicate your understanding of the benefits of the argument and bring both sides together.

WANT TO KNOW MORE? Remember that long, hot summer evening by the seashore when you talked long into the night, debating this and that, and maybe getting quite animated at one point in the evening?

Cut to the Roman port of Ostia sometime soon after 200 CE.

There's a lively debate, and it's about religion.

Oops. Don't they advise steering clear of politics, sex and religion when enjoying a lively debate? (What's left to debate, you might ask … ?)

Back to Ostia. An agnostic and a chap called Octavius, a Christian, are debating. Octavius wins the argument (he was always going to).

Minucius Felix is not a major Latin writer, but his book, *Octavius*, is a lively and readable work and offers us a glimpse into social and religious attitudes in early 3rd cenruty Rome.

> **Anyone who thinks that his close competitor knows nothing, and that he is the only one to craft clever strategic plans, is an idiot, his common sense deeply flawed.**
>
> *(ὅστις τοι δοκέει τὸν πλησίον ἴδμεναι οὐδέν,ἀλλ᾽ αὐτὸς μοῦνος ποικίλα δήνε᾽ ἔχειν,κεῖνός γ᾽ ἄφρων ἐστί, νόου βεβλαμμένος ἐσθλοῦ·)*
>
> Theognis. Elegies 221-223

THEME: COMPETITORS

CHECKPOINT: Never, ever, underestimate the competition.

They might be struggling.

They might be losing customers, or key employees.

Their products or services could be mauled by social media pundits.

No matter. You still shouldn't underestimate them. The competition has a way of biting you on the behind just when you least expect it. Keep a constant eye on what is happening.

And don't define your sector too narrowly when you determine who your threats are.

You are not the only one who has a clever idea, or a winning way with customers.

Competitors can spring up suddenly from the most suprising places.

WANT TO KNOW MORE? The *Ludi Plebeii*, that started back on November 4, ended yesterday, and, as usual, the big markets came rolling back into town.

Three days of busy market trading would occupy the streets and the minds of the Romans.

Way back in Rome's history, you simply bartered goods. Twelve sheep would be worth one cow, and so on.

The Latin for cattle is '*pecus*', which led to '*pecunia*', meaning money, from which we now get the word 'pecuniary'.

The earliest form of money was a bar of copper of a standard weight – one pound – stamped with an impression of a cow. One bar = 12 sheep.

Some time around 350 BCE, copper was cast into a coin, called an '*as*'.

One twelfth of an '*as*' was an '*uncia*', from where we get both 'ounce' and 'inch'.

Over the years, as the economy grew, the '*as*' depreciated in value and led to the Latin expression '*ad assem*' meaning 'to the last farthing'.

'Ace', when counted as the lowest card in the pack, is also derived from '*as*'.

....

> ### To accumulate you have to speculate.
>
> *(necesse est facere sumptum qui quaerit lucrum)*
>
> Plautus. The Comedy of Asses 217

THEME: FINANCE

CHECKPOINT: Most people who run businesses are not expert at financial investments.

And that includes the team in the Finance Department.

The talent in a company is usually there to focus on running the business.

So phrases like 'you have to speculate to accumulate' don't really help if you don't know how various investment strategies work.

Therefore, get some outside specialist advice.

Because if you do nothing, either inflation or low interest rates will erode the value of the hard-earned money you have built up.

Be careful not to take your eye off your business when you start thinking about financial investments.

Your business will have a core purpose and unless you are in specialist financial services, this core purpose will not be 'making money on the money'.

WANT TO KNOW MORE? It's the second day of *Mercatus* the three-day market festival in Rome.

By Plautus' time, you will be using money to buy goods and not bartering sheep for cattle.

Silver coins were certainly in use by 250 BCE.

There were two types, the sestertius, worth 2.5 asses and the denarius, worth 10 asses.

It is from the 'd' in denarius that the pre-decimal one penny coin was written as 1d.

As the economy grew in size and sophistication, the sestertius became worth 4 asses and the denarius 16 asses.

The Emperor Augustus reformed the coinage system in 23 BCE and the silver sestertius became a bronze coin, and bigger in size.

> **You ask: what is the appropriate limit for wealth?**
> **First it is to have what is necessary, secondly to have what is enough.**
>
> *(quis sit divitiarum modus, quaeris?*
> *Primus habere quod necesse est, proximus quod sat est)*
>
> Seneca. Epistles 3.2.6

THEME: PERSONAL DEVELOPMENT

CHECKPOINT: We live in an age of overnight millionaires. But for most people, the principal source of wealth will be defined by their salary.

However, you can plan for future wealth. You need to put a personal finance strategy in place at the earliest possible time. Yet few do that.

But, for the purpose of today's thought piece, let's assume you are the sort of person who wants to build up a secure financial position.

The key here is that it isn't about the amount of money you earn, it's about what you do with it.

And here's my advice: Think Small (as opposed to so many financial products whose marketing position is Think Big).

Establishing a plan that secures the basics in life is where you start, rather than beating yourself up because you don't yet have the boat and fancy pad in the Caribbean.

WANT TO KNOW MORE? Today is the final day of the three-day *'Mercatus'*.

Rome would be filled with traders of all types, selling fish, meat, clothes, etc., who would have come into the city from out of town. They would have swelled the number of market traders normally to be found in Rome.

One place a Roman shopper would know very well would be the *'taberna'*.

The word immediately makes us think of 'taverns' but these places were much more diverse in nature and usage.

'Tabernae' would house all sorts of trades: butchers, doctors and wood-carvers, for example. And yes, they could be drinking houses too. The shops could change hands as quickly as our high-street retailers do. They would use the outside space to display their wares and entice customers – a little like the modern-day 'souks' or 'bazaars'.

> **Don't set your heart and mind on things that can't be made to happen. They're unachievable.**
>
> *(μήποτ᾽ ἐπ᾽ ἀπρήκτοισι νόον ἔχε μηδὲ μενοίνα*
> *χρήμασι· τῶν ἄννσις γίνεται οὐδεμία)*
>
> Theognis. Elegies 461

THEME: PERSONAL DEVELOPMENT

CHECKPOINT: You may be the sort of person who sets personal targets.
You want that pay grade by this time, or that promotion before this age.
Sometimes your plan doesn't go according to plan.

In all matters of your personal growth and development, you need to remain flexible.

Setting targets and hoping to achieve them is admirable. But there are so many moving parts in any workplace that you are not always in control of your own destiny.

The positive aspect of reaching self-imposed targets is that it gives you drive and direction.

But don't get stuck.

Banging your head against the brick wall of an unachievable objective won't make it happen.

It'll just make your head hurt.

WANT TO KNOW MORE? Theognis was a poet from an aristocratic background who was raised in Megara, Greece, and was writing sometime around 550 BCE.

We have just under 1,500 lines of verse attributed to Theognis, but we know very little about him.

When you compare the works of Homer and Hesiod to those of Theognis, you can sense that Theognis is a writer communicating different, more personal matters.

Whether that's because social life in Greece was changing, or because Theognis is just the first to relate concepts that had been around for a while, we just don't know.

Theognis addressed many of his poems to a boy called Cyrnus.

He also wrote about drinking wine, friendship and love.

Theognis is the first Greek poet we have to open up and show us what his personal passions were.

> **I tell you this, propositions and seeds are the same things; they both produce a great deal, and yet they are such delicate things.**
>
> *(eadem est, inquam, praeceptorum condicio quae seminum; multum efficiunt, et angusta sunt)*
>
> Seneca. Epistles 38.2

THEME: STRATEGY

CHECKPOINT: Any successful strategy has to have a champion.

A strategy is a very delicate thing.

It's just a set of words. Well worked-out words, but just words nonetheless.

A strategy has to be clearly understood.

Words can mean different things to different people.

A strategy has a rationale, and it's usually well put together. Like any construction, it has to be well built, with strong arguments and firm foundations.

Every strategy starts with the seed of a good idea. You can get people to agree to the seed of an idea. But remember, as the idea develops, it might not flourish into exactly what everyone had expected. People bring their own imagination to nascent thoughts.

A good strategy will involve a number of people. It will generate a great deal of work.

It might end up as a huge document or a multi-media presentation.

All this from just an idea. Make sure your idea is properly looked after, and nurtured.

WANT TO KNOW MORE? Seneca was a rich man.

He amassed a serious amount of money during the reign of Nero, for whom he worked.

How much was a serious amount of money in Roman times?

Well, Seneca was worth over 300 million sestertii; he owned a number of properties, both prime real estate in Rome and big villas in the countryside.

How much was 300 hundred million sestertii?

Despite many attempts to try and work out an exchange rate into today's currency, it's not as simple as that. We just don't know enough about the purchasing power of Roman money.

Suffice it to say that it was a phenomenal amount of money.

Let's assume Seneca was at least a multimillionaire.

> **This life of ours is on a stage. It's just a play.
> So, either go for it and learn the play or stay unhappy, forever.**
>
> *(Σκηνὴ πᾶς ὁ βίος καὶ παίγνιον· ἢ μάθε παίζειν,τὴν
> σπουδὴν μεταθείς, ἢ φέρε τὰς ὀδύνας).*
>
> Palladas. Fragment Greek Anthology 10.65

THEME: PERSONAL DEVELOPMENT

CHECKPOINT: So much of what happens in your work life is a game. Crazy isn't it?

You have to act the part of the enthusiastic candidate in a job interview. You have to learn the set pieces in the workplace, like who to impress, who to avoid. You might have to stand up and give a presentation on something you knew absolutely nothing about only a month ago, like an actor learning his lines and getting immersed in the part.

Getting promoted is also often about negotiating your way around various people and obstacles, as if you are moving yourself through a game of chess.

How many times have you heard people say: 'I got dealt a bum set of cards' or 'You've got to know how to play the game'?

To make things harder, this Game of Work has no written rules. And what rules there are pop up suddenly and need to be interpreted very quickly. And then the rules change. Yes, it is crazy, but it's how it is.

You might not want to fully play 'the game', but whatever you do, don't kick against it, or try to change the rules to suit yourself. You might find you're 'out' faster than you anticipated.

WANT TO KNOW MORE? Does today's quote ring any bells?

You're right. Look at these famous lines from the play *As You Like It*:

> All the world's a stage,
> And all the men and women merely players.

Shakespeare knew his classics.

> **There hasn't been a great genius who didn't have a touch of madness.**
>
> *(nullum magnum ingenium sine mixtura dementiae fuit)*
>
> Seneca. De Tranquillitate Animi 17.10

THEME: INNOVATION

CHECKPOINT: Mavericks. Don't ya just love 'em?

Of course. Without Steve Jobs' crazy vision and obsessive drive would we have the Apple we have today?

But they are difficult to work with.

History throws up genius minds who persist with their ideas against all odds and eventually win through. They might have created the innovation of the century, but if your job is to work with them, it will be, what shall we say, 'a ride'.

They say Thomas Edison never slept. Nice. What do you think his working hours were?

Being in a company where you have a genuine genius will be not be easy. They don't understand the niceties of conventional behaviour. But beware the false mavericks. The ones who think they are a genius, or a uniquely talented individual, but are in fact just a regular person aspiring to be someone else. You'll spot them very easily.

They're the ones working in a conventional company.

WANT TO KNOW MORE? Seneca thought a great deal about the meaning of life.

Take a look at the titles of some of his works:
- *On The Tranquillity Of The Mind*
- *On The Shortness Of Life*
- *On The Happy Life*
- *On Mercy*
- *On Anger*

Seneca also had a way with words and was able to encapsulate big thoughts in easy, communicable bite-sized chunks. This makes so much of what he has to say intelligible to the snappy demands of the Twitter age.

> **Managing a good ship is an art, just like any other skill.**
>
> *(τὸ δὲ ναυτικὸν τέχνης ἐστίν, ὥσπερ καὶ ἄλλο τι)*
>
> Thucydides. The Peloponnesian War 1.142.9

THEME: LEADERSHIP

CHECKPOINT: You can learn a great deal from the brightest educators at the best business schools, but as every business leader will tell you, at some point the job becomes a skill, nuanced by experience.

No business book has ever provided all the answers. How could they? There are simply too many moving parts in a business that in the end combine to create a unique entity.

Think about it.

Today's thought by the historian Thucydides goes on to say that you need to keep learning the skill of leadership through continued practice.

When you are at the helm of the ship, nothing can take priority over keeping up the skills to keep on course. It should never be a sideshow.

So, if you're in charge, never take your eyes off the instrument panels, keep your destination in clear view and maintain the course you have set for yourself and the crew.

WANT TO KNOW MORE? One day, so the story goes, Herodotus, 'the father of history', was giving a public reading of sections of his innovative account of the Persian Wars (499 BCE – 449 BCE).

In the audience was a certain Thucydides, who is said to have left the event in tears, so overwhelmed was he by the stimulating wealth of information that Herodotus had assembled.

Thucydides was from a family that had made millions from gold and silver mines.

He could have done anything he wanted with his life.

But as the Peloponnesian War broke out in 431 BCE, he chose to follow Herodotus into the new literary genre of history, believing, with great foresight, that this would be an important war to write about and more significant than any other war that had preceded it.

> **What a large number of high achievers lie unnoticed,
> fame unknown, because of their modesty and unassuming lives.**
>
> *(o quantum eruditorum aut modestia ipsorum aut quies
> operit ac subtrahit famae!)*
>
> Pliny The Younger. Letters 7.25.1

THEME: HUMAN RESOURCES

CHECKPOINT: There are two sides to the coin of personal achievement.

On one side, it has to be driven by personal ambition. You have to really want to get on and climb the ladder of success.

On the other side of the coin, you will need a helping hand to pull you up and to point out fast-track routes ahead.

Not everyone is given to promoting themselves. And not everyone who is clambering up that ladder is necessarily better than the next.

One of the biggest positive roles senior executives can play in people's lives is to proactively seek out those people who have talent. There is a strong business argument behind this.

Latent talent is one of a company's biggest assets. Those businesses that have a policy of discovering and nurturing talent save time and money.

And, most importantly, they improve the competitive prospects of the business.

WANT TO KNOW MORE? You may have heard of the famous book about ancient Rome by Edward Gibbon, *The History of the Decline and Fall of the Roman Empire*, written towards the end of the 18th century.

Gibbon describes the period of time after the death of the controversial Emperor Domitian as "the period in the history of the world during which the condition of the human race was most happy and prosperous."

Wow. That would have been a time to have lived. And fortunately for Pliny, that's exactly the time when he was flourishing.

Pliny's letters are a wonderfully refreshing account of ordinary Roman life and they sit in stark contrast to his predecessors Juvenal, Martial and Tacitus, who often reveal a bitterness and unhappiness about the Roman society they grew up in.

> **Job done. To perfection.**
>
> *(exegi)*
>
> Horace. Odes 3.30.1

THEME: **PROJECT MANAGEMENT**

CHECKPOINT: Work occupies a huge part of our waking life. If you can't care about what you do, you are relegating a large chunk of your life to a meaningless existence.

People who take pride in their work enjoy their work. They care. They like to see a job done well. And it goes without saying that such people tend to do well.

If you treat your work life as simply a means to an end, you deprive yourself of a number of things that can actually add value to your life.

Not everything you do in your job can be fulfilling. But surely there are some aspects, including occasional projects, that you can throw yourself into and give 100% of yourself to make it go well?

Try it.

WANT TO KNOW MORE? The wonderful Roman poet Horace died on this day in 8 BCE, aged 57.

Six years before he died, Horace wrote this: *"natalis gratis numeras?"* – "Do you count your birthdays gratefully?"

You get a strong feeling that although Horace made a point of addressing his poetry to other people, the person he was really trying to communicate to was himself.

Horace pondered death a great deal.

He could see it coming.

His view was that you should live life to the full until old age approaches, when you should live a gentler and better life.

Horace knew his body of work was exceptional and that it would outlive him. "I shan't completely die," he wrote. "A greater part of me will bypass death."

He was absolutely right. His poetry has survived him for over 2,000 years.

> **Let's hope we get what we want; but, let's be prepared
> to take onboard whatever happens.**
>
> *(speremus, quae volumus, sed, quod accident, feramus)*
>
> Cicero. Pro Sestio 68.143

THEME: STRATEGY

CHECKPOINT: Well it looks like Cicero was saying, 'Hope for the best, prepare for the worst' a long time before our modern politicians and CEOs, who seem to use this expression an awful lot.

Having a contingency plan is a sensible move. Protecting the company at all costs is a duty as much as a corporate responsibility.

As an expression, it makes sense, but it is a little fuzzy. For me, it only comes into focus if you pair it with another thought: 'Plan as much as you can, execute the plan just once.'

'Hope' is not really a business thought. It smacks of inaccurate or incomplete planning.

This might sound harsh, but in truth, there is no reason why a well thought-out strategy should not go according to plan.

Contingency planning is less effective when it is about damage limitation and is more valuable when it's about other proactive options.

So maybe we should be saying something more like: 'Plan for the best, prepare a good alternative.'

Although, admittedly, it's not quite so snappy.

WANT TO KNOW MORE? Today's thought from Cicero comes from one his legal defence speeches in the courts of Rome.

Cicero is defending a character called Publius Sestius, who had been accused of using armed force within the city of Rome.

Cicero's speech is one of his grandest, and at one point seems to go off on a tangent that looks and smells like Cicero making a completely separate political point.

Cicero was as clever as they come when it came to arguing his case.

He demonstrated that Sestius was only using force to protect the very institutions of Rome that prohibit the use of force. Ha!

Sestius was cleared of all charges.

> ### There are four presentation styles: 'abundant'... 'brief'... 'dry'... 'rich and florid'.
>
> *(quattuor sunt genera dicendi:*
> *copiosum ... breve ... siccum ... pingue et floridum)*
>
> Macrobius. Saturnalia 5.7

THEME: PRESENTATIONS/MEETINGS/DOCUMENTS

CHECKPOINT: There are many different ways to deliver a presentation. You can stand. Sit. Speak from notes. Have lots of hi-tech. Have no tech at all. Give handouts. Go solo, or be part of a team. And so on.

But unless you are given a specific request to make your delivery in a certain way, the best advice is 'to be yourself'.

It is rare that you are criticized for presenting in your own unique style. And here's why:

Almost no one enjoys giving a presentation.

So while you have the floor, you will also have the tacit support of the audience in the room.

Be yourself and you will almost certainly get across your message in an endearing and intelligible way.

WANT TO KNOW MORE? Macrobius lived some time around 400 CE. Today's quote comes from a piece he wrote concerning different styles of oratory.

He gives examples of people who fit the categories he outlined.

Cicero was '*copiosum*'. His style was to be generous and provide abundant elaboration.

The historian Sallust (see July 22 and March 21) kept things brief, '*breve*'.

Fronto was regarded as '*siccum*' (dry) although his love letters to his young pupil seem far from arid. (Fronto was tutor to the young Marcus Aurelius).

Pliny the Younger was thought to have spoken in a rich and florid way, '*pingue et floridum*'.

But Vergil, says Macrobius, was able to cover all styles, such was his mastery of the Latin language.

> No intelligent person – and there's been a great deal
> written about this – has ever said that changing
> your plan demonstrated inconsistency.
>
> *(nemo doctus umquam – multa autem de hoc genere scripta*
> *sunt – mutationem consili inconstantiam dixit esse)*
>
> Cicero. Letters To Atticus 16.7.3

THEME: STRATEGY

CHECKPOINT: You need to put the right resources behind a strategy and you need to execute your plan with directness and determination. Having said that, it takes a great person to stand up and say: 'You know what? The strategy is not right. We need to rethink what we are doing.'

This does not demonstrate inconsistency or hesitancy.

This demonstrates confidence and leadership.

It is better to press the pause button and review, or even to press the stop button and halt everything, if you feel you need to change direction.

WANT TO KNOW MORE? Cicero wrote at least 461 letters to his friend Atticus. We have 16 letters from Atticus to Cicero, although he must have written many more.

Atticus was Cicero's great friend from schooldays. Born in November 110 BCE (and so four years older than Cicero), Atticus moved to Athens when he was 25, after his father's death, although he made regular visits to Rome.

Atticus was born Titus Pomponius, from a long-standing Roman family, but because he adopted Athens as his home town, falling in love with all things Greek, he earned the nickname 'Atticus', Attica being the Greek name for the territory in which Athens was located. In 65 BCE he returned to Rome and decided to make it his permanent home.

Atticus never got involved in politics. He was a man of considerable private means who loved antiquarian and cultural pursuits (he was said to have written a history of Rome and a study of Roman families).

After Cicero's execution he lived on in Rome until his death in 32 BCE, aged 78.

....

> ## Where have I come from and where am I going to?
>
> ### *(unde quo veni?)*
>
> Horace. Odes 3.27.37

THEME: **PERSONAL DEVELOPMENT**

CHECKPOINT: At some point in your career, probably at several points, you'll need to ask yourself these two questions:

1. What has the sum of my past made me?
2. Where do I want to end up at age 65?

There are a few reasons you'll need to do this self check-up. You might feel 'stuck', neither hating nor loving your work. You're just hanging on. You might feel under-appreciated. You have skills that others don't realize, or which you haven't had time to develop yourself.

You might feel the need to assert yourself. To go for that promotion or pay rise.

You might be about to start a family. Or say goodbye to the last offspring fleeing the nest.

Make a strategy for yourself. Make it a three-, five- or ten-year plan.

Open up a spreadsheet and start doing some calculations.

The more you understand your own motivations, and the more you are in control of what you're doing, the better you will feel about yourself.

WANT TO KNOW MORE? There were no public games held in December.

And the half dozen religious observances became more obscure as time went on.

December was the beginning of winter. The days were shorter, with fewer working hours, and there would have been less travel and trade in a month when the sea could be wild, and the weather was colder.

The climate of ancient Rome was much like it is there today. In the winter it would rain, and they would have snow at times too.

Only the wealthy would have underfloor heating. The majority of Romans would have made small fires in their homes and wrapped themselves up in woollen clothes.

Further north of Rome, it was not unusual for Romans to wear trousers in the winter.

....

> **King Cyrus knew the names of every single soldier in his army.**
>
> *(Cyrus rex omnibus in exercitu suo militibus nomina reddidit)*
>
> Pliny The Elder. Natural History 7.24

THEME: LEADERSHIP (PART 1)

CHECKPOINT: I've always been amazed by the way so many schoolteachers can remember the names of each and every pupil they teach.

I've even seen headmasters stroll through the playground and reel off a number of names as if they were close family.

It's impressive. But it's also important. Particularly in the workplace.

To feel that you can be personally identified gives you value and significance.

To be just another employee makes you feel like an insignificant cog in the wheel.

You might not expect the chairman to know everybody in person, but certainly your department head should know not just your name, but something about you as well.

The personal touch takes time and effort.

But that's the point.

If you demonstrate that you have invested time and effort into getting to know the people who work with you, you will increase the chances of having a team that is more committed to the work they have to do and more loyal to the person they work for.

WANT TO KNOW MORE? Cyrus the Great was not called 'the Great' for no reason.

In an all-conquering career of some 25 years he subdued territory that today stretches from the east coast of the Mediterranean to the Indus River in Pakistan.

Put simply, he created a vast empire and inspired considerable respect for his achievements.

Cyrus lived sometime between 600 BCE and 530 BCE and his military success garnered him the following titles:

Great King; King of Kings; King of Persia; King of Anshan; King of Media; King of Babylon; King of Sumer and Akkad.

As a neat summary, he was also known as King of the Four Corners of the World. Not bad.

DECEMBER 3

> Whenever you have an exceptional senior manager, departmental
> administration runs perfectly; when the manager is less able,
> the departments fall apart.
>
> (ὅταν μὲν ὁ ἐπιστάτης βελτίων γένηται, καθαρώτερον τὰ νόμιμα
> πράττεται· ὅταν δὲ χείρων, φαυλότερον)
>
> Xenophon. Cyropaedia 8.1.8

THEME: LEADERSHIP (PART 2)

CHECKPOINT: Yesterday we looked at how simply making the effort to remember people's names can pay dividends. Here are nine more ideas, to make up a top-ten chart.

1. Be on time for meetings. (Not too early, that's intimidating, and not late, as that shows contempt for the meeting and those attending.)
2. Show equanimity. A calm composure and a level head will both inspire confidence.
3. Demonstrate impartiality. If you have 'favourites' you create division and a lack of motivation.
4. Don't take all the credit. You're only as good as the people who work for you.
5. Be good-humoured. Your emotions will define the mood of the day.
6. Define exactly what the personal review system will be and don't change it.
7. Stick to agreements.
8. Lead by example. If you want a top performing team, be a top performer yourself.
9. Take your holidays. An over-present workaholic boss is passively confrontational.

WANT TO KNOW MORE? Xenophon wrote a kind of retro-fit biography of Cyrus the Great. His *Cyropaedia* was an opportunity for him to outline what he felt were the right characteristics to be a great ruler and what were the circumstances needed to have great government.

The fictional nature of this work, imprinted onto the life of an extraordinarily famous king of history, makes for choppy waters when trying to separate fact from fiction.

The Greeks saw Cyrus the Great as a successful and powerful Persian (therefore 'foreign') leader. As part of his expansionist programme, Cyrus conquered the Greek-inhabited region of Ionia in 547 BC. He seemed to be a permanent threat.

Persia was to stand in opposition to Greece as a natural foe for 100 years until the Persian invasion force was decisively beaten in 449 BCE.

> **So often it's better to have just one person than a whole crowd of people.**
>
> *(plus esse in uno saepe quam in turba boni)*
>
> Phaedrus. Fables 4.5.1

THEME: PRESENTATIONS/MEETINGS/DOCUMENTS

CHECKPOINT: A recurring problem throughout many companies is who exactly to take to the meeting.

On the surface, it should be so simple. You only want those people who are actively going to make a contribution. But it doesn't work out like that, does it?

The boss wants to come because it's an 'important' meeting. Two colleagues both want to give the presentation because they both contributed to it. Someone feels you need IT support, because the meeting location is out-of-office.

The other side is fielding six people, so your side should field the same number.

Meeting management is a classic example of the need for a strong Project Manager. It's very simple. The team that is fielded is the team that can win the meeting. And the person who leads the meeting should be the one who has the most compelling part to play.

In the military, tasks are commanded by those with the expertise, independent of rank. Businesses can learn from this. Sending the entire army to the meeting, or just all the top brass, or one lone redundant general, may not give your best performers the opportunity to shine.

WANT TO KNOW MORE? Phaedrus is a source for Aesop's fables.

Aesop never wrote them down, so they survive through copied versions and fragments in other literature.

Phaedrus wasn't referred to much by later writers and he dedicated his books of fables to a couple of people we know nothing about. Phaedrus sounds less than exciting.

But every now and then Phaedrus looks like he wants to try a little experimentation.

He puts Aesop himself into the fables, sometimes as the storyteller and other times as an integral part of the story itself.

DECEMBER 5

THEME: LEADERSHIP

CHECKPOINT: Sometimes you just want to throw your hands up into the air and bemoan how things are done nowadays.

Maybe the prevalent and persistent use of social media is driving you mad. Or the attitudes of the younger people toward work. Or you just don't understand the way customers are making decisions. It could be anything.

Modern life is constantly re-inventing itself.

To be an effective leader in business you need to understand how things are changing.

There are real changes happening every day that require thinking through and understanding.

And there are subtle, confusing changes that simply reskin, or relabel attitudes which you previously understood. *'Plus ça change'*, you might say.

Try to diarize time to understand the times and the prevailing attitudes.

WANT TO KNOW MORE? The Catiline Conspiracy was Cicero's big, early career-defining moment. We know that because he told us it was.

Catiline was a Roman senator with a distinguished military career. His attempts to reach the highest political position had been constantly thwarted.

He planned to rally the poor and dispossessed of Rome (there had been a constant drain on Rome's funds for a number of years due to internal strife) so that he could put himself into a position of political strength. His campaign slogan was 'Debt Relief'.

When this idea failed, he and a few fellow conspirators plotted a violent takeover.

Cicero was the man of the moment. He discovered the plot and wiped it out before it really started. Catiline was killed (somewhat heroically, in fact) and the other conspirators were put to death. The name Catiline became synonymous with political plotting, in a similar way as Guy Fawkes is in the UK today.

> **So who will double-check on those who are in charge?**
>
> *(sed quis custodiet ipsos custodes?)*
>
> Juvenal. Satires 6.347

THEME: HUMAN RESOURCES

CHECKPOINT: Today's quote by Juvenal ranks amongst the best known of all quotes. It is usually translated as "who will guard the guards?"

At its heart lies something most companies experience in one form or another.

Double-checking. Auditing. Compliance.

Companies operate in the public domain under a legal framework that needs to be adhered to. This framework protects all involved – investors, owners, managers, employees, suppliers and customers.

Auditing makes sure the financial footprint of the company satisfies the regulations that are in force. There are other forms of auditing as well that are not legally required. Social, Ethical and Environmental Auditing, for example.

How much you decide to have outsiders inside your businesses, beyond the statutory ones, is up to you. But if you do, be sure that such extra double-checking is done in service to the company and its commercial needs. It could well be that demonstrating you are an open and transparent business is actually good for business.

WANT TO KNOW MORE? Juvenal wrote 16 satires. Satire Six was his longest and possibly most talked about. The subject matter is women and marriage.

He writes the satire to advise his friend not to get married because women are a nightmare. (I'm being polite.)

His line about 'who will guard the guards' is actually about chaperones. All well and good for ladies to go out in public with female chaperones – but who'll keep an eye on the chaperones? They can be complicit when the women are being, ahem, 'naughty'.

Some say that the satire is subtle. That's it's not about marriage, it's about Roman women and how they became hardened by life.

DECEMBER 7

> **Was the business matter so important that people had to be dragged from their sick beds? I'm guessing Hannibal was outside our gates!**
>
> *(an ea res agebatur ut etiam aegrotos deferri oporteret?*
> *Hannibal, credo, erat ad portas)*
>
> Cicero. Philippic 1.11

THEME: LEADERSHIP

CHECKPOINT: Don't panic!

How you are seen to handle emergencies reflects on your overall management style.

At some point a serious threat will emerge, an alarm will go off and there will be a frenzy of activity. Assuming there is not an instant threat to life, give yourself a few minutes to think things through calmly. Don't drag people from their sickbeds to attend an emergency meeting; that's panicking.

Pull together two or three capable associates.

Talk it through. Plan your next steps. Don't rush around like a mad person.

The process at this point is all about how you will be seen to act; therefore, that is what will matter most.

WANT TO KNOW MORE? It is sometimes easy to forget that amongst the brilliant poetry, the architectural wonders and the intellectual genius of the Romans, there was also abhorrent brutality.

To have been a Roman in Cicero's time would have been to witness horrors that today we would find very hard to stomach.

The greatest intellect of his day, the finest example of Republican pride, Cicero, was butchered this day on the orders of Mark Antony and his military junta.

Cicero knew it was coming. He was 63, and in his final days he knew he was fighting a losing battle for the soul of the Roman Republic.

He bared his neck to his executioners as he leaned out of his carriage. They decapitated him and chopped off his hands. Both were displayed in the Forum in Rome. His tongue was cut out and given to Antony's wife who, it is told, repeatedly stabbed it with a hair pin.

In this way, Cicero's weapons – his head for thinking, his hands for writing and his tongue for speaking – could wage war against the anti-Republicans no more.

> **In tough times show you have spirit and strength.**
>
> *(rebus angustis animosus atque fortis appare)*
>
> Horace. Odes 2.10.21

THEME: LEADERSHIP

CHECKPOINT: There is an old saying that goes: 'A ship is safe in a harbour, but that's not what ships are made for.'

Ships go to sea, businesses go to work.

To captain a boat, you need a licence. In business, your 'licence' is your previous track record.

You need to learn how to navigate through choppy seas; how to understand the various distress signals there are.

You need to know the rules of the sea. What the signals from lighthouses and buoys mean.

What you don't do is pass your test just by navigating gently through calm waters on a clear day.

A leader is exposed in tough times. It's make or break time.

Make sure you have all the training you can get.

Every employee knows that if the business goes down, there won't be lifeboats.

So they'll be looking to you to make sure the enterprise stays afloat.

WANT TO KNOW MORE? If you have time when you're next on holiday, go to Puglia in southern Italy, and take a drive up to Venosa.

To be honest, it's quite a hike. It's a good hour from the coast.

In fact, it's a good hour from anywhere. But take the trip anyway.

Venosa is dissected north-south by the Strada Provinciale 168 and on the eastern half, just off the Via Giuseppe Garibaldi, you'll find a tiny lane, the Vico Sallustio.

Wander down this lane for a few yards until the space opens out to a lovely small square.

There'll be a bar in the corner somewhere.

Take a seat and with a cold drink in your hand raise a glass to the statue in front you.

It's the statue of the extraordinary poet Horace, born this day, 8th December, in this place, Venosa, in 65 BCE.

> **When I nod something through, my word is my bond.**
> **There'll be no reneging on the deal, no smoke and mirrors.**
>
> *(οὐ γὰρ ἐμὸν παλινάγρετον οὐδ᾽ ἀπατηλὸν οὐδ᾽ ἀτελεύτητον,*
> *ὅ τί κεν κεφαλῇ κατανεύσω)*
>
> Homer. Iliad 1.526

THEME: LEGAL

CHECKPOINT: The best way of securing a deal is to get it in writing. Preferably overseen by a lawyer.

But you might want to make a verbal commitment too.

That's fine and there are plenty of examples of honourable executives committing to something verbally and sticking to their agreements.

But, I'm afraid, there are examples of the opposite too.

Going back on your word or reneging on a commitment is the lowest form of management.

It makes you untrustworthy in everything you do – not just making agreements.

But, again, the opposite is true as well.

People who are known to keep to their word are very highly regarded.

The best advice here is never to commit to something unless you know 100% that you are able to keep to your word.

WANT TO KNOW MORE? When we talk about Homer, it's hard not to think about a person.

But it is questionable whether Homer was in fact a single person.

The identity of Homer is a huge mystery.

He is first referred to in Greek literature some 200 years after the *Iliad* and *Odyssey* were written. He was a mystery to the likes of Herodotus, Plato and Aristotle.

Homer uses many different Greek dialects, maybe suggesting that many hands were at work in the stories. Or were the dialects widely known and used to appeal to a wide audience?

What is certain is that the *Iliad* and the *Odyssey* were famous stories transmitted over hundreds of years by travelling storytellers.

The stories survived through an incredible oral tradition – the tales being repeated over and over again by experts. These experts were trained to understand the way Homer needed to sound. Reciting lengthy passages by heart was a skill by any standards.

> **Truth hates delays.**
>
> *(veritas odit moras)*
>
> Seneca. Oedipus 850

THEME: HUMAN RESOURCES

CHECKPOINT: When the truth of any situation, good or bad, is finally out, it should be made available to those who need it as quickly as possible. This is because when it's 'out there' it becomes available to more people than you might at first expect.

Businesses need to act fast and sitting on any data or information is pointless.

You will have noticed how good news travels faster than the speed of sound.

But you might also have observed that bad news can sometimes travel very slowly and often it takes a less than direct route. It is sat on, pondered, edited even.

When you put delay into news transmission, weird things happen.

You might get falsification or distortion.

Obviously, sometimes you don't get the full picture immediately. That's fine. As you pass the information on, just explain that it is only part of the story and that you will relate the remaining part as soon as you have it.

WANT TO KNOW MORE? If you were an ancient Roman and you decided to write a tragedy, your first port of call would be the tragedies already written by the Greek masters.

You might think this was somewhat unoriginal, but that is what the public wanted, and if you were a smart writer with a commercial head, you gave the public what they wanted.

Seneca's play *Oedipus* follows closely the version written by Sophocles.

But Sophocles' version was far, far superior.

Seneca gets sidetracked and spends too much time writing about obscure occult rituals.

His drama fails to put the, well, drama, into Oedipus' discovery that he has in fact married his mother.

Which, let's be fair, is one of the cornerstone moments of the entire Oedipus story.

....

> **A not inconsiderable part of the art of conversation is knowing, and sticking to, good taste when it comes to asking questions and making jokes.**
>
> *(οὐ γάρ τι μικρόν τῆς ὁμιλητικῆς μόριον ἡ περὶ τὰς ἐρωτήσεις καὶ τὰς παιδιὰς τοῦ ἐμμελοῦς ἐπιστήμη καὶ τήρησις)*
>
> Plutarch. Moralia 8 Table Talk 629

THEME: ENTERTAINING

CHECKPOINT: There is nothing worse than that awkward silence when someone sticks their foot right in it and tells a completely inappropriate joke.

When you're with a customer the indiscretion is magnified, making it twice as bad.

After all, think about it, it could cost you that customer.

People are easily offended. They always have been.

In conversation with a customer at a relaxed event, steer clear of these obvious danger zones: Politics. Religion. Personal Finance. Sex. Major Illnesses. Death.

Stick to: The Weather. Holidays. Entertainment (movies, books, games, etc). Sport. Current Affairs. Hobbies.

If you have to tell a joke, there are some rules here too.

Avoid the sensative subjects above.

Avoid including any real people in the joke.

Don't tell any joke unless you have told it before and it is guaranteed to get a laugh.

WANT TO KNOW MORE? Today in Rome, you might have witnessed a festival but might not have participated.

The '*Septimontium*' was an 'invitation-only' party for residents living on seven particular hills in Rome (not the famous seven hills of Rome, a different seven!).

It seems to have been somewhat elitist and may have had its roots in the early days of Rome, when the city was first colonized and established.

The Emperor Domitian seemed to like this festival.

He arranged an expensive and exclusive dinner for the upper echelons of Roman society. The menu was clearly far superior to that of the everyday citizen.

Domitian would kick off proceedings by eating first and then inviting the others to tuck in.

....

> **Make sure you say and do whatever you would like your company to think and do.**
>
> *(πάνθ᾽ ὅσα τοὺς ἀρχομένους καὶ φρονεῖν καὶ πράττειν βούλει, καὶ λέγε καὶ ποίει)*
>
> Maecenas (Quoted by Dio Cassius. Roman History 52.34.1)

THEME: LEADERSHIP

CHECKPOINT: Ah. The art of persuasion. In order to successfully lead a team, you need to bring them on a journey, with you leading from the front.

Speaking and doing as you want your team to speak and do is the first step in ensuring that everyone is aligned.

This means you have to regularly keep in touch with the mindset of everyone involved.

Keeping aligned means remaining attentive to what's going on.

As a manager, how you act and the messages you give out are openly observed – and discussed. If you suddenly and inexplicably change tack, expect confusion to follow.

WANT TO KNOW MORE? Gaius Clinius Maecenas is a major figure in Roman cultural history. Born about 68 BCE, he died aged 60 a few weeks before the poet Horace in 8 BCE. Horace was a close friend, and for a reason.

Maecenas was responsible for sponsoring many of the most important poets of his day.

With justification, he can be seen as the leading light in arts patronage.

Maecenas was born into a very established noble family. His ancestors were respected, ancient royalty. He enjoyed inherited wealth, but never officially went into politics.

At some point in his early twenties, he became a close friend of Augustus and a kind of minister without portfolio. Augustus used the arts to promote his vision of a reborn, revitalized Rome, based on traditions, but with a forward-looking perspective. Maecenas supported Vergil, Horace and Propertius, ensuring they were looked after financially, and connecting them into the highest echelons of power.

The patronage paid off. Vergil's epic the *Aeneid* was a work of genius and promoted Augustus into the ranks of the exalted and sublime.

DECEMBER 13

THEME: LEADERSHIP

CHECKPOINT: It is quite an eye-opener when you realize that you have been deceived by the leadership of your company. Of course, you'll be told there was a sound reason behind it. Security. Competitive Advantage. Sensitive HR issues. But there is no excuse for it. Management is as much about the management of information as it is the management of people.

There is always sensitive information in any business, but the trick is to confine it to where it is most needed whilst galvanizing the workforce around the information that you know you can safely give out.

As these passages have mentioned many times, when trust between colleagues at any level breaks down, you have a fault line in the organization that will inevitably lead to a reduction of effort, and therefore profitability.

WANT TO KNOW MORE? Today we meet the mighty Marcus Vipsanius Agrippa, the muscle behind Augustus, his trusted general.

Augustus, with Agrippa and Maecenas, operated a kind of triangular power centre, with each covering for the other at times.

Agrippa's birth and childhood are shrouded in mystery – and maybe he liked it that way. But what we do know is that he very early became a friend of Augustus and was with him when they heard the news that Julius Caesar had been assassinated. The two travelled together to Rome to assert Augustus' rights as heir to Caesar's inheritance. They stayed together through thick and thin. Just about every battle that Augustus needed to win was won for him by Agrippa, including the famous sea battle of Actium that confirmed Augustus as master of the world.

The combination of Augustus, Agrippa and Maecenas ensured that every new agenda that needed to be promoted was executed with expert precision.

> **Whether it be a contract or a transaction,
> if it's agreed by word of mouth, it's agreed.**
>
> *(cum nexum faciet mancipiumque,
> uti lingua nuncupassit, ita ius esto)*
>
> Twelve Tables. Table 6.1a

THEME: LEGAL

CHECKPOINT: Be careful when you make a verbal commitment.

Most people in business are not lawyers and this means that you can make an expensive mistake by agreeing to something that you later do not want to continue with.

Whether a verbal agreement is binding or not is something you can pay expensive lawyers to debate until the cows come home.

But this is the point. It's not the sort of debate or expenditure you want to get into.

Play safe.

Don't make verbal agreements unless you have a signed piece of paper in your pocket with at least an outline of what you had in mind.

Better still, whenever you do make an agreement, make sure it is covered by legal advice.

WANT TO KNOW MORE? While the Greeks far away over the seas were defining democracy, polishing up philosophical positions and delivering drama of genius, the Romans were just beginning to organize themselves into some form of ordered society.

The legal history of Rome begins in 445 BCE with the Twelve Tables.

The idea was to end the longstanding differences between the ordinary citizens and the noble, aristocratic rulers – a struggle that would continue to rumble on through Rome's early history.

A board of 10 men was commissioned to write up a code, and one story is that they were packed off to Athens to see how it was done properly.

The agreed 'rules' or 'statutes' were put onto bronze tablets and enshrined as a legal charter.

Cicero tells us that at school, every upper-class Roman schoolboy learned the Twelve Tables by heart, chanting it the way we (used to?) learn our twelve times table.

> For I noted that those who do their jobs carelessly lose out,
> while I discovered that those who seriously focus accomplish
> them more quickly, more easily, and more profitably.
> If you choose to learn from the latter, I think, god willing,
> you too would become a seriously formidable businessman.
>
> *(τοὺς μὲν γὰρ εἰκῇ ταῦτα πράττοντας ζημιουμένους ἑώρων, τοὺς δὲ γνώμῃ*
> *συντεταμένῃ ἐπιμελουμένους καὶ θᾶττον καὶ ῥᾷον καὶ κερδαλεώτερον*
> *κατέγνων πράττοντας. παρ᾽ ὧν ἂν καὶ σὲ οἶμαι, εἰ βούλοιο, μαθόντα,*
> *εἴ σοι ὁ θεὸς μὴ ἐναντιοῖτο, πάνυ ἂν δεινὸν χρηματιστὴν γενέσθαι.)*
>
> Xenophon. Economics 2.18

THEME: **PERSONAL DEVELOPMENT**

CHECKPOINT: Work can become a chore for anyone, at any level. The challenge for us is to maintain our level of commitment to what we are doing when the day seems just that little too boring for our liking. Focusing on what you are doing produces much better results. If necessary, divide your workload up in to bite-sized chunks and focus on each section at a time.

You might think that by focusing on what you need to do you will spend longer doing it, but in fact it will get you through the work faster.

Whatever you do, don't get careless. If you cannot concentrate on what you are doing, take a break. Have a coffee, or whatever. Go for a walk, if you can.

Lack of concentration produces poor work and you might end up having do it all over again – the worst possible outcome.

People who have the ability to apply themselves to any and every task always do better than those who don't.

WANT TO KNOW MORE? Today in 37 CE, the Emperor Nero was born.

One big change that Augustus (his great-great grandfather) brought to the Roman Empire was inherited succession.

Up until Augustus, the two consuls (and occasional limited-term dictators) were appointed by, and within, an electoral process.

After Augustus, there's no voting to be done. The next in line was either obvious (a family member) or, after a lot of back-stabbing (literally), was made obvious. You'd want the Praetorian Guard (the imperial security service) to be on your side to guarantee success.

Nero succeeded his great-uncle Claudius, who had adopted him. Adoption was just as legitimate a process of providing a successor as having your own naturally-born son.

> **Oh the stresses of life. There is so much nonsense going on!**
>
> *(O curas hominum! O quantum est in rebus inane!)*
>
> Lucilius. Satires 1.2

THEME: **THE WATERCOOLER**

CHECKPOINT: Work can be stressful at times. Let's not make light of this. For some, the stress is serious and requires professional input.

Stress comes to us from so many different sources – home life, work life, private life, virtual life. What you don't need is to add any unnecessary pressure to what you do.

Avoid those colleagues who seem to add to your stress through nonsensical rants or unverifiable gossip.

Speak out as soon as you feel anxious or depressed. Sometimes you can get wound up by something that doesn't exist.

At all times, when you feel things are getting too much, seek professional advice.

WANT TO KNOW MORE? The literary output of ancient Greece after the time of Alexander the Great is more limited, but still important and influential. There were superb writers, such as Menander, Polybius, Apollonius of Rhodes, and the poets Callimachus and Theocritus, but the literary action now begins to shift over to the west coast of Italy.

In Rome, there was plenty to write about. Rome was becoming ever more influential, throwing up controversial characters, eventful power struggles and multicultural politics.

Enter Lucilius, who was born around 180 BCE and died as Cicero and Caesar were entering the world, in about 102 BC.

Lucilius' work survives only in fragments. He wrote frankly about the Roman society of his day. He spoke his mind. He was a satirical commentator and diarist on the growing and changing nature of Roman society, making the loss of his work even more frustrating.

Lucilius gave the Romans their own genre of literature: satire.

....

> ### It's all Greek to me.
>
> *(Graecum est; non legitur)*
>
> Marginalia (Written in the margins of Greek and Latin manuscripts by monks in the Middle Ages who could not understand what was written.)

THEME: PRESENTATIONS/MEETINGS/DOCUMENTS

CHECKPOINT: When putting together any form of document that has to be read by another person, the cardinal sin is to make it difficult to understand.

Often, it's the convoluted calculations. How on earth did you get to that profit margin?!

Sometimes it's the overlong sentence with no punctuation or paragraphs in sight.

Many times, I've seen a visual that is meant to clarify something actually ending up needing a five-minute explanation itself.

The truth is that we are not all gifted at putting information together in a digestible way.

Build in time to bounce your work off someone else.

Build in even more time to go back and edit what you have done to make it comprehensible.

If necessary, enlist the help of another to fill in the parts you are less able to complete.

After all, the purpose of a presentation or document is to communicate. And you want your communication to be crystal-clear.

WANT TO KNOW MORE? How have the classics, some 2,500 years old (some older) come down to us through the ages?

The quick answer is that monasteries preserved many texts, and monks made copies.

There is another answer, that might sit alongside the 'monk' tradition.

Writing was big business in Rome. There were a number of libraries and many booksellers. Even after the invasion of the Goths and the downfall of Rome, there were booksellers, stationers, antiquarians, copyists and so on. There is written evidence of these from 500 CE right up to the invention of printing.

Schools and universities needed books to educate the wealthy in the 'proper' literature that was available.

There was a huge demand for books! It was education that kept many manuscripts alive.

....

> **Don't talk too much at the client dinner.**
>
> *(pauca in convivio loquere)*
>
> Cato. Collectio Distichorum Vulgaris. I.51

THEME: **ENTERTAINING**

CHECKPOINT: We are coming to the season of entertaining and there will be plenty of opportunities to take colleagues and customers out for a lunch or dinner. Maybe there will be a party too.

What can I say? Don't be stupid!

Too much alcohol can make you say and do things you later regret.

Remember, work is work. How you behave in your private life is up to you.

Avoid talking too much and taking over the event. No one appreciates someone making themselves the centre of attention.

Have fun. Enjoy yourself.

But be prepared to face yourself the following morning!

WANT TO KNOW MORE? "Io Saturnalia!"

We have now entered the season of *Saturnalia*.

Saturnalia, December 17 – 23 was the festival of the god Saturn. Yesterday was the strict, religious day; today and for the next six days it was party time.

The shops, law courts and schools of Rome would shut; gambling in the streets would be permitted; there would be widespread feasting and fun. It was a time for families to party together. Hilariously, Pliny the Younger tells us how he hid himself away in a separate room to get away from the noise of the party at his house.

Masters would wait upon the servants at table; the entire household, slaves included, would be treated as equals. A Master of Fun would be appointed; small gifts given; wine would flow.

Saturnalia coincided with the Winter Solstice and the last sowing of the season. The merriment and getting-together may have had its roots in ancient ceremonies when the master and farmhands could at last relax and appreciate each other's work.

"The best of days," said the love poet Catullus.

> **It's very true what they say 'a liar should have a good memory'.**
>
> *(verumque est illud quod vulgo dicitur, mendacem memorem esse oportere.)*
>
> Quintilian. Institutio Oratoria 4.2.91

THEME: **PERSONAL DEVELOPMENT**

CHECKPOINT: Telling the truth is so much easier than lying.

For most people, remembering what time the meeting is due to start is hard enough.

To carry an elaborate storyline in your head, with alternative versions for different likely outcomes, is a skill indeed. But not one that endears you to your colleagues.

The staggering thing is that we have all encountered liars who persist in their storyline even after it has been evidenced to be completely false!

These people need to get help.

Telling the truth is a powerful tool. It confers honesty and trust. You are listened to more.

When things aren't going well, the advice of a trustworthy person is followed more readily.

Telling the truth is not the same as 'telling it as it is'. Sometimes you need to apply a little diplomacy.

WANT TO KNOW MORE? Quintilian was widely known and respected. He was a highly successful teacher of rhetoric in Rome, who lived roughly between 35 CE and 100 CE.

Born in the Rioja region of Spain, he was sent to Rome for his education, which he then took back to Spain where he started to practice law.

In his mid-thirties, Quintilian returned to Rome in the retinue of the short-lived Emperor Galba and, sensibly avoiding politics, he opened a school of rhetoric.

Quintilian wrote the standard textbook of his day on oratory, the *Institutio Oratoria*. Running to 12 volumes, it is a cornerstone work of Latin, not just for its teachings on oratory but also for its insights into the social life of ancient Rome.

> ### Call this accounting?
> ### The figure in the 'total column' is wrong and calculated badly.
>
> *(hoc est ratio? perversa aera summae et subducta inprobe)*
>
> Lucilius. Satires 29. 907

THEME: FINANCE

CHECKPOINT: Always double-check. There's never a reason not to go over something that is important. No one is infallible. This advice holds particularly true of any work done by someone else which you yourself need to present.

Once you've accepted the work as it is, and presented it on to other people, then it becomes your work.

Blaming someone else at that stage for a mistake is actually blaming yourself.

Besides, it never looks good to pass the blame. It begs the question: why didn't you check everything first yourself?

One thing definitely worth checking over is financial information.

It is so easy to input a wrong figure, to misplace a decimal point or to construct the wrong formula on a spreadsheet.

Look at the information and ask yourself first: 'Does this look roughly right?' Big mistakes are usually easy to spot.

If it looks good, go through the information at your own speed until you are satisfied that everything is accurately expressed.

WANT TO KNOW MORE? "Phew, at least satire is totally ours," wrote yesterday's famous Roman grammarian, Quintilian. Satire was Roman. But more importantly, it wasn't Greek. That made it special.

Satire comes from the Latin word '*satura*' meaning 'a medley of different dishes'.

It was a form of writing that was flexible enough to include comic sketches, dialogues, rants, political jokes and sarcasm.

Think of *Last Week Tonight With John Oliver*, a medley of sketches, some serious, some rude, some just plain slapstick. This mix of ideas is contained in a TV show of fixed length, just as Lucilius, the first pure poet of satire, contained his medley within the fixed metre of poetry.

....

> ### The fox may change his fur, but never his nature.
>
> #### *(vulpem pilum mutare, non mores)*
>
> Suetonius. Vespasian 16.3

THEME: HUMAN RESOURCES

CHECKPOINT: When you are looking at people who are 'promotion material' remember that past performance does, in fact, give a very clear indication of future expectations.

We all form early patterns of behaviour which are difficult to edit or remove completely.

Mostly, we keep them under control, but stress or anger can reveal traits we thought we'd left behind in the school playground.

Our version of Suetonius' phrase is that 'a leopard cannot change his spots'.

What we all hope and expect is that as we gain experience and learning, we also understand ourselves a little better.

If you are thinking of giving someone a senior position, particularly a position that interacts with a large number of people, do your very best to fully understand that person so that the company can provide support whenever and wherever needed.

WANT TO KNOW MORE? Vespasian, declared emperor this day in 69 CE, was one of the good guys.

His most famous legacy is the Colosseum, the largest amphitheatre ever built.

He was an affable man, with a robust sense of humour (and a penchant for vulgar and obscene jokes).

His biographer, Suetonius, while giving us a candid picture of the emperor, has a laugh at his expense: "He had a well-built, well-proportioned body, with muscular arms and legs. His facial expression was of someone sitting on the toilet and straining. Because of that, when Vespasian asked some comedian to make a joke about him, the comic replied: "I will when you've finished relieving your bowels." Vespasian enjoyed excellent health without doing very much to look after himself, except getting a regular face and body massage whenever he played ball. He also fasted one full day every month."

....

> **They say changing your job changes your luck.**
>
> (φασὶ γὰϱ ἅμα ταῖς τῶν ἐπιτηδευμάτων ἀλλαγαῖς
> καὶ τὰς τύχας μετασχηματίζεσθαι)
>
> Alciphron. Letters 2.10

THEME: PERSONAL DEVELOPMENT

CHECKPOINT: So many times in my business life I've come across the situation where an employee leaves for no reason other than they need a change.

And that is as valid a reason as any.

Sometimes, your internal body clock just winds down, an alarm goes off, and you hear yourself saying, 'it's time to move on'.

Other times, a great offer comes up and you'd be a fool not to take it.

I would always advise people to think twice before leaving a job, particularly if you're doing well.

You never know what is coming up around the corner, and loyalty normally pays dividends.

But, as they say, a change is as good as a rest, and a move to a new environment can allow you to open up and develop new skills.

WANT TO KNOW MORE? Alciphron wrote letters to imaginary people.

To fishermen, farmers and prostitutes.

They cover a wide range of subjects, but if he can smuggle a sexual reference into his letters, he will.

He certainly wrote the letters to be read by a wide audience and, I guess, for posterity.

You could say he was an early pioneer of Romantic prose.

Although his work is lively and imaginative, it is frustrating that we know absolutely nothing at all about him.

Zilch. Nada.

We don't even know which century he was born in, or where he lived.

You'd think that with all the letters he wrote, he could at least have left us his address.

....

> **It's said that gifts persuade even the gods.**
>
> *(πείθειν δῶρα καὶ θεοὺς λόγος)*
>
> Euripides. Medea 964

THEME: HUMAN RESOURCES

CHECKPOINT: Have you done your Secret Santa yet? Surely things are closing down in the office now?

You might have wondered who in the company deserves a gift.

The answer is, unless there is a pre-established tradition, no one.

No, I'm not being Scrooge, it's just that Christmas gifts really belong to home, not the workplace

You might want to give a small thank you to someone who has gone out of their way to help.

The company itself might decide to give corporate gifts. But again, be careful. Such gifts are wonderful when times are good, but in downturns you'll need to keep the gifts coming, or risk sending out a distress signal!

And just in case you had any ideas, giving gifts will not persuade your customers that your product or service is any better. A gift is just a gift, and no more.

My best advice? Avoid business-related gift giving. But keep the fun entertainment going!

WANT TO KNOW MORE? Today's quote comes from one of the most brilliant and enduringly modern of all the Greek tragedies, Euripides' *Medea*.

The Greeks, and the Romans too, loved Euripides.

He was a playwright who got straight to the heart of real characterization.

Medea is the story of a woman burdened by complete dependency on her husband and who is then scorned in favour of a younger model. It could have been written yesterday.

Medea seeks revenge. She is an enormously powerful woman, with an intelligence that Athenian audiences would have expected of heroic men.

As Medea exacts her revenge, there is blood and gore and violence on a quite unbelievable scale.

If you've seen the movie *Carrie*, you're beginning to head in the right direction.

Utterly wonderful.

....

First and foremost, it is essential to keep quiet and not to reveal
your master plan to anyone who is not involved with it.
It doesn't matter that you're thrilled with it, or that you can see an
exciting opportunity, or even that you may have concerns about it,
or that someone in the team is personally close to you – could even
be a family member. Only communicate it to those essential to
its execution and leave it right up until the last moment.

*(ἔστι δ᾽ ἀρχὴ μὲν τῶν προειρημένων τὸ σιγᾶν, καὶ μήτε διὰ χαρὰν
παραδόξου προφαινομένης ἐλπίδος μήτε διὰ φόβον μήτε διὰ συνήθειαν
μήτε διὰ φιλοστοργίαν μεταδιδόναι μηδενὶ τῶν ἐκτός, αὐτοῖς δὲ κοινοῦσθαι
τούτοις, ὧν χωρὶς οὐχ οἷόν τε τὸ προτεθὲν ἐπὶ τέλος ἀγαγεῖν, καὶ τούτοις
μὴ πρότερον, ἀλλ᾽ ὅταν ὁ τῆς ἑκάστου χρείας καιρὸς ἐπαναγκάζῃ.)*

Polybius. Histories 9.13.2

THEME: STRATEGY

CHECKPOINT: It's Christmas Eve.

Don't give away too many hints.

'Nuff said.

Oh, and in a work context, keep your master plan safe and secure until
it's time to make it public.

WANT TO KNOW MORE? Think of Polybius' *Histories* as a kind of gift to
the Greeks. This race that gave the world Homer, Socrates, Plato, Aristotle, Herodotus, Thucydides, Aeschylus, Sophocles, Euripides, Aristophanes, Archimedes ... the list goes on, was by 200 BCE a mere shadow
of its former self.

Having fought off the Persians, suffered under the Spartans and been
humiliated by Alexander the Great, this race of cultural giants was now
on the point of coming under, gasp, Roman rule. They wouldn't know it,
but the 'Roman' domination of Greece would last in some form (mainly
Byzantine) until the fall of Constantinople in 1453 CE.

It was over, and Polybius saw the signs. He had friends in Rome. He
had cultivated relationships while he had been a political detainee there for
17 years. He personally witnessed the sack of Carthage in 146 BCE. He
knew more than most Greeks about the Roman mindset.

If there was one thing he knew he could give his compatriots, it was
information. He wrote his history to explain to his fellow countrymen
what was happening and what they should expect.

DECEMBER 25

> **Your stomach does not listen to advice.**
>
> *(venter praecepta non audit)*
>
> Seneca. Epistles 21.11

THEME: ENTERTAINING

CHECKPOINT: Happy Christmas!

WANT TO KNOW MORE? December 25 was just another day in the life of the Greeks and Romans until 275 CE, when the Emperor Aurelian officially declared '*Sol Invectus*' – 'The Unconquered Sun' – to be an official cult, celebrated on this day.

As cults go, it enjoyed a relatively short life (just 113 years).

It wasn't until 336 CE that Christmas Day was celebrated as a religious festival.

There is some slight evidence that Christmas Day in Rome borrowed some of the trappings of the Roman festival of *Saturnalia*.

During *Saturnalia*, families would feast together and give gifts, and light-weight hats would be worn.

Ring any bells?

As we observe, when people drink, they become flush with cash, they are immensely successful, they win lawsuits, they're blissfully happy and they help their friends ...

(ὁρᾷς, ὅταν πίνωσιν ἄνθρωποι, τότε πλουτοῦσι, διαπράττουσι, νικῶσιν δίκας, εὐδαιμονοῦσιν, ὠφελοῦσι τοὺς φίλους)

Aristophanes. Knights 92

THEME: THE WATERCOOLER

CHECKPOINT: Remember the guy from work who'd had a few at the office party?

Remember what he told you about himself?

How he didn't really need to work? (He was privately very wealthy.)

The villa with pool in the south of France?

How his top lawyers had dealt with 'any problems'?

How he'd splashed the cash when his friends were in trouble?

Oh dear. There is an equation which you might like to remember. The level of nonsense spouted is directly proportional to the level of alcohol consumed. Take it easy over the festive period.

WANT TO KNOW MORE? Three of Aristophanes' plays – *Λυσιστράτη* (*Lysistrata*), *Θεσμοφοριάζουσαι* (*Thesmophoriazusae* or *Women Celebrating the Festival of the Thesmophoria)* and *Ἐκκλησιάζουσαι* (*Ecclesiazusae,–* or *The Assembly Women*) – feature women turning the Greek established order upside down.

In *Lysistrata*, the women try to bring an end to the deleterious Peloponnesian War by depriving their men of sex.

In *Thesmophoriazusae*, the women are plotting some form of revenge on the playwright Euripides for portraying women as sexually depraved.

In *Ecclesiazusae*, the women take control of the government and bring in new laws that ban private wealth and enforce sexual equality for all old and unattractive people.

Much as we might want to invest Aristophanes with the honour of spearheading an early form of women's liberation, that was almost certainly not his objective.

Aristophanes just took pleasure in stirring things up and upsetting the cosy norms of Athenian (male) life.

> **Remember to keep a level head when things get steep.**
>
> *(aequam memento rebus in arduis servare mentem)*
>
> Horace. Odes 2.3.1

THEME: PERSONAL DEVELOPMENT

CHECKPOINT: At some point in your work life, you'll face an uphill struggle. It's human nature to brood on these things and then to explode.

Unfortunately, so often the explosion happens at the wrong time and in the wrong place.

When you hit tough times, diarize a day or two out of the office that is specifically set aside to work through these issues.

Find someone you know who is level-headed. It doesn't have to be a close friend, just a sensible one.

I found writing down or even drawing the situation on paper helps. It provides a kind of third-party objectivity.

Whatever you do, don't get into a flap and make a sudden knee-jerk decision.

Just think things through calmly.

WANT TO KNOW MORE? Today's quote from Horace comes from the type of poem we are so used to getting from this poet.

"No point worrying, we're all going to die. So get on with it."

There's something else in this poem which makes it interesting. It shines a light on a smaller, lesser-known character in Roman history called Quintus Dellius.

Dellius flip-flopped through the muddy waters of Roman political intrigue, changing sides so many times he must have either had a death wish or a strong belief in his own ability to talk his way out of a paper bag.

He wins out in the end and (like many others) he is re-absorbed back into society by the Emperor Augustus. In 23 BCE Dellius hits a rough patch, as Horace's poem shows. Whether he kept a level head or not, we may never know.

> **It's lovely to let your hair down on occasion.**
>
> *(dulce est desipere in loco)*
>
> Horace. Odes 4.12.28

THEME: ENTERTAINING

CHECKPOINT: Life is, of course, much more than just working nine to five, five days a week, 40 weeks a year until you retire.

Although I confess, it may not seem like that at times.

But sometimes enjoying life takes some work too.

If you don't plan ahead, or build in the time to have fun, then those opportunities will pass you by.

As John Lennon said: "Life is what happens to you while you're busy making other plans."

Take those holidays. Go to those parties. Start that hobby. Socialize with colleagues.

And if your colleagues are being stuffy, boring or lazy, or all three, organize something.

And if you really need to justify any of this to anyone, just point them to the many websites and books that explain how having fun every now and then can increase productivity!

WANT TO KNOW MORE? There's been a lot of Horace in this book.

Well, you could probably rewrite this book using only quotes from Horace. He is the sort of poet who lends himself to the clever, succinct comment that starts you thinking.

This is the last quote from Horace for the year.

It comes from his wonderful fourth book of *Odes*, written when Horace had turned 50.

He's having a think.

He's getting on a bit. His sex life isn't going well.

Did it ever go well? Could it ever go well again? Probably not, he muses.

Horace never married but had plenty of sexual partners, both female and male.

His sexuality pervades his poetry, winding through his life like a permanent teasing thread.

....

> **Management of inanimate objects is a finance function, whereas the management of people is a political one.**
>
> *(τὴν γὰρ οἰκονομικὴν ἐν ἀψύχοις χρηματιστικὴν οὖσαν, ἐν ἀνθρώποις πολιτικὴν γιγνομένην ὁρῶμεν)*
>
> Plutarch. Crassus 2.7

THEME: HUMAN RESOURCES

CHECKPOINT: Financial strategy can be so simple and straightforward when human beings aren't part of the picture. Assets stay still and depreciate. Building costs stay still for long periods of time. Goods and services can be costed.

The price of a can of beans is the same for all the cans of beans you are making. You change the price and they all go up together.

Neat.

Then people come along. They're messy. They want pay rises. Benefits. Resources. They leave unexpectedly, bringing unforeseen recruitment costs. They're ill – adding to productivity issues.

But then people are the one asset that really make a difference.

Finance chiefs who really understand people management are themselves a superb asset for any business.

WANT TO KNOW MORE? The Roman general and politican Marcus Licinius Crassus (born around 115 BCE – died 53 BCE) was all about money. Lots of it.

On paper, it looks like he had a formidable military career.

He played a significant part on the winning side of some bitter Roman civil wars, when he was in his early thirties. He joined a three-person junta with Julius Caesar and Pompey the Great.

It was Crassus who brought an end to the famous slave uprising led by Spartacus.

But it was money he was after. And he used his military roles to deliberately source and build up seriously huge wealth. He became a billionaire.

As governor of Syria, he invaded Parthia to gain, you guessed it, more wealth.

He went too far. The Parthians defeated and killed him. As a sign of their disdain for his wealth-creating activities they poured molten gold down the throat of his lifeless body.

....

> **Through his affability and approachability, he inspired loyalty both in and out of the workplace, often mingling gregariously with the troops, without undermining his position as leader.**
>
> *(comitate et adloquiis officia provocans ac plerumque in opere, in agmine gregario militi mixtus, incorrupto ducis honore)*
>
> Tacitus. Histories 5.1

THEME: LEADERSHIP

CHECKPOINT: Being a leader means leading people. It doesn't mean sitting behind a desk and pushing pieces of paper around. All businesses are made up of people.

You can convince yourself that your job is super-complicated and that you need to concentrate 100% on strategy and dealing with investors. There are others who can do 'the people stuff'. Fatal mistake.

The people in the business are an endless source of energy and imagination. They make it all happen.

When you are strategizing, you are looking at ways of deploying your people.

Investors are looking for the return that the sweat of each worker has made.

Never forget the people who are really making the money and get out and meet them!

WANT TO KNOW MORE? Today's quote is about the Emperor Titus, born this day 39 CE. He had one very unique claim.

He was the first emperor to succeed his biological father (Vespasian). All the previous emperors had gained their position through adoption or intrigue.

Titus had a short but exemplary reign of just over two years. He was an honest man, a good soldier and a keen reader. He was generous, not personally greedy, publicly prudent and was greatly appreciated. He was 'the people's darling'.

He died relatively young, aged 41. Natural causes? Poisoning? Certainly a mystery.

"ἓν μόνον ἐπλημμέλησα," history records him saying. "I have made one mistake." What was it? Who knows? But the looming, threatening figure of his brother Domitian may have had something to do with it.

Maybe the nice Titus should have executed Domitian for plotting against him?

But then, Titus didn't do that sort of thing.

Oops.

> **When we are working on something important that requires eloquence of thought and expression, we could do well to ask ourselves how Homer would have said it. Or how might Plato, Demosthenes or the historian Thucydides have given it an elevated tone?**
>
> (ἡνίκ' ἂν διαπονῶμεν ὑψηγορίας τι καὶ μεγαλοφροσύνης δεόμενον, καλὸν ἀναπλάττεσθαι ταῖς ψυχαῖς, πῶς ἂν εἰ τύχοι ταὐτὸ τοῦθ᾽ Ὅμηρος εἶπεν, πῶς δ᾽ ἂν Πλάτων ἢ Δημοσθένης ὕψωσαν ἢ ἐν ἱστορίᾳ Θουκυδίδης)
>
> Longinus. On The Sublime 1.14

THEME: PERSONAL DEVELOPMENT

CHECKPOINT: The classical world has so much more to tell us than the 365 quotes so far in this book.

Plato, Cicero, Horace or Seneca could alone fill a book of business advice.

Writing this book, it became even clearer to me that we have progressed no further than the ancient Greeks and Romans in terms of intellectual ability.

Just a handful of technological interventions have fast-tracked us to where we are now: e.g. the printing press, steam engine, oil, electricity and the internet.

You can pick up the Classics at any time and at any age.

In fact, Classics today has become more open, and in my view more exciting, than ever before.

There are books and courses for all levels.

There are many free classes. Sign up, try one out!

And if you are by chance at school, weighing up your course options, put Classics on the list.

It worked for JK Rowling, Martha Lane Fox (lastminute.com) and Chris Martin (Coldplay) as a starter list of famous classicists that could go on for many pages.

WANT TO KNOW MORE? If you want to know more about the ancient worlds of the Greeks or Romans try these books from two eminent scholars:

Mary Beard	*Classics: A Very Short Introduction*
Mary Beard	*SPQR: A History of Rome*
Edith Hall	*Introducing The Ancient Greeks*
Edith Hall	*Aristotle's Way*

Also take a look at The Cambridge Schools Classics Programme (www.cambridgescp.com), or any of the free online resources that have sprung up over the past few years.

APPENDIX

QUOTES BY THEME		
THEME	AUTHOR	DATE
Communicating	Euripides. Aeolus 28.	Jan-29
Communicating	Galen. On The Natural Faculties 1.2	Jan-02
Communicating	Horace. Epistles 1.18.68	Jan-21
Communicating	Pliny The Younger. Letters 8.2.5	Jan-23
Communicating	Varro. On The Latin Language 6.56	Jan-25
Competitors	Aristophanes. Birds 375	Mar-24
Competitors	Caesar. The Gallic War 7.20	Oct-03
Competitors	Hesiod. Works And Days 24	Jun-29
Competitors	Isocrates. Discourses 5 To Philip 121	Jun-02
Competitors	Publilius Syrus. Sententiae 680	Sep-05
Competitors	Tacitus. Annals 1.67	Sep-09
Competitors	Theognis. Elegies 221-2	Nov-18
Competitors	Vergil. Aeneid 11.387	Jan-24
Consumer Insights	Caesar. The Gallic War 3.18	Jan-10
Consumer Insights	Persius. Satires 1.63	Mar-13
Disputes	Macrobius. Saturnalia 5.4	May-02
Disputes	Martial. Epigrams 2.90	Jan-18

Disputes	Menander. Men In Arbitration 219	Jan-30
Entertaining	Cato. Collectio Distichorum Vulgaris. I.19	Jun-18
Entertaining	Cato. Collectio Distichorum Vulgaris. I.51	Dec-18
Entertaining	Cicero. Pro Murena 13	Mar-08
Entertaining	Horace. Odes 1.37.1	May-01
Entertaining	Horace. Odes 4.12.28	Dec-28
Entertaining	Juvenal. Satires 10.80	Feb-17
Entertaining	Menander. Sententiae 554	Apr-23
Entertaining	Plautus. The Comedy of Asses 835	Aug-13
Entertaining	Plutarch. Moralia 8 Table Talk 629	Dec-11
Entertaining	Seneca. Epistles 21.11	Dec-25
Finance	Aeschylus. Prometheus Bound 997	Mar-03
Finance	Aristotle. Economics 2.1346a	May-27
Finance	Columella. On Agriculture 3.3.6	Sep-26
Finance	Demosthenes. Against Timotheus 5	Jun-11
Finance	Horace. Epistles 1.10.47	Nov-11
Finance	Juvenal. Satires 14.200	Feb-05
Finance	Lucilius. Satires 29. 907	Dec-20
Finance	Plautus. The Comedy of Asses 217	Nov-19
Finance	Pliny the Younger. Panegyrics. 36.1	Apr-06
Finance	Seven Sages	Mar-09
Finance	Xenophon. Economics 1.12	Feb-01
Finance	Demosthenes. On Organization 2	Jun-05
Finance	Petronius. Satyricon 14	Jul-03
HR	Aristophanes. Wasps 471	Nov-03
HR	Aristotle. Politics 1.1	Jan-12
HR	Aristotle. Rhetoric 1.11.25	Feb-25

HR	Caecilius Statius	Aug-18
HR	Cicero. In Vatinium 36	May-22
HR	Cicero. Tusculan Disputations 3.21	Aug-05
HR	Euripides. Medea 964	Dec-23
HR	Hesiod. Works And Days 354	Feb-12
HR	Horace. Epistles 1.1.80	Jan-15
HR	Horace. Epistles 1.11.25	Jul-01
HR	Juvenal. Satires 10.54	Mar-02
HR	Juvenal. Satires 13.26	Oct-17
HR	Juvenal. Satires 6.347	Dec-06
HR	Minucius Felix. Octavius 13.2	Mar-07
HR	Minucius Felix. Octavius 14.7	Nov-17
HR	Ovid. Heroides 2.9	Mar-20
HR	Plato. Meno 97c	Jul-17
HR	Plautus. The Captives 165	Oct-10
HR	Plautus. Truculentus 493	Apr-17
HR	Pliny The Younger. Letters 7.25.1	Nov-26
HR	Plutarch. Crassus 2.7	Dec-29
HR	Propertius. Elegies 2.5.20	Nov-10
HR	Seneca. De Beneficiis 4.34.1	Sep-02
HR	Seneca. Oedipus 850	Dec-10
HR	Suetonius. Gaius Caligula 55.3	Mar-23
HR	Suetonius. Vespasian 16.3	Dec-21
HR	Sulpicia. Poems 1	Aug-29
HR	Tacitus. Agricola 9.3	Oct-28
HR	Tacitus. Histories 2.7	Apr-30
HR	Theocritus. Idylls 21.2	Jun-30

HR	Varro. On Agriculture 2.1.3	May-23
HR	Vergil. Eclogues 3.93	Apr-26
HR	Xenophon. Memorabilia 4.4.10	Sep-04
Innovation	Callimachus. Aetia 1.25	Jan-05
Innovation	Cicero. De Officiis 1.44.157	Jun-07
Innovation	Demosthenes. On The Navy Boards 31	Jan-11
Innovation	Homer. Odyssey 1.351	May-09
Innovation	Lucian. Zeuxis 1	May-06
Innovation	Musaeus	Oct-21
Innovation	Plato. Phaedrus 274a	Nov-15
Innovation	Pliny The Elder. Natural History 8.17	Jun-13
Innovation	Publilius Syrus. Sententiae 83	Jul-30
Innovation	Seneca. De Tranquillitate Animi 17.10	Nov-24
Innovation	Socrates (Plato Apology 38a)	May-25
Innovation	Tacitus. Agricola 30.3	May-24
Innovation	Vergil. Aeneid 1.278	Feb-23
Innovation	Vitruvius. On Architecture 1.2.2	Jun-27
Internet	Anaxagoras. Testimonia 2. D14	Aug-07
Internet	Aristophanes. Wasps 314	Jul-25
Internet	Cato. Collectio Distichorum Vulgaris. 1.4	Apr-01
Internet	Dio Chrysostom. Discourses 32.36	Sep-29
Internet	Euripides. Chrysippus Frag. 839	Feb-24
Internet	Horace. Epistles. I.18.71	Feb-19
Internet	Juvenal. Satires 7.157	Aug-04
Internet	Lucretius. On The Nature Of Things 1.221	May-16
Internet	Plautus. The Rope 943	Jul-15
Internet	Pliny The Younger. Letters 3.14.5	Sep-27

Internet	Plutarch. Sayings Of The Spartans. 215	Jul-04
Internet	Seneca. Epistles 2.2	Jan-13
Internet	Seneca. Epistles 2.2	May-03
Leadership	Aeneas Tacticus. Fortified Positions 14.1	Jun-06
Leadership	Agrippa	Dec-13
Leadership	Aristophanes. Wasps 725	Aug-12
Leadership	Babrius. Fables 6.16	Apr-09
Leadership	Catullus. Poems 73	May-18
Leadership	Chabrias	May-10
Leadership	Cicero. In Catilinam 1.2	Dec-05
Leadership	Cicero. Philippic 1.11	Dec-07
Leadership	Cicero. Philippic 8.4	Aug-11
Leadership	Claudian	Apr-29
Leadership	Demosthenes. Third Olynthiac 16	Oct-26
Leadership	Ennius. Fragment	May-07
Leadership	Homer. Iliad 2.204	Jan-19
Leadership	Horace. Epistles 1.7.44	Aug-30
Leadership	Horace. Odes 2.10.21	Dec-08
Leadership	Juvenal. Satires 13.1	Jul-02
Leadership	Lucilius. Satires.1.23	Sep-06
Leadership	Maecenas	Dec-12
Leadership	Marcus Aurelius. Meditations 1.12	Aug-26
Leadership	Onasander. The General 13.3	Jul-08
Leadership	Ovid. Amores 2.61	Oct-20
Leadership	Petronius. Satyricon 43	Aug-27
Leadership	Petronius. Satyricon 45	Aug-17
Leadership	Phaedrus. Fables 3.9.1	May-31

Leadership	Phaedrus. Fables 4.3.5	Apr-07
Leadership	Phaedrus. Fables 4.2.5	Jul-09
Leadership	Pindar. Pythian Odes 1.86	Sep-03
Leadership	Plautus. The Ghost 181	Aug-09
Leadership	Pliny The Elder. Natural History 7.24	Dec-02
Leadership	Plutarch. Caesar 60.5	Mar-25
Leadership	Publilius Syrus. Sententiae 43	Jan-27
Leadership	Quintus Curtius. History Of Alexander 8.5.6	May-21
Leadership	Sallust. Jugurthine War 10.6	Jul-22
Leadership	Seneca The Elder. Controversiae 1.1.3	Oct-14
Leadership	Seneca. Epistles 20.1	Mar-12
Leadership	Seneca. Epistles 47.11	Jun-25
Leadership	Seneca. Hercules 276	Oct-19
Leadership	Seneca. Natural Questions 2.39.4	May-29
Leadership	Seneca. Natural Questions 3.27	Jul-21
Leadership	Seneca. Natural Questions Preface 3.7	Aug-16
Leadership	Sophocles. Ajax The Locrian Frag. 14	Jan-17
Leadership	Sophocles. Antigone 277	Apr-10
Leadership	Sophocles. Oedipus Tyrannus 1521	Nov-14
Leadership	Statius. Thebaid 1.130	Jun-03
Leadership	Suetonius. Domitian 23.2	Sep-18
Leadership	Suetonius. The Deified Augustus 28.3	Apr-21
Leadership	Tacitus. Agricola 16.1	Jul-06
Leadership	Tacitus. Histories 5.1	Dec-30
Leadership	Theocritus. Idylls 11.75	Sep-12
Leadership	Thucydides. The Peloponnesian War 1.142.9	Nov-25
Leadership	Thucydides. The Peloponnesian War 2.36.4	Apr-25

Leadership	Vergil. Aeneid 6.95	Oct-15
Leadership	Xenophon. Cyropaedia 8.1.15	Aug-06
Leadership	Xenophon. Cyropaedia 8.1.8	Dec-03
Legal	Aristotle. Politics 1.1	Feb-22
Legal	Aristotle. Rhetoric 1.15.21	Jul-16
Legal	Hesiod. Works And Days 370	Oct-08
Legal	Homer. Iliad 1.526	Dec-09
Legal	Lysias. Against Philocrates 14	Feb-10
Legal	Pliny The Elder. Natural History 7.32	Aug-22
Legal	Propertius. Elegies 4.8.81	Apr-03
Legal	Twelve Tables. Table 3	May-30
Legal	Twelve Tables. Table 6.1a	Dec-14
Personal Development	Aeschylus. Agamemnon 584	Feb-08
Personal Development	Aeschylus. Persians 598	Mar-30
Personal Development	Alciphron. Letters 2.10	Dec-22
Personal Development	Ammianus Marcellinus. History 14.11.12	Jul-27
Personal Development	Appius Claudius Caecus. Sententiae	Sep-13
Personal Development	Aristotle. Nichomachean Ethics 1109b	Sep-14
Personal Development	Aristotle. Nicomachaen Ethics 1140a	Jun-19
Personal Development	Cato. Collectio Distichorum Vulgaris. 1.33	Jul-18
Personal Development	Cato. Distichs 4.48	Jul-19
Personal Development	Catullus. Poems 22	Feb-26
Personal Development	Catullus. Poems 40	Apr-24
Personal Development	Chilon	Nov-09
Personal Development	Chilon	Mar-11
Personal Development	Cicero. Philippic 2.116	Mar-15
Personal Development	Cicero. Pro Murena 60	Oct-31

Personal Development	Cicero. Pro Murena 65	Oct-22
Personal Development	Columella. On Agriculture 11.1.4	May-11
Personal Development	Decimus Laberius.	Oct-13
Personal Development	Demosthenes. Third Olynthiac 6	Oct-12
Personal Development	Diogenes Laertius. Pythagoras 23	Mar-16
Personal Development	Epictetus. Discourses 1.12.26	Apr-05
Personal Development	Heraclitus	Mar-27
Personal Development	Herodotus. Histories 7.203	Sep-08
Personal Development	Hesiod. Theogony 27	May-20
Personal Development	Hesiod. Works And Days 381	Aug-10
Personal Development	Homer. Iliad 15.741	Aug-20
Personal Development	Homer. Iliad 6.339	Jun-24
Personal Development	Homer. Iliad 9.443	Apr-14
Personal Development	Homer. Odyssey 5.360	Jul-23
Personal Development	Horace. Epistles 1.17.37	Jun-21
Personal Development	Horace. Odes 1.11	Feb-29
Personal Development	Horace. Odes 1.19.13	Jul-28
Personal Development	Horace. Odes 1.7.27	Apr-20
Personal Development	Horace. Odes 2.3.1	Dec-27
Personal Development	Horace. Odes 3.1.25	May-12
Personal Development	Horace. Odes 3.27.37	Dec-01
Personal Development	Horace. Odes 3.29.49	Jun-09
Personal Development	Horace. Satires 1.1.92	Jan-04
Personal Development	Horace. Satires 2.5.88	Jun-22
Personal Development	Inscription on the Temple of Apollo	Jan-16
Personal Development	Isocrates. Panegyricus 9	Oct-29
Personal Development	Jerome. Letters 54.13	Apr-28

Personal Development	Jerome. Letters 54.6	Sep-25
Personal Development	Juvenal. Satires 10.356	Mar-19
Personal Development	Juvenal. Satires 2.8	Apr-18
Personal Development	Juvenal. Satires 8.76	May-08
Personal Development	Livy. History Of Rome 4.2.11	Mar-31
Personal Development	Longinus. On The Sublime 14.1	Dec-31
Personal Development	Lucretius. On The Nature Of Things 3.94	May-14
Personal Development	Macrobius. Saturnalia 2.5	Oct-30
Personal Development	Marcus Aurelius. Meditations 1.8	Aug-31
Personal Development	Otho	Apr-15
Personal Development	Ovid. The Art of Love 2.107	Feb-14
Personal Development	Pacuvius. Periboea Frag. 316	Jul-26
Personal Development	Palladas. Greek Anthology 10.65	Nov-23
Personal Development	Petronius. Poems 6	Jan-31
Personal Development	Phocylides. Fragments 8	Jul-05
Personal Development	Pindar. Pythian Odes 4.286	Mar-22
Personal Development	Plato. Cratylus 402a	Jan-28
Personal Development	Plato. Sophist 263E	Jun-08
Personal Development	Pliny The Elder. Natural History 7.25	Mar-06
Personal Development	Pliny The Younger. Letters 1.18.6	Mar-26
Personal Development	Plutarch. Caesar 11.3	Jul-13
Personal Development	Plutarch. Marius 23.1	Oct-06
Personal Development	Polybius. Histories 5.4.13	Aug-21
Personal Development	Publilius Syrus. Sententiae 133	May-26
Personal Development	Publilius Syrus. Sententiae 83	Sep-22
Personal Development	Publilius Syrus. Sententiae 9	Feb-21
Personal Development	Quintilian. Institutio Oratoria 4.2.91	Dec-19

Personal Development	Rutilius Namatianus. De Reditu Suo 491	Sep-20
Personal Development	Seneca. De Brevitate Vitae 2.2	Oct-07
Personal Development	Seneca. Epistles 13.4	Nov-02
Personal Development	Seneca. Epistles 3.2.6	Nov-20
Personal Development	Seneca. Epistles 31.3	Nov-04
Personal Development	Seneca. Epistles 32.2	Aug-03
Personal Development	Seneca. Epistles 6.5	Apr-12
Personal Development	Seneca. Epistles 7.8	Jul-11
Personal Development	Seneca. Hercules 437	Oct-27
Personal Development	Seneca. Natural Questions 3.11	Oct-01
Personal Development	Seneca. Oedipus 847	Nov-13
Personal Development	Sophocles. Acrisius. Frag. 65	Oct-05
Personal Development	Sophocles. Oedipus Tyrannus 1124	May-28
Personal Development	Statius. Thebaid 10.703	Aug-23
Personal Development	Symmachus. Relationes 3.4	Sep-01
Personal Development	Terence. The Self-Tormentor 675	Jul-12
Personal Development	Theocritus. Idylls 4.42	Aug-01
Personal Development	Theognis. Elegies 461	Nov-21
Personal Development	Vergil. Aeneid 2.65	Feb-02
Personal Development	Vergil. Eclogues 9.51	Feb-18
Personal Development	Vergil. Georgics 2.490	Sep-21
Personal Development	Vergil. Georgics 3.8	Mar-01
Personal Development	Xenophon. Economics 2.18	Dec-15
Personal Development	Xenophon. Memorabilia 4.4.10	Sep-17
Presentations/Meetings/Documents	Aristophanes. Wasps 631	Sep-07
Presentations/Meetings/Documents	Cicero. De Finibus Bonorum et Malorum 1.15	Jan-03
Presentations/Meetings/Documents	Macrobius. Saturnalia 5.7	Nov-29

Presentations/Meetings/Documents	Marginalia	Dec-17
Presentations/Meetings/Documents	Ovid. The Art of Love 1.574	May-19
Presentations/Meetings/Documents	Pacuvius. Antiopa Frag. 7-10	Sep-15
Presentations/Meetings/Documents	Persius. Satires 1.2	Jun-12
Presentations/Meetings/Documents	Phaedrus. Fables 4.5.1	Dec-04
Presentations/Meetings/Documents	Phocion	May-13
Presentations/Meetings/Documents	Polybius. Histories 1.60.5	Mar-10
Presentations/Meetings/Documents	Thucydides. The Peloponnesian War 2.35.2	May-04
Presentations/Meetings/Documents	Quintilian. Institutio Oratoria 8.3.24	Jun-04
Project Management	Augustus. Suetonius 2.25.4	Mar-28
Project Management	Cicero. Letters To Atticus 7.22	Feb-09
Project Management	Euripides. Aeolus 32	Oct-02
Project Management	Heraclitus	Apr-02
Project Management	Herodotus. Histories 7.157	Jan-07
Project Management	Horace. Ars Poetica 139	Aug-14
Project Management	Horace. Epistles 1.2.40	Jun-15
Project Management	Horace. Odes 3.30.1	Nov-27
Project Management	Lucilius. Satires 2.75	Jun-26
Project Management	Manlius. Astronomica 4.155	Feb-11
Project Management	Martial. Epigrams 4.82.8	Feb-03
Project Management	Ovid. Heroides 2.85	Jul-20
Project Management	Plato. Republic 377a	Jan-01
Project Management	Plautus. The Brothers Menaechmus 247	Jan-08
Project Management	Plautus. The Persian 659	Apr-11
Project Management	Pliny The Younger. Letters 10.41.2	Sep-28
Project Management	Polybius. Histories 2.4.5	Jul-29
Project Management	Popilius Laenas	Oct-23

Project Management	Propertius. Elegies 2.10.6	Mar-18
Project Management	Propertius. Elegies 4.10.3	Jun-28
Project Management	Sallust. The War With Catiline 44.5	Mar-21
Project Management	Seneca. Epistles 77.13	Oct-09
Project Management	Thucydides. The Peloponnesian War 3.54.5	Feb-15
Project Management	Vergil. Eclogues 10.69	Nov-01
Project Management	Vergil. Eclogues. 8.63	Jan-20
Project Management	Xenophon. Cyropaedia 1.6.10	Jun-17
Reorganization	Demosthenes. First Philippic 25	Jan-26
Risk	Herodotus. Histories 50.19	Mar-05
Risk	Solon. Fragment 13.65	Jan-09
Risk	Vergil. Aeneid 2.48	Mar-14
Selling	Juvenal. Satires 14.203	Aug-08
Selling	Plautus. Trinummus 1004	Jun-23
Social and Environmental	Isocrates. To Demonicus 1.1	Mar-04
Social and Environmental	Statius. Silvae 2.3	Feb-13
Social and Environmental	Tacitus. Agricola 30.4	Apr-22
Strategy	Aristotle. Nicomachean Ethics 1098a	Jun-01
Strategy	Bion. Frag. 4	Feb-28
Strategy	Cato the Elder. (Florus. Epitome 1.31.5)	Apr-04
Strategy	Cicero. De Divinatione 1.128	Jul-31
Strategy	Cicero. Letters To Atticus 14.6	Aug-19
Strategy	Cicero. Letters To Atticus 16.7.3	Nov-30
Strategy	Cicero. Philippic 5.53	Jan-14
Strategy	Cicero. Pro Sestio 68.143	Nov-28
Strategy	Horace. Ars Poetica 350	Jun-14
Strategy	Juvenal. Satires 6.165	Jul-07

Strategy	Livius Andronicus. Ajax. Frag. 15	Sep-10
Strategy	Livius Andronicus. Frag. 7	Feb-27
Strategy	Marcus Aurelius. Meditations 2.14	Mar-17
Strategy	Naevius. The Punic War. Frag. 65-66	Sep-11
Strategy	Plutarch. Lucullus 14.1	Feb-04
Strategy	Polybius. 9.13.2	Dec-24
Strategy	Publilius Syrus. Sententiae 124	Oct-25
Strategy	Publilius Syrus. Sententiae 141	Mar-29
Strategy	Publilius Syrus. Sententiae 151	Oct-04
Strategy	Publilius Syrus. Sententiae 188	Jun-16
Strategy	Seneca. Epistles 1.2	Jun-10
Strategy	Seneca. Epistles 38.2	Nov-22
Strategy	Sophocles. Oedipus Tyrannus 617	May-17
Strategy	Suetonius. The Deified Julius 37.2	Aug-02
Strategy	Terence. The Eunuch 255	Jul-14
Strategy	Thucydides. The Peloponnesian War 1.84.3	Nov-06
The Watercooler	Anacharsis	Oct-24
The Watercooler	Aristophanes. Knights 92	Dec-26
The Watercooler	Aristophanes. Wasps 642	Sep-30
The Watercooler	Aristotle. Metaphysics 980a.22	Sep-16
The Watercooler	Cato. Distichs 1.17	Jul-24
The Watercooler	Cicero. De Legibus 3.16	Jun-20
The Watercooler	Cicero. De Officiis 1.45.161	May-05
The Watercooler	Cicero. Pro Q. Roscio Comoedo 10.29	May-15
The Watercooler	Demosthenes. First Philippic 14	Oct-16
The Watercooler	Euenus. Fragments 1	Sep-24
The Watercooler	Homer. Iliad 20.248	Nov-16

The Watercooler	Livy. History Of Rome 22.39.19	Aug-28
The Watercooler	Lucilius. Satires 1.2	Dec-16
The Watercooler	Martial. Epigrams 12.12	Nov-08
The Watercooler	Ovid. Metamorphoses 4.64	Apr-27
The Watercooler	Pliny The Elder. Natural History 14.142	Oct-11
The Watercooler	Homer. Iliad 7.358	Aug-25
The Watercooler	Plutarch. Cato The Younger 1.5	Jul-10
The Watercooler	Sophocles. Acrisius Frag. 62	Apr-08
The Watercooler	Theophrastus. Characters 8.1	Feb-07
The Watercooler	Vergil. Aeneid 4.174	Feb-20
Time Management	Accius. Diomedes Frag. 270	Feb-06
Time Management	Augustus. Suetonius 2.25.4	Sep-23
Time Management	Cicero. Philippic 2.38	Apr-13
Time Management	Ennius. Annals 10.348	Nov-05
Time Management	Epictetus. Discourses 1.15.7	Oct-18
Time Management	Homer. Iliad 1.141	Nov-07
Time Management	Homer. Iliad 2.435	Jan-22
Time Management	Moschus. Megara 41	Sep-19
Time Management	Ovid. Amores 1.11	Jan-06
Time Management	Persius. Satires 5.153	Aug-15
Time Management	Pliny The Younger. Letters 1.9.3	Apr-19
Time Management	Seneca. Epistles 84.11	Feb-16
Time Management	Socrates (Plato. Theaetetus 187E)	Apr-16
Time Management	Xenophon. Cyropaedia 8.2.5	Nov-12

ENDNOTES

1 A rising tricolon consists of three evenly structured words or phrases which build in intensity to deliver a verbal punch. A wonderful example in advertising comes from a 1940s Chevrolet slogan: 'Eye it. Try it. Buy it!'

2 Professor Niall Rudd was Chair of Latin and Director (Head of Department) of the Department of Classics and Ancient History, Bristol University, 1973-1989.

3 Throughout the book I use the the modern method of renaming BC 'BCE' and AD 'CE', denoting a time Before the Christian Era and a time in the Christian Era.

4 Scheidel, Walter; Friesen, Steven J. (Nov. 2009): *The Size of the Economy and the Distribution of Income in the Roman Empire*, The Journal of Roman Studies, Vol. 99, pp. 61–91.

5 Philip Parker. *The Empire Stops Here*. Pub. Pimlico 2010.

6 Epistles 2.1.156.

7 Cicero. De Legibus 1.5.

8 Literally: 'Don't seek a knot in a bulrush'. The saying was repeated a generation later in Terence's play *The Girl From Andros* (And. 5.4.38).

9 The more literal translation is 'Jackdaws always (stay) with jackdaws'.

10 *Implosion* (London: LID Publishing, 2013). *Upgraded* (London: LID Publishing, 2016).

ABOUT
THE AUTHOR

Described by Theodore Zeldin as "one of our boldest business gurus," Andy Law is an Ernst & Young Entrepreneur of the Year.

During his 40 years working first in advertising and then global business consulting, he has been profiled by the *Harvard Business Review*, has chaired plenary sessions at Davos, advised in Downing Street, shared the podium with world leaders, managed communications innovation for global companies and written a number of highly acclaimed business books. His first book, *Open Minds*, was described as "a 20th century equivalent of John Foxe's *Book of Martyrs* (1563), a business book which is literature."

His final goal, to retire as near as possible to 60, has now been achieved and at last he can return to his first love, Classics, which he read at university.

Andy now lives in the UK and Italy and spends his time writing.